"At a time when the need for independent jo[urnalism]
outlets unaffiliated with and untainted by the [corpo]-
rate sponsors is greater than ever, Project C[ensored provides]
context for reporting the complete truths in all matters that matter. . . .
It is therefore left to us to find sources for information we can
trust. . . . It is in this task that we are fortunate to have an ally like
Project Censored."—Dahr Jamail

"Activist groups like Project Censored . . . are helping to build the
media democracy movement. We have to challenge the powers that be
and rebuild media from the bottom up."—Amy Goodman

"Project Censored is one of the organizations that we should listen to,
to be assured that our newspapers and our broadcasting outlets are
practicing thorough and ethical journalism."—Walter Cronkite

"[Censored] should be affixed to the bulletin boards in every newsroom
in America. And, perhaps read aloud to a few publishers and television executives."—Ralph Nader

"[Censored] offers devastating evidence of the dumbing-down of mainstream news in America. . . . Required reading for broadcasters,
journalists, and well-informed citizens."—Los Angeles Times

"One of the most significant media research projects in the
country."—I. F. Stone

"A terrific resource, especially for its directory of alternative media and
organizations. . . . Recommended for media collections."—Library
Journal

"[Project Censored's] efforts to continue globalizing their reporting
network could not be more timely or necessary."—Kristina Borjesson

"A distant early warning system for society's problems."—American
Journalism Review

"Project Censored goes where the media conformist angels fear to tread. . . . It's the kind of journalism we need."—Norman Solomon

"Project Censored shines a spotlight on news that an informed public must have . . . a vital contribution to our democratic process."—Rhoda H. Karpatkin, president, Consumer's Union

"Hot news, cold truths, utterly uncensored."—Greg Palast

"Buy it, read it, act on it. Our future depends on the knowledge this collection of suppressed stories allows us."—*San Diego Review*

"Those who read and support Project Censored are in the know." —Cynthia McKinney

"This volume chronicles 25 news stories about events that could affect all of us, but which we most likely did not hear or read about in the popular news media."—*Bloomsbury Review*

"Censored serves as a reminder that there is certainly more to the news than is easily available or willingly disclosed. To those of us who work in the newsrooms, it's an inspiration, an indictment, and an admonition to look deeper, ask more questions, then search for the truth in the answers we get."—*Creative Loafings*

"This invaluable resource deserves to be more widely known." —*Wilson Library Bulletin*

CENSORED2012
Sourcebook for the Media Revolution

The Top Censored Stories and Media Analysis of 2010–2011

MICKEY HUFF AND PROJECT CENSORED

Introduction by Peter Phillips
Cartoons by Khalil Bendib

Seven Stories Press
NEW YORK

Seven Stories Press
140 Watts Street
New York, NY 10013
www.sevenstories.com

ISBN 978-1-60980-347-6 (paperback)
ISBN 978-1-60980-358-2 (electronic)

ISSN 1074-5998

9 8 7 6 5 4 3 2 1

Book design by Jon Gilbert

Printed in the USA

Contents

SECTION I
Censored News and Media Analysis

Chapter 1
Project Censored News Clusters and
the Top Censored Stories of 2010 and 2011
by Peter Phillips, Mickey Huff, Elliot D. Cohen, Dean Walker, Andy Lee
Roth, Elaine Wellin, Kristen Seraphin, Joel Evans-Fudem, Amy Ortiz, Kenn
Burrows, and Tom Atlee, with additional research and editing by Trish
Boreta, Bill Gibbons, Craig Cekala, Melody J. Haislip,

Introduction

CENSORED NEWS CLUSTER: Human Costs of War and Violence

CENSORED NEWS CLUSTER: Social Media and Internet Freedom

CENSORED NEWS CLUSTER: Economics and Inequality
by Dean Walker, with research assistance by Bill Gibbons

CENSORED NEWS CLUSTER: Power, Abuse, and Accountability

CENSORED NEWS CLUSTER: Health and the Environment

CENSORED NEWS CLUSTER: Women and Gender Issues

CENSORED NEWS CLUSTER: Collaboration and Common Good

SECTION III
Project Censored International
Human Rights and the Right to Know
Introduction by Mickey Huff with an introduction to the
Fair Sharing of the Common Heritage by Mary Lia

Chapter 16

Censorship of the True State of Maternity Care in the US

Dedicated to the first real rebel and truth teller I ever knew:
my father,
Jesse Francis "Mickey" Huff (1939–2004)

and to the next generations that continue in
that same vein—Meg, Molly, and . . .

Moving Beyond Media Reform for *Censored 2012*

by Mickey Huff

> *In the final analysis, each scholar, just like every citizen,*
> *has to take a long, hard look in the mirror and consider*
> *the following: If we act as if social change for the better*
> *is impossible, we guarantee it will be impossible. That is*
> *the long-standing human dilemma, except that in crit-*
> *ical junctures our powers increase and the odds can*
> *swing dramatically in democracy's favor. We hold*
> *immense power in our hands. Let's not blow this oppor-*
> *tunity. Let's have a real communication revolution.*[1]
> —ROBERT MCCHESNEY, media scholar

> *Reformers who are always compromising, have not yet*
> *grasped the idea that truth is the only safe ground to*
> *stand upon.*
> —ELIZABETH CADY STANTON

As we approach the historically prophetic and now mass media-hyped "End of Times" year of 2012, hysterical speculation abounds. The failed prediction of a preacher in Oakland, California, who claimed the Rapture was upon us come May 21, 2011, was quite metaphoric as it exposed, yet again, how someone in American society is always able to captivate the corporate media by spinning doomsday yarns, whether it be Y2K or the upcoming 2012 end of the Mayan calendar (further manifest in the outpouring of Hollywood apocalypse films). Though, to be clear, it is not merely the entertainment media that succumb to this lowest common denominator (fear sells), it is the news media as well, in the forms of Junk Food News and News Abuse (see chapter 3) and relentless power elite propaganda (see the Truth Emergency section of this volume).

In the realm of the "serious" traditional institutional news media in the US, increasingly, speculation masquerades as fact, gossip, and tripe stand in for analysis, and the titillating and inane trump the sober and sane. The ongoing corporate media feeding frenzy at the trough of the factually groundless and absurd has only intensified over the past decade, whether promulgating faux fears—from killer bee attacks to various flu viruses—or pushing nonexistent weapons of mass destruction and the Orwellian, nebulously defined yet unending War on Terror. Fear and innuendo rule the headlines of the day while television news programs are dominated by opinion journalism, empty technological displays, and elaborate computer graphics (perhaps casting the shadows in Plato's cave). In short, for establishment "news" as we have known it in the last quarter of the twentieth century, it really *is* the "end of times," and no amount of "reform" attenuating the current commercially dominated system from the top down will likely resuscitate it, at least in journalistic terms.

That there *is* a crisis in journalism seems to be understood by many scholars and independent journalists, while many in the corporate media don't seem to notice, or at least don't mention it much. Further, they do not divulge much in terms of the challenges we face in the twenty-first century as the corporate media flood the airwaves with celebrity tales and misinformation. The overall so-called "mainstream" reporting in the United States is the equivalent to fiddling while Rome burns. And make no mistake, the US is an empire, and we are in decay. We the People of these United States already stand at a very real precipice—the potential end of what has been deemed the Great American Experiment, the institutional embodiment of human freedom protected by government of, by, and for the people. Meanwhile, the corporate media fill so-called news time with faux-angst, Astroturf platforms, cult-of-personality disorders, and one manufactured irrelevant crisis after another in what appears to be a Herculean effort to avoid telling the public what is really going on at home and abroad—with the economy, with the environment, in Afghanistan, Libya, or in Fukushima, Japan. In short, the establishment press in America is not telling people what is really going wrong and how, and what we can start doing about it as a society. The Fourth Estate is dead to the people.

America in the first decade of the twenty-first century is experiencing a decline of epic proportions in terms of the performance and accessibility of its economy, the efficacy of its civil institutions under constitutional law, and the ability to deliver the promise of what was known as the American Dream to all that strove for it in earnest. But, perhaps this is not so surprising given the recent past, at least for those that know it in spite of the fact that the so-called mainstream media in America has done a good deal to not report on what is really going on in the world, and at home. The late comic and critic George Carlin once said, "It's called the 'American Dream' because you have to be asleep to believe it." Based on our current circumstances, Carlin's quip seems sage.

Of course, for many, the promises of equality and democracy that lie within the American Dream ethos never existed in the history of the United States. Certainly, racism, sexism, classism, and imperialism, have all played the role of antagonist to said promises. However, America's founding documents were particularly rife with rhetorical flourishes that were supportive of liberty, freedom of expression, the pursuit of happiness—all of which actually sprouted many social and political movements that changed American culture by striving toward those founding principles, achieving them in varying degrees. In this regard, America has succeeded in realizing the essence of some of its promises. But in reality, the US, in historical terms, has fallen short in myriad ways across the demographic spectrum and that trend is not abating. This is in large part due to Americans' reliance on institutional reform over implementation of revolutionary ideals and actions as tools for change. We are in need of such radical action now.

Arguably, the root of these aforementioned problems within democracy, beyond exclusion or manipulation of the franchise, chiefly resides in the controlling of public information and education, and access to it. Thomas Jefferson once offered a possible solution to these issues when he wrote, "The functionaries of every government have propensities to command at will the liberty and property of their constituents. There is no safe deposit for these but with the people themselves, nor can they be safe with them without information. Where the press is free, and every man able to read, all is safe." The focus then is to achieve a truly free press and a literate citizenry in maintenance of democratic government.

More recently, this was purportedly the focus of the organizers and A-list participants of the National Conference on Media Reform this past spring in the historic (once revolutionary?) city of Boston. Certainly groups like Free Press and the Media Consortium, among many others, have pursued laudable media democracy causes. However, and most respectfully stated, some of the reformers and key participants of the event are also part of the establishment media and political system (Federal Communications Commission [FCC], Congress). These people have fallen short of achieving reform goals, noble as they may be, by working through the current system.

We the People should go straight to the root of our problems with media, which means taking a radical approach in dealing with the current problems of our supposed free press, to ensure that all are, as Jefferson put it, safe. For starters, we should move well beyond reformist calls for attenuating institutional dials, changing a few metaphorical channels, or appointing new FCC commissioners. This has not worked. The root of democracy is with the people, in education, in media literacy, in civic awareness. The path to change comes from the people, not the president. That we move beyond a reform ethos concentrated on elite media control must be agreed upon by all those aware of the problem in order for real change to take place. And while moving beyond reform, we cannot succumb to a top-down-initiated "hope and change we can believe in," which was promised yet never delivered after the 2008 election, on which many reformers focused great efforts to no avail. These eventual outcomes of reform serve to create a subculture of acceptance in defeat, living to fight again . . . in another four years.

That is a cyclical game. And we have played it for a long time. It is true that reforms play a role in radical changes, though they are merely steps to paradigmatic shifts. The time to unite, face reality, and act to rebuild a new and relevant democracy on the foundation of a truly free press is upon us as we are now in dire straits as a country, as a world, from economic collapse to environmental destruction. A People's Media Revolution is the vehicle for such a change—and it is, in some parts of the world, indeed in America, at the tips of our fingers.

Like falling empires of old, the US today is mired in multi-front, unilateral wars and is engaging in new ones that are ongoing, all while living well beyond its means at home, ignoring domestic affairs when not outright waging internal wars against those who actually expect elected and appointed officials to live up to our founding Enlightenment principles. These current so-called "wars on terror" have cost over $3 trillion to date and occupy a great deal of time of political leaders. All the while, the US boasts record declines in middle- and working-class incomes and opportunities; a jobless "recovery" in the wake of the economic collapse of 2008 (caused in large part by the biggest banks on Wall Street, which subsequently were not held accountable and instead bailed out at taxpayer expense); a crumbling infrastructure; failing schools (including public and private charter schools); abysmal records on access and quality of health care given the overall wealth and technological prowess of the country; rising infant mortality rates; increasing homelessness; skyrocketing foreclosures; collapse of community development and nonprofit support systems; faulty elections procedures; the use of torture abroad and at home; an encroaching police state and erosion of the rule of law; an increasing lack of transparency with more attacks on whistleblowers . . . the list goes on and on. Though don't expect to hear this on the ever-consolidating, oligopoly-owned "news" media.

Last but not least, we suffer a hyperreal condition as a society, spurred on by fearful, factless, and feckless news programming by the nation's supposed leading journalistic outlets. This is why most people in America do not seem to notice the inevitable descent. America is so disconnected that, even while individuals may suffer in large numbers, they lack a collective adhesive in a modern media landscape. They erroneously believe they suffer alone, and thanks to corporate media propaganda, are often afraid of the wrong things. Yet, a truly free press should help build and protect democracy for the people, not destroy it.

All this is taking place in what appears to be absolute decline across the board for most Americans as the upper few percent of the population control most of the nation's wealth. A real free press would tell us to forget the gross domestic product (GDP) and focus on community building, local banking, and public works programs, not abstract market fluctuations and foreign exchange rates. America is a debtor nation within its population and has not made much outside of weapons and related technologies accompanied by military-industrial-media complex propaganda/advertising for years—all masquerading as official foreign policy and the "news." The US government, along with this massive military-industrial-media complex, has now armed the world to the teeth to justify a permanent warfare state. As I write this, we are involved in six wars . . . and counting. (According to the Nation Institute's Tom Engelhardt, these include Iraq, Afghanistan, Pakistan, Yemen, Libya, and what used to be called the Global War on Terror, which may mark a record for simultaneous wars in US history—unbeknownst to the public.) However, the Obama administration and its media lapdogs are careful not to refer to any of these as "wars," even if that is exactly what they are, and they are bankrupting the empire.

America, its government of and by corporations over the people (especially after the Citizens United case), is now locked in a self-created, last-ditch effort to occupy the nether regions of oil, industrial capitalism's dwindling lifeblood. The US forces the rest of the world to trade on the dollar to maintain global hegemony, funding its expansion of over a thousand military bases in over 130 countries. Meanwhile, China, Russia, and several South American countries are already operating outside this monetary imposition, which, as the late scholar and author of the *Blowback* trilogy Chalmers Johnson argued, is what would spell the end of American empire: fiscal bankruptcy. The collapse of the dollar would hasten that, as was reported in last year's most censored story in *Censored 2011*. Indeed, that time draws nigh. The cry for austerity from ostentatious leaders rings hollow across the land as US leaders spend billions (and now trillions) on the wars for empire. But at home, it's all "tightening of the belts," belts that are slowly becoming tourniquets for democracy.

Don't expect the so-called mainstream media to explain all this to the public. After all, according to the mainstream media in the US, there are teachers to blame and public workers to vilify, and there is an ever-ready supply of immigrant populations to enslave or deport as well as invasions to carry out on exotic lands Americans can't find on a map in efforts to rout evildoers who supposedly cause our current calamities. (And let's not forget that in actuality, it is the *corporate* media, but the term "mainstream" is used so often people tend to forget it is not at all mainstream.) And when this "news" gets too heavy, big media in the US can intersperse a steady diet of Junk Food News on which Americans can vicariously feast—celebrity gossip and sport spectacles ranging from Charlie Sheen's Tiger Blood meltdown and Bristol Palin's *Dancing with the Stars* scandal to the next Super Bowl and more March Madness, all in hopes that the problems we all face in the real world will simply just go away. But they won't. They only get bigger.

These are the same issues many in the media reform movement also decry, and rightfully so. Reform efforts have been laudable, and there are many that continue to work toward creating better, more truthful, and democratic media (see chapter 5). But the solutions many reformers offer mostly seem to involve "fixing the system," by focusing on the influence of advertisers or regulating ownership, which to date have not achieved reformer objectives. Other reformers want the government to step in to "fix the system" by creating a public media, without noting that government has played a big role in the current problem; even while public media is under attack by Congress, Public Broadcasting Service (PBS) and National Public Radio (NPR) have hardly stood out in major ways to challenge the plutocracy in the name of the people. A publicly subsidized free press is a good idea, but getting there is another story, one that likely does not involve the current, or a future, Congress or the FCC, at least if the past is prologue.

These reform notions do not go to the root of the problem, they do not map out a radical solution. And, despite reformers' benevolent instincts and intentions, don't always expect reformers that criticize the big media messengers' behaviors to realize that the system they spend so much time trying to repair is now defunct—not that it ever existed in a democratically utopian means in the first place. This is why we, the media-literate citizens of this dying republic, must now move beyond reform to create a new way.

We need to Be the Media in word and deed (as David Mathison has said), not lobby those in power to reform their own current establishment megaphones for their own power elite agendas, as that will not happen, and indeed, has not, for the most part, in the past. In order to achieve real change, we need not have elaborate conferences that rely on power elite voices, their foundation monies, and their apologetic reformist rhetoric. We need to embody the true change channeled by nineteenth-century American activist Elizabeth Cady Stanton when she said, "Reformers who are always compromising have not yet grasped the idea that truth is the only safe ground to stand upon." Indeed.

The time to speak truth to power—to media power elites, their political allies, and their funders—is now. Media Reform is an important movement, but it should not be seen as the only path to creating a more just and democratic media system. More radical approaches are needed at this point. So just say "no" to reform-driven agendas delivered as so much managed news propaganda, and instead embrace the possibilities of a radical media democracy in action, of, by, and for the people. Show it with actions through citizen journalism and through support of local and independent, non-corporate, community media. Real change only begins with radical action on the local level. That's the only way a truly free press can be created, preserved, and nurtured to be a tool of the people and not the reformers with their unrequited overtures to the media power elite. The time to act is now. As Robert McChesney said, "Let's have a real communication revolution." We may not have time enough for the next reform conference to save us, despite all the best intentions. We are the media revolution of tomorrow. But we must act today.

Notes on Recent Literature Concerning Media Reform

The topic of a failing free press system, or the shortcomings of the so-called mainstream media, has been the subject of many works, including scholarly works from esteemed, academic, establishment publishing houses over the past few years. Two key works include Alex S. Jones's *Losing the News: The Future of the News That Feeds Democracy*, and W. Lance Bennett, Regina G. Lawrence, and Steven Livingston's *When the Press Fails: Political Power and the News Media from Iraq to Katrina*.[2] Both works have legitimate critiques but operate within the confines of a traditional media system—that is, a corporate media system.

Jones in particular calls for a return to accountability (and accountability is certainly not a bad thing, though whether or not we are returning to it, as if it existed prior, is another question, and this accountability is referred to as an "iron core," which has eroded, thus the unproven "return" concept). Bennett et al. focus on the corporate media failures in covering Abu Ghraib and Hurricane Katrina, specifically on the role of the White House and political spin machines. A notable section is the inclusion of Kristina Borjesson in an interview with Ron Suskind, who tries to explain the role of the Fourth Estate in the lead up to the Iraq War, and ends up saying the press utterly failed, as its real role was to prevent both the American people and Congress "from seeing clearly the true reasons and motivation that ultimately drove us to war." Even with this damning inclusive observation, the authors here cite how the same establishment press do a stellar job on other political issues like abortion, and are rife with diverse views, but without giving any real evidence. Again, the notion is that the establishment press, the corporate media, are not really all that bad and do a mostly good job, but that they have had a rough first decade on a couple major issues in the twenty-first century. Even using the same examples Bennett et al. use, another conclusion seems highly possible, one leaning more toward not just "when the press fails," but rather, toward a sentiment of "when does the press not fail so miserably?"

While both are good works on a number of levels in calling out the failures of the establishment press, neither go so far as to critique the overarching structure within which the media they critique actually operate—that of capitalism and the private, for-profit model for journalism in a supposedly free and egalitarian society. Both works are heavily sourced with establishment journalists, politicians, scholars, publications, etc. One will find similar critiques coming out of Harvard, Columbia, and the Annenberg Schools, all leaving out consideration of the latter issue (though not everyone associated with those institutions would agree, there is a pattern leading in the direction described). These major institutions all miss a big piece of the puzzle that has also contributed to the collapse of modern journalism: the reliance on establishment sources and exclusion of vernacular views.

On the other hand, works by media scholars like Robert W. McChesney do such a critique, and include different sources, as have others like Edward S. Herman and Noam Chomsky, all of whom are also at major academic institutions, but these were mostly ignored in the two highly praised academic works cited above. Both the previous works paid lip service to McChesney, Herman, and Chomsky, towering figures in the field of media criticism to be sure, but only on one or two pages of their overall analysis which, again, called for subtle changes in the current media system regarding journalism. And, to be fair, even the establishment-based changes suggested in Jones and Bennett et al., which are hardly revolutionary, have not been adopted in the corporate media. Perhaps this is why McChesney, Chomsky, and others in similar fashion are framed as "radical" (read "untenable" if one is in the establishment media or academia), even though much of what they put forward is either merely a deconstruction of the current free press problem in America, or a solution that utilizes current existing models of journalism, including government subsidization, which has proven to be quite tepid in its implementation due to the overarching problems of the for-profit, privatized philosophical tyranny that exists in what passes for American discourse.

The above-cited books above are worthy of reading as they offer insightful commentary on recent media failures and the collapse of traditional journalism. However, a thorough reading of *Will the Last Reporter Please Turn Out the Lights: The Collapse of Journalism and What Can Be Done to Fix It*, edited by Robert W. McChesney and Victor Pickard, and *The Death and Life of American Journalism: The Media Revolution that Will Begin the World Again*, by Robert W. McChesney and John Nichols, will leave the reader with a much broader understanding of the problem of the failures of the free press in America and what one can do about it.[3] Further, samplings from the Truth Emergency and Project Censored International sections of this work, and *Censored 2011*, may do the same. Reading these works together, the reader may seriously begin to make up his or her mind about the current state of affairs for the supposed free press in the US, and what can be done to change or improve it, which is ultimately the purpose of this *Censored 2012* volume—to generate a more media-literate public.

Indeed, we at Project Censored are suggesting that we need to go even further than that which is proffered by the recent McChesney works, at least in terms of citizen journalism—having people become the media—though the group he helped found, Free Press, has made great strides in the realm of media freedom. That said, we need to utilize our systems of education to produce accurate and quality information in our local communities, news production from the bottom up, to further diminish reliance on imposed, corporate-man aged news platforms, especially those on cable television, but also including the major networks and even national broadcasts from NPR and PBS. These institutions have ritually kept the public in the dark on some of the most crucial issues of our times. McChesney himself noted, in *The Problem of Media in the 21st Century*, that the quality of reporting by major media sources about key matters, like the nation going to war, has sadly not changed much over the past hundred years, and that the tendencies toward so-called yellow journalism are still alive and well:

> Journalists who question agreed-upon assumptions by the political elite stigmatize themselves as unprofessional and political. Most major US wars over the past century have been sold to the public on dubious claims if not outright lies, yet professional journalism has generally failed to warn the public. Compare the press coverage leading up to the Spanish-American War, which is a notorious example of yellow journalism—before the advent of professional journalism to the coverage leading up to the 2003 Iraq war and it is difficult to avoid the conclusion that the quality of reporting has not changed much.[4]

We are in need of a true media revolution, neither controlled by the corporations nor the moneyed foundations, liberal or otherwise. We need the free press promised and protected by America's founders in pure, radical fashion. And we can't just ask the powers-that-be to give it to us. We have to not only demand it; we must rid ourselves of corporate media dominion and create a new, democratic system of media of, by, and for the people. Media literacy and democracy must be part of a vibrant, diverse, and inclusive program of public education and civic action. We must work together to be the media revolution of the twenty-first century if our democracy is to survive.

Inside Censored 2012

This year, we continue to divide our annual publication into three sections as we broaden, grow, and diversify efforts to illuminate examples of censorship in the corporate mainstream US press. Further, we continue to promote ways of improving our systems of reporting and communicating to the public at large about the most crucial issues we face as a society.

Former director of Project Censored, Dr. Peter Phillips, kicks off Censored 2012 in a no-holds-barred introduction that frames this year's volume. His call for a media revolution to dismantle empire is clear, and his noting of how we can get there, through our collective cultures of resistance, is advice we should heed.

The first section of this year's book—the News that Didn't Make the News and Why—houses the traditional top censored news stories from the past year, which are, for the first time, analyzed in what we call Censored News Clusters. Within these Clusters, Project Censored's team of media experts and their student interns analyze and connect the dots among stories based on similar themes or topics, flushing out why some topics are prone to such underreporting, and what we might do about this problem, rather than simply list the top stories as ranked in importance by Project Censored judges. This year, our chapter 1 writing team includes Peter Phillips, Elliot D. Cohen, Dean Walker, Andy Lee Roth, Elaine Wellin, Kristen Seraphin, Joel Evans-Fudem, Amy Ortiz, Kenn Burrows, and Tom Atlee, with additional research and editing by Trish Boreta, Bill Gibbons, Craig Cekala, Melody J. Haislip, Nolan Higdon, and Casey Goonan. Of course, it also involves hundreds of students and professors from colleges across the United States.

In chapter 2, Censored Déjà Vu, we check for any new or increased coverage of previously underreported top stories. Most receive little if any coverage in the corporate mainstream press, but if they do, we monitor and remark upon it here, ever in hopes that the corporate media may be improved, but not waiting for such a change to take place as we advocate for the coming media revolution.

In chapter 3, Adam Bessie joins the Project Censored director, Abby Martin of Media Roots, and student interns Nolan Higdon and Clifton Roy Damiens to analyze the ubiquity of Junk Food News and the growing problem of News Abuse, including framing and propaganda in the US media. This year we include a case study of how pubic workers—teachers especially—have been negatively portrayed in the corporate press as a major example of News Abuse.

Chapter 4, by San Francisco State University professor of holistic studies Kenn Burrows, brings out the best in underreported news as we look at the positive, the signs of health and community building as published in the independent press, which the corporate media tend to deride, downplay, or outright ignore. The problems we face do not only include the sordid stories the corporate media fail to report; they also include the many positive things going on often right in front of us. When the corporate media do not acknowledge these stories, they contribute to a sense of disconnection among many in society.

Chapter 5 brings back our media activism showcase, of examples of media democracy in action, highlighting what other activists, scholars, and organizations are doing to achieve the media revolution and support the First Amendment, in maintenance of self governance and democracy. This year we include Abby Martin of Media Roots, Tracy Rosenberg of Media Alliance, Jeff Cohen of the Park Center for Independent Media (Cohen was also the founder of Fairness and Accuracy In Reporting, which just celebrated its twenty-fifth anniversary), Lisa Graves of PR Watch, Josh Wolf, Khalil Bendib of the *Voices of the Middle East and North Africa* radio program, and the pro-transparency group supporting Bradley Manning and Wikileaks, Courage to Resist.

Section 2 focuses on what we call the Truth Emergency.[5] This Truth Emergency we face is a result of the lack of factual reporting by the so-called mainstream media over the past decade. Americans are subjected to mass amounts of propaganda, from misinformation to disinformation, on a daily basis, about some of the most significant issues of the day. Whether this involves the post-9/11 wars in the Middle East, the health care debate, election fraud, or economic collapse, most Americans are unaware of all the facts of how we got where we now are as a society. It is the duty of the constitutionally protected free press to report factually to the public on these matters. However, as shown by Project Censored's work dating back to 1976, that is not happening.

One way of combating this Truth Emergency is by understanding the nature of propaganda. This year, our Truth Emergency section is a primer on Propaganda Studies, which includes a brief history, theory, application, and case studies all presented to enhance media literacy among the general public. We are pleased to bring some of the best and brightest in the field to offer insight on this ever-important area of study. Randal Marlin gives a brief history of propaganda; Jacob Van Vleet looks at one of the key theorists of propaganda, Jacques Ellul. Robert Abele offer a philosophical and structural analysis of propaganda for readers, while Elliot D. Cohen and Anthony DiMaggio look at specific areas, the importance of net neutrality and Astroturf activism in the so-called Tea Party respectively, where understanding communication politics and media literacy really matter if a society is to be truly democratically functional, able to operate outside the propaganda matrix of the corporate media and establishment public relations machine.

The final section of the book is Project Censored International, which is a collection of various studies and media commentary that not only look at problems of global media censorship but also examine how these important issues are handled, or ignored, in the US corporate press. This section brings us a diverse group of scholars and activists and also introduces our work on the Fair Share of the Common Heritage awards. This year, we welcome Mary Lia, Cynthia Boaz, Ann Garrison, Jon Elmer, Robin Andersen, Margaret Flowers, and Ina May Gaskin. The significant issues in this section include the Fair Sharing of the Common Heritage, on moving toward an embrace of the human commons; understanding nonviolence and how media depict such movements for peace and social justice; and the deconstruction of various myths—from the incredibly biased reporting on Africa to distorted views of recent disaster coverage, plus the ongoing skewed coverage concerning Israel/Palestine. This section continues on issues of health with an analysis of the top-down denial of mass public support for single payer health care, and we round out *Censored 2012* by looking at how corporate media distort life itself, from birth, by either ignoring or demonizing the efficacy of natural childbirth and midwifery in the US, despite facts surrounding home birth culture that clearly refute the mass media's biased coverage.

All in all, this is a work in progress (all thirty-five years of it), and it involves hundreds of dedicated scholars, students, activists, and people from all walks of life across the globe who have at least one thing in common: the belief in democracy and the role a free press plays in the creation, protection, and maintenance of it. Thanks to all who made this work possible, to all the tireless and selfless contributors, to all the readers and supporters of a free and vibrant people's press, one that is always and only uncensored. Please pass it on . . .

Mickey Huff
Berkeley, CA
June 2011

Notes

1. Robert McChesney, *Communication Revolution: Critical Junctures and the Future of Media* (New York: New Press, 2007), 221.
2. Alex S. Jones, *Losing the News: The Future of the News That Feeds Democracy* (Oxford: Oxford University Press, 2009); and W. Lance Bennett, Regina G. Lawrence, and Steven Livingston, *When the Press Fails: Political Power and the News Media from Iraq to Katrina* (Chicago: University of Chicago Press, 2007).
3. Robert W. McChesney and Victor Pickard, eds., *Will the Last Reporter Please Turn Out the Lights: The Collapse of Journalism and What Can Be Done to Fix It* (New York: New Press, 2011); and Robert W. McChesney and John Nichols, *The Death and Life of American Journalism: The Media Revolution that Will Begin the World Again* (New York and Philadelphia: Nation Books, 2010).
4. Robert W. McChesney, *The Problem of the Media: US Communication Politics in the 21st Century* (New York: Monthly Review Press, 2004), 74.
5. See Peter Phillips, Mickey Huff, et al., "Truth Emergency Meets Media Reform," chap. 11 in *Censored 2009: The Top 25 Censored Stories of 2007–08*, eds. Peter Phillips and Andrew Roth (New York: Seven Stories Press, 2008), 281–95. Also see Peter Phillips and Mickey Huff, "Truth Emergency: Inside the Military Industrial Media Empire," chap. 5 in *Censored 2010: The Top 25 Censored Stories of 2008–09*, eds. Peter Phillips and Mickey Huff (New York: Seven Stories Press, 2009), 197–220.

Introduction to Censored 2012

by Peter Phillips

The international concentration of wealth and military power is endangering not only the personal freedoms and life chances of billions of people, but the potential for life on earth to simply exist. The US-NATO military-industrial-media empire operates in support of transnational corporations and the central banks primarily as the enforcer of the International Monetary Fund's and World Bank's fiscal policies, and as the protector of transnational capital flow. Considering capital's need for constant growth and profits, the combination of the private owners of production in partnership with empire enforcers—military and police, both public and private—is resulting in a tragic decline of humanity into a freedomless state of global corporate fascism.

The alarmists featured in *Censored 2012*, with their Paul Revere voices, are echoing the warnings of global catastrophe. Chris Hedges and Cord Jefferson raise the issue of the human costs of the 9/11 empire wars. Peter Dale Scott and Allen Roland astound us with documentation regarding the preparation for marshal law and military control in the US. Tim Reid and Michael Evans document the worldwide deep penetration of empire forces deployed in seventy-five countries. Tina Mather, Kimberly Daniels, and Shannon Pence disclose the systemic waste of food by corporate capitalism. Nick Fielding, Ian Cobain, Darlene Storm, and Stephen Webster warn of the immediate penetration of empire enforcers into cyberspace for propaganda control. Regionally, we are reminded of the ongoing apocalypse in central Africa by Keith Harmon Snow, while E. Eduardo Castillo and Martha Mendoza address the massive US involvement in Mexico's war on drugs.

The overall environmental disasters of empire expansion featured in *Censored 2012* are seemingly beyond comprehension, ranging from new diseases to massive life-threatening pollution of the oceans, air, and earth. We, in our bodies, are all Fukushima, Gulf oil, plastics, and electromagnetic waves. No one is safe, including the children of our children. Without immediate mass interventions, humankind is in danger of permanent extinction.

Also documented in *Censored 2012* are the very human efforts around the world to counter the empire of destruction. There are movements to ban plastic bags, protect the environment, develop local banks, and establish community-based budgeting, as well as many other efforts to protect the commons and encourage collaborations. The democracy movements of young people in the Middle East, Greece, and Spain are inspiring other attempts to counter the empire of destruction. These social movements in resistance to power, crossing ideological lines, are a manifestation of grassroots radical democracy. They are community-based reality checks by human beings sharing inequality in the face of overwhelming power.

During the movement's May 15, 2011, protests in Madrid, Spain, Project Censored affiliate professor Concha Mateo wrote from the M15 camp in the Puerta del Sol ("Gate of the Sun"), just before it was taken down on June 12:

> [A]fter five hours debate, the Assembly of Sol decided on the continuity of "acampadasol" as it is known in the web. . . . One more step forward. . . . The local assemblies are working. The 15M goes on.
>
> The energy will never disappear—it only gets transformed.
>
> We are moving out of Puerta del Sol. We will leave the *Puerta* but will take the *Sol* with us. The 15M goes on.
>
> One sign over the wall says: The sun can rise up whatever night.
>
> The night: democratic deficits, collective efforts required to rescue banks but no collective profit, economic austerity measures imposed by the government dictated by financial capitalism, 4 million unemployed [in Spain], corrupt politicians. . . . We are not anti-system, the system is anti-us.[1]

While we can be encouraged by the emerging awareness of the need for democratic challenges to empire, we cannot ignore the extreme danger of total economic collapse, chaos, and environmental destruction that potentially undermines human rights and civil societies everywhere. This empire of destruction seems to many to be unstoppable. Over a million civilians have died in Iraq since the US invasion. US-NATO wars continue in Afghanistan, Libya, and Pakistan, with alarming daily civilian death rates. Over three billion people live on less than two dollars a day. Human misery expands inside the empire of destruction, while the transnational corporate class—less than 1 percent of the world's population—relishes in wealth, opulence, and greed protected by both private and public military forces and cooperative governments doing the bidding of empire.

But, we can draw strength through mutual recognition of our resistance movements. Iara Lee's new film, *Cultures of Resistance*, is a heartwarming look at the daily efforts of people worldwide to protect humanness in the face of fascism and repression, and is symbolically representative of the efforts that need to be manifested in real life, around the world, as well. Without strong democratic movements of resistance worldwide, the chaos resulting from the empire of destruction will inevitability move from Kabul and Palestine to Paris and San Francisco.

Time and again, *Censored 2012* heeds the call for the global truth and justice movement to become self-informed, radically democratic, and culturally resistant to the empire of destruction.

We are not going to reform the empire of destruction globally through corrupt capital-protecting legislative bodies controlled by millionaires and corporate money. We are not going to change the propaganda messages of corporate media—as they are just as deeply embedded in the destructive empire of power as the transnational corporate elite.

Corporate media (singular) is the information control wing of the global power structure. The corporate media systematically censors news stories that challenge the propaganda of empire. Some of the mythologies of empire are that we live in democratic societies with fair elections, that governments are primarily transparent and seek to protect the public, that evil lurks in the world waiting to challenge our freedoms, that we fight fairly and morally while the others are evil terrorists, that governments would never do anything to harm their own citizens, that wealth trickles down, that we are all trying to be green, and that capitalism will save us.

Many of the stories that Project Censored has covered over the past thirty-five years have challenged the core myths of empire. These are stories about election fraud, transnational elite planning and control, 9/11, torture, extensive civilian deaths in wars, state crimes against democracy, massive military misspending, corporate tax evasion and misappropriation or economic resource (capital flight), unsustainable practices and environmental damage, and the denegation of world leaders who fail to cooperate with neoliberal economic policies. We are in an era of total information control and top-down managed news throughout the empire. It is not against the law to lie to the public or to prepackage news to match empire propaganda myths.

The time is right for democracy movements to build their own news, and their own systems of decision-making from the bottom-up. We no longer need a majority to make change inside the empire. We need only active, informed populations in the 10 to 20 percent range of society to initiate change producing social movements of resistance and noncooperation with empire.

Individually and collectively we can disconnect from employment that supports the empire of destruction, and we can instead keep our work with community-based efforts at local sustainability, economic development, and caring. We can shop locally and never enter the Walmarts of empire. We can organize for resistance to counter the billions of dollars a year spent by the military to deceive our children into serving the empire of destruction. We can turn off the corporate media filled with its propaganda and lies and seek our own sources of news from within democracy movements worldwide.

We can un-censor the news, utilizing the efforts of our colleges and universities validating independent news within the Project Censored/Media Freedom network. We can invite activists and those concerned with the empire of destruction to speak truth to power with news and stories of the abuses of empire and the successes of our efforts of resistance. Telling our stories openly and transparently will be vital to a global democratic movement. We will share the wealth of humanness to build democratic change to save our grandchildren's grandchildren and ourselves. We are all protégé of the Sol.

PETER PHILLIPS is a professor of sociology at Sonoma State University and recent past director of Project Censored (1996–2010). He teaches classes in Media Censorship, Investigative Sociology, Sociology of Power, Political Sociology, and Sociology of Media. He has published fourteen editions of the *Censored* yearbooks with Seven Stories Press. He has also published, with Seven Stories Press, the books *Impeach the President: The Case Against Bush and Cheney* (2006) and *Project Censored Guide to Independent Media and Activism* (2003).

Peter Phillips co-hosts the Project Censored show on Pacifica Radio and is a frequent writer and blogger on numerous websites worldwide. In 2009, Phillips received the Dallas Smythe Award from the Union for Democratic Communications. Dallas Smythe is a national award given to researchers and activists who, through their research and/or production work, have made significant contributions to the study and practice of democratic communication.

Phillips is president of Media Freedom Foundation, the nonprofit corporation that supports Project Censored and the following websites:

Project Censored: www.projectcensored.org

Daily News: www.censorednews.org

Validated News and Research: www.mediafreedominternational.org

Daily Censored Blog: www.dailycensored.com

Daily News in Spanish: www.proyectocensurado.org

Fair Share of the Common Heritage: www.fairsharecommonheritage.org

Note

1. Concha Mateo, "Spanish 15M Goes Out of Puerta del Sol: An Ethical Revolution Spread its Wings," *Daily Censored*, June 9, 2011, http://dailycensored.com/2011/06/09/spanish-15m-goes-out-of-puerta-del-sol-an-ethical-revolution-spread-its-wings/.

Censored News and Media Analysis

CHAPTER I

Project Censored News Clusters and the Top Censored Stories of 2010 and 2011

by Peter Phillips, Mickey Huff, Elliot D. Cohen, Dean Walker, Andy Lee Roth, Elaine Wellin, Kristen Seraphin, Joel Evans-Fudem, Amy Ortiz, Kenn Burrows, and Tom Atlee, with additional research and editing by Trish Boreta, Bill Gibbons, Craig Cekala, Melody J. Haislip, Nolan Higdon, and Casey Goonan

> *No experiment can be more interesting than that we are now trying, and which we trust will end in establishing the fact, that man may be governed by reason and truth. Our first object should therefore be, to leave open to him all the avenues to truth. The most effectual hitherto found, is the freedom of the press. It is, therefore, the first shut up by those who fear the investigation of their actions.*
> —THOMAS JEFFERSON, 1804

> *The truth comes as conqueror only because we have lost the art of receiving it as guest.*
> —RABINDRANATH TAGORE, Indian poet, 1924

INTRODUCTION

by Mickey Huff, director of Project Censored

Project Censored has compiled a list of stories absent from the United States establishment news media each year since 1976. The annual Top 25 Censored Stories have become our tagline as an organization, despite that we do much more in the field of media studies, communications, journalism, and sociology. This year, we divide our top stories into categories, and analyze them in what we call Censored News Clusters, which relate closely with the additional contents of our media research. We added the Censored News Clusters, encompassing our top censored stories each year, because we couldn't help but notice that simply ranking the stories did little to tie them all together, to illuminate topical patterns of censorship. That is, there are several topics, or clusters, that almost always have stories within them, and the numerical ranking of stories can act to obscure the connections among many of the stories. The top stories and their runners up over the years are all important, and they have all been underreported, if reported at all, by the seemingly ubiquitous corporate news media. We believe that analyzing the stories through Censored News Clusters, we can better understand the architecture of censorship in the US.

Project Censored founder Dr. Carl Jensen originally grouped the top stories topically though they were still enumerated and ranked by Project Censored researchers and judges. Dr. Peter Phillips, Jensen's successor, commented on thematic groupings of stories, noting their reoccurrence. This year at Project Censored, we quite purposefully discuss and organize the top censored stories within topical categories to draw particular attention to the nature of censorship in the US press, highlighting the type of story likely to be underreported, distorted, or outright ignored. While we continue to have our Top 25 Stories ranked by Project Censored judges and college and university affiliates, we include related stories that were nominated this past year in topical clusters to show a pattern among the types of stories that are slighted by the corporate media, and take a look at why this is so.

Censorship, as defined by the Project, includes anything that interferes with the free flow of information in a society that purports to have a free press, and America has protections for such freedom in its Constitution (specifically under the First Amendment). When the free press fails to function factually in the public interest, it acts as a propaganda organ of the private sector owners and investors of big media, and even of their supposed government overseers.

It is important to consider, though, that censorship, by its very nature, is a form of propaganda—deceptive communication used to sway or influence public opinion to benefit a special interest, party, or individual. Propaganda, and this type of censorship, is intentional by nature, and is oft the result of a plan hatched to achieve certain objectives to the gain of one party at the expense of another (see Section II of this volume). In essence, this is a conspiracy. We use this term fully aware that it has unfortunately become a buzzword for propagandistic attacks against any story that is outside the realm of conventional wisdom—in other words, out of bounds for consideration regardless of factual content. Such exclusion is also a clear violation of the freedom of expression and free press principles ensconced in the First Amendment.

In short, the decision by media institutions to run—or to not run—a particular news story, or to include—or to exclude—a certain view, based on anything other than the desire to report the full truth, is censorship and functions as a form of propaganda. Censorship includes many techniques, such as framing, slighting of content, and appealing to emotion over logic, among other tactics of media manipulation, including what is referred to as spin.[1] These methods are used to create matter-of-fact conspiracies to manipulate or withhold information. These are not the "conspiracy theories" as used in the pejorative, comprised of wild speculation or paranoia. And if wild speculation dominates a particular message, when unsupported theories present themselves as solid truths rather than as possibilities requiring further investigation, sober challenges based on all the known facts should be put forth to tame them in free debate—not dismissively ignore or attack them a priori. Simply put, censorship of any kind must be confronted and dismantled.

The great playwright George Bernard Shaw once wrote, "All great truths begin as blasphemies." If we cannot get past the stage at which controversial stories are merely blasphemies, we may never arrive at the truth of many important matters. To lump all potentially conspiratorial topics together does a disservice to free speech, as factual conspiracies (proven to have censored information about wrongdoings) have a long past. This type of labeling acts to censor further investigation. This labeling comes from a place of fear—fear of the facts and to where they may lead. A free press cannot tolerate such restrictive forms of communication and must resist them at all turns, lest that system fall into disrepute with the public and fail at its constitutionally protected mission of keeping the electorate informed. The corporate media have failed in this task. These problems of censorship and the use of propaganda also have long-proven pasts. We need to act in concert to overcome these dual demons for democracy, purge ourselves of the plagues of fear and secrecy, and truly come out into the light of knowledge and hope.[2]

We would do well to recall and ponder the four freedoms enunciated by President Franklin D. Roosevelt seventy years ago. On January 6, 1941, Roosevelt addressed the US Congress in the context of a world on the verge of serious crisis, on how America should move forward:

> In the future days, which we seek to make secure, we look forward to a world founded upon four essential human freedoms. The first is freedom of speech and expression—everywhere in the world. The second is freedom of every person to worship God in his own way—everywhere in the world. The third is freedom from want—which, translated into world terms, means economic understandings, which will secure to every nation a healthy peacetime life for its inhabitants—everywhere in the world. The fourth is freedom from fear—which, translated into world terms, means a worldwide reduction of armaments to such a point and in such a thorough fashion that no nation will be in a position to commit an act of physical aggression against any neighbor—anywhere in the world. That is no vision of a distant millennium. It is a definite basis for a kind of world attainable in our own time and generation. That kind of world is the very antithesis of the so-called new order of tyranny, which the dictators seek to create with the crash of a bomb. To that new order we oppose the greater conception—the moral order. A good society is able to face schemes of world domination and foreign revolutions alike without fear.

Those words have become both apt and prescient. But we cannot face schemes of world domination abroad without also examining them right here at home, especially when those ambitions emanate from our very own leaders and government—indeed from our own empire—which is, to be sure, everywhere in the world. Future days are here now, in 2011, and we still have much work to do to fulfill the promise of Roosevelt's four freedoms; we cannot wait for that distant millennium as it has already arrived. One way to face our current challenges is by seriously adopting these four freedoms. By considering free speech and expression, by providing the public with honest, fact-based information that is accurately reported by the free press, perhaps we shall overcome the many challenges we face.

In the end, we must lift the veil that censors and propagandists create for democracy to thrive. Thomas Jefferson once wrote, "Our liberty depends on the freedom of the press, and that cannot be limited without being lost." The only way our republic will have a viable future is through the creation, protection, and public support of an uncensored press. In that spirit, Project Censored presents the top censored stories and Censored News Clusters for 2010–2011, in an effort to make better known these significant yet underreported stories. The Clusters include:

- ▶ Human Costs of War & Violence
- ▶ Social Media and Internet Freedom
- ▶ Economics and Inequality
- ▶ Power, Abuse, and Accountability
- ▶ Health and the Environment
- ▶ Women and Gender Issues
- ▶ Collaboration and Common Good

The authors and journalists of *Censored 2012* (especially here in chapter one) exemplify the kind of future we need in a free press. We hope these people and their reports embolden others in the news media and the citizenry at large to at long last lift the veil, see the truth of our times, and act in a democratic spirit to create a better world.

Notes

1. For more on these tactics, see political scientist and former Project Censored judge, Michael Parenti, "Monopoly Media Manipulation," May 2001, online at http://www.michaelparenti.org/MonopolyMedia.html; for a more detailed analysis on the phenomenon of "spin," see Stuart Ewen, *PR!: A Social History of Spin* (New York: Basic Books, 1996).
2. Thomas Jefferson, in his first inaugural address in 1801, said, "If there be any among us who would wish to dissolve this Union, or to change its republican form,

let them stand undisturbed as monuments of the safety with which error of opinion may be tolerated, where reason is left free to combat it." This sentiment clearly favors free expression and debate over censorship. It encourages factual transparency and the creation of public consensus in maintenance of democratic self-governance. The free press plays a crucial role in this free expression.

For further reading on issues surrounding conspiracy labeling and research, and in particular concerning potential State Crimes Against Democracy and the censorship of other controversial issues that have great impact on our society, please see Paul Craig Roberts, "9/11 and the Orwellian Redefinition of 'Conspiracy Theory,'" Global Research, June 20, 2011, http://www.globalresearch.ca/index.php?context=viewArticle&code=ROB20110620&articleId=25339; Dr. Robert Abele on "Conspiracy Theory," (in two parts), *The Daily Censored*, written for the *Project Censored Show* on Pacifica Radio, May 18 and 21, 2011, available online at http://dailycensored.com/2011/05/18/conspiracy-theory/ and http://dailycensored.com/2011/05/21/conspiracy-theory-ii/, and especially note Dr. Abele's "Further Reading" list at the links.

Dr. Mark Crispin Miller talks about the genesis of the label "conspiracy theory" coming from the CIA after the JFK assassination, and the term has been used ever since as a term to discredit anyone that investigates unpopular subjects. Miller discusses this at the "How the World Changed After 9/11: A Critical Thinking Symposium" panel discussion and the "Distrust Your Government: How Conspiracy Theorists Become Conspiracy Realists" conference hosted by *INN World Report* in New York City, September 11–12, 2010, http://www.howtheworld-changed.org/. For more on Miller's remarks, see http://tangibleinfo.blogspot.com/2011/02/word-conspiracy-theory-was-invented-by.html, and especially for audio of the panel from 5:25 to 26:33, online at http://www.radio4all.net/files/cheryl@ct911truth.org/4212-1-911WUC_20110217_Miller.mp3. Miller quotes James Madison: "The fetters (the chains) on liberty at home have ever been forged out of the weapons used in defense against real, pretended, or imaginary enemies from abroad." The term "conspiracy theory" acts as a cudgel to curtail and censor open and honest debate (a fetter on liberty). Similarly, scholar Peter Dale Scott has written and spoken a great deal about conspiracy research in what he calls "Deep Politics," which he expands upon in many of his books, but for an introduction, see http://www.maryferrell.org/wiki/index.php/The_War_Conspiracy.

Further reading includes Peter Phillips and Mickey Huff, "Response to Chip Berlet's 'Toxic to Democracy: Conspiracy Theories, Demonization, and Scapegoating,'" Project Censored, July 29, 2010, http://www.projectcensored.org/top-stories/articles/a-response-to-chip-berlet's-"toxic-to-democracy"/; Dr. Peter Phillips, "Conspiracies, Plots and Other Anti-democratic Notions" Global Research, Nov 10, 2002, http://www.globalresearch.ca/articles/PHI211A.html; Dr. Michael Parenti, "Conspiracy and Class Power," lecture in Berkeley, CA, 1993, recorded by Maria Gilardin of TUC Radio, http://www.tucradio.org/081015_ConspiracyONE.mp3 and http://www.tucradio.org/081022_ConspiracyTWO.mp3.

The Top Censored Stories of 2010–2011

Censored #1: More US Soldiers Committed Suicide than Died in Combat

Censored #2: US Military Manipulates the Social Media

Censored #3: Obama Authorizes International Assassination Campaign

Censored #4: Global Food Crisis Expands

Censored #5: Private Prison Companies Fund Anti-Immigrant Legislation

Censored #6: Google Spying?

Censored #7: US Army and Psychology's Largest Experiment—Ever

Censored #8: The Fairy Tale of Clean and Safe Nuclear Power

Censored #9: Government-Sponsored Technologies for Weather Modification

Censored #10: Real Unemployment: One Out of Five in US

Censored #11: Trafficking of Iraqi Women Rampant

Censored #12: Pacific Garbage Dump: Did You Really Think Your Plastic Was Being Recycled?

Human Costs of War and Violence
by Peter Phillips and Craig Cekala

Censored #1
More US Soldiers Committed Suicide than Died in Combat

Sources:
Chris Hedges, "Death and After in Iraq," *Truthdig*, March 21, 2011, http://www.truthdig
.com/report/item/the_body_baggers_of_iraq_20110321.
Cord Jefferson, "More US Soldiers Killed Themselves Than Died in Combat in 2010,"
Good, January 27, 2011, http://www.good.is/post/more-us-soldiers-killed-themselves-
than-died-in-combat-in-2010/.

Student Researcher: Bay Ewald (San Francisco State University)

Faculty Evaluator: Kenn Burrows (San Francisco State University)

Censored #3
Obama Authorizes International Assassination Campaign

Sources:

William Fisher, "Judge Declines to Rule on Targeted Killings of US Citizens," Inter Press Service, December 8, 2010, http://ipsnorthamerica.net/news.php?idnews=3426.

"Letter to President Obama—Targeted Killings," Human Rights Watch, December 7, 2010, http://www.hrw.org//en/news/1210/12/07/letter-obama-targetedkillings.

Glenn Greenwald, "Confirmed: Obama Authorizes Assassination of US Citizen," *Salon*, April 7, 2010, http://www.salon.com/news/opinion/glenn_greenwald/2010/04/07/assassinations.

Philip Alston, Project on Extrajudicial Executions, *UN Special Rapporteur on Extrajudicial Executions Handbook*, March 30, 2010, www.extrajudicialexecutions.org/application/media/Handbook%20Chapter%201%20Use%20of%20Force%20Duri ng%20Armed%20Conflicts5.pdf.

Francis A. Boyle, "Extrajudicial Killings: US Government 'Death List' for American Citizens," Global Research, February 10, 2010, http://www.globalresearch.ca/index.php?context=va&aid=17527.

"Obama Administration Claims Unchecked Authority to Kill Americans Outside Combat Zones," Common Dreams, November 8, 2010, http://www.commondreams .org/headline/2010/11/08-4.

Student Researchers: John M. Curtin, Molliann Zahm, Maria Rose, Vincent Caruso, and George Antzoulis (Niagara University); Jason Corbett (Sonoma State University)

Faculty Evaluators: Brian Martin Murphy (Niagara University); Cynthia Boaz (Sonoma State University); Mickey Huff (Diablo Valley College)

For more information on the case, including fact sheets and legal papers, visit www.aclu.org/targetedkillings and www.ccrjustice.org/targetedkillings.

Censored #7
US Army and Psychology's Largest Experiment—Ever

Sources:

Jeremy McCarthy, "Comprehensive Soldier Fitness: A Holistic Approach to Warrior Training," The Psychology of Wellbeing, August 17, 2010, http://psychologyofwellbeing.com/201008/comprehensive-soldier-fitness.html.

Roy Eidelson, Marc Pilisuk, and Stephen Soldz, "The Dark Side of Comprehensive Soldier Fitness," *Truthout*, April 1, 2011, http://www.truthout.org/dark-side-comprehensive-soldier-fitness/1301814000.

Jason Leopold, "Army's Spiritual Fitness Test Comes Under Fire," *Truthout*, January 5, 2011, http://www.truth-out.org/armys-fitness-test-designed-psychologist-who-inspired-cias-torture-program-under-fire66577.

Student Researcher: Rene Arellano (San Francisco State University)

Faculty Evaluator: Kenn Burrows (San Francisco State University)

Censored #25:
Extension of DU to Libya

Sources:
Dave Lindorff, "Toxic Intervention: Are NATO Forces Poisoning Libya with Depleted Uranium as They 'Protect' Civilians?," This Can't Be Happening, March 23, 2011, http://www.thiscantbehappening.net/node/530.
Souad N. Al-Azzawi, "Crime of the Century: Contaminating Iraq with Depleted Uranium," B*Russells* Tribunal, September 19, 2010, http://www.brusselstribunal.org/pdf/DU-Azzawi.pdf.

Student Researchers: Nathasha Terry-Ulett (Florida Atlantic University); Rosa Caldera (Sonoma State University)

Faculty Evaluators: James Tracy (Florida Atlantic University); Elaine Wellin (Sonoma State University)

Related Validated News Stories

T. Christian Miller and Daniel Zwerdling, "Aftershock: The Ticking Time Bomb of Soldiers' Traumatic Brain Injuries," AlterNet, March 27, 2011, http://www.alternet.org/world/150391/aftershock%3A_the_ticking_time_bomb_of_soldiers%27_traumatic_brain_injuries/?page=1.
James Cogan, "Suicide Claims More US Military Lives than Afghan War," World Socialist Web Site, January 6, 2010, http://www.wsws.org/articles/2010/jan2010/suic-j06.shtml.
Ernesto Carmona, "Dejad que los niños vengan a mi," Proyecto Censurado, translated by Project Censored, February 1, 2011, http://www.proyectocensurado.org/america-latina/dejad-que-los-ninos-vengan-a-mi/.
Mathew Nasuti, "American Military Creating an Environmental Disaster in Afghan Countryside (Part 1 of 3)," *Kabul Press*, April 25, 2010, http://kabulpress.org/my/spip.php?article7985.
Nasuti, "American Military Burn Pits Pollute Afghan Countryside (Part 2 of 3)," *Kabul Press*, May 2, 2010, http://kabulpress.org/my/spip.php?article9030.
Nasuti, "American Military Burn Pits Pose Risk to Future Generations of Afghans (Part 3 of 3)," *Kabul Press*, May 4, 2010, http://kabulpress.org/my/spip .php?article9421.
US Government Accountability Office, *Afghanistan and Iraq: DOD Should Improve Adherence to Its Guidance on Open Pit Burning and Solid Waste Management*, October 2010, http://www.gao.gov/new.items/d1163.pdf.
Christine Parthemore, "Promoting the Dialogue: Climate Change and US Ground Forces" (working paper, Center for a New American Security, April 2010), http://www.cnas.org/files/documents/publications/Promoting_Dialogue_Climate-Change&GroundForces_Parthemore_April2010_code408_workingpaper.pdf.
"Afghan Civilian Killings at Record Level," *Democracy Now!*, February 28, 2011, http://www.democracynow.org/2011/2/28/headlines#8.
Amanda Terkel, "Afghan Civilian Deaths Hit Record Levels in 2010," *Huffington Post*, February 1, 2011, http://www.huffingtonpost.com/2011/02/01/afghan-civilian-deaths-record-levels-2010_n_816813.html.

ARM Annual Report: Civilian Casualties of War, January–December 2010, Afghanistan Rights Monitor, February 1, 2011, http://www.arm.org.af/file.php?id=4.

Student Researchers: Karen Kniel, Josh Crockett, Ana Elliott, and Amy Ortiz (Sonoma State University); Joan Pedro and Luis Luján (Complutense University of Madrid)

Faculty Evaluators: Peter Phillips, Heather Flynn, and Jim Preston (Sonoma State University); Dr. Ana I. Segovia (Complutense University of Madrid)

For the second year in a row, the year ending 2010, more US soldiers killed themselves (468) than died in combat, reported Cord Jefferson on January 27, 2011. Excluding accidents and illness, 462 soldiers died in combat, while 468 committed suicide. Veterans who, after serving, suffer post-traumatic stress disorder (PTSD) are also at high risk. The study showed that 47 percent of veterans with PTSD had thoughts of suicide before they found help. The internal anguish a soldier experiences after returning from Iraq and Afghanistan can be far more severe than that experienced during live external combat.

More than two million troops have been deployed to Iraq and Afghanistan since 2001. Those who do return often suffer from physical, psychological, and cognitive trauma. More than 40 per 100,000 men from the ages of 20 to 24 take their lives each year. Some deaths, which are not counted in these statistics, are due to driving while under the influence of alcohol consumed due to depression. In 2008, Iraq and Afghanistan veterans were 75 percent more likely to die in a car accident and 148 percent more likely to die in a motorcycle accident. By making the calculations of 40 per 100,000 per year, the numbers of veteran suicides reaches into the tens of thousands nationwide since the beginning of the 9/11 wars.

In 2009, there were 381 military personnel suicides, a number that also exceeded the number of combat deaths. While the military has acknowledged an increase in suicides for some years, the corporate media tends to downplay the seriousness of these deaths by pointing to improvements and blaming the victims themselves. *USA Today* reporter Gregg Zoroya wrote on July 29, 2010, "After nine years of war, the Army attracts recruits ready for combat but inclined toward risky personal behavior. It's a volatile mix that led to more deaths from suicide, drug overdoses and drinking and driving than from warfare, an Army review concludes."[1]

Zoroya followed up half a year later: "The Marine Corps reported a decline in suicides from 52 in 2009 to 37 confirmed or suspected cases in 2010. Among active-duty Army soldiers, there were 156 potential suicides in 2010, down slightly from 162 in 2009."[2]

In his *Truthdig* article "Death and After in Iraq," Chris Hedges quoted former mortuary unit marine Jess Goodell: "War is disgusting and horrific. . . . It never leaves the people who were involved in it. The damage is far greater than the lists of casualties or cost in dollars. It permeates lifestyles. It infects cultures and people and worldviews. The war is never over for us. The fighting stops. The troops get called back. But the war goes on for those damaged by war."

Goodell also described how the Marines have exploited young people, "Every single Marine I know goes to Iraq to help," she said. "While I was there that is what I thought. That is why I volunteered. I thought I was going to help the Iraqis. I know better now. We did the dirty work. We were used by the government. The military knows that young, single men are dangerous. We breed it in Marines. We push the testosterone. We don't want them to be educated. . . . We cannot question anyone. We do what we are told."

In corporate media, coverage of suicide rates among the troops, a comprehensive analysis of the nature of the war and occupations itself, is absent, though there has been basic acknowledgment that "the Army and the Marine Corps, which have borne the heaviest burden in Iraq and Afghanistan, have been hit the hardest, reporting a record number of suicides in 2008. This year (2009), the toll is on pace to climb even higher. When combined, the figures paint a stark portrait of loss. More than 2,100 members of the armed forces have taken their own lives since 2001, nearly triple the number of troops who have died in Afghanistan and almost half of all US fatalities in Iraq."[3]

Post-traumatic stress disorder is also widely covered in the corporate media with the focus on the soldiers themselves and not on the US government's position in these wars and occupations. Corporate media's framing of the impact on soldiers never questions the US policy of maintaining a military empire of occupations and wars worldwide.

A bipartisan group of senators is asking President Barack Obama to change the current "insensitive" policy of not sending condolence letters to families of service members who commit suicide. A letter signed and sent May 25 by eleven senators—ten Democrats and one Republican—urged the president to "take immediate steps to reverse the long-standing policy of withholding presidential letters of condolence" to families of troops who killed themselves.[4]

In the January 2011 issue of *American Psychologist*, the American Psychology Association (APA) dedicated thirteen articles to detailing and celebrating a $117 million collaboration with the US Army, "Comprehensive Soldier Fitness" (CSF), marketed as resilience training to reduce, if not prevent, adverse psychological consequences to soldiers who endure combat. Because of the CSF emphasis on "positive psychology," advocates call it a holistic approach to warrior training.

Criticism arose shortly after the initiative was announced—including ethical questions about whether soldiers should be trained to become desensitized to traumatic events. Psychologist Bruce Levine loudly warned politicians, military brass, and the nation that if soldiers and veterans discover that they have been deceived about the meaningfulness and necessity of their mission, it is only human for them to become more prone to emotional turmoil, which can lead to destructive behaviors for themselves and others.

When asked during a National Public Radio interview whether CSF would be "the largest-ever experiment," Brigadier General Rhonda Cornum, who oversees the program, responded, "Well, we're not describing it as an experiment. We're describing it as training."[5]

"It is highly unusual for the effectiveness of such a huge and consequential intervention program not to be convincingly demonstrated first in carefully conducted, randomized, controlled trials—before being rolled out under less controlled conditions," wrote Roy Eidelson, Marc Pilisuk, and Stephen Soldz in *Truthout*.

The Obama administration has quietly put into practice an escalation of policy left over from the Bush II presidency: creating a de facto "presidential international assassination program." Court documents, evidence offered by Human Rights Watch, and a special United Nations report allege that US citizens suspected of encouraging "terror" had been put on "death lists." Reports of these death lists show that Obama's director of national intelligence told a congressional hearing that the program was within the rights of the Executive Branch of the government and did not need to be revealed. At least two people are known to have been murdered by Central Intelligence Agency (CIA) operatives under this program. When the program was challenged in a New York City court, the judge refused to rule, saying, as reported by William Fisher for the Inter Press Service: "There are circumstances in which the executive's unilateral decision to kill a US citizen overseas is 'constitutionally committed to the political branches' and judicially unreviewable."

A moral, ethical, and legal analysis of assassinations seems to be significantly lacking inside corporate media. The unquestioned announcement that the Obama administration had authorized assassinations of supposed terrorists, including US citizens, was on the front page of the *Washington Post* on January 27, 2010, by Dana Priest:

> After the Sept. 11 attacks, Bush gave the CIA, and later the military, authority to kill US citizens abroad if strong evidence existed that an American was involved in organizing or carrying out terrorist actions against the United States or US interests, military and intelligence officials said. The evidence has to meet a certain, defined threshold. The person, for instance, has to pose "a continuing and imminent threat to US persons and interests," said one former intelligence official.
>
> The Obama administration has adopted the same stance. If a US citizen joins al-Qaeda, "it doesn't really change anything from the standpoint of whether we can target them," a senior administration official said. "They are then part of the enemy."
>
> Both the CIA and the JSOC maintain lists of individuals, called "High Value Targets" and "High Value Individuals," whom they seek to kill or capture. The JSOC list includes three Americans, including Aulaqi, whose name was added late last year. As of several months ago, the CIA list included three US citizens, and an intelligence official said that Aulaqi's name has now been added.[6]

The Center for Constitutional Rights (CCR) and the American Civil Liberties Union (ACLU) are currently challenging this notion in the US District Court for the District of Columbia. This lawsuit stems from the killing of Nasser Al-Aulaqi's son, a US citizen, who was targeted and killed by the United States government. It is interesting to note that according to CCR staff attorney Pardiss Kabriaei, "the Supreme Court has repeatedly rejected the government's claim to an unchecked system of global detention, and the district court should similarly reject the administration's claim here to an unchecked system of global targeted killing." The ACLU and CCR hope the court will rule that the US government can only kill a US citizen if there is proof of an imminent threat to life.

Focusing on American targets in a February 4 press release, Ben Wizner, a staff attorney for the ACLU National Security Project, emphasized, "It is alarming to hear that the Obama administration is asserting that the president can authorize the assassination of Americans abroad, even if they are far from any battlefield and may have never taken up arms against the US, but have only been deemed to constitute an unspecified 'threat.'"[7]

Francis A. Boyle at the University of Illinois College of Law wrote, "This extrajudicial execution of human beings constitutes a grave violation of international human rights law and, under certain circumstances, can also constitute a war crime under the Four Geneva Conventions of 1949. In addition, the extrajudicial execution of US citizens by the United States government also violates the Fifth Amendment to the United States Constitution mandating that no person 'be deprived of life, liberty, or property, without due process of law.'"

There has been no correlation drawn by corporate media between the US policy of presidential assassinations and the on-ground troop engagement in outrageous human rights violations, which was made public when the German magazine *Der Spiegel* released images of smiling US soldiers kneeling next to naked children they had just massacred. The soldiers not only took the village children's lives but also ripped out their teeth and fingertips as keepsakes, and took pictures of themselves holding the dead bodies up by their hair. Jeremy Morlock, one of the soldiers in that group who participated in these incidents, has agreed to negotiate his declaration against his colleagues and superiors, to reduce his sentence for the murders. This group of soldiers referred to themselves as "Team Death."

Luke Mogelson from the *New York Times* covered the trial of Jeremy Morlock on May 1, 2011:

In a military courtroom at Joint Base Lewis-McChord near Tacoma, Wash., 22-year-old Jeremy Morlock confessed to participating in the premeditated murder of Mullah Allah Dad, as well as the murders of two other Afghan civilians. In exchange for his agreement to testify against four other soldiers charged in the crimes, including the supposed ringleader, Staff Sgt. Calvin Gibbs, the government reduced Morlock's mandatory life sentence to 24 years, with the possibility of parole after approximately 8. The rest of the accused, who are still awaiting trial, contest the allegations against them.

The story that has been told so far—by Morlock in his confession and by various publications that relied heavily on the more sensational accusations from interviews hastily conducted by Army special agents in Afghanistan—is a fairly straightforward one: a sociopath joined the platoon and persuaded a handful of impressionable subordinates to join him in sport killing as opportunities arose. There may indeed be truth to this, though several soldiers in the platoon give a more complicated account. Certainly it's a useful narrative, strategically and psychologically, for various parties trying to make sense of the murders —parents at a loss to explain their sons' involvement and lawyers advocating their clients' innocence and a military invested in a version of events that contains and cauterizes the problem.[8]

While the tragic events of "Team Death" received widespread coverage in world news, most US coverage focused on the individuals as rogue deviants and included official apologies from the US military.

Additionally, Afghan civilian deaths are usually reported in the US corporate media as isolated incidents, and/or mistakes. A comprehensive evaluation of the human and environmental costs of the war in Afghanistan is mostly ignored by the corporate media.

Afghan civilians are facing the deadliest period since the US-led invasion began more than nine years ago. According to the Afghanistan Rights Monitor, at least 2,421 civilians were killed in Afghanistan last year, and more than 3,270 civilians were injured in conflict-related security incidents. This means that, every day, 6–7 non-combatants were killed and 8–9 were wounded in the war. In addition to the casualties, hundreds of thousands of people were forced from their homes, or deprived of health care, education services, and livelihood opportunities due to war, affected in various ways by the intensified armed violence in 2010.

Armed opposition groups were blamed for 63 percent of the total reported civilian deaths, US/NATO forces for 21 percent, pro-government Afghan forces for 12 percent, and about 4 percent could not be attributed to an identifiable armed group and were labeled "unknown" in the report. Improvised explosive devices (IEDs) were the most lethal tools, which killed more than 690 civilians and wounded more than 1,800. At least 217 noncombatants died in air strikes, and 192 were killed in direct/indirect shooting by US/NATO forces in 2010.

The American military presence in Afghanistan consists of fleets of aircraft, helicopters, armored vehicles, weapons, equipment, troops, and facilities. Since 2001, these together have generated millions of kilograms of hazardous, toxic, and radioactive wastes. Matthew Nasuti asks a simple question in *Kabul Press*: "What have the Americans done with all that waste?" The answer is chilling in that virtually all of it appears to have been buried, burned, or secretly disposed of into the air, soil, groundwater, and surface waters of Afghanistan. Even if the Americans begin to withdraw next year, the toxic chemicals they leave behind will continue to pollute for centuries. Any abandoned radioactive waste may stain the Afghan countryside for thousands of years. Afghanistan has been described in the past as the graveyard of foreign armies. Today, according to Nasuti, Afghanistan has a different title: "Afghanistan is the toxic dumping ground for foreign armies."

Hundreds of tons of depleted uranium (DU) were used during the invasions of Iraq and Afghanistan. The US forces forbid any kind of DU-related exploration programs or research. They have also covered up and denied DU's damaging health effects, and refused to release information on the amounts, types, and locations of these weapons. As a consequence, thousands of Iraqi and Afghan children and their families are suffering from various diseases related to low-level radiation (LLR), such as malignancies, congenital heart diseases, chromosomal aberration, and multiple congenital malformations.

Women in the contaminated areas suffered high rates of miscarriages and sterility.

DU weapons are manufactured from radioactive waste generated during the enrichment process of natural uranium, as part of the nuclear fuel cycle. American and British armed forces fired DU bullets and projectiles for the first time against a human population in Iraq during the 1991 Gulf War. When DU munitions hit their target, they ignite prophetically and generate heat that reaches a temperature of 3000–6000 degrees Celsius. This heat causes the DU and other metals to form a gas or aerosol of nanoparticles. These nanoparticles cross the lung-blood barrier, gain entrance to the cells, and create free radicals. Some effects that the people are facing are immune and hormonal systems damage; disruption of thyroid function; and tetrogenic toxicity, as soluble DU oxides cross the placenta to the fetus, resulting in damages that range from behavioral problems to mental retardation and congenital malformations.

President Obama's undeclared and congressionally unauthorized war against Libya may be compounded by the crime of spreading toxic uranium oxide in populated areas of that country. Concern is being voiced by groups such as the International Coalition to Ban Uranium Weapons, which monitors military use of DU antitank and bunker-penetrating shells.

As of late March 2011, the US has not introduced its A-10 Thunderbolts, known also as Warthogs, into the Libyan campaign, probably because these subsonic, straight-wing craft, while heavily armored, are vulnerable to the shoulder-fired antiaircraft missiles that Libyan forces are known to possess in large numbers. Once the air-control situation is improved by continued bombardment, however, these specialized ground-attack aircraft will probably be added to the attacking forces. The A-10 has a particularly large automatic cannon, which fires an unusually large 30 mm shell. These shells are often fitted with solid uranium projectiles.

Notes

1. Gregg Zoroya, "Army Suicides Linked to Risky Behavior, Lax Discipline," *USA Today*, July 29, 2010, http://www.usatoday.com/news/military/2010-07-29-army-suicides_N.htm.
2. Gregg Zoroya, "More Army Guard, Reserve Soldiers Committing Suicide," *USA*

Today, January 20, 2011, http://www.usatoday.com/news/military/2011-01-20-suicides20_ST_N.htm.

3. "Military Suicides Increase as US Soldiers Struggle with Torment of War," *Star-Ledger*, November 22, 2009, http://www.nj.com/news/index.ssf/2009/11/us_military_suicides_increase.html.

4. Adam Levine, "Obama Urged to Reverse Policy on No Condolence Letters for Suicides," CNN, May 26, 2011, http://articles.cnn.com/2011-05-26/politics/president.suicides.letters_1_condolence-letters-suicide-rate-policy?_s=PM:POLITICS.

5. "Army to Train Soldiers in Emotional Resiliency," *Talk of the Nation*, National Public Radio, September 10, 2009, http://www.npr.org/templates/story/story.php?storyId=112717611.

6. Dana Priest, "US Military Teams, Intelligence Deeply Involved in Aiding Yemen on Strikes," *Washington Post*, January 27, 2010, http://www.washingtonpost.com/wp-dyn/content/article/2010/01/26/AR2010012604239_pf.html.

7. "Intelligence Official Acknowledges Policy Allowing Targeted Killings Of Americans," American Civil Liberties Union, February 4, 2010, http://www.aclu.org/national-security/intelligence-official-acknowledges-policy-allowing-targeted-killings-americans.

8. Luke Mogelson, "A Beast in the Heart," *New York Times*, May 1, 2011, New York edition, MM34.

Social Media and Internet Freedom

by Elliot D. Cohen

Censored #2:
US Military Manipulates the Social Media

Sources:

Persona Management Software, Department of the Air Force, Air Mobility Command, Federal Business Opportunities, June 22, 2010, http://www.rawstory.com/rs/wp-content/uploads/2011/03/personamanagementcontract.pdf.

Nick Fielding and Ian Cobain, "Revealed: US Spy Operation that Manipulates Social Media," *Guardian*, March 17, 2011, http://www.guardian.co.uk/technology/2011/mar/17/us-spy-operation-social-networks.

Darlene Storm, "Army of Fake Social Media Friends to Promote Propaganda," Computerworld, February 22, 2011, http://blogs.computerworld.com/17852/army_of_fake_social_media_friends_to_promote_propaganda.

Stephen Webster, "Exclusive: Military's 'persona' software cost millions, used for 'classified social media activities,'" Raw Story, February 22, 2011, http://www.rawstory.com/rs/2011/02/22/exclusive-militarys-persona-software-cost-millions-used-for-classified-social-media-activities/.

Student Researchers: Ashley Nelson, Alex Miller (Sonoma State University); Michael Smith (San Francisco State University); Wend-Kouni Deo-Gratias Nintiema (St. Cloud University)

Faculty Evaluators: Peter Phillips (Sonoma State University); Kenn Burrows (San Francisco State University); Julie Andrzejewski (St. Cloud State University); Mickey Huff (Diablo Valley College)

Censored #6:
Google Spying?

Sources:

Eric Sommer, "Google's Deep CIA Connections," *Pravda Online*, January 14, 2010, http://english.pravda.ru/world/asia/14-01-2010/111657-google_china-o/.

David Vladeck to Albert Gidari, October 21, 2010, Office of the Director Bureau of Consumer Protection, United States Federal Trade Communication, http://www.ftc.gov/os/closings/101027googleletter.pdf.

Nicholas Carlson, "Google's Marissa Mayer Hosting Obama At $30,000-A-Head Fundraiser Tonight (GOOG)," *San Francisco Chronicle*, October 21, 2010, http://www.sfgate.com/cgi-bin/article.cgi?f=/g/a/2010/10/21/businessinsider-googles-marissa-mayer-to-host-president-obama-for-30000-a-head-fundraiser-2010-10.DTL.

Student Researchers: James Dobbs (Indian River State College); Keith Garrett (Sonoma State University)

Faculty Evaluators: Elliot D. Cohen (Indian River State College); John Kramer (Sonoma State University); Mickey Huff (Diablo Valley College)

Related Validated News Stories, 2009–2011

"Andrew McLaughlin '94 Leaves Google to Join Obama Administration," Harvard Law School, June 18, 2009, http://www.law.harvard.edu/news/2009/06/18_mclaughlin.html.

Alissa Bohling, "First, Your Shoes; Next, Your DNA: Elliot Cohen on How Surveillance Is Erasing Freedom and Autonomy, Step by Incremental Step," *Truthout*, January 5, 2011, http://archive.truthout.org/first-your-shoes-next-your-dna-elliot-cohen-how-surveillance-erasing-freedom-and-autonomy-step-incre.

James Temple, "FTC Closes Investigation into Google's Street View Data Collection," *San Francisco Chronicle*, October 27, 2010, http://www.sfgate.com/cgi-bin/blogs/techchron/detail?entry_id=75580.

Noah Shachtman, "Exclusive: US Spies Buy Stake in Firm that Monitors Blogs, Twitter," *Wired*, October 19, 2009, http://www.wired.com/dangerroom/2009/10/ exclusive-us-spies-buy-stake-in-twitter-blog-monitoring-firm/.

Juan Gonzalez and Amy Goodman, "CIA Invests in Software Firm Monitoring Blogs, Twitter" *Democracy Now!*, October 22, 2009, http://www.democracynow.org/2009/10/22/cia_invests_in_software_firm_monitoring.

Marcia Hofmann, "EFF Posts Documents Detailing Law Enforcement Collection of Data from Social Networks," Electronic Frontier Foundation, March 16, 2010, http://www.eff.org/deeplinks/2010/03/eff-posts-documents-detailing-law-enforcement.

Murry Wardrop, "Facebook Could be Monitored by Government," *Telegraph*, March 25,

2009, http://www.telegraph.co.uk/technology/facebook/5046447/Facebook-could-be-monitored-by-the-government.html.

Nigel Morris, "Now 'Big Brother' Targets Facebook," *Independent*, March 25, 2009, http://www.independent.co.uk/news/uk/politics/now-big-brother-targets-facebook-1653407.html.

Mike Elgan, "'Pre-Crime' Comes to the HR Dept.," Datamation, September 29, 2010, http://itmanagement.earthweb.com/features/article.php/12297_3905931_1/Pre-crime-Comes-to-the-HR-Dept.htm.

Tom Burghart, "Big Brother Only a Mouse Click Away?," Sky Valley Chronicle, October 17, 2010. http://www.skyvalleychronicle.com/FEATURE-NEWS/BIG-BROTHER-ONLY-A-MOUSE-CLICK-AWAY-br-Invasive-cyber-technologies-may-mean-Big-Brot her-has-his-eye-on-you-in-ways-you-never-thought-possible-494357.

Rick Rozoff, "US Cyber Command: Waging War In The World's Fifth Battlespace," Global Research, May 27, 2010, http://www.globalresearch.ca/index.php?context=va&aid=19360.

"US to Set Up Secret 'Big Brother' Surveillance System to Monitor Internet for Cyber-attacks," *Daily Mail*, July 9, 2010, http://www.dailymail.co.uk/sciencetech/article-1293344/Perfect-Citizen-US-set-secret-Big-Brother-surveillance-monitor-internet-cyber-attacks.html.

Richard Adhikari, "NSA: Perfect Citizen Is All About R&D, Not Eavesdropping," Tech-NewsWorld, July 9, 2010, http://www.technewsworld.com/story/NSA-Perfect-Citizen-Is-All-About-RD-Not-Eavesdropping-70384.html.

Noah Shachtman, "Your Guide to Crimeware Apps," *Wired*, January 31, 2011, http://www.wired.com/magazine/2011/01/st_crimeware/.

Angeline Grace Close, George M. Zinkhan, and R. Zachary Finney, "Cyber-Identity Theft: A Conceptual Model and Implications For Public Policy," paper, University of Nevada, Las Vegas, http://faculty.unlv.edu/angeline/Close%5B1%5D%5B1%5D.Zinkhan.CyberIDTheft.pdf.

Andy Beckett, "The Dark Side of the Internet," *Guardian*, November 26, 2009, http://www.guardian.co.uk/technology/2009/nov/26/dark-side-internet-freenet.

Steve Aquino, "Should Obama Control the Internet?" *Mother Jones*, April 2, 2009, http://motherjones.com/politics/2009/04/should-obama-control-internet.

Stephanie Mencimer, "Is Obama Plotting to Shut Down the Internet?" *Mother Jones*, October 27, 2009, http://motherjones.com/mojo/2009/10/obama-plotting-shut-down-internet.

Eric Sinrod, "Presidential Powers During Cybersecurity Emergencies," Findlaw, October 6, 2009, http://blogs.findlaw.com/technologist/2009/10/presidential-powers-during-cybersecurity-emergencies.html.

Cybersecurity Act of 2009, S. 773, 111th Cong., 1st sess. (2009), http://www.opencongress.org/bill/111-s773/show.

William D. Hartung, "Is Lockheed Martin Shadowing You?," *Mother Jones*, January 12, 2011, http://motherjones.com/politics/2011/01/lockheed-martin-shadowing-you.

John Lasker, "US Space Weapon Now Circling the Globe," Toward Freedom, May 27, 2010, http://www.towardfreedom.com/home/special-reports/1980-us-space-weapon-now-circling-the-globe.

Student Researchers: Lynn Demos, Ben Solomon, Steve Wojanis, (DePauw University); Tinya Clements and Nick Gedo (Indian River State College); Bradley Shadoan, Shah Baig, Tyler Head, Andrew Nassab, Taylor Falbisaner, and Craig Cekala (Sonoma

State University); Jamaal Rawlings (Indian River Community College); Ryan Shehee (Diablo Valley College)

Faculty and Professional Evaluators: Kevin Howley and Jeff McCall (DePauw University); Elliot D. Cohen (Indian River State College and Indian River Community College); Noel Byrne, Peter Phillips, and Kelly Bucy (Sonoma State University); Glenn Cekala (IPT Leader, Boeing)

Under a veil of corporate media censorship, the United States military has contracted the development of software to secretly manipulate social media websites by using fake internet personas in order to influence online conversations and spread pro-military/corporate propaganda.

According to Lieutenant Commander Bill Speaks, spokesperson for the US Central Command (CENTCOM), the contract was awarded to Ntrepid, a newly formed corporation located in Los Angeles. The so-called "online persona management service" can allow a single US serviceperson to control up to ten separate identities. The contract stipulates that up to fifty US-based controllers could operate false identities from their workstations, and that each fake online persona has a convincing background, history, and supporting details. The contract further requires that the personas "be able to appear to originate in nearly any part of the world and can interact through conventional online services and social media platforms."

"The technology," said Speaks, "supports classified blogging activities on foreign-language websites to enable United States Centcom to counter violent extremist and enemy propaganda outside the US." The software potentially allows US service personnel, working around the clock in one location, to respond to emerging online conversations with a host of coordinated blog posts, tweets, re-tweets, chat room posts, and other interventions. "Details of the contract suggest this location would be MacDill air force base near Tampa, Florida, home of US Special Operations Command."[1]

The multiple persona contract was allegedly "awarded as part of a programme called Operation Earnest Voice (OEV), which was first developed in Iraq as a psychological warfare weapon against the online presence of al-Qaeda supporters" and other "extremists" resisting the US military and political presence in Iraq. According to Speaks, none of the interventions can be in English, as it would be unlawful to "address US audiences" with such technology, and any English-language use of social media by CENTCOM must be clearly identified. However, even if CENTCOM does not directly target US persons in English, the web is seamless, and one language could be electronically translated into another, thereby allowing ease in dissemination of American propaganda throughout the world.

Web experts have compared the "online persona management service" project to China's attempts to monitor and control the internet, as it has the potential to create a false online consensus by crowding out opposing opinions, commentaries, and reports. Creation of such false persons or "sock puppets" may also encourage other governments, companies, and organizations to follow suit.

Speaks refused to say which social media sites are potential targets, but claimed that CENTCOM would not target Facebook or Twitter. However, once the "online persona management service" program is up and running (and it is not clear whether it has already been deployed) there is presently no safeguard in place against these or other popular social media sites being expressly targeted by the military, especially if done in the name of "national security."

Given such dangerous potential with the military effort to manipulate social media, and with hundreds of millions of people now using social media, one might think that the corporate media would have covered this story. But, even after the story was posted and discussed widely on the internet by independent media websites, the corporate media remained mum.

Still, the plot thickens. The US government is not only interested in manipulating social media by injecting doses of military propaganda; In-Q-Tel, "the investment arm of the CIA," has also invested in a company that monitors social media as part of the CIA's effort to access more "open source intelligence." Visible Technologies, a firm created in 2005, with offices in New York, Seattle, and Boston, will help the CIA monitor information that gets overlooked in the massive number of documents transferred on the web. More specifically, Visible will score postings, labeling them as positive, negative, mixed, or neutral, and will even attempt to determine how influential an author is and "who really matters." Visible can monitor over half a million sites per day. Site access includes any open social websites, such as Twitter or Flickr, but excludes closed social networking sites such as Facebook.[2]

While In-Q-Tel claims it will only target foreign social media, the software can also be pointed to domestic social media—and is, in fact, already being used by private companies such as Microsoft, AT&T, and Verizon to monitor postings that conflict with company interests. The CIA also claims it will be gathering information that is legally open for anyone to view. But the possibility remains that this information could be used for illegal or nefarious political purposes, such as conducting unauthorized, domestic investigations into public figures and journalists whose views conflict with government interests.

This is not a stretch considering that the Obama administration's Department of Justice recently obtained the personal records of *New York Times* reporter James Risen in an effort to find out who leaked government information to the press.[3] They accessed Risen's telephone, credit, and bank records, as well as credit reports from Equifax, TransUnion, and Experian. It is therefore unfortunate that corporate media have failed to give consistent and thorough coverage and analysis of the growing trend toward the abridgment of freedoms of speech and press by the US government, especially as it now threatens internet freedom and privacy.

But this movement toward government usurpation of internet freedom and privacy is not confined to the US; the British government, too, has plans to monitor the online activities of approximately twenty-five million British citizens who use popular websites such as MySpace, Bebo, and Facebook. Through a directive called the Interception Modernisation Programme (IMP), all e-mail and internet usage would be monitored, with the information saved in a massive government database, ostensibly to uncover terrorist plots. However, according to Vernon Coaker, the United Kingdom's shadow minister of state for policing and criminal justice (essentially, the UK's chief security officer), this directive has left a security loophole of social networking sites not covered by the IMP. Coaker wants to close this loophole by adding the monitoring of social networking sites to the directive.[4]

As in the US, civil liberties advocates are alarmed by the plan. According to Isabella Sankey, policy director for the British human rights organization Liberty, "Even before you throw Facebook and other social networking sites into the mix, the proposed central communications database is a terrifying prospect. It would allow the Government to record every e-mail, text message and phone call and would turn millions of innocent Britons into permanent suspects."

Not only are social media sites being monitored by the government, they are also being exploited by an emerging new industry that assists employers in hiring and firing their employees. Evolving software now has the capacity to profile and predict future behavior of current and prospective employees for purposes of hiring and firing.

In the article "'Pre-Crime' Comes to the HR Dept.," Silicon Valley–based columnist Mike Elgan discussed how one California start-up called Social Intelligence provides a service it calls "Social Intelligence Hiring." This company utilizes proprietary parsing technology to troll through Facebook, Twitter, Flickr, YouTube, LinkedIn, blogs, and numerous other online sources, searching for evidence of bad character and creating a detailed profile on prospective employees. Elgan explained that humans then review the reports that have been automatically generated to eliminate false positives. Dredging up racy photos, comments about drugs and alcohol, and other negative evidence, the reports use classifications such as "Poor Judgment," "Gangs," "Drugs and Drug Lingo," and "Demonstrating Potentially Violent Behavior" to paint a portrait of what kind of person the target is. The company, however, is cautious to avoid legal challenges by using only publicly shared data, and does not "friend" targets to obtain additional negative information.

Elgan also reported that, as Social Intelligence is advertised as "a way to enforce company social media policies," it also provides a "social intelligence monitoring" service for continuous surveillance of existing employees. The service includes "real-time notification alerts," which notify the employer as soon as something unseemly about an employee appears on the internet.

Other emerging companies use online data to predict the future behavior of employees, and in turn use these predictions as bases for firing them. The Massachusetts-based firm Recorded Future utilizes a "temporal analytics engine" for such purposes. Google also claims to be developing an inference engine that trolls through personnel records, examining such things as employee reviews and promotion and salary histories to predict with high probability which of its employees will quit.

Such technologies draw conclusions about the future performance of employees and, rather than wait until the events actually happen, the employer fires the employee preemptively, based on these predictions. This is tantamount to punishing people for crimes they have not committed. There is no trial; the employee is simply fired.

Yet, according to Elgan, such "pre-crime" analytics will soon become standard practice for human resource departments. "Following the current trend lines," claimed Elgan, "very soon social networking spiders and predictive analytics engines will be working night and day scanning the internet and using that data to predict what every employee is likely to do in the future. . . . When the software decides that you're going to quit, steal company secrets, break the law, post something indecent on a social network or lie on your expense report, the supervising manager will be notified and action will be taken—before you make the predicted transgression."

Again, the corporate media have failed to cover this emerging spy industry, let alone present a thorough analysis of its dangerous implications for freedom and privacy on the internet. Moreover, even when the corporate media have covered stories about employers spying on their employees, it has largely reflected a bias toward minimizing the dangers. For example, NBC Chicago published a story titled, "Your Boss is Likely Spying on You," about a man who volunteered for a charity organization and was terminated after posting a remark condemning the shooting of Congresswoman Gabrielle Giffords in Arizona last January. Far from exploring the dangerous implications for internet freedom and privacy raised by such cases, the brief article instead quoted a civil rights attorney who denied that nongovernment employees have the right to freedom of speech. "Almost all employees, understandably, think that we have a freedom of speech right that extends to all areas of our life, including employment. That's not the case," said attorney Kristin Case. "Unless somebody is a public employee, unless somebody works for a governmental entity, the federal government, state, local, generally they have no free speech rights," she determined. The article then reported how things "ended on a positive note" when, after much discussion with his superiors, the volunteer was allowed to resume his volunteer work.[5]

Similarly, Jenna Wortham for the *New York Times* covered the issue of employers spying on employees by weakly admonishing prospective employees: "To be on the safe side, it's probably wise to use the new privacy settings offered by Facebook to keep everything but the most innocuous content away from the public eye."[6] No mention was made of companies such as Recorded Futures with its "temporal analytics engine" or Google's trolling through employees' records to make future forecasts about employees' "pre-crimes." With such powerful surveillance engines coming to market, it is remarkable that the *Times* had no more to warn about than being "on the safe side" by adjusting the privacy settings on Facebook.

Now, as the private sector continues to advance into the spying business, the alliance of industry and government calls into question the government's capacity to protect millions of Americans against having their right to privacy abridged. Internet search engine giant Google is a case in point.

Earlier this year, the Federal Trade Commission (FTC) investigated Google for illegally collecting personal data such as passwords, e-mails, and other online activities from unsecured Wi-Fi networks in homes and businesses across the United States and around the world. Google claims that the data was accidentally picked up by their Street View cars while driving the world's streets for the Google Maps website, but has not denied that the data collection was an invasion of the public's privacy.

Nevertheless, the FTC failed to take legal action against Google. Instead, in late October 2010, David Vladeck, director of the FTC Bureau of Consumer Protection, sent a two-page letter to Google attorney Albert Gidari saying that the FTC had ended their inquiry into the matter with little more than an assurance from Google that it will make "improvements to its internal processes" and "continue its dialogue with the FTC." Why was nothing more done? Well, perhaps it was because, according to Nicholas Carlson in a *San Francisco Chronicle* article, less than a week before the FTC's decision to drop the inquiry, President Barack Obama attended a $30,000-per-person Democratic Party fundraiser at the Palo Alto, California, home of Google executive Marissa Mayer.

Furthermore, Google's former head of public policy, Andrew McLaughlin, joined the Obama administration as the deputy chief technology officer in mid-2009. Moreover, other Obama administration officials include Eric Schmidt, Google's chief executive, who serves as a member of the President's Council of Advisors on Science and Technology, and Katie Jacobs Stanton, who joined the administration after serving as a Google project manager. Stanton, who now heads international strategy at Twitter, is also currently the director of Citizen Participation, an Obama administration initiative designed to promote greater citizen involvement in government and lessen the influence of special interest groups and lobbyists. The former head of Google.org's global development team, Sonal Shah, is now the head of the White House's Office of Social Innovation. Google also has close business ties with US intelligence: federal agencies, including the CIA and the FBI, maintain a shared intranet database called Intelink. This massive database includes a social networking component for spies and related personnel called Intellipedia, which Google helped to build in 2008. Google supplies the software, hardware, and even the tech support for this component of Intelink.

In addition, Google Earth and Google Maps software were originally created by a company called Keyhole, Inc., which received financial backing from the CIA's investment company, In-Q-Tel. Keyhole was acquired by Google in 2004—thus, Google owes some of its technology to funding from the CIA. Google and the CIA's In-Q-Tel also have staff connections. In 2005, then the director of technology assessment at In-Q-Tel, Rob Painter, became a senior manager for Google's federal government division.

These close ties to Google suggest that the Obama administration has a conflict of interest in the handling of Google's civil rights violations.

Meanwhile, the Obama administration's predilection for policing the private sector has taken a new turn, as it is now poised to police military and civilian computer networks, including air-traffic control networks, subway systems, electricity grids, and nuclear power plants.

On May 21, 2010, "the world's first comprehensive, multi-service military cyber command operation," CYBERCOM, was launched. Based at Fort Meade, Maryland, home to the National Security Agency (NSA), CYBERCOM is, according to Deputy Defense Secretary William J. Lynn III, "a milestone in the United States being able to conduct full-spectrum operations in a new domain." Lynn added that the "cyber domain . . . is as important as the land, sea, air and space domains to the US military, and protecting military networks is crucial to the Defense Department's success on the battlefield."

According to the Pentagon, CYBERCOM will achieve "unprecedented unity of effort and synchronization of Army forces operating within the cyber domain." The US Air Force said that "it has transferred at least 30,000 troops from communications and electronics assignments to 'the front lines of cyber warfare.'"[7]

A significant thrust behind this military effort is the possibility of moving cyber war onto a physical battlefield. According to Deputy Under Secretary of Defense for Policy James Miller, the Pentagon would consider a military response to a cyber attack against the United States. "We need," said Miller, "to think about the potential for responses that are not limited to the cyber domain." And according to former North Atlantic Treaty Organisation (NATO) Secretary General Jaap de Hoop Scheffer, an attack on a civilian system, such as a nation's energy supply, "can destroy the economic and social fabric of a country in a way that resembles a war—yet without a single shot being fired. It is therefore vital that NATO defines what added value it can bring, for example in terms of protecting critical infrastructure or securing choke points through which supply lines run."

Consistent with the aims of CYBERCOM is an NSA initiative called Perfect Citizen, for which Massachusetts defense contractor Raytheon received a $100 million contract. Initial reports described this project as a cyber security system that would protect America's infrastructure from cyber attacks through the installation of sensors in civilian and military networks that were vital to national security. Subsequently, amid criticisms that the program would inject "Big Brother" into the private sector, a spokesperson for the NSA claimed that the project was just for "research and engineering" purposes. The spokesperson declined to say whether the present project would culminate in guidelines or actual solutions to be implemented later, or whether further actions would need to be taken to implement Perfect Citizen.

In any event, the main goal of CYBERCOM and projects such as Perfect Citizen is clear—the militarization of cyberspace, including the civilian sector. Critics see this as symptomatic of an overreaching, intrusive trend of the US military. As Global Research writer Rick Rozoff explained, "placing computer security, including in the civilian sector, under a military command is yet another step in the direction of militarizing the treatment of what are properly criminal or even merely proprietary and commercial matters."

The invasive cyber practices of military, government, private corporations, and employers are not the only threats posed to internet freedom and privacy. As the cyber age advances, there has also been a hike in identity theft over the web. Millions of Americans every year lose their identity to hackers. Previously, knowledge of computer and web programming was necessary in order to steal someone's identity over the web. But now it has become as easy as downloading a program.

There are presently a variety of programs available that can track keystrokes, spoof wire transfers, and steal credit card information straight from hard drives. These programs cost anywhere from five hundred to seven thousand dollars, and offer large payoffs. A German gang, for example, intercepted nearly $6 million in banking transactions with the help of a program called ZeuS.

The prevalence and ease of obtaining such "crimeware" applications have allowed cyber thieves to access millions of confidential documents and steal billions of dollars. As regulations and government interventions attempt to reduce or stop these crimes, it has become an arms race between the two opposing sides. Whenever regulations are put into effect, cyber thieves manage to circumvent them. Consequently, the consumer bears the responsibility to stay informed and take precautions against identity and other forms of cyber theft.

While internet monitoring has increased exponentially in the past decade, there is still an unmonitored side of the internet. However mysterious and dark this "other" internet may be, Ian Clarke released his innovative idea of a "distributed, decentralized information storage and retrieval system," with the hope of unlocking what he considered to be the true purpose of the internet—"freedom to communicate." Clarke explained that, back in the late 1990s, "the internet could be monitored more quickly, comprehensively, and cheaply than dated versions of communication like the mail."

Clarke named his software Freenet and allowed it to be downloaded free of charge so that people all over the world could gain anonymous access to a previously hidden internet. Once downloaded, the software prompts you to set the amount of security you think you need, acknowledging the fact that you may be violating laws in your country by accessing the information that you are looking for.

Although the majority of the "other" internet is said to contain an immense amount of child pornography, virus sharing, media piracy, organized cyber crime, and incomprehensible acts of privacy invasion, there are still people using the veil of mystery and obscurity created by darknets and other forms of the "deep web" to communicate and share ideas and opinions about governments, politics, and conspiracy theories, as well as human and animal rights, some more radical than others. Clarke and others have openly defended the freedoms of the "hidden," claiming they need to be defended absolutely. Clarke also admits that child pornography exists on Freenet and that a virus could, theoretically, be constructed to target and destroy any child pornography. This, however, will likely never be implemented because, according to Clarke, "To modify Freenet, would be to end Freenet."

As both the government and private sector, often cooperatively, monitor the internet, including social media, the dark side of the internet may become its only bright side. This cluster of news stories shows that policing activities have increased exponentially over the past few years and that this dangerous trend can be expected to accelerate as new, even more formidable means of surveillance become available.[8] The implication is an Orwellian state where internet freedom and privacy have evaporated and been replaced with a police state that is capable of watching every activity of every citizen. This is not speculation. The seeds have been set and are sprouting luxuriantly. But the corporate media are still not covering the story!

Notes

1. Nick Fielding and Ian Cobain, "Revealed: US Spy Operation that Manipulates Social Media," *Guardian*, March 17, 2011, http://www.guardian.co.uk/technology/2011/mar/17/us-spy-operation-social-networks.
2. Noah Shachtman, "Exclusive: US Spies Buy Stake in Firm that Monitors Blogs, Twitter," *Wired*, October 19, 2009, http://www.wired.com/dangerroom/2009/10/exclusive-us-spies-buy-stake-in-twitter-blog-monitoring-firm/.
3. Michael Isakof, "DOJ Gets Reporter's Phone, Credit Card Records in Leak Probe," NBC News, February 25, 2011, http://www.msnbc.msn.com/id/41787944/ns/us_news-security/.
4. Murry Wardrop, "Facebook Could be Monitored by Government," *Telegraph*, March 25, 2009, http://www.telegraph.co.uk/technology/facebook/5046447/Facebook-could-be-monitored-by-the-government.html.
5. Alex Perez, "Your Boss is Likely Spying on You," NBC Chicago, January 19, 2011, http://www.nbcchicago.com/news/tech/cyber-spying-empoyer-facebook-twitter-social-network-114235219.html#ixzz1OesK1KND.

6. Jenna Wortham, "More Employers Use Social Networks to Check Out Applicants," *New York Times*, August 20, 2009, http://bits.blogs.nytimes.com/2009/08/20/more-employers-use-social-networks-to-check-out-applicants/.

7. Rick Rozoff, "US Cyber Command: Waging War In The World's Fifth Battlespace," Global Research, May 27, 2010, http://www.globalresearch.ca/index.php?context=va&aid=19360.

8. Elliot D. Cohen, *Mass Surveillance and State Control: The Total Information Awareness Project* (New York: Palgrave Macmillan, 2010).

Economics and Inequality

by Dean Walker, with research assistance by Bill Gibbons
and editing by Melody J. Haislip

Censored #4
Global Food Crisis Expands

Source:
David Moberg, "Diet Hard: With A Vengeance," *In These Times*, March 24, 2011,
http://www.inthesetimes.com/article/7112/.

Student Researcher: Aluna Soupholphakdy (Sonoma State University)

Faculty Evaluator: Peter Phillips (Sonoma State University)

Censored #10:
Real Unemployment: One Out of Five in US

Source:
Greg Hunter, "9% Unemployment Rate is a Statistical Lie," Information Clearing House, February 7, 2011, http://www.informationclearinghouse.info/article27435.htm.

Student Researcher: Ashley Wood (Sonoma State University)

Faculty Evaluator: Peter Phillips (Sonoma State University)

Censored #18
Monsanto Tries to Benefit from Haiti's Earthquake

Sources:
Julio Rojo, "Monsanto hace negocio en Haití tras el terremoto," Diagonal Web, translated by Project Censored, July 28, 2010, http://www.diagonalperiodico.net/Monsanto-hace-negocio-en-Haiti.html.

Thalles Gomes, "Monsanto y el Proyecto Vencedor," América Latina en Movimiento, translated by Project Censored, May 19, 2010, http://www.alainet.org/active/38266.

Student Researchers: Joan Pedro and Luis Luján (Complutense University of Madrid)

Faculty Evaluator: Dra. Ana I. Segovia (Complutense University of Madrid)

Related Validated News Stories

Tina Mather, Kimberly Daniels, and Shannon Pence, "Food Waste Remains Persistent Problem at Farms, Grocery Stores and Restaurants," California Watch, March 31, 2010, http://californiawatch.org/health-and-welfare/food-waste-remains-persistent-problem-farms-grocery-stores-and-restaurants.
Russ Baker, "Giving Chase: Egypt, OK—But What About America's Oligarchs?" WhoWhatWhy, February 10, 2011, http://whowhatwhy.com/2011/02/10/giving-chase-egypt-ok-but-what-about-america%E2%80%99s-oligarchs-3/.
Agence France-Presse, "World Food Prices Hit Record Highs Amid Oil Jitters," Common Dreams, March 3, 2011. http://www.commondreams.org/headline/2011/03/03-1.
Alan Collinge, *The Student Loan Scam: The Most Oppressive Debt in U.S. History—and How We Can Fight Back* (Boston: Beacon Press, 2009).
Jared Bernstein, *Crunch: Why Do I Feel So Squeezed? (And Other Unsolved Economic Mysteries)* (San Francisco: Berrett-Koehler Publishers, Inc., 2008).
C. Alonzo Peters, "To Hell With Student Loans—It's Time for College to Be Free," AlterNet, November 18, 2010, http://www.alternet.org/economy/148918/to_hell_with_student_loans_-_it%27s_time_for_college_to_be_free.
Agence France-Presse, "Global Poverty Doubled Since 1970s: UN," Information Clearing House, November 26, 2010, http://www.informationclearinghouse.info/article26918.htm.
Christine Vestal, "Collapse in Living Standards in America: More Poverty by Any Measure," Global Research, July 14, 2010, http://www.globalresearch.ca/index.php?context=va&aid=20124.

Student Researchers: Elizabeth Fernwood (College of Marin); Aluna Soupholphakdy,

Jordan Hall, Dane Steffy, and Danielle Frisk (Sonoma State University); Brittany Bardin, Christan Zbytniewski, and Gabrielle Vono (Siena College)

Faculty Evaluators: Susan Rahman (College of Marin); Peter Phillips, Andy Deseran, Shelia Katz, and Heather Flynn (Sonoma State University); Dr. Mo Hannah (Siena College)

According to the United States Department of Labor's Bureau of Labor Statistics (BLS), unemployment in the US has hovered around 9 percent during the first four months in 2011. This number is what the BLS calls the U-3 statistic. The U-3 statistic, considered the "official unemployment rate," measures "total unemployment, as a percentage of the civilian labor force." However, when the BLS adds the total number of discouraged workers along with the marginally employed and part-time labor force—all reflected in the U-6 statistic— the unemployment number rises to an average 15.9 percent.[1]

Nonetheless, the BLS's U-6 number might not be the whole story. One article that made it onto Project Censored's top 25 stories, "Real Unemployment: One out of Five in the US," claims the real unemployment number may be as high as 22.1 percent. This story links to author Greg Hunter's articles, published at InformationClearinghouse.info and his own USAWatchdog.com.[2] In interviews with economist John Williams from Shadow Government Statistics (SGS), Hunter delves into why the SGS's unemployment numbers are considerably higher than the BLS's U-6 rate, and, when looking deeper into the numbers, it is harder to see the turnaround picture. In fact, just the opposite is going on. In his latest report, Williams estimated that the government routinely overstates job growth by "230,000 jobs" a month. In a recent interview from his San Francisco office, Williams told Hunter that when it comes to calculating unemployment numbers, the BLS is "flying blind." Williams admitted, "It is hard to put an exact number on the actual job losses last month, but we likely lost jobs—not gained them." He added, "The job losses could be as high as 30,000 for last month."[3]

Over the course of researching this news summary, the authors of this article searched nearly thirty corporate and independent media sites. We compared the underreported stories, which might have briefly appeared in independent media outlets like Common Dreams, IndyMedia, or AlterNet, with the spin presented by the more corporate media outlets like MSNBC News, Reuters, Associated Press, the *New York Times*, the *Washington Post*, and Fox News. Given the wide range of topics covered in this summary, as primary representatives of the corporate media, we have limited this focus to how the *New York Times*, Fox News, and the *Washington Post* covered the stories. As representative of the independent media, we use Common Dreams, AlterNet, and *Mother Jones*.

When it came to reporting the unemployment numbers, both the corporate and the independent media reported the U-3 statistics and often alluded to the U-6 discouraged statistics, as in this *New York Times* article published on May 13, 2011: "Dig a little though and the foundation looks wobblier. Economists point out that some of the drop in state unemployment merely reflects people's giving up on the job search or retiring early, as well as an aging work force with fewer young people hunting for jobs."[4] The press often glosses over the U-6 numbers; rarely does anyone delve into the subject, let alone the alternative statistics provided by economist John Williams at SGS. The independent media covered the unemployment numbers with the same glossing-over of the U-6 numbers and an avoidance of any alternative statistics. Not surprisingly, with President Barack Obama in office, Fox News has actively promoted the higher U-6 statistics but has left the SGS numbers to the left- and right-wing bloggers.

For many people, the SGS unemployment rate of 22.2 percent seems to be a more accurate number. In a related story, the US Census Bureau reported that for three consecutive years, from 2006 to 2009, the poverty rate in the US rose. (At publication time, the 2010 poverty rate had not yet been released.) According to the Census Bureau, the official 2009 poverty rate stood at 14.3 percent, up from 13.3 percent in 2008. In real terms, in 2009, 43.6 million people were living in poverty—up from 39.8 million in the previous year, and the largest number of people living in poverty in fifteen years. Anticipating the 2010 rate, most predict a fourth consecutive year of increases in the poverty rate.

A closer look at the poverty rate in the US reveals a significant racial component to the numbers. The Census Bureau reported that while the poverty rates rose in nearly all ethnic groups, the highest rates and increases were reflected in blacks (from 24.7 percent to 25.8 percent) and Hispanics (from 23.2 percent to 25.3 percent). In comparison, the poverty rate for non-Hispanic whites rose only 0.8 percent (from 8.6 percent to 9.4 percent). All the while, Asians stayed statistically the same (12.5 percent) from 2008 to 2009.

Interestingly, the Census Bureau estimated that the poverty rate for people aged sixty-five and older decreased (from 9.7 percent to 8.9 percent), though the rate for children under the age of eighteen increased (from 19.0 percent to 20.7 percent).[5]

In September 2011, President Obama plans to release the 2010 poverty numbers. The current formula used by the government to determine the poverty line has been unchanged since 1963. Essentially, the formula takes the cost of food and multiplies it by the number of household members. In an article published by Global Research, Christine Vestal explained the problem with this calculation:

> While the formula may have been a good way to estimate a subsistence cost of living in the early 1960s, experts say food now represents only one-eighth of a typical household budget, with expenses such as housing and childcare putting increasing pressure on struggling families.
>
> In addition, the official measure fails to account for regional differences in the cost of housing, it doesn't include medical expenses or transportation, and at $22,000 for a family of four, the poverty line is considered by many to be simply too low.[6]

President Obama's plan was developed by the National Academies of Sciences (NAS) in 1995, thus the product of a study funded by Congress nearly twenty years ago. Obama's plan calculates many of the additional costs of living and subtracts government aid like food stamps and money received from other stimulus programs. Obama is hoping that with the new NAS formula, along with the 2009 stimulus bills, poverty numbers will soften in the forthcoming poverty report. Even if this is true, Vestal points out that now that most of the stimulus money has been spent, the poverty numbers will likely spike up again.

Opinion polls have shown that for the last seven years American voters have listed the economy as the first or second most important issue. In the same polls, roughly 50 percent of Americans have believed that taxes on the middle class should be cut and that government should be downsized.[7] One of the most important government programs affected by the gradual downsizing is education. Cutting education is extremely shortsighted and can only lead to America forfeiting its competitive advantage to better-educated nations. In fact, this is already happening. Dr. C. Alonzo Peters, founder of Mocha-Money.com—a personal finance website dedicated to helping black Americans gain financial independence—wrote in an AlterNet article published on November 18, 2010:

> Let's not forget that increasing the pool of college-educated workers improves the ability of the country to discover the next breakthrough in biology, nanotechnology, or computer science—a process that would create entire new industries and promote further prosperity. Currently only 4 of the top 10 companies receiving US patents in 2009 were American companies. Without a well-educated workforce there is the risk that the next great technology will be invented overseas and then imported here to America.[8]

Dr. Peters pointed out that after World War II, the government provided free college education through the GI Bill. Some seven million returning veterans took advantage of the bill, helping to create a wide and prosperous middle class. Peters continued, "In fact, it's estimated that the GI Bill returned nearly $7 to the economy for every $1 spent on it." Peters then referred to a US Census study that reported that a person who receives a college education earns, on average, more than $900,000 more than a person with only a high school education.[9] Someone with $900,000 more in her pocket ends up spending that much more in their community, which in turn stimulates the whole economy.

For most Americans, the Great Recession is not over. Budget cuts from both federal and state governments have forced colleges to increase tuition. From 1996 to 2006, higher education costs increased by over 80 percent. The average college graduate received both a diploma and a bank statement with an average of over $26,000 in debt coming due in monthly payments to Sallie Mae. One popular article on Project Censored's website, reported by Siena College student researchers Brittany Bardin, Christan Zbytniewski, and Gabrielle Vono, pointed out how student debt made private student loan companies incredibly wealthy, all the while leaving millions of college-educated citizens as, essentially, indentured servants to the high-powered and politically connected bankers.[10]

Once again, few corporate media outlets have focused on the rise in student debt, and none of the corporate media outlets seem to have presented the proposal for free college education. *The New York Times* published an article suggesting, "Many economists say student debt should be seen in a more favorable light." *The New York Times* quoted Sandy Baum, a higher-education policy analyst and senior fellow at George Washington University, as saying she was not concerned that student debt was growing so fast.[11] At the *Washington Post*, columnist Michelle Singletary actually brought up the idea of free education in her May 18, 2011, article, "Higher Education: Right or Privilege?" Singletary argued, "The majority believes the federal government, states, private donations and endowments, or some combination of the four, should cover the cost."[12]

On the independent media site AlterNet, Les Leopold published an excellent piece titled, "Free College on Wall Street's Tab?" However, even progressive sites like *Mother Jones* seemed to barely cover the issue of rising student debt. Kevin Drum of *MoJo* wrote a few paragraphs on how one of the components of the Affordacare bill that passed in Congress forced commercial banks like Sallie Mae and Nelnet out of the government-subsidized student loan business. Drum presented this as a bonus for education and college students, yet he failed to go into any of the dozens of countermeasures that continue to make going to college less and less accessible to everyday, Main Street Americans.[13] In fact, to find any article on one of the most progressive websites and magazines in the country, *Mother Jones*, doing a simple search of the words "college loans" and "college debt" takes you back to a brief 2006 blog post entitled "Generation Debt" by Jim Rossi.[14] Certainly the financial situation for college students in 2011 has become considerably worse.

Another underreported story relating to poverty and hunger exposed the persistent problem of food waste in America. According to a California Watch article published on March 31, 2010, California's "largest single source of waste" is food. While poverty and hunger are on the rise in the US, California alone throws away more than six million tons of food each year.[15]

According to Jonathon Bloom, author of the book *American Wasteland*, "Americans waste more than 40 percent of the food we produce for consumption. That comes at an annual cost of more than $100 billion. At the same time, food prices and the number of Americans without enough to eat continues to rise."[16]

Worldwide, the problem of food waste and poverty is not much different. On May 11, 2011, the Food and Agriculture Organization of the United Nations (FAO) released a stunning report that received almost zero coverage from the corporate media. According to the report titled *Global Food Losses and Food Waste*: "Roughly one third of the food produced in the world for human consumption every year—that's approximately 1.3 billion tonnes—gets lost or wasted." Interestingly, the FAO report stated among its key findings, "Industrialized and developing countries dissipate [waste] roughly the same quantities of food—respectively 670 and 630 million tonnes."[17]

While Americans throw away roughly 40 percent of the food produced in the US, and the rest of the world tosses out 33 percent of their food, the price of food has skyrocketed. Another *Censored 2012* top 25 story explores the fact that food prices are creating a global crisis. In a web-only article for the magazine *In These Times* titled "Diet Hard: With a Vengeance," senior editor David Moberg unraveled the web of interwoven factors that have created global food prices, noting that according to a February 2011 FAO report, the food price index rose to its highest level since 1990. Moberg wrote:

> As a result, since 2010 began, roughly another 44 million people have quietly crossed the threshold into malnutrition, joining 925 million already suffering from lack of food. If prices continue to rise, this food crisis will push the ranks of the hungry toward a billion people, with another two billion suffering from "hidden malnutrition" of inadequate diets, nearly all in the developing countries of Africa, Asia and Latin America.[18]

Moberg attributed the rise in malnutrition to climate change and the rise in food prices, referencing an October 2010 FAO report from the

Committee on World Food Security that claimed climate change will affect, "the livelihoods, food security, and way of life of billions of people." The FAO committee concluded, "climate change multiplies existing threats and . . . increases the vulnerability . . . to food insecurity."[19]

However, the FAO committee determined that the single greatest factor in the current food crisis is not the threat of global warming, or the diversion of 40 percent of US corn into biofuels, which has been problematic. The number one threat to food security worldwide, and the cause of much of the world's food shortages and starvation, turns out to be bad policies and unregulated free-market speculation. While there is no lack of food, millions of people die each year from malnutrition and starvation as a result of decades-old bad policies that have allowed multinational corporations and Wild West speculators to enter food staples into commodities markets.

"By contrast," Moberg wrote, "many countries, civil society groups, environmentalists, advocates for the poor, and representatives of peasants and small farmers say that food should be treated as a human right. And countries should strive for food security and as much self-sufficiency as can reasonably be achieved, as Karen Lehman, former senior fellow at the Minneapolis-based Institute for Agriculture and Trade Policy, argues."

The primary conclusion from the October 2010 FAO report is that government policies that have led to mismanaged and unregulated trade systems have resulted in less self-sufficiency and less food security globally. The report states that increased volatility created by free-market speculators "threatens farm viability (low prices), food security (high prices), undermines investment decisions, and threatens domestic security and political stability." As Tim Wise— director of the Research and Policy Program for Tufts University's Global Development and Environment Institute—illuminated in Moberg's article, "The big picture about rising food prices is that one of the things that globalization has done is increasingly to put food reserves in private hands. . . . You get speculation and hoarding if people feel there's a shortage of supply."

Moberg's article concluded by pointing out that "new global investments in agriculture derivatives reached $2.6 billion in December 2010, double the level a year earlier." He then suggested immediate limits on financial speculators in commodity future index derivatives—and ultimately a complete ban on such agricultural derivatives. In addition, he suggested that individual countries and even local communities go back to maintaining their own food reserves and demand the domestic freedom to control their own food polices, in order to assure self-sufficiency.

In a related and underreported story, world food prices have now hit a record high. An article published on Common Dreams via Agence France-Presse, on March 3, 2011, reported that the FAO has partly blamed the eight consecutive months of increased food prices on the fact that oil exports from Libya were cut between "850,000 and one million barrels per day." According to the FAO, "higher oil prices affect all aspects of the food production chain, from fertilizer to transport."[20]

As in the US, global poverty rates rose substantially. Another article that caught Project Censored's attention was first reported in November 2010 by Agence France-Presse, who declared that global poverty has doubled since 1970. According to Supachai Panitchpakdi, secretary-general of the United Nations Conference on Trade and Development (UNCTAD), the failure of the least-developed countries (LDCs) in the world is a result of the International Monetary Fund's free-trade model of development policy, which needs to be reassessed.

Searching corporate media on articles addressing both food waste and the true rising costs of food came up blank. *The New York Times* has noted the rise in food costs but has also glossed over the reasons that prices are increasing. In May 2011, the *Washington Post* hosted a Future of Food conference at Georgetown University, which featured over thirty speakers including Prince Charles, Secretary of Agriculture Tom Vilsack, top chefs, and experts in food policy, distribution, organic farming, and nutrition. Yet, judging from the excerpts provided by the *Washington Post* for each of the speakers, not a single speaker addressed the problem of free-market speculators affecting the price of food. Nor, for that matter, was the subject of food waste presented in any substantial measure at the Future of Food conference.[21]

In contrast to the US, where the cost of food has decreased, food in the LDCs often comprises more than half of an individual's cost of living. Panitchpakdi explained, "What happened is that in the past thirty to forty years, the number of LDCs have doubled so it [the situation] has actually deteriorated, the number of people living under the poverty line has doubled from the 1980s."[22] Oxfam International's report recently declared that the planet is entering an era of so-called "permanent food crisis" where the price of food is likely to double by 2030.

In fact, the May 2011 annual report stated, "LDCs' share of the global population living in extreme poverty has doubled since 1990." This is a dramatically darker picture than what Panitchpakdi expressed in November. The UNCTAD report also stated that, "Using the World Bank data, the overall trend remains the same: the share of the global population living in extreme poverty which is located in LDCs increased from 18% in 1990 to 30% in 2005." By 2007, that number increased to 36 percent.[23]

The earthquake-ravaged nation of Haiti is one LDC that is not only fighting the problem of increased poverty, but now has to contend with predatory multinationals attempting to make a buck on Haiti's misfortunes. There is perhaps no more egregious example of the predatory business dealings than US-based agricultural biotechnology corporation Monsanto's so-called "gift" to Haiti in May of 2010: a donation of sixty tons of corn and vegetable hybrid seed.

According to an in-depth report on the Monsanto "gift" by Haiti Grassroots Watch, "Among the dangers presented, the Environmental Justice Institute for Haiti, the National Lawyers Guild–Environmental Justice Committee and the Lawyers Earthquake Response Network noted that, 'The unrestricted flow of seeds from outside the country presents a high risk that plant pathogenic organisms or their vectors will be introduced.'"

The report added that the organizations also deplored the use of "large quantities of commercial hybrid seeds," which necessitate "purchase of new seeds the following year," as well as the uncontrolled use of dangerous chemicals that "present risk for contamination of Haiti's scarce water and food supply."[24] Haiti Grassroots Watch pointed out that the hybrid seeds require additional water and fertilizers. Plus, nearly 90 percent of the seeds are coated with a fungicide that is hazardous and should be handled with gloves and a gas mask. The label found on one bag of hybrid maize read, "DO NOT use treated seed for animal or human consumption. . . . DO NOT allow treated seed to contaminate grain or other seed intended for animal or human consumption. DO NOT feed treated seed, or otherwise expose, to wild or domestic birds."

Yet, Haiti Grassroots Watch located farmers who had received hybrid seeds. They found sacks of maize and vegetable seeds in an open shed with children playing just outside. Inside the shed, coated pink maize seeds were spilled out onto the floor along with other seeds. Haiti Grassroots Watch reported, "Asked about the open sacks of seed, Farmer [the interviewed farmer] said [the] Association intended to grind up the sorghum and maize seed for chicken feed because it was 'expired' (although there were no dates on the sacks)."

One month after the May 2010 donation, the nation's largest farmers' movement, Papaya Farmers, held a demonstration during which about ten thousand Haitian farms symbolically burned maize seed in protest.

While all or most of the independent media sites represented in this news summary—AlterNet, Common Dreams, as well as *Truthout*—covered the Monsanto deal in Haiti, the independent *Mother Jones* and pretty much all of the corporate media outlets appeared to have completely avoided reporting on the issue.

One of the most effective ways the media—either corporate or independent—censor news is by simply not reporting on the stories. But one aspect of the economy that had some traction in corporate media was the corruption in the banking system. While the US government has done virtually nothing to criminally prosecute the individuals involved in writing fraudulent, predatory, subprime home loans, or the securities traders that misrepresented bundled derivatives, corporate media have put a good deal of ink on the page regarding these scandals.

For example, in May 2011 the *Washington Post* published an Associated Press article covering the growing shareholder protests at Wells Fargo, Bank of America, and JPMorgan Chase over their roles in the foreclosure crisis[25]—though a search of the *Washington Post* website in June 2011 showed the story to be no longer available. Also in May 2011, the *New York Times* published a Bloomberg News piece revealing that JPMorgan Chase was negotiating a deal with the Securities and Exchange Commission (SEC), which is currently investigating how mortgage-linked securities were packaged and sold. The article reported that, as with Goldman Sachs, the SEC is looking for a deal in which JPMorgan Chase admits it made some mistakes and pays a relatively small fine.[26]

On top of the securities investigation and the home foreclosure scandal, JPMorgan Chase finds itself in another civil and criminal investigation. In February 2011, the *New York Times* reported on a civil suit brought against JPMorgan involving Bernard Madoff's Ponzi scheme. Apparently, the bank had been Madoff's primary bank since 1986, and legal documents revealed that internal investigations by two high-level risk management officers had already previously suggested that Madoff's numbers did not add up. As a result of JPMorgan's own analyses, the bank withdrew from Madoff-linked hedge funds all but $35 million of the once $276 million it had invested. Yet, JPMorgan maintained Madoff's accounts up until Madoff's arrest. Essentially, the bank had denied any knowledge of Madoff's fraud, though the risk management reports suggested the bank had turned a blind eye to the crime.[27]

The question not being asked by the corporate media is, "Why are the banks getting bailouts and not jail time?" After $700 billion in government bailouts, the banking industry logged record profits in 2011. In January 2011, JPMorgan reported a record year in profits, up 48 percent from the previous year. While billions of dollars in bonuses are being handed out to the very same executives that created the Great Recession, foreclosures, poverty, and hunger are on the rise. As reported by the independent media site Think Progress, CEO bonuses rose nearly 20 percent, while unemployment and wages remained stagnant. Income inequality in the US is now the highest since the Great Depression.[28] With all the money going into the political coffers of both the Democratic and Republican parties, it should be apparent why the real problems with the free-market system and growing worldwide inequality is underreported, or simply not covered in the corporate media.

Notes

1. Bureau of Labor Statistics, "Table A-15. Alternative Measures of Labor Underutilization," *The Employment Situation*, United States Department of Labor, June 3, 2011, http://www.bls.gov/news.release/empsit.t15.htm.
2. Greg Hunter, "9% Unemployment Rate is a Statistical Lie," Information Clearing House, February 7, 2011, http://www.informationclearinghouse.info/article27435.htm.
3. Hunter, "Flying Blind," USA Watchdog, March 9, 2011. http://usawatchdog.com/unemployment-rate-flying-blind/.

4. Motoko Rich, "Encouraging Numbers, at First Glance," *New York Times*, May 13, 2011, http://www.nytimes.com/2011/05/14/business/economy/14unemployed.html.

5. "Poverty," United States Census Bureau, September 16, 2010, http://www.census.gov/hhes/www/poverty/about/overview/index.html.

6. Christine Vestal, "Collapse in Living Standards in America: More Poverty by Any Measure," Global Research, July 14, 2010, http://www.globalresearch.ca/index.php?context=va&aid=20124.

7. Scott Rasmussen, "Importance of Issues: Economy, Health Care, Taxes Continue to Be Top Issues for Voters," Rasmussen Reports, April 15, 2011, http://www.rasmussenreports.com/public_content/politics/mood_of_america/importance_of_issues.

8. C. Alonzo Peters, "To Hell With Student Loans—It's Time for College to Be Free," AlterNet, November 18, 2010, http://www.alternet.org/economy/148918/to_hell_with_student_loans_-_it%27s_time_for_college_to_be_free.

9. Jennifer Cheeseman Day and Eric C. Newburger, "The Big Payoff: Education Attainments and Synthetic Estimates of Work-Life Earnings," United States Census Bureau, July 2002, http://www.census.gov/prod/2002pubs/p23-210.pdf.

10. Brittany Bardin, Gabrielle Vono, and Christan Zbytniewski, "Student Loan Debt: Indentured Servitude," Project Censored, December 19, 2010, http://www.mediafreedominternational.org/2010/12/19/student-loan-debt-indentured-servitude/.

11. Tamar Lewin, "Burden of College Debt on Graduates Grows," *New York Times*, April 12, 2011, http://www.nytimes.com/2011/04/12/education/12college.html.

12. Michelle Singletary, "Higher Education: Right or Privilege?" *Washington Post*, May 18, 2011, http://www.washingtonpost.com/business/economy/the-color-of-money/2011/05/18/AFrw8h6G_story.html.

13. Kevin Drum, "All This and College Loans Too," *Mother Jones*, March 25, 2010, http://motherjones.com/kevin-drum/2010/03/all-and-college-loans-too.

14. Jim Rossi, "Generation Debt," *Mother Jones*, January 2006, http://motherjones.com/media/2006/01/generation-debt.

15. Tina Mather, Kimberly Daniels, and Shannon Pence, "Food Waste Remains Persistent Problem at Farms, Grocery Stores and Restaurants," California Watch, March 31, 2010, http://californiawatch.org/health-and-welfare/food-waste-remains-persistent-problem-farms-grocery-stores-and-restaurants.

16. Jonathan Bloom, "About," Wasted Food, http://www.wastedfood.com/about/.

17. Jenny Gustavsson et al., "Global Food Losses and Food Waste," Swedish Institute for Food and Biotechnology, Food and Agriculture Organization of the United Nations, 2011, http://www.fao.org/fileadmin/user_upload/ags/publications/GFL_web.pdf.

18. David Moberg, "Diet Hard: With A Vengeance" *In These Times*, March 24, 2011, http://www.inthesetimes.com/article/7112/.

19. *Policy Roundtable: Managing Vulnerability and Risk to Promote Better Food Security and Nutrition*, Committee on World Food Security, Food and Agriculture Organization of the United Nations, October 16, 2010, http://www.fao.org/docrep/meeting/019/k8953e.pdf.

20. "World Food Prices Hit Record Highs Amid Oil Jitters," Agence France-Presse, Common Dreams, March 3, 2011, http://www.commondreams.org/headline/2011/03/03-1.

21. Mary Jordan, ed., "Excerpts from Future of Food conference," *Washington Post*, May 10, 2011, http://www.washingtonpost.com/lifestyle/food/editors-note-on-the-future-of-food-conference/2011/05/09/AFEmnojG_story.html.

22. "Global Poverty Doubled Since 1970s: UN," Agence France-Presse, Information

Clearing House, November 26, 2010, http://www.informationclearinghouse.info/article26918.htm.

23. Committee on Trade and Development, *UNCTAD Policy Brief: Least Developed Countries Series*, United Nations, May 2011, http://www.unctad.org/en/docs/presspb20118_en.pdf.

24. "Monsanto in Haiti," Haiti Grassroots Watch, *Truthout*, May 5, 2011, http://www.truth-out.org/monsanto-haiti/1304605989.

25. Andrew Welsh-Huggings and Pallavi Gogoi, "Protester Handcuffed at Chase Shareholders Meeting," Associated Press, *Seattle Post-Intelligencer*, May 17, 2011, http://www.seattlepi.com/business/article/Protester-handcuffed-at-Chase-shareholders-meeting-1382977.php.

26. "JPMorgan in Talks to Settle S.E.C. Inquiry Into Securities," Bloomberg News, *New York Times*, May 6, 2011, http://www.nytimes.com/2011/05/07/business/07bank.html.

27. Diane B. Henriques, "JPMorgan Hid Doubts on Madoff, Documents Suggest," *New York Times*, February 4, 2011, http://www.nytimes.com/2011/02/04/business/04madoff.htm.

28. Marie Diamond, "CEO Bonuses Rose By Nearly 20% in 2010, While Average Worker Saw Income Stagnate," Think Progress, May 9, 2011, http://thinkprogress.org/2011/05/09/ceo-pay-350-companies/.

Power, Abuse, and Accountability

by Andy Lee Roth

Censored #5:
Private Prison Companies Fund Anti-Immigrant Legislation

Source:
Peter Cervantes-Gautschi, "Wall Street and the Criminalization of Immigrants," Counterpunch, October 15, 2010, http://www.counterpunch.org/gautschi10152010.html.

Student Researcher: Caitlin Morgan (Sonoma State University)

Faculty Evaluator: Peter Phillips (Sonoma State University)

Censored #9:
Government Sponsored Technologies for Weather Modification

Sources:
Rady Ananda, "Atmospheric Geoengineering: Weather Manipulation, Contrails and Chemtrails," Global Research, July 30, 2010, http://www.globalresearch.ca/index.php?context=va&aid=20369.
"Global Warming: An Effect of Weather Manipulation," *European Union Times*, January 3, 2010, http://www.eutimes.net/2010/01/global-warming-an-effect-of-weather-manipulation.
Rosalind Peterson, "Contrails & Man-Made Clouds Change Climate, Harming Agriculture," News with Views, July 12, 2009, http://www.newswithviews.com/Peterson/rosalind117.htm.

Student Researcher: Noe Otero (San Francisco State University)

Faculty Evaluator: Kenn Burrows (San Francisco State University)

Censored #13
Will a State of Emergency Be Used to Supersede Our Constitution?

Sources:
Peter Dale Scott, "Continuity of Government: Is the State of Emergency Superseding our Constitution?" Global Research, November 24, 2010, www.globalresearch.ca/index.php?context=va&aid=22089.
Allen Roland, "HR 645 / U.S. Preparing for Civil Unrest," People's Voice, March 16, 2010, www.thepeoplesvoice.org/TPV3/Voices.php/2010/03/16/hr-645-u-s-preparing-for-civil-unrest.
Scott, "War, Martial Law, and the Economic Crisis," Global Research, February 23, 2011, http://www.globalresearch.ca/index.php?context=va&aid=23354.
Scott, "Supplanting the United States Constitution: War, National Emergency and 'Continuity of Government,'" Global Research, May 19, 2010, http://www.globalresearch.ca/index.php?context=va&aid=19238.

Student Researchers: Robert Usher and Brittney Barsotti (San Francisco State University)

Faculty Evaluators: Kenn Burrows (San Francisco State University); Mickey Huff (Diablo Valley College)

Censored #16
Sweatshops in China Are Making Your iPods While Workers Suffer

Sources:
Dan Margolis, "Rotten Apple: iPod Sweatshops Hidden in China," People's World, January 25, 2011, http://www.peoplesworld.org/rotten-apple-ipod-sweatshops-hidden-in-china/.

Student Researcher: Aluna Soupholphakdy (Sonoma State University)

Faculty Evaluator: Elaine Wellin (Sonoma State University)

Censored #19
Oxfam Exposes How Aid Is Used for Political Purposes

Sources:
Mike Lewis, "Oxfam warns against trend in using aid for political & military purposes," Oxfam International, March 10, 2011, http://www.oxfam.org/en/pressroom/press-release/2011-02-10/oxfam-warns-against-trend-using-aid-political-military-purposes.

Student Researcher: Nzinga Dotson-Newman (Sonoma State University)

Faculty Evaluator: Peter Phillips (Sonoma State University)

Censored #20
US Agencies Trying to Outlaw GMO Food Labeling

Sources:
Mike Adams, "GMO Alert: U.S. Attempting Global Censorship of GMO Food Labeling," *Natural News*, May 4, 2010, http://www.naturalnews.com/z028716_GMOs_food_labels.html.

"US Opposes Honest Labeling of GMO Foods," Ethan A. Huff, *Natural News*, July 9, 2010, http://www.naturalnews.com/z029168_GMO_foods_labeling.html.

Student Researcher: Brittney White (San Francisco State University)

Faculty Evaluator: Kenn Burrows (San Francisco State University)

Related Validated Independent News Sources

Tim Reid and Michael Evans, "Obama Secretly Deploys US Special Forces to 75 Countries Across World," *Times* (London), June 5, 2010, http://www.timesonline.co.uk/tol/news/world/us_and_americas/article7144445.ece.

Keith Harmon Snow, "Apocalypse In Central Africa," *Z Magazine*, July 2010, http://www.zcommunications.org/apocalypse-in-central-africa-by-keith-harmon-snow.

E. Eduardo Castillo and Martha Mendoza, "US Law Enforcement Role in Mexico Drug War Surges," Associated Press, *Yahoo! News*, March 20, 2011, http://news.yahoo.com/s/ap/lt_drug_war_us_cops_in_mexico.

Bill Conroy, "Pentagon Fingered as a Source of Narco-Firepower in Mexico," Narcosphere, February 12, 2011, http://narcosphere.narconews.com/notebook/bill-conroy/2011/02/pentagon-fingered-source-narco-firepower-mexico.

Erin Rosa, "US Teaching 'Counterinsurgency' Courses To Mexican Military in Drug War," Narcosphere, February 12, 2011, http://narcosphere.narconews.com/notebook/erin-rosa/2011/02/us-teaching-counterinsurgency-courses-mexican-military-drug-war.

Michael Werbowski, "Is Mexico a Narco-State?" Global Research, March 29, 2011, http://www.globalresearch.ca/index.php?context=va&aid=19430.

Sherwood Ross, "America's Special Prisons for Muslims and Arabs," Global Research, March 26, 2011, http://www.globalresearch.ca/index.php?context=va&aid=23960.

Wayne Pacelle, "Big Ag Wants To Make It a Crime to Expose Animal Abuse at Factory

Farms," AlterNet, March 21, 2011, http://www.alternet.org/food/150312/big_ag _wants_to_make_it_a_crime_to_expose_animal_abuse_at_factory_farms.

Will Potter, "Minnesota Bill Targets Anyone Who Exposes an 'Image or Sound' of Animal Suffering at Factory Farms, Puppy Mills," Green Is The New Red, April 6, 2011, http://www.greenisthenewred.com/blog/minnesota-bill-factory-farm-photos/ 4626/.

Yvonne Yen Liu, "America's Food Sweatshops and the Workers of Color Who Feed Us," AlterNet, February 18, 2011, http://www.alternet.org/food/149970/america%27s _food_sweatshops_and_the_workers_of_color_who_feed_us.

Mike Adams, "GMO Alert: U.S. Attempting Global Censorship of GMO Food Labeling," Natural News, May 4, 2010, http://www.naturalnews.com/z028716_GMOs_food _labels.html.

Ethan A. Huff, "US Opposes Honest Labeling of GMO Foods," Natural News, July 9, 2010, http://www.naturalnews.com/z029168_GMO_foods_labeling.html.

Student Researchers: Shah Baig, Erica Chavez, Chante Noel, and Elizabeth Michael (Sonoma State University); Brittney White (San Francisco State University)

Faculty Evaluators: Peter Phillips, Ronald Lopez, and Elenita Strobel (Sonoma State University); Kenn Burrows (San Francisco State University)

Control over another person's body is, as Michel Foucault has shown, perhaps the most elementary form of power.[1] But even the late French theorist might have been surprised by the machinations of the Corrections Corporation of America (CCA) and GEO Group, the United States' two largest companies that design, build, finance, and operate prisons. As Peter Cervantes-Gautschi originally reported, the CCA (based in Nashville, Tennessee) and Geo Group (a global corporation based in Boca Raton, Florida) are crucial forces in the covert organization of the current wave of anti-immigrant legislative efforts. CCA's top management contributed the largest block of out-of-state campaign contributions received by Governor Jan Brewer as she sought election in November 2010. Brewer has been an outspoken champion of Senate Bill 1070 (SB 1070), the Arizona state law that is the most expansive and strict proposed anti-illegal immigration legislation in recent US history. Furthermore, two of Governor Brewer's aides who helped sign SB 1070 into law are former CCA lobbyists. As Cervantes-Gautschi shows, both CCA and GEO rely almost exclusively on revenue from tax dollars at local, state, and federal levels, and they directly profit from the incarceration of immigrants apprehended by US Immigration and Customs Enforcement (ICE). Since 2006, roughly a million immigrants have been incarcerated in dangerous detention facilities, in what Cervantes-Gautschi characterizes as "a tax-payer-financed private prison system."

Though corporate media eventually reported on the lobbying efforts of CCA and GEO and how private companies like these benefit from the criminalization of immigrants, what Cervantes-Gautschi's report reveals, and what corporate media ignored, is the extent to which CCA and GEO are integrated into Wall Street. The principal investor in CCA is a hedge fund, Pershing Square Capital Management, run by Bill Ackman, who plays a powerful role in Target Corporation and Kraft Foods. Wells Fargo is the principal investor in GEO. Thus, many Americans are invested in CCA and GEO through their pensions without knowing it. The same is true, as Cervantes-Gautschi reports, of Congress. Most members of Congress have personal investments in one or more of CCA's or GEO's major shareholders. Thus, in addition to the substantial campaign contributions that congressional leaders receive from the private prison industry, many stand to gain from the dubious economic successes of companies like CCA and GEO.

In May 2011, the *New York Times* did report that previous claims that Arizona's private prison system save the state money are misleading or even false: "Data there suggest that privately operated prisons can cost more to operate than state-run prisons—even though they often steer clear of the sickest, costliest inmates."[2] According to one estimate cited, inmates held in private prisons cost the state as much as $1600 more per year. Moreover, five of Arizona's eight private prisons do not accept the state's most costly prisoners, those with "limited physical capacity and stamina," severe physical illness, or chronic conditions.

The global atmosphere, including the air that we breathe, exemplifies what many people envision when they champion protection of the commons—i.e., forms of wealth that belong to all of us and must therefore be protected and managed for the good of all. Rising global temperatures, increasing population, and degradation of water supplies have created broad support for the growing field of weather modification. One such program is atmospheric geo-engineering, or cloud seeding, which involves using airplane contrails to seed cirrus clouds. Advocates claim that geo-engineering could be employed to counteract global warming, while critics raise concern about public health effects and potential military applications.

Coverage in the corporate media has been almost nonexistent: the *New York Times*, for instance, ran a 2007 opinion piece advocating geo-engineering as "an insurance policy, a backup plan for climate change."[3] More recently, *Newsweek* offered a skeptical account of geo-engineering's potential to block sunlight and thus counteract global warming, while WTEN, an ABC affiliate based in Albany, New York, broadcast a report on activists who believe that geo-engineering may actually be a covert military operation.[4]

Rady Ananda reported on an international symposium hosted in Belgium during May 2010, where scientists gathered to "force public debate" on geo-engineering. At the conference, Dr. Coen Vermeeren of the Delft University of Technology stated that "weather manipulation through contrail formation . . . is in place and fully operational." The Case Orange Report concluded that "manipulation of climate through modification of Cirrus clouds is neither a hoax nor a conspiracy theory" and warned that the United States aims to "control the weather by the year 2025, both for civil and military purposes." Reviewing the history of efforts at weather modification dating back to 1915, Ananda wrote, "The only conspiracy surrounding geo-engineering is that most governments and industry refuse to publicly admit what anyone with eyes can see."

The European Union Times reported on China's extensive cloud seeding projects and the US government's covert weather modification experiments over the past half century. One of the latest US programs is HAARP, the High Frequency Active Aural Research Program. This technology, the *European Union Times* reported, could potentially trigger floods, droughts, hurricanes, and earthquakes. The scientific idea behind HAARP is to "excite" a specific area of the ionosphere and observe the physical processes in that excited area with intention of modifying ecological conditions. *The Times* report described HAARP as having the potential to be used as "a weapon of mass destruction on a global scale."

After the March 11, 2011, earthquake and tsunami that devastated Japan's northeast coast, MSNBC reported that "the atmosphere above the epicenter . . . underwent unusual changes in the days leading up to the disaster," according to preliminary data being examined by Dimitar

Ouzounov, a professor of earth sciences at Chapman University in California.[5] MSNBC's report emphasized Ouzounov's claim that scientists could study the ionosphere, part of the earth's upper atmosphere, to predict earthquakes, while noting that the research had not yet been published or formally reviewed by other scientists. The MSNBC report did not address whether increases in both the concentration of electrons and infrared radiation in the ionosphere in the days before the earthquake might have been caused by the sort of technologies identified in the Case Orange Report or the *European Union Times* story, cited above.

"Peacekeeping" provides cover for the potential consolidation of power by political elites and the domestic mobilization of the US military. Peter Dale Scott and Allen Roland, in articles from Global Research and the People's Voice, respectively, revealed how a federal program of emergency measures—originally implemented during the Eisenhower administration as a legitimate response to the threat of nuclear attack—is being adapted to bestow far-reaching powers on the executive branch in response to any situation that the president considers an emergency. The National Emergency Centers Establishment Act (HR 645), introduced by Representative Alcee Hastings (D-FL) in January 2009, proposed to establish emergency centers to provide "temporary housing, medical, and humanitarian assistance to individuals and families dislocated due to an emergency, major disaster," or to "meet other appropriate needs, as determined by the Secretary of Homeland Security." In his report, Roland described the proposed legislation as "the militarization of FEMA [Federal Emergency Management Agency] internment facilities."

Scott's reports traced the history of "Continuity of Operations" or "Continuity of Government" (COG) programs, dating back to their formation under the Eisenhower administration, to their transformation during Reagan's presidency, to the implementation of COG following 9/11 by the Bush executive. COG plans are the probable source for the USA PATRIOT Act, presented to Congress five days after 9/11, and also for the Department of Homeland Security's Project Endgame—a ten-year plan, initiated in September 2001, to expand detention camps, at a cost of $400 million in Fiscal Year 2007 alone. The consequences include the removal of time-honored constitutional protections and increased militarization of civilian law enforcement.

Nearly a decade since 9/11, aspects of COG remain in effect. COG plans are still authorized by a proclamation of emergency that has been extended each year by presidential authority, most recently by President Barack Obama in September 2010.[6] *The New York Times* reported that "President Obama called for tolerance" and declared that the US was "not—and never will be—at war with Islam," but made no mention of the president's continuation of the national emergency with respect to terrorism.[7]

Congress is also to blame. The National Emergencies Act requires that "not later than six months after a national emergency is declared, and not later than the end of each six-month period thereafter that such emergency continues, each House of Congress shall meet to consider a vote on a joint resolution to determine whether that emergency shall be terminated." As Peter Dale Scott documented, since implementation of COG in the days following 9/11 nearly a decade ago, Congress has not once met to discuss the state of emergency declared by George W. Bush in response to 9/11. Thus, the state of emergency remains in effect today.

Under these conditions, US military troops can engage in police actions in US cities, operations that would otherwise violate long-standing Posse Comitatus statutes. Scott's reports alerted us to antecedents of the current militarization of US domestic law enforcement and to the challenges that this militarization presents to our cherished conception of the United States as a nation governed by laws and its Constitution.

A deadly explosion on May 20, 2011, at a Chinese factory where workers assemble Apple's iPads and iPhones, garnered attention in the corporate media. However, while noting that the blast in the Foxconn plant killed three workers and injured fifteen others, most corporate news focused on the question of whether the accident would negatively impact Apple's ability to supply its much sought-after iPads and iPhones.[8]

By contrast, before the Foxconn disaster, Dan Margolis reported on the systemic conditions that threaten workers' health in factories contracted with Apple. On a daily basis, factory conditions expose Chinese workers to poisonous chemicals as they assemble Apple iPods. Citing a report by China's Institute of Public & Environmental Affairs, Margolis revealed how Apple hides mistreatment of workers and environmental damage behind a "secretive supply chain." According to this report, management in factories subcontracted by Apple forced workers to use n-hexane, a neurotoxin and irritant, in place of alcohol as a cleaning agent. Margolis reported that forty-nine workers from one plant were admitted to a hospital after falling ill, while more were likely poisoned but pushed out of work before they fell ill. The manufacturer, Lian Jian, forced the latter group to sign papers saying they would not hold the company accountable for their health. Management at factories producing Apple products also forced workers to work more overtime than legally permitted under Chinese law, and subjected workers to humiliating surveillance, including strip searches when leaving work.

The Institute of Public & Environmental Affairs concluded that Apple is able to get away with abuses of workers and the environment due to its "culture of secrecy," which makes monitoring of Apple's production unusually difficult. For example, while hundreds of other companies that operate in China (including Walmart and Nike) participate in the Green Choice Alliance, a nongovernmental organization that monitors corporate polluters, Apple does not. As Margolis noted, Apple's practices contradict the image it markets to the public of itself as "a benevolent corporate giant . . . that does more than its part to better the world."

Abuses of power in the name of "peacekeeping," "diplomacy," and "development" demonstrate how elites not only take advantage of military and economic crises but also contribute to their formation in the first place. Thus Mike Lewis reported on the politicization of international aid by donor governments pursuing their own political and military purposes. The nongovernmental relief organization Oxfam International found that national governments spent billions of dollars in international aid—which could have transformed the lives of people in some of the world's poorest countries—on unsustainable, expensive, and dangerous projects that supported those governments' own short-term foreign policy and security objectives.

The politicization and militarization of aid has made it harder for aid agencies to provide help to those in need. For example, after the United States identified armed groups operating in central and southern Somalia as terrorists, US aid to Somalia in 2010 dropped to an eighth of what it was in 2008. Moreover, by blurring the distinction between military and civilian activities, politicized aid potentially makes aid workers and intended beneficiaries targets. The Oxfam report showed that 225 aid workers were killed, injured, or kidnapped in violent attacks during 2010, compared with 85 in 2002.

Although commitments of international aid by wealthy countries have risen steadily since 2002, more than 40 percent of the $178 billion went to just two countries, Afghanistan and Iraq, which figure prominently in the donor nations' foreign policy and national security interests. Equally insecure, impoverished, and conflict-inflicted countries that fall outside of the donor nations' immediate interests are, by contrast, relatively neglected.

The Guardian reported Oxfam's findings, but otherwise major newspapers in the US and the UK passed over the report's critical analysis of the politicization of international aid.[9]

As President Barack Obama publicly emphasizes diplomacy, his administration has expanded the United States' global military presence, as documented in the first Censored News Cluster, "Human Costs of War and Violence." While corporate media lavished attention on the killing of Osama bin Laden and SEAL Team Six as a single, dramatic military operation, Tim Reid and Michael Evans reported that President Obama has secretly sanctioned a huge increase in the number of US forces carrying out search-and-destroy missions against al-Qaeda around the world. American troops now operate in seventy-five countries. This dramatic expansion goes far beyond the covert missions authorized by President George W. Bush, and reflects how aggressively the Obama administration is pursuing al-Qaeda behind the public rhetoric of global engagement and diplomacy.

Keith Harmon Snow documented the lethal consequences of US foreign policy in central Africa, where millions of dollars in military hardware provided by the United States under the veil of the "War on Terror" has contributed to atrocities in the Congo, Uganda, and Rwanda.[10] The United States African Command (AFRICOM) projects an image of US troops in Africa undertaking exclusively humanitarian and peacekeeping operations, but as Snow's report indicated, under cover of the long shadow of the 1994 Rwandan genocide, US military operations actually include "overseeing strategic minerals (essential for US military stockpiles) and covert missions in northeastern Congo." Snow wrote that "Pentagon-trained African proxy warriors" operate not only throughout Africa, but also as far away as Afghanistan, Iraq, and Haiti.

Closer to the United States' own borders, a trio of news stories revealed the scope of the US military's involvement in Mexico's war on drugs. Together, Bill Conroy, Erin Rosa, E. Eduardo Castillo, and Martha Mendoza documented the unprecedented numbers of US law enforcement agents active in Mexico since President Felipe Calderón launched a crackdown on drug trafficking four years ago.[11] More than thirty-five thousand people have been killed in drug-related violence during that time. US agents generally provide intelligence and training to the Mexican military. Although the exact number of US agents operating in Mexico is not known with certainty, journalists using the Freedom of Information Act, federal budget requests, government audits, congressional testimony, and agency accountability reports have been able to establish a figure of several hundred agents. Michael Werbowski showed how narcotics traffickers in Mexico have ruthlessly exploited the increasing economic interdependence among Mexico, the United States, and Canada.

The Federal Bureau of Prisons (BOP) has been targeting Arabs and Muslims for detention in "Communication Management Units," which deny inmates virtually all communication with their families and the outside world, according to Sherwood Ross. Muslim prisoners in BOP facilities in Terra Haute, Indiana, and Marion, Illinois are not being punished because of terrorist acts. "The vast majority of these folks are there due to entrapment or material support convictions," said Center for Constitutional Rights attorney Rachel Meeropol, who has communicated with most of them. These are "terrorism-related convictions that do not involve any violence or injury." Nonetheless, under communication management, BOP authorities at the Indiana facility limit inmates to mailing one six-page letter per week, making one fifteen-minute phone call per month, and receiving only one sixty-minute visit per month. The Center for Constitutional Rights contended that BOP officials are shifting Muslim inmates to these facilities "based on their religion and/or perceived political beliefs." The extreme nature of the BOP restrictions raises the issue of cruel and unusual punishment, forbidden by the US Constitution.

Animal rights activists constitute another group at risk of unjust incarceration and prejudicial treatment when they are imprisoned. Wayne Pacelle, president and CEO of the Humane Society of the United States, reported that Iowa and Florida have proposed new laws intended to make illegal the undercover recording of animal abuses in industrial agricultural factories. Lawmakers in both states have introduced bills to establish criminal penalties for going undercover at agricultural facilities and simply taking pictures. As Pacelle noted, corporate management of factory farms "want to prevent their very own customers, America's consuming public, from learning about the production practices that bring food to their tables and plates." Will Potter reported that Minnesota is following Iowa and Florida's lead, with even stronger proposed legislation cracking down on activists who attempt to document animal suffering. Potter linked the current spate of antiactivist legislation to previous "ecoterrorism" bills and the Animal Enterprise Terrorism Act, and he documented how the legislators championing the Minnesota bill include the past president of the Minnesota Pork Producers.[12]

Not all forms of incarceration restrict humans behind bars in prisons or jails. Economic servitude constitutes another indirect form of incarceration in which workers, although formally free, have little control over their own lives and health. Yvonne Yen Liu reported on a survey of the US food system that shows food workers in all phases of the system working in "sweatshop-like conditions."[13] Examining the race, gender, and class of workers along the supply chain, the study by the Applied Research Center documented a significant wage gap between whites and workers of color in food production, processing, distribution, and service, and a concentration of people of color in low-wage jobs within the system. Liu concluded that, despite advances in assuring that our food is locally sourced and sustainably produced, the movement for good food must also encompass food workers, the "often-invisible labor that help bring our food to the table."

In contrast with the global atmosphere, which is widely recognized as a commons to be protected and managed for the good of all, food has been widely accepted as a private commodity. As one commons advocate acknowledged, food is "grown, processed, packaged, and sold for a profit, usually by large corporations."[14] However, with growing concern over the health impacts of genetically modified (GM) foods, many environmentalists and social justice advocates now champion the inclusion of food as part of the commons. The World Health Organization has identified allergenicity, antibiotic resistance, gene transfer, outcrossing, GM genes introduced into the wild population, gene stability, susceptibility of nontarget organisms (insects), and loss of biodiversity as possible risks associated with GM seeds.[15] In response to these potential risks, countries including Japan, Australia, China, and those of the European Union require mandatory labeling for products made with genetically modified organisms (GMOs).

In sharp contrast to this precautionary approach, the United States' Food and Drug Administration (FDA) and Department of Agriculture (USDA) officially contend that there are no differences between GMOs and non-GMOs. In separate stories, both Mike Adams and Ethan A. Huff reported that the FDA and USDA not only oppose domestic labeling of products containing GMO ingredients, they also seek to prevent other nations from doing so. The two federal agencies have proposed to the Codex Alimentarius Commission (the United Nation's top committee on food and agriculture) that no country should be able to require GMO labeling on food items, arguing that such labels would be "false, misleading, and deceptive." In his report, Huff wrote that, through their appeal, the FDA and USDA are "trying to outlaw truth in labeling and are openly working to deceive the public." Adams reported that, if successful in its Codex appeal, the FDA could "seize any products in the US that make 'non-GMO' claims," and the federal government could file lawsuits through the World Trade Organization against any country that allows non-GMO labeling or claims on its products.

Notes

1. Michel Foucault, *Discipline & Punish: The Birth of the Prison* (New York: Norton, 1979).
2. Richard A. Oppel Jr., "Private Prisons Found to Offer Little in Savings," *New York Times*, May 19, 2011, http://www.nytimes.com/2011/05/19/us/19prisons.html.
3. Ken Caldeira, "How to Cool the Globe," *New York Times*, October 24, 2007, http://www.nytimes.com/2007/10/24/opinion/24caldiera.html.
4. Sharon Begley, "A Climate Cure's Dark Side," *Newsweek*, January 30, 2011, http://www.newsweek.com/2011/01/30/a-climate-cure-s-dark-side.html. See also "Secrets in the Sky," WTEN, Albany, New York, May 3, 2011, http://www.wten.com/global/story.asp?s=14547467.
5. Stephanie Pappas, "Did Atmosphere Give Warning of Japan Quake?" Science on

MSNBC.com, May 18, 2011, http://www.msnbc.msn.com/id/43083235/ns/tech-nology_and_science-science/t/did-atmosphere-give-warning-japan-quake/.

6. Barack Obama to Nancy Pelosi, Letter from the President on the Continuation of the National Emergency with Respect to Certain Terrorist Attacks, September 20, 2010, http://www.whitehouse.gov/the-press-office/2010/09/10/letter-president-continuation-national-emergency-with-respect-certain-te.

7. Ann Bernard and Manny Fernandez, "On Sept. 11 Anniversary, Rifts Amid Mourning," New York Times, September 12, 2010, http://www.nytimes.com/2010/09/12/nyregion/12sept11.html.

8. "Fatal Blast and Fire Halt Work at Chinese Plant That Makes iPads," Bloomberg News, New York Times, May 20, 2011, http://www.nytimes.com/2011/05/21/technology/21foxconn.html.

9. Richard Norton-Taylor, "Military priorities are distorting aid budgets, says Oxfam," Guardian, February 10, 2011, http://www.guardian.co.uk/global-development/2011/feb/10/military-aims-distorting-aid-priorities.

10. Peter Phillips and Andrew Roth, eds., "AFRICOM: US Military Control of Africa's Resources," Censored 2008: The Top 25 Censored Stories of 2006–07 (New York: Seven Stories, 2007), 44–48.

11. For further Project Censored coverage on this topic, see Peter Phillips, Andrew Roth, and Project Censored, eds., "Security and Prosperity Partnership: Militarized NAFTA," Censored 2009: The Top 25 Censored Stories of 2007–08 (New York: Seven Stories Press, 2008), 25–29.

12. For further Project Censored coverage on this topic, see Peter Phillips and Andrew Roth, eds., "Terror Act Against Animal Activists," Censored 2008: The Top 25 Censored Stories of 2006–07 (New York: Seven Stories, 2007), 109–14.

13. Jay Walljasper, "Commons for a Small Planet," On the Commons, August 14, 2008, http://onthecommons.org/commons-small-planet.

14. "20 Questions on Genetically Modified Foods," World Health Organization, http://www.who.int/foodsafety/publications/biotech/20questions/en/; "GE Food," Center for Food Safety, http://truefoodnow.org/campaigns/genetically-engineered-foods.

15. For further Project Censored coverage on this topic, see Peter Phillips and Project Censored, "Dangers of Genetically Modified Food Confirmed," Censored 2007: The Top 25 Censored Stories of 2005–06 (New York: Seven Stories, 2006), 72–74.

Health and the Environment
by Elaine Wellin and Kristen Seraphin

Censored #8
The Fairy Tale of Clean and Safe Nuclear Power

Sources:

Lindsey Blomberg, "Germany Backs Away from Nuclear," *Environmental Magazine*, May 31, 2011, http://www.emagazine.com/daily-news/germany-backs-away-from-nuclear.

Jeff Goodell, "America's Nuclear Nightmare," *Rolling Stone*, April 27, 2011, http://www.rollingstone.com/politics/news/america-s-nuclear-nightmare-20110427.

Matthew Hick, "Advantages and Disadvantages of Renewable Energy," Renewable Energy Today, April 4, 2011, http://renewableenergy-today.com/Renewable-Energy/ Advantages-Disadvantages-Renewable-Energy.html.

Michael Mariotte, "Nuclear Energy Is Dirty Energy (and Does Not Fit into a 'Clean Energy Standard')," Nuclear Information and Resource Service (NIRS), January 25, 2011, http://www.nirs.org/factsheets/nuclearenergyisdirtyenergy.pdf.

"Nuclear Reactor Crisis in Japan FAQs," Union of Concerned Scientists, April 7, 2011, http://www.ucsusa.org/nuclear_power/nuclear_power_risk/safety/nuclear-reactor-crisis-faq.html.

"Radiation Exposure and Cancer," US Nuclear Regulatory Commission, October 20, 2010, http://www.nrc.gov/about-nrc/radiation/health-effects/rad-exposure-cancer.html.

Jeffrey St. Clair, "Inside America's Most Dangerous Nuclear Plant," *Counterpunch*, March 24, 2011, http://www.counterpunch.org/stclair03242011.html.

Student Researchers: Aaron Peacock (San Francisco State University); Taylor Falbisaner (Sonoma State University)

Faculty Evaluators: Kenn Burrows (San Francisco State University); Peter Phillips (Sonoma State University)

Censored #12:
Pacific Garbage Dump: Did You Really Think Your Plastic Was Being Recycled?

Sources:
Fabien Cousteau, "TEDxGreatPacificGarbagePatch: Fabien Cousteau: Ocean Animals and Plastic Pollution," YouTube video, 10:10, from a TEDx talk for GreatPacific-GarbagePatch given on November 6, 2010, posted by TEDxTalks, December 17, 2010, http://www.youtube.com/watch?v=BXv4Xc_6oC8.

David de Rothschild, "Message on a Bottle," United Nations Environment Programme, UNEP: Our Planet, April 2011, http://unep.org/pdf/op_april/EN/OP-2011-04-EN-ARTICLE7.pdf.

"Seven Misconceptions about Plastic and Plastic Recycling," Ecology Center, April 2011, http://www.ecologycenter.org/ptf/misconceptions.html.

Jaymi Heimbuch, "The Great Pacific Garbage Patch Is Bigger Than the Continental US: Here's What We Can Do About It," AlterNet, July 13, 2010, http://www.alternet.org/water/147528/the_great_pacific_garbage_patch_is_bigger_than_the_continental_us%3A_here%27s_what_we_can_do_about_it/.

Jocelyn Kaiser, "The Dirt on Ocean Garbage Patches," *Science* 328, no. 5985 (June 18, 2010).

"Plastic Debris in the Ocean," United Nations Environment Programme, UNEP Year Book 2011, http://www.unep.org/yearbook/2011/pdfs/plastic_debris_in_the_ocean.pdf.

Stiv Wilson, "The Fallacy of Gyre Cleanup: Part One, Scale," 5 Gyres, July 5, 2010, http://5gyres.org/posts/2010/07/05/the_fallacy_of_gyre_cleanup_part_one_scale.

Student Researchers: Laralyn Yee (University of California, Berkeley); Allison Holt (San Francisco State University)

Faculty Evaluators: Kenn Burrows (San Francisco State University); Mickey Huff (Diablo Valley College)

Censored #15
Big Polluters Freed from Environmental Oversight

Sources:
Kristen Lombardi and John Solomon, "Big Polluters Freed from Environmental Oversight by Stimulus," Center for Public Integrity, November 28, 2010, http://www.publicintegrity.org/articles/entry/2565/.

Student Researcher: Courtney Rider (Sonoma State University)

Faculty Evaluator: Keith Gouveia (Sonoma State University)

Censored #17
Superbug Bacteria Spreading Worldwide

Sources:
Michelle Roberts, "Europe 'Losing' Superbugs Battle," *BBC News*, April 6, 2011, http://www.bbc.co.uk/news/health-12975693.
Associated Press and Reuters, "Scientists Worry New Superbug Could Spread Worldwide," MSNBC, August 11, 2010, http://www.msnbc.msn.com/id/38655676/ns/health-infectious_diseases/t/scientists-worry-new-superbug-could-spread-worldwide/.

Student Researcher: Nzinga Dotson-Newman (Sonoma State University)

Faculty Evaluator: Peter Phillips (Sonoma State University)

Censored #21
Lyme Disease: An Emerging Epidemic

Sources:
"Statement of the National Non Profit Lyme Disease Association on the IDSA Guidelines Panel Decision," Lyme Disease Association, April 22, 2010, http://www.lymediseaseassociation.org/index.php?option=com_content&view=article&id=616:idsa-guidelines-panel-decision-4-22-10&catid=7:conflict-report&Itemid=398.
"MA Governor Signs Lyme Disease Doctor Protection Bill into Law," Lyme Disease Association, June 30, 2010, http://www.lymediseaseassociation.org/index.php?option=com_content&view=article&id=670:ma-governor-signs-lyme-disease-doctor-protection-bill-into-law-june-30-2010&catid=7:conflict-report&Itemid=398.
"Bay Area Lyme Disease Patient Fights Insurer," CBS-San Francisco, November 23, 2010, http://sanfrancisco.cbslocal.com/2010/11/23/healthwatch-bay-area-lyme-disease-patient-fights-insurer.
"Reported Cases of Lyme Disease by Year," Centers for Disease Control and Prevention, August 26, 2010, http://www.cdc.gov/ncidod/dvbid/lyme/ld_UpClimbLymeDis.htm.

Student Researcher: Ashley Myers (San Francisco State University)

Faculty Evaluator: Kenn Burrows (San Francisco State University)

Related Validated News Stories

Agence France-Presse, "Scientists Warn Naked Body Scanners May Cause Cancer," November 12, 2010, http://www.google.com/hostednews/afp/article/ALeqM5ho8khPyF-PinX_4vNYd1JZwn8hV4Q?docId=CNG.442824fa7c08853af96322d7315a6f02.461.
Mike Adams, "Radiation Scientists Agree TSA Naked Body Scanners Could Cause Breast Cancer and Sperm Mutations," *Natural News*, December 3, 2010, http://www.naturalnews.com/030607_naked_body_scanners_radiation.html.

Brian Merchant, "50% of the New Congressmen Deny Climate Change," Treehugger, November 5, 2010, http://www.treehugger.com/files/2010/11/50-percent-new-congressmen-deny-climate-change.php.

"Don't Order The Gulf Shrimp No Matter What BP Tells You," Media Freedom International, http://www.mediafreedominternational.org/2011/04/09/don%E2%80%99t-order-the-gulf-shrimp-no-matter-what-bp-tells-you/.

Dahr Jamail, "BP Blamed for Toxification," Al Jazeera English, November 9, 2010, http://english.aljazeera.net/indepth/2010/11/201011872121964396.html.

Amy Goodman, "Goodman: On Weather and Longfellow," Press Democrat, http://www.pressdemocrat.com/article/20110613/WIRE/110619873?Title=GOODM AN-On-weather-and-Longfellow.

Bill McKibben, "A Link Between Climate Change and Joplin Tornadoes? Never!" *Washington Post*, http://www.washingtonpost.com/opinions/a-link-between-climate-change-and-joplin-tornadoes-never/2011/05/23/AFrVC49G_story.html.

Maria Cheng, "Superbug Gene found in New Delhi Drinking Water," *Huffington Post*, April 7, 2011, http://www.huffingtonpost.com/2011/04/07/superbug-gene-water-india_n _846056.html.

Melly Alazraki, "Glaxo Smith Kline finds Compound," Daily Finance, August 6, 2010, http://www.dailyfinance.com/2010/08/06/glaxosmithkline-finds-compound-fight-superbugs.

Student Researchers: Alyssa Andrews (Florida Atlantic University); Courtney Rider and Keith Garrett (Sonoma State University); Rashanah Baldwin, Maureen Foley, and Monica Macellari (DePaul University)

Faculty Evaluators: James Tracy (Florida Atlantic University); Eric Williams and Ervand Peterson (Sonoma State University); Marla Donato (DePaul University); Mickey Huff (Diablo Valley College)

Corporate media frame environmental issues, disasters, and especially health outcomes as isolated events, denying what even today's school children know about the complex interconnectedness of the world's ecosystems and the effects on individuals within them. Of particular concern to Project Censored are the ways that environmental waste and contamination, and its subsequent effects, are ignored, wrongly framed, or deeply flawed and misrepresented by the corporate media. Examples include the global spread of superbug bacteria, the emerging Lyme disease epidemic, oil and toxic dispersant contamination from the British Petroleum (BP) oil explosion disaster, and the unfolding effects of one off the world's worst nuclear reactor accidents since Chernobyl, the Fukushima Daiichi nuclear plants in Japan.

Half of the United States' newly elected Congress members deny climate change, and the federal government has released big polluters from oversight and accountability. Analyses of corporate responsibility and the true cost to human health and the environment are rarely addressed. For instance, after provoking the worst environmental disaster in American history, BP ultimately got off the hook; the company continued drilling throughout the disaster and installed new rigs within a year. The fundamental connection between reckless corporate behavior and its impact on the environment was ignored, with dire consequences for humans and the planet. Environmental catastrophes are framed as isolated events, with a beginning, maybe a bit of passing human interest, and an end, and the ongoing environmental damage seldom hits the press.

Middlebury College professor and 350.org campaign founder Bill McKibben reminds us that it is vitally important to connect the dots among massive weather events, government negligence, corporate greed, and environmental degradation of land, air, and oceans. But what happens more often is that media "greenwashes" dirty energy sources (coal, gas, nuclear power) as "clean"—a particularly dangerous notion because it belies the threat they pose to our planet and human health.

Radiation—whether from naked body scans at airports by the Transportation Security Administration (TSA); or the Fukushima Daiichi nuclear power plant in Japan; or Indian Point, one of America's most dangerous nuclear plants—affect health and well-being. No levels are safe. There is nothing "clean" about it. And nuclear power leaves a byproduct that is toxic for millennia and is capable of killing hundreds of thousands of people. Yet, industry backers are promoting a "Clean Energy Standard," to endorse nuclear power. They champion nuclear energy as carbon-free and, therefore, pollutant-free. This proposal suffers from three fundamental misconceptions: 1) that pollutants other than carbon dioxide are irrelevant when defining "clean energy," 2) that because radiation is invisible and odorless, it is not a toxic pollutant, and 3) that nuclear power is carbon-free. These statements are not true. The earthquake and tsunami in Japan are a stark reminder of the risks inherent in nuclear power. Recently, the Japanese government admitted to three full nuclear meltdowns at Fukushima.

Fukushima is now considered equal to, if not worse than, the catastrophe at Chernobyl. The devastation at Chernobyl forms the basis for estimates of the number of deaths from radiation and cancer. With thirty-one deaths directly attributed to the accident, projected outcomes include the following:

The United Nations Scientific Committee on the Effects of Atomic Radiation (UNSCEAR) 2008 report confirmed sixty-four deaths from Chernobyl's radiation.

The World Health Organization (WHO) suggested the figure could reach 4,000.

The 2006 TORCH report by European Greens predicted 30,000 to 60,000 cancer deaths as a result of Chernobyl fallout.

Tragically, the Japanese now face similar consequences, as will, inevitably, human populations and environs near future nuclear reactor meltdowns anywhere in the world.

As a result of the Fukushima disaster, American concern for the safety of nuclear power facilities in the US has intensified. However, the Nuclear Regulatory Commission (NRC), the federal agency responsible for ensuring that US nuclear plants are operated as safely as possible, gets mixed reviews. In a March 2011 Union of Concerned Scientists (UCS) report, *The NRC and Nuclear Power Plant Safety in 2010: A Brighter Spotlight Needed*, UCS's Director of Nuclear Safety Project David Lochbaum examined fourteen "near misses" at US nuclear plants during 2010 alone, then evaluated the NRC regulatory response in each case. The report revealed a variety of shortcomings: inadequate training, faulty maintenance, poor design, and failure to investigate problems thoroughly. Clearly, the failures in oversight of all US nuclear reactors represent major problems affecting the safety and "cleanliness" of nuclear energy.

One of the NRC's most egregious oversight problems concerned Entergy's Indian Point nuclear power plant on the Hudson River. One of the five most dangerous nuclear reactors in the United States, Indian Point made headlines for its faulty emergency cooling system that was deemed "certain to fail" by nuclear engineers. According to engineers, the head company Entergy has known about these mechanical issues and lackluster nuclear meltdown plan for over six years yet has continued to downplay its controversial meltdown scenarios, as well as the need for repairs on their cooling system. The NRC has known about these hazards since 1996 but has joined Entergy in claiming that there is no rush to fix them because a breakdown isn't likely. Indian Point is only about thirty miles from Manhattan. A nuclear accident could expose millions of Americans to cancer-causing radiation. Despite safety hazards and security risks, the Obama administration continues to back nuclear energy as clean and carbon-free.

The myth of carbon-free nuclear energy was endorsed by Entergy's campaign for Affordable Energy and Economic Justice in response to protesters' demands to close Indian Point. The campaign advertised nuclear energy as a clean alternative to coal with benefits including revitalizing impoverished neighborhoods and maintaining good health through the prevention of respiratory illnesses. Campaign representatives used fear and misinformation to gather support for keeping Indian Point open and in business. Entergy's alliance with politicians such as Hillary Clinton—who accepted affiliated campaign contributions—has also allowed the plant to operate with little oversight. Corporate media support this dubious conception. Matthew Daly of the Associated Press wrote, "The US Nuclear Regulatory Commission said inspections conducted after the Japan nuclear crisis found reason for concern, although it continues to believe that the nation's 104 nuclear reactors are safe."

Inspectors found that many plant operators have neither done enough to train their staff on the voluntary emergency guidelines nor updated their procedures, said Eric Leeds, director of the NRC's Office of Nuclear Reactor Regulation. The guidelines—intended to contain or reduce the impact of accidents that damage a reactor core—were put in place in the 1990s.

"While overall we believe plants are safe . . . we are concerned that our inspectors found many of the plants have work to do in either training their staff on these procedures or ensuring the guidelines are appropriately updated," Leeds said.[1]

According to the Associated Press and the NRC, proper safety training at nuke plants will keep us safe. The NRC story received widespread coverage in the corporate media in the US.

A crucial detail to those promoting nuclear power as "clean" is corporate media's rubber stamp of the myth that nuclear power is carbon-free. But nuclear power is not carbon-free—it releases small amounts of radioactive carbon. Building nuclear facilities is carbon-intensive and requires enormous amounts of concrete, steel, and carbon-based fuels for transport of materials. The nuclear fuel chain necessary to operate and support reactor operations (e.g. uranium mining, processing, enrichment, and fuel fabrication), as well as the millennia of radioactive waste storage, all result in substantial and unavoidable carbon emissions. The nuclear food chain itself is a massively polluting process. Nuclear power results in water pollution because reactors require large amounts of water to cool their red-hot nuclear cores—some twenty thousand to five hundred thousand gallons per minute are diverted from rivers, lakes, or oceans, then spewed back out again, discharged five to ten degrees warmer than when it went in, causing havoc among marine environments and affecting downstream industrial uses and drinking water.

Carbon dioxide is not the only pollutant to be considered when assessing a "Clean Energy Standard"; singling it out ignores fifty years of accumulated knowledge of the effects of other long-lasting and toxic pollutants, not least of which are the carcinogens released by radionuclides from nuclear reactors: Tritium, Strontium-90, Ceisim-137, Plutonium-239, and dozens more. It doesn't take an accident to become contaminated by them. Nuclear reactors emit radiation into our air and water as part of their routine operations, made all the more dangerous because it cannot easily be detected or avoided. The 2005 report from the US National Academy of Sciences indicated that no safe level of radiation exposure exists—every exposure increases the risk of cancer, birth defects, and other disease. The NRC's adoption of the Linear No Threshold Hypothesis (LNTH) to calculate risk is conservative: any increase in dose of radiation, no matter how small, results in incremental increase in risk. As corporations and media dismiss science that does not support their interests, ignoring how ecosystems function and how pollution is spread, they neglect to address bioaccumulation, the process by which the concentration of many contaminants increases as one moves up the food chain.

Contaminants such as radioactive iodine, cesium, and strontium—all beta emitters—become concentrated in the food chain due to bioaccumulation. At the top of the food chain are humans, also encompassing fetuses and human breast milk. In 1963, one week after an atmospheric nuclear bomb test in Russia, scientists observed the magnifying power of bioaccumulation when they detected radioactive iodine in the thyroids of North American mammals, even though they could not detect smaller amounts in the air or on vegetation. Bioaccumulation is one reason why it is dishonest to equate the danger to humans living five thousand miles away from Japan with the minute concentrations measured in our air. If we tried, we would now likely be able to measure radioactive iodine, cesium, and strontium bioaccumulating in human embryos in this country.

In particular, radioactive tritium releases have been identified from existing nuclear reactors, releases that exceed safe drinking water standards at thirty-seven different nuclear plants—more than half of all those now in operation. Normal background levels of radioactive tritium in drinking water are three to twenty-four picocuries per liter. Astonishingly, radioactive tritium levels above one million picocuries per liter were measured at nine sites covering eighteen reactors. The cumulative effect of exposure to radiation in air and water is not restricted to these vectors.

In his article "There is No 'Safe' Exposure to Radiation," Brian Moench noted that radiation from Japan is now detectable in the atmosphere, rainwater, and food chain in North America. Fukushima's four reactors, still out of control months after the earthquake and tsunami that killed thousands and crippled the plants, hold ten times more nuclear fuel than had been at Chernobyl, thousands of times more than the bomb dropped on Hiroshima.

In an interview on June 3, 2011, Arnie Gundersen, a licensed reactor operator and energy advisor with thirty-nine years of nuclear power engineering experience, said that the average human being breathes about ten cubic meters of air daily. Air filters measuring air in the Seattle area in April 2011, when they pulled ten cubic meters through them, had ten hot particles in them.[3]

The official refrain carried by major corporate media? "No worries here, perfectly harmless."

In a related bioaccumulation matter, the Transportation Security Administration (TSA) began rolling out full-body scanners at US airports in 2007, but stepped up deployment of the devices this year when stimulus funding made it possible to buy another 450 of the advanced imaging technology scanners. Former Homeland Security Secretary Michael Chertoff represents Rapiscan Systems, who profits from every machine that is installed at airports. Current Homeland Security Secretary Janet Napolitano has discussed putting them in malls, schools, subways, and train stations. Some 315 "naked" scanners are currently in use at sixty-five US airports, according to the TSA.[2]

Beyond the demeaning nature of a "naked" body scan are the potential health dangers of backscatter scanning raised by X-ray imaging specialists from the University of California and Johns Hopkins University School of Medicine. Author Karin Zeitvogel cited Dr. Michael Love, who runs an X-ray lab at the department of biophysics and biophysical chemistry at Johns Hopkins University, saying that air passengers risk cancer and gene mutations by subjecting themselves to these scanners. Government officials, on the other hand, have said that the scanners have been tested and meet safety standards. Their interest in protecting the public may be obstructed by business relationships—such as Chertoff's alliance with Rapiscan.

In an April 2011 letter addressed to Obama's science and technology adviser John Holdren, X-ray imaging specialists from the University of California, San Francisco—Drs. Russell Blaylock, John Sedat, David Agard, and Robert Stroud—and Dr. Marc Shuman maintained that naked body scanners may be dangerous to human health and that their safety has never been demonstrated, especially not by an independent panel of qualified scientists. The doctors claimed that the ionizing radiation emitted by these devices could alter your DNA and cause sperm and breast mutations.

Americans are, and should remain, uneasy, as real dangers are neither reflected nor addressed by major corporate media. Instead, as TSA body scan concerns are ignored, and as daily news of the Fukushima disaster disappears, paid advertisements by power generation companies, such as Entergy's greenwashing media campaign, dominate air time. These ads tout clean nuclear power and America's stake in nuclear power generation for jobs and income—leading Americans to connect all the wrong dots.

DID YOU REALLY THINK YOUR PLASTIC WAS BEING RECYCLED?

Many people have not heard that there is a swirling mass of plastic in the middle of the Pacific Ocean that qualifies as the planet's largest garbage dump. The Great Pacific Garbage Patch is not even the only trash vortex out there: there are *five* giant trash gyres. Located in the North and South Pacific, Atlantic, and Indian oceans, these trash gyres now contain an estimated 315 billion pounds of plastic. Much of the world's trash has accumulated in part of the Pacific Ocean—roughly 135° to 155°W and 35° to 42°N, based on the movement of ocean currents.

How did the plastic get to these trash gyres? Not all plastic in the recycling bin gets recycled, and people carelessly toss plastics away. Plastic litter often ends up in the waterways and currents carry it out into the ocean. How much plastic is in the Great Pacific Garbage Patch? No one really knows, but, according to researchers, surface area estimates determine the North Pacific trash gyre to be as large as the continental United States. According to HowStuffWorks.com, every square mile of ocean hosts forty-six thousand pieces of floating plastic, constituting 90 percent of all trash floating in the world's oceans.

These pieces of plastic have a dire effect on marine life. Turtles confuse plastic bags for jellyfish, and birds confuse bottle caps for food. They ingest but can't digest, so their stomachs fill with plastic and they starve to death. Evidence is mounting that trash vortexes also have significant impacts on human health.

How do five massive oceanic garbage patches exist, most as big as the continental US, with so few people aware of them? Can ocean gyres be cleaned up? No, probably not. The only way to prevent further large-scale global garbage pollution is to stop humans from throwing away plastic (or to simply stop using it) and clean up waterways and beaches before the plastic reaches the sea. It will take a massive public interest campaign to change our throwaway behaviors and the most effective avenue is the major media, which thus far are not addressing this critical issue.[4]

Unfortunately, the corporate media blocks all hope of stemming the tide of plastics and other refuse going into our waterways and into the gyres. The media, by not actively and comprehensively covering the garbage patches of the world, directly inhibits the only known and effective solution to the problem—creating awareness around changing human habits.

NO MATTER WHAT, DON'T ORDER
THE GULF SHRIMP

Corporate spin for British Petroleum was in top form with a media blitz that included a "Voices from the Gulf" campaign and politicians parroting ad slogans claiming it was business as usual in the Gulf of Mexico, after BP's *Deepwater Horizon* oil disaster in April 2010. The campaign ignored the volatile organic compounds (VOCs) and showcased happy residents assuring the public that "fishermen are working," "local shrimp is on the menu," and beaches are back just in time for spring break! Idyllic shots of contented fishermen hauling in crab, a restaurant owner ladling steaming gumbo into a bowl, and a hotel owner promoting sparkling white beaches created an ambiance to combat what would have otherwise been a public relations and public health nightmare.

Government and media complicity in this campaign included statements from Mississippi Governor Haley Barbour who declared, "The coast is clear . . . come on down." Images from the movie *Jaws* come to mind, except that in this scenario, shark and human are the victims of a blob of oil and chemical dispersant the size of 312 Olympic swimming pools. The trinity of government, big business, and corporate media colluded to deny reality while creating a deadly illusion of clean, safe beaches and seafood. This type of gaslighting—a term used to describe the process by which psychopaths deny their victims reality—is crazy making.

In order to sell "crazy," BP hired advertising agency Purple Strategies and spent $50 million on its campaign after an estimated 185 million gallons of oil were dumped into the Gulf.[5] Their strategies to cap the well and their solution for cleanup were equally "crazy." A media critique addressing company knowledge of safety hazards at the Macondo Prospect and on the *Deepwater Horizon* rig was mostly absent except for in congressional hearings, which showed a somewhat apologetic BP Chief Executive Officer Tony Hayward. A scientific analysis providing an accurate number of barrels spilled per day was ignored, and in-depth reporting about the dangerous use of dispersants—which experts say should not have been used at all—was left out. Finally, the serendipitous branding of the spill itself protected those who were responsible.

Branding is critical to invoking particular frames. Corporate media's misrepresentation of the oil "spill" helped maintain the BP spin. Essential to this was also leaving out the words British Petroleum, Halliburton, or Transocean to protect those responsible. A "spill" doesn't conjure up the image of the millions of gallons of oil and chemicals that flowed into the sea for three months. Today, the gusher is still referred to as the "Gulf Oil Spill."

Central to maintaining the brand was the obfuscation of the number of barrels spilled per day and of the most effective methods of cleanup. BP's spin doctor Bill Salvin confidently asserted, "We've said . . . that there is no way to estimate the flow coming out of the pipe accurately." Utilizing science and software, Eugene Chiang, associate professor of astronomy and Earth and planetary science at UC Berkeley, and Steven Werely, associate professor of mechanical engineering at Purdue University, estimated the number of barrels—at minimum twenty-nine thousand and at most one hundred thousand per day.[6] The oil slick stretched hundreds of miles long.

Media were so focused on BP's frantic efforts to clean up the spill that they neglected to focus on alternatives less toxic to the environment than the chemical dispersant Corexit 9500. The tragic reality of the cleanup—that Corexit's formula was more toxic than the oil itself—was completely ignored, as was the fact that this dispersant spreads after being broken up into small droplets, depending on the currents of the oceans. The long-term toxic effects on human health and the environment were downplayed and replaced by reporting that BP was going to "make it right," and that the spill had been cleaned up. An analysis of the reckless profit-driven decision-making process by corporate heads, with government agency support, was completely absent.

Corporate media didn't connect the dots between the revolving doors on the BP board of directors and the Nalco Holding Company (NHC), producer of the oil dispersant Corexit. One month before the "Gulf Oil Spill," BP CEO Tony Hayward sold approximately one-third of his holding in the company.[7] So did Goldman Sachs, selling 250 million of their BP shares. BP's former chairman Peter Sutherland is now chairman of Goldman Sachs International. Former BP board member Rodney Chase is on the board of NHC. After the spill, BP purchased NHC's entire inventory of the toxic oil dispersant Corexit. The NHC's stock jumped 18 percent. Corporate media did not investigate these relationships, which benefited former BP shareholders and the NHC, but not public health. In the biggest environmental catastrophe in history, they did not search for the least toxic alternative—they looked for the most profitable outcome. Why did BP go with Corexit instead of the myriad of less toxic options—like the water-based Dispersit by Polychem?[8] An examination of stock trading and past and present board members makes the insane sane, all framed by corporate media as a desperate attempt to clean up the oil. Ignoring deadly toxic effects to human health allowed corporate owners to dump 1.9 million gallons of Corexit into the Gulf. The stamp of approval from the Environmental Protection Agency (EPA) and the lack of scientific-based evidence of the environmental impact provided complicity in this mendacious behavior. The EPA's approval of Corexit, showing government compliance and potential criminal negligence, was never discussed.

The corporate media instead followed federal and state politicians who said that the BP oil has dispersed and that there is no longer a problem. Alongside these declarations of safety, however, are scores of studies showing high levels of dangerous chemicals in seafood, as well as stories about increasing illnesses and mounting environmental destruction. Media have not only failed to connect these dots but have also colluded in the cover-up.

In his article "BP Blamed for Toxification," Dahr Jamail illustrated the complicity among mainstream media, Gulf state officials, BP, and the Obama administration. "This is the biggest cover-up in the history of America," Plaquemines Parish President Billy Nungesser told reporters. Many of the chemicals in the oil and dispersants, samplings of which have been found along the Mississippi Coast, are known to be teratogenic, mutagenic, and carcinogenic. Exposure to the dispersants occurs through inhalation, ingestion, and skin and eye contact. Workers on BP's Vessels of Opportunity (VoO) have found VOCs in their blood after tests revealed the presence of ethylbenzene, p-Xylene, and hexane.

Dr. Riki Ott, a toxicologist, marine biologist, and *Exxon Valdez* survivor, said, "People are being made sick in the Gulf because of the unprecedented release of oil and toxic chemicals, in response to BP's disaster." Corexit 9500 made the problem worse because, according to Dr. Ott, the dispersant is like a delivery system, bringing oil deeper into the body. The effects on the human body are staggering: nausea, headaches, vomiting, diarrhea, abdominal pain, chest pain, respiratory system damage, hypertension, skin sensitization, central nervous system depression, cardiac arrhythmia, cardiovascular damage, and neurotoxic effects.

BIG POLLUTERS FREED FROM ENVIRONMENTAL OVERSIGHT

What the public did not know as the Obama administration doled out billions in economic stimulus packages to corporations is that known big polluters were categorically freed from EPA oversight as they received those funds.

Passed by Congress in 1969, the National Environmental Policy Act (NEPA) provides one of the few proactive protections in an environmental enforcement system that typically relies on penalties after harm has already afflicted the environment and human health. NEPA requires companies to study possible benefits and threats to landscape, wildlife, or human health before proceeding with a major federal project, giving officials one last chance to intervene if the work imposes a "significant impact." Ultimately, the federal law is meant to ensure that environmental factors weigh as much as economic ones.

Because industry groups complained that NEPA compliance could delay projects by months or years, tying up companies with public notices and scientific studies costing millions of dollars, the Obama administration was thus influenced to ignore federal law and grant NEPA exemptions—more than 179,000 "categorical exclusions"—to streamline the environmental review process for "shovel-ready" stimulus projects that could create jobs quickly in a recession and yield "green energy" benefits down the road. Among the firms that won blanket NEPA exemptions were coal-burning utilities like Westar Energy and Duke Energy, chemical manufacturer DuPont, and ethanol maker Didion Milling—all despite histories of serious environmental violations. A project at BP's refinery in Texas City, Texas, secured a waiver for a carbon capture experiment, even with its poor safety record and deadly 2005 explosion.

The so-called "stimulus" funding came from the $787 billion legislation officially known as the American Recovery and Reinvestment Act, passed in February 2009. Documents show that the administration devised a speedy review process that relied on voluntary disclosures by companies to determine whether stimulus projects posed environmental harm. Corporate polluters often omitted mention of health, safety, and environmental violations from their applications and were able to do so because administration officials chose to ignore companies' environmental compliance records in making grant decisions and issuing NEPA exemptions, saying they considered such information irrelevant. In the words of Energy Secretary Steven Chu, the Obama administration's main goal was to "get the money out and spent as quickly as possible."

LYME DISEASE: AN EMERGING EPIDEMIC

Lyme disease is growing, with new cases appearing faster than AIDS and West Nile virus combined. Lyme—one of the most political and controversial diseases of our times—is ostensibly transmitted through the bite of an infected tick. Insurance companies maintain that while Lyme disease is hard to catch, it is easy and fast to cure. Yet, Lyme is difficult to diagnose because it can lie dormant in the body. When it does produce symptoms, it can mimic a bevy of mental and physiological conditions: neurodegenerative disorders such as multiple sclerosis, Parkinson's, or Lou Gehrig's disease, or mental disorders such as schizophrenia and bipolar. Patients may be misdiagnosed with lupus, Crohn's disease, chronic fatigue, fibromyalgia, or rheumatoid arthritis. The bacteria have been found in the brain tissue of Alzheimer's victims. Current diagnostic tools are inadequate to identify whether or not a patient is infected. Even if a diagnosis is obtained, arbitrary standards of treatment apply. Infectious Diseases Society of America (IDSA) designed these guidelines.

Since Lyme is onerous enough to diagnose and treat, the IDSA's guidelines simply reinforce this enigma by punishing physicians who diagnose and treat Lyme. Physicians who treat chronic Lyme patients recognize scientific research showing that, even with the two- to four-week course of treatment, some Lyme bacteria can survive in persistent infections. Despite physicians' understandings that Lyme disease patients may need longer-term care, insurance companies, along with "lockstep" medical panels such as the IDSA, have taken strong actions to limit treatment to short-term antibiotic therapy.

Indeed, most treating physicians understand that IDSA guidelines were written not with patient health in mind but for profit. Thus the IDSA's guidelines are meant to restrict treatment, penalize doctors who recognize and treat chronic Lyme, and deny coverage for treatment. Physicians risk having their licenses suspended by state medical boards and being sued by insurance companies.

For Massachusetts's 2011 budget, Governor Deval Patrick signed into law language on doctor protection for Lyme disease-treating physicians. The law permits doctors to clinically diagnose and treat patients long term. The state medical board in Massachusetts cannot bring charges against a doctor solely for prescribing long-term antibiotic treatment for Lyme disease. However, Lyme still remains a controversial disease—spirochete bacteria, of the same phylum as syphilis, leave room for speculation about the route of transmission. Scientists predict that Lyme disease will increase with global warming. The lack of attention to this lethal and debilitating disease is another "dot" the corporate media have dismissed in their dissemination of information.

SUPERBUG BACTERIA SPREADING WORLDWIDE

In samples taken from drinking water and puddles on the streets of New Delhi, a gene that could turn many types of bacteria into deadly superbugs was discovered, according to a new study. First identified in 2008, the bacteria armed with this gene, known as New Delhi metallo-beta-lactamase 1 (NDM-1), is now widely circulating in the environment and could spread to the rest of the world. Superbugs such as NDM-1 are resistant to carbapenem antibiotics, which is of major concern to experts because they are used for persistent infections that evade other drugs. Guenael Rodier, director of communicable diseases at the World Health Organization's (WHO) Copenhagen office, said, "It's like asking in the 1980s if a few HIV cases should be a big worry . . . the fact that NDM-1 has emerged is worrisome, but forecasting what it will do is very difficult."

Emerging in India, the superbug has made some appearances in North America. London-based pharmaceutical company GlaxoSmithKline currently holds the patent on a chemical compound, which, if processed, could treat NDM-1. Yet the super drug for the superbug remains in chemical form with no human trials underway.

There is no profit in the generation and testing of new antibiotics; profit is measured in sales volume, therefore a market must exist independent of the need. Thus, pushing current drugs that contribute to antibiotic resistance takes precedence over clinical trials for new drugs that might cure diseases.[10]

Each year in the European Union (EU), over twenty-five thousand people die of bacterial infections that are able to outsmart even the newest antibiotics. That figure will increase unless more powerful antibiotics are developed. According to the WHO, the situation has reached a critical point and a united push to make new drugs is urgently needed because there are now a number of bacteria resistant to all existing drugs.

While doctors and patients are blamed for overuse of antibiotics, the real cause for urgent action is the lack of development of new drugs, an issue largely unknown outside relevant medical communities. Corporate media portrays superbugs and climate change similarly, as isolated events, invisible to the eye and therefore a deceptively distant threat. The reality is that with the planet heating up from carbon emissions, there is a clear association between climatic conditions and infectious diseases. The link between malaria and climate change has long been studied in India. Excessive monsoon rainfall and humidity are factors, contributing to mosquito breeding and survival. If the NDM-1 gene can turn bacteria into superbugs, then vectors of transmission influenced by climate change will contribute to their spread.

HALF OF NEWLY ELECTED GOP CONGRESS MEMBERS DENY CLIMATE CHANGE

While mainstream medicine denies the connection between human health and the environment, 50 percent of newly elected GOP congressmen deny the impact of human-made emissions on the health of the Earth, ThinkProgress discovered. Eighty-six percent reject climate change legislation that would increase government revenue. These Congress members have gone on record rejecting the decades of sound evidence compiled by scientists, which shows human-made emissions are warming the atmosphere, and they have done so in a year slated to become the hottest ever recorded.

In summary, GOP congressmen's environmental myopia mirrors the corporate media view that environmental issues, if acknowledged, are framed as isolated events, with a beginning and isolated cause, an estimated cost, maybe a bit of passing human interest, and an end. The real and ongoing stories, the remaining and growing damage, and especially the cumulative effects on health and wellbeing of people and the planet, seldom hit corporate controlled headlines and stories. Americans have a right to, and in many studies say they want to, connect the dots and to react reasonably to environmental calamities. But without transparency and accurate information, society cannot adequately meet the clearly escalating environmental challenges today.

Rarely, if ever, is accountability included in stories and analyses. Despite responsibility for the worst environmental disaster in American history, government and the media lets BP off the hook, with continued drilling in the Gulf throughout the disaster, new rigs going up within a year, and, in the face of studies to the contrary, continued assurances to Americans that everything is safe. At perhaps even greater magnitudes, the levels and effects of radiation contamination in Japan, the US, and elsewhere by the Fukushima Daiichi nuclear power plant and by US reactors, are largely ignored, denying as well citizens' rights to know both the extent of dangers and ways to protect themselves and the environment.

The most basic of accepted ecological principles, that everything is interrelated so that any event has impacts and inevitable implications in the interconnected web of life, is most often ignored or unheeded by corporate media in America. This is a lesson with terminal consequences and there may not be more opportunities to learn from our misguided energy policies. While Switzerland and Germany phase out of nuclear energy, and China, Germany, and Japan move forward with research and deployment for renewables, the Obama administration invests in a losing game throwing billions in subsidies toward the oil, coal, gas, and nuclear industries.

In between media coverage of New York Congressman Anthony Weiner's sexual peccadilloes, Sarah Palin's flubbing about Paul Revere, and TV commercials greenwashing "clean" energy contributing to climate change are the stories of extreme weather events—tornadoes in the Midwest, fires in Texas and Arizona. Bill McKibben asks why we

didn't see pictures of disasters in Sri Lanka, Vietnam, or the Philip
pines, or of the megafloods in Brazil. Amy Goodman wonders why TV
meteorologists don't connect the dots—"by following the words
extreme weather with another two—climate change." As she astutely
points out, "we need modern day eco-Paul (or Paula) Reveres to rouse
the populace to this imminent threat."

Notes

1. Matthew Daly, "NRC: Nuke Plants Need More Training on Emergencies," Associated
   Press, June 6, 2011, http://hosted2.ap.org/APDEFAULT/Article_2011-06-06-
   Nuclear%20Plants-Safety/id-p874d5a0dbc094a95b127e79d43791eb2.
2. Cindy Sheehan, "Cindy Sheehan Takes on TSA," *Daily Censored*, December 4, 2010,
   http://dailycensored.com/2010/12/04/cindy-sheehan-takes-on-tsa/.
3. Chris Martenson, "Exclusive Arnie Gundersen Interview: The Dangers of
   Fukushima Are Worse and Longer-lived Than We Think," ChrisMartenson.com,
   June 3, 2011, http://www.chrismartenson.com/ blog/exclusive-arnie-gundersen-
   interview-dangers-fukushima-are-worse-and-longer-lived-we-think/58689.
4. These corporate media articles touch on the subject by revealing the existence of
   the plastic garbage patch but do little to question the underlying causes and efforts
   to fix the problem: Shelby Lin Erdman, "Scientists Study 'Garbage Patch' in Pacific
   Ocean," CNN, August 4, 2009, http://articles.cnn.com/2009-08-04/tech/
   pacific.garbage.patch_1_plastic-bits-and-pieces-pacific-ocean; Lindsey Hoshaw,
   "Afloat in the Ocean, Expanding Islands of Trash," *New York Times*, November 9,
   2009, http://www.nytimes.com/2009/11/10/science/10patch.html.
5. Jake Tapper, "BP Turns to Political Shop for $50 Million Ad Buy to Convince You the
   Company 'Will Get This Done' and 'Make It Right,'" ABC News, June 4, 2010,
   http://blogs.abcnews.com/politicalpunch/2010/06/bp-turns-to-political-shop-for-
   50-million-ad-buy-to-convince-you-the-company-will-get-this-done-and-.html.
6. Richard Harris, "Gulf Spill May Far Exceed Official Estimates," National Public Radio,
   May 14, 2010, http://www.npr.org/templates/story/story.php?storyId=126809525.
7. Jon Swaine and Robert Winnett, "BP Chief Tony Hayward Sold Shares Weeks
   Before Oil Spill," *Telegraph* (UK), June 5, 2010, http://www.telegraph.co.uk/
   finance/newsbysector/energy/oilandgas/7804922/BP-chief-Tony-Hayward-sold-
   shares-weeks-before-oil-spill.html.
8. "Media Ignores Goldman Sachs' ties to Corexit Dispersant," War on You, May 20,
   2010, http://waronyou.com/topics/media-ignores-goldman-sachs-ties-to-corexit-
   dispersant/.
9. "Statement of the Lyme Disease Association, Inc. on the IDSA Guidelines Panel
   Decision 4-22-10," Lyme Disease Association, April 22, 2010, http://www.lymedis-
   ease.org/news/lyme_disease_views/400.html.
10. Steve Sternberg, "Drug-resistant 'Superbugs' Hit 35 States, Spread Worldwide,"
    USA Today, September 17, 2010, http://www.usatoday.com/yourlife/health/med-
    ical/2010-09-17-1Asuperbug17_ST_N.htm.

Women and Gender Issues

by Joel Evans-Fudem and Amy Ortiz

Censored #11
Trafficking of Iraqi Women Rampant

Source:

Sebastion Swett and Cameron Webster, "Trafficking of Iraqi Women Rampant Despite US Commitment To End It," AlterNet, August 25, 2010, www.alternet.org/news/147962/trafficking_of_iraqi_women_rampant_despite_u.s._commitment_to_end_it.

Student Researcher: Allison Holt (San Francisco State University)

Faculty Evaluator: Kenn Burrows (San Francisco State University)

Censored #14:
Family Pressure on Young Girls for Genitalia Mutilation Continues in Kenya

Sources:
Erick Ngobilo, "Parents Disown Girls for Evading 'the Cut,'" *Daily Nation*, February 6, 2011, http://www.nation.co.ke/News/Parents%20disown%20girls%20for%20evading%20th e%20cut/-/1056/1102708/-/kdcr7jz/-/index.html.
"We Must Intensify Fight Against FGM," *Daily Monitor*, December 6, 2010, http://www.monitor.co.ug/OpEd/Editorial/-/689360/1066970/-/8yt6kg/-/index.html.
"Female Genital Mutilation," fact sheet, World Health Organization Media Centre, February 2010, http://www.who.int/mediacentre/factsheets/fs241/en/.

Student Researcher: Nzinga Dotson-Newman (Sonoma State University); Amanda Avery (State University of New York, Potsdam)

Faculty Evaluator: Matthew Paolucci (Sonoma State University); Dr. Christina Knopf (State University of New York, Potsdam)

Censored #24:
South Dakota Takes Extreme Measures to Be the Top Anti-Abortion State

Source:
Tanya Somanader, "The Five Ways That The GOP Is Trying To Eradicate A Woman's Right To Choose," ThinkProgress, February 15, 2011, http://thinkprogress.org/2011/02/15/five-ways-eradicate-choice/.

Student Researcher: Taylor Wright (Sonoma State University)

Faculty Evaluator: Don Romesburg (Sonoma State University)

Related Validated News Stories

Ángel Páez, "Women Sterilised Against Their Will Seek Justice, Again," Inter Press Service, October 15, 2010, http://ipsnews.net/news.asp?idnews=53177.
Cléo Fatoorehchi, "Women's Health in Crosshairs of Republican Congress," Inter Press Service, February 18, 2011, http://www.ipsnews.net/print.asp?idnews=54533.
Nick Baumann, "House GOP Declares War on Planned Parenthood," *Mother Jones*, February 9, 2011, http://motherjones.com/mojo/2011/02/house-gop-slashes-planned-parenthood-family-planning-funding-zero.
Jodi Jacobson, "The Pregnancy Police and the Citizens' Arrest of Pregnant and Nursing Women," *Truthout*, January 14, 2011, http://www.truth-out.org/the-pregnancy-police-and-citizens-arrest-pregnant-and-nursing-women66902.
"American Women Must Not be Fooled: Smeal Calls for National Reform in Rape Reporting and Investigating," Feminist Majority Foundation, Choices Campus, September 14, 2010, http://www.choicescampus.org/know/news/newstory.asp?id=12626.
J. Richard Cohen, "The Injustice on Our Plates," *Huffington Post*, November 24, 2010, www.huffingtonpost.com/J-richard-cohen/the-injustice-on-our-plat_b_787665.html.
Jill Richardson, "Why Women Who Pick and Process Your Food Face Daily Threats of Rape, Harassment and Wage Theft," AlterNet, January 26, 2011, http://www.alternet.org/story/149693.

"Injustice on Our Plates: Immigrant Women in the US Food Industry," Southern Poverty Law Center, Fall 2010, http://www.splcenter.org/sites/default/files/downloads/publication/Injustice_on_Our_Plates.pdf.

Anna Mulrine, "Exclusive: 1 in 5 Air Force Women Victim of Sexual Assault, Survey Finds," *Christian Science Monitor*, March 17, 2011, http://www.csmonitor.com/USA/Military/2011/0317/Exclusive-1-in-5-Air-Force-women-victim-of-sexual-assault-survey-finds.

Agnes Odhiambo, "Human Rights Violations Lead to Obstetric Fistula," Media Freedom International, April 5, 2011, http://www.mediafreedominternational.org/2011/04/17/human-rights-violations-lead-to-obstetric-fistula/.

Paul Breer, "With Support From Anti-Gay Foundation, West Virginians Can Sexually Discriminate For Another Year," ThinkProgress, March 14, 2011, http://wonkroom.thinkprogress.org/2011/03/14/wv-discrimination/.

Joey L. Mogul, Andrea J. Ritchie, and Kay Whitlock, "Queer Injustice: The Widespread Sexual Abuse LGBT People Face in Prison," AlterNet, March 11, 2011, http://www.alternet.org/story/149873/queer_injustice%3A_the_widespread_sexual_abuse_lgbt_people_face_in_prison/.

Student Researchers: Jordan Hall, Cynthia Solano, Taylor Wright, Amy Ortiz, Cameron Cleveland, and Yuliana Zamudio (Sonoma State University); Cara Peracchi Douglas, Sarah Schmidt, and Katie Whitney (Fresno State University); Ashley Noble and Jessica Capers (Indian River State College)

Faculty Evaluators: Sheila Katz, Andrew Deseran, Don Romesburg, Lena McQuade, James Dean, and Peter Phillips (Sonoma State University); Steven D. Walker (Fresno State University); Elliot D. Cohen (Indian River State College)

The corporate-owned media system has largely failed at the task of providing information about stories that do not reinforce heteronormativity and female submission. The lack of adequate coverage stems from how the media is organized and how news is created, but it is also a reflection of our culture's deeply entrenched problems of sexism, racism, and classism, as well as our inability to critique the realities of capitalism. The corporate media often trivializes news stories about women and marginalizes them within the media structure through their framing and omission of issues of concern to women. This lackadaisical attitude toward gender inequity and sexual violence has historically allowed many of the worst atrocities against human life and society to go unanalyzed and underreported.

The lack of a critical mass of women participating equally on all levels of news creation furthers a cultural missive in which no institutionalized understanding or inclusion of women's issues in the mainstream media's news agenda is necessary. The distorted portrayal of women and gender issues in the corporate press is not accidental;

it is the product of how journalism is practiced, how newsrooms are run and by whom the stories are chosen and edited, as well as who owns the company. "Women have been successful in gaining access to US news companies in numbers approaching those of men overall, but they are not yet at parity with men in their status across occupational levels. Most vividly, women encounter a glass ceiling in senior management that prevents their upward mobility into top decision-making posts. Women are fewer than a fourth of those in top management, and only about a third of those in governance."[1]

The United States is ranked thirty-sixth out of 175 in freedom of the press, seventieth among nations in women holding national office, and sixty-fourth in wage equality.[2] The corporate media are preoccupied with the appearance of women within the male gaze and trivializing women in power positions by focusing on their perceived attitudes, appearance, or questioning their mothering capabilities, and this allowable sexism prevents real women's issues from being discussed in substantive terms. Only by comparing corporate media coverage of issues relating to women or gender to the coverage we found from independent sources, can we begin to see how issues such as rape, sexual violence, reproductive rights, and gender inequity are framed in the mainstream media.

Since the midterm elections in November 2010, a broad rash of legislative actions aimed at restricting the reproductive rights of women has been introduced and signed into law in governments all across the United States by Republican-controlled legislative houses and governors. While it has been impossible for corporate media to ignore these developments as factual news, these outlets have published little analysis of the rhetoric used to impose these laws or of the concrete impacts they are likely to have.

For instance, one quote from an anti-abortion activist published by a corporate news outlet in a story on their website directly says, "Americans [want to] make sure our legal system protects the weakest members of our society, which is the unborn child."[3] On its face, this assertion appears to be simply the opinion of a prominent activist. However, left unquestioned by critical analysis, this statement makes multiple contentions with regard to national citizenship and the protections guaranteed to such members of our society. Fetuses cannot justly be given protections through our legal system on the basis of

their class as members of our society since they can have no citizenship and, at the very least, no consciousness of their status in a
hierarchical world. Women, themselves, only recently came under the
protections of the Constitution as citizens of this country. Publishing
statements like the example noted above, without a critical framework
in which to place them, promotes a view of these new laws, which
restricts the reproductive rights of women in America, as just another
debate over morality between different factions.

Reporting within this framework undermines the concept that protections and rights are granted to peoples in the US and cannot be
abridged or restricted based on prejudicial religious beliefs. While
reproductive rights are surely not the only protections abridged in this
way, these attacks affect a salient majority of persons in this country
whose rights to bodily integrity and full personhood are relatively
recent developments in our history; namely, women.

Another way that major corporate outlets frame the issue of the
abridgement of constitutional rights and protections is through the lens
of controversy. *The New York Times*, in a story on state bills restricting
abortion on the basis of pain felt by the fetus, has said, "The question
of fetal pain . . . is one of intense, unresolved debate among researchers
and among advocates on both sides of the abortion question."[4] This
obscures the issue behind a cloud of "scientific controversy."

Medical scientists have actually stated, however, that "pain perception requires conscious recognition or awareness of a noxious stimulus
[and] fetal awareness of noxious stimuli requires functional thalamocortical connections. Thalamocortical fibers begin appearing between
23 to 30 weeks' gestational age."[5] There appears to be no scientific controversy surrounding the issue of fetal pain, but anti-abortion activists
who also happen to hold medical degrees may very well be claiming
otherwise. That does not mean that there is evidence such pain exists.
Even if it did, the fundamental constitutional rights of a woman should
take precedence over that of a preconscious fetus.

The notable exception to the mass of reporting, which places this
issue within the framework of competing conceptual discourses, is
that of Rachel Maddow on her corporate-owned television program,
The Rachel Maddow Show. Her constant reporting on these laws as they
develop shies away from placing them in an abstract, conceptual,

moral frame, and reports on the harsh actualities that women seeking to utilize their rights will face.

In some cases, such as those in South Dakota, which does not have even one full-time abortion provider in the entire state, women are subjected to waiting periods of multiple days, legislature-scripted lectures by their doctors, forced ultrasounds, and mandated visits to unregulated pregnancy crisis centers run by anti-abortion activists who provide dubious and unscientific information, and do not provide an assurance of privacy or confidentiality. These new policies have already been signed into law and are to take effect July 1, 2011, unless a court injunction is imposed. Planned Parenthood and the American Civil Liberties Union have said that they will file a lawsuit.[6]

While this law appears to be one of the most radical and potentially unconstitutional attacks on women's reproductive rights that this country has seen in years, South Dakota proposed a bill earlier in the legislative session that would have allowed a relative or spouse of a pregnant woman, even against the woman's will, to defend the life of the fetus. Called, "justifiable homicide," the bill was intended to intimidate doctors who perform abortions in the state, and may have been proposed in the expectation of an eventual decision overturning *Roe v. Wade* by the Supreme Court. After public backlash, South Dakota shelved this bill and passed the restrictions noted above.

This type of legislation did not end with South Dakota; both Nebraska and Iowa have taken up similar bills. Nebraska Senator Mark Christensen introduced a bill that would allow any third party to use deadly force to stop harm or death from being inflicted on a fetus. Nebraska has already passed a bill (LB 1103) banning the termination of a pregnancy after twenty weeks, regardless of the viability of the fetus outside the womb.

Iowa has two bills on the table regarding this issue. The first, House File 153, mandates that the state recognize the personhood of a fetus from the moment of conception and requires that it provide the same protections to that fetus as to any person in the state. Iowa House File 7 expands the legal definition of self-defense to include the use of deadly force in defense in any place that a person is legally allowed to be. Taken together, the two laws would make the murder of abortion providers legal and mandatory for the state and/or its citizen.[7]

Justifiable homicide is not a new idea in anti-abortion circles. In the case of Dr. George Tiller in Kansas in 2009, his convicted murderer attempted to claim that his actions were justified because he was saving the lives of unborn children who were in imminent danger from the doctor. The judge in the case ultimately refused to allow this defense and the suspect was convicted of murder. Kansas, however, has restrictive laws regarding abortion as well.

Kansas has enacted a full ban on abortions after twenty-two weeks; consent for a minor seeking an abortion must be obtained by both parents; the abortion provider must read a state-written, unscientific script to their patients; and private insurance providers are disallowed from offering abortion services in their regular insurance plans.[8] Additionally, a new law, SB 36, will likely shut down most health clinics in the state due to building code and requirements of proximity to a nearby hospital.

There is a slew of other signed, passed, or pending legislative actions restricting a woman's right to a safe and private abortion across the country. What is listed here is by no account an exhaustive list of the current or pending abortion restrictions in state governments. What is clear is that these are not isolated pieces of legislation created by communities with their own best interests in mind. This is a conspicuously concerted effort throughout the country to rescind the constitutional rights of female citizens of the United States of America and to impose the morals of a certain religious faction onto the rest of the population. The New Right wasted no time in enacting these policies all over the country after their windfall election in November 2010.

In fact, the newly Republican-controlled House of Representatives passed House Resolution 3, the No Taxpayer Funding for Abortion Act. This resolution takes aim at any tax credits that a person may be able to claim for medical expenses that might have been abortion services. Any health insurance plan, whether private or small-business employer-based, that covers abortion would not be considered tax-exempt. Tellingly, the taxable status of employer-based health insurance does not apply to corporations, only small businesses.

In effect, this would eliminate most insurance coverage for abortion across the nation. The bill does allow for tax exemption exceptions in cases of rape or incest, as is the historical norm. However, in an unreported committee statement of intent, language was reinserted to alter the definition of the word "rape" used in the bill to specifically apply only to forcible rape in which the woman had to be physically subdued, fought constantly, and could prove it through medical exams. Although this bill has passed the House of Representatives, it is unlikely that the Senate will pass it and President Barack Obama has promised to veto it.

These legislators, through hypocritical rhetoric of libertarian mores coupled with an overt religious authoritarianism, are attempting to flood state legislatures with blatantly unconstitutional laws in order to force abortion rights defenders into a court battle. They are well aware that the current composition of the Supreme Court led by John Roberts makes *Roe v. Wade* vulnerable to being overturned completely if it reaches their court. Abortion rights defenders are aware of this as well, and have been wary of challenging any of these laws in court. The concrete results of these laws will be that scores of women will be left to abort their own fetuses; birth children to whom they bear no moral responsibility for raising because their options were restricted by the state; or undoubtedly be abused by the underground market that must inevitably grow to deal with unwanted pregnancies.

Conceptually, the Republicans passing these laws believe that they can, through legislation, stop abortion. That is their stated goal. However, they are attacking the only institutions that can potentially effect a solution: family planning clinics. The endgame here is the overturning of *Roe v. Wade* in its entirety, a return to unlicensed and dangerous abortions, and the criminal prosecution of any woman who would deny a fetus its full-term birth.

Apart from decisions regarding abortion, American women are being increasingly policed and harassed by their fellow citizens and institutions. In January 2011, a woman who was eight months pregnant met her friends at The Coach House Restaurant in Roselle, Illinois. While sipping water at the bar and talking with her friends, the bouncer approached and asked that she come outside to speak with him. Once outside he proceeded to ask her if she was pregnant and she answered in the affirmative. The bouncer then told her that she had to leave, ostensibly because he felt that the restaurant was not safe for a pregnant woman, but he most likely believed that she would drink alcohol while there and thereby damage her fetus.[9]

Though she said that she had no intention of drinking that night (which she has the right to do regardless), and the law enforcement officials in Roselle told her later that there are no regulations against pregnant women in bars, the bouncer felt he had the right to make decisions for this woman based on her reproductive status.

Among the many recent incidents involving women breastfeeding their children in public, two Ohio mall security guards forced a mother to leave the facility in February 2011 when they said that they had received complaints from shoppers about her exposed cleavage. Knowing her rights, the woman protested and told them that there were laws in place that protect her right to breastfeed in any area that she is personally allowed to be in any other instance. They forced her to exit the mall regardless and she later contacted city authorities and mall officials who both reiterated that she was legally allowed to breast-feed anywhere she liked.[10]

In both of these cases the legal rights of pregnant or nursing women were infringed upon by citizens who, armed with their own mores, values, and assumptions, believed they could make decisions for women based on their reproductive status regardless of the laws and protections that the US government has afforded women. That few people come to the aid of pregnant or nursing women during these incidents speaks to a cultural ambivalence toward this issue that often defers to those in positions of authority. However, when authorities are pursuing ends not codified in our laws, it should be everyone's duty to uphold the rights of pregnant and nursing women.

Corporate media coverage of sexual assault in the military is quick to report the steps the military is taking to prevent and punish sexual assault. According to our story, "New Recourse Option for Victims of Military Sex Assault," military sexual assaults in war zones rose 26 percent from 2007 to 2008, and another 33 percent over the following year, according to annual reports from the US Department of Defense.[11] In 2005 the Department of Defense created the Sexual Assault Prevention and Response Office (SAPRO), the military's first lead office to deal strictly with sexual assault. There are two recourse options available for victims of rape or sexual assault: restricted and unrestricted reporting. Restricted reporting is the new system, which bypasses the chain of command by permitting a victim to call a sexual assault response hotline coordinator, or to tell a victim's advocate, and receive medical care. With restricted reporting, however, no investigation is conducted into the incident and the accused assailant is free to potentially assault other service members. Unrestricted reporting forces service members who desire an investigation along with medical care services to first notify their commanding officers, as well as the person or people they are accusing—the investigation is often conducted on a "he-said" "she-said" basis. Without video proof or a multitude of witness testimonies, these investigations seldom determine the truth and are discontinued without conviction. In these situations, it is very dangerous to be the accusing party, as backlash assaults (subsequent assaults which take place because of attempts to prosecute the first assault) are common and accusers are often denigrated by their units and officers.

In the article "New Study: Sexual Assault in Air Force Goes Unreported," we see that according to the United States Military, one in five US Air Force servicewomen is a victim of sexual assault, and nearly half of rape victims—mostly females who are assaulted by males—never report the crime. Of the nearly 20 percent of servicewomen who admitted being assaulted, 58 percent reported being raped and 20 percent reported being sodomized, which the military classifies as "nonconsensual oral or anal sex."[12] This raises the question of how our troops can defend our country when there isn't an appropriate means for them to defend themselves against threatening forces within the military itself.

The New York Times reported:

> The Pentagon attributed the rise [in sexual assaults] largely to an upward trend in the reporting of incidents, and said the jump did "not necessarily" reflect an increase in the number of incidents. The Pentagon offered no evidence that reporting rather than sexual assault itself was on the rise in the military, and there have been multiple reports in recent years suggesting that the strains between close quartered men and women in war zones have exacerbated the problem. As they are quick to note, since 2004 the Defense Department has radically changed the way it handles sexual abuse in the mil-

itary, including encouraging victims to come forward, expanding access to treatment and toughening standards for prosecution.[13]

Yet, these changes are far from perfect and military culture expressly prohibits any public sign of weakness or a break in rank loyalty. These standards revisions from the Department of Defense are utilized more as a shield from criticism and inquiry than as a form of protection for assaulted men and women in the armed forces.

Corporate media coverage of domestic rape rates parrots the same misleading and inaccurate statistics as those reported by the federal government. According to the *Washington Post*:

> The number of rapes per capita in the United States has plunged by more than 85 percent since the 1970s . . . according to federal crime data. This seemingly stunning reduction in sexual violence has been so consistent over the past two decades that some experts say they have started to believe it is accurate, even if they cannot fully explain why it is occurring.[14]

Although this article states that rapes are one of the most underreported crimes, they qualify the reduced rape statistics reported by state and the federal law enforcement by stating that one school of thought holds that rape has declined for the same reasons that other violent offenses have: a reduction in the lawlessness associated with crack cocaine, a shrinking population of young people and an increased number of criminals in jail.[15]

The racialized connotations in this quote cannot be easily obscured, as the war on drugs and the prison-industrial complex have both targeted young, poor men of color. What has been said here is that the government has incarcerated a lot of black men; the underlying assumption being that it is predominantly black men that rape women; an assumption that remains unsupported by statistics.

In the article "Women Take Heed: Rape Reports Mislead," we learn that the US continues to report decreased numbers of rape, but Eleanor Smeal, president of Feminist Majority Foundation, says the numbers are misleading. In a hearing before [the] Senate Subcommittee on Crime and Drugs, Smeal called for a national reform of rape reporting. Specifically, Smeal argued the current definition of rape is outdated, excluding many types of rape. The definition has not been updated since 1927. It does not include forced anal or oral sex, vaginal or anal fisting, rape by an object, sexual assault, statutory rape, rape by men against men, any rape by a woman, the use of drugs or alcohol to subdue a victim, nor does it include rape of children younger than twelve. Smeal argues that underreporting of rape "threatens the safety and lives of millions of women. Without adequate reports, we cannot know the magnitude of the problem and therefore cannot adequately address it." The national definition of rape must be updated.[16]

Most of the United States' rape laws were first codified in the early twentieth century and have since seen little revision that acknowledges the major shifts in sexology, juvenile justice, and the rights of women.

Just as the high level of institutionalism in the military promotes acts of sexual violence more than it deters it, incarcerated prisoners in American correctional institutions are many times more likely than the general population to be raped or sexually assaulted. Within the national prison population, more than 18 percent of self-identified homosexual inmates (male and female) report being forced into sexual acts against their will compared with just over 2 percent of the self-identified heterosexual population. Self-identified homosexual inmates are not only victims of sexual violence from other prisoners, but also of routine acts of violence and negligence by prison guards and officials.[17] Again, this relates to the culture of hypermasculinity and rigid gender codes that are enforced in masculinist institutions like prisons or the military. In both institutions, the exemplar agent is one who embodies masculine stereotypes to the extreme, who uses violence and intimidation to enforce his will and abhors femininity in any of its forms. It is no great wonder that women and feminized men in either the military or the prison system are attacked and used for coerced sexual purposes at an inordinate rate and that the perpetrators of these crimes are left unpunished.

The fact that homosexual men are raped and assaulted in prison more often than heterosexual men is no great surprise. Given the history of pathologization and violence directed at homosexuals in the

United States and the continuing stigmatization and legal discrimination against them, acts that negatively effect male or female homosexuals are perceived as less damaging and more justified by American culture. In February 2011, a West Virginia coal miner claimed that he was threatened, verbally mistreated, and his property vandalized because of his sexual orientation. He was unable to bring a formal legal complaint against his employer because West Virginia's antidiscrimination laws do not apply to anyone on the basis of sexual orientation.[18] Although a number of states and municipalities have included sexual orientation and gender presentation in their antidiscrimination policies regarding employment, education, and housing, West Virginia failed this year to pass two bills that would have included sexual orientation in their antidiscrimination laws.

Of course, one of the major organizations opposing these bills was the West Virginia Family Foundation, which said its opposition was based on its endorsement of "deviant behavior."[19] Although the Kinsey reports of the 1950s dispelled the myth that homosexual acts were deviant or abnormal, multiple "family" foundations and organizations continue to use the rhetoric of mental illness, deviance, and criminality to convince legislators that certain persons should continue to be treated as second-class citizens based on their sexuality. This is an issue that will not be solved without a formal amendment to the Civil Rights Act that includes sexual orientation. Although numerous executive orders and interpretations of the Civil Service Reform Act of 1978 by the Office of Personnel Management supposedly bar discrimination in federal employment based on sexual orientation, they have never been expanded to include private sector workplaces and are rarely enforced within federal workplaces.[20] Until homosexual persons or persons who engage in same-sex acts are afforded the same rights and protections as all other citizens of the United States, we will continue to see violence perpetrated against them en masse, as well as their exclusion from global and domestic policy decisions and their continued denigration as deviants or criminals.

While the United States' formal eugenic program of sterilization, castration, and detention of the poor, "feebleminded," and "criminally inclined" citizens ran between the mid-nineteenth century and the mid-twentieth century, right up until we entered World War II and backed away from any scientific discourse that resembled that of the Nazi regime, we continue to subtly endorse population control initiatives in the third world and Global South, where we believe human lives are less valuable than our own. Our endorsement of the Peruvian sterilization program was indirect, but part of a larger global push to stem the growth of the population in other parts of the world in order to allow the US to have continued access to dwindling global resources.

The United States must take responsibility for fostering eugenic policies across the globe through our endorsement of population control campaigns in the Global South and through our key role in United Nations policymaking.[21] One of the most recent of these instances occurred between 1995 and 2000 when the Peruvian government, in compliance with the UN Population Fund directives, embarked on a campaign of mass, forced sterilization of mostly poor and indigenous women and men in the province of Anta.[22] The Peruvian government's National Programme for Reproductive Health and Family Planning issued quotas and payment-per-operation guidelines for doctors who were required to locate and sterilize as many Peruvians as possible, using deceit and coercion when necessary.

In 2009, the Women's Association of Forced Sterilisation Victims of Anta brought a lawsuit against four government officials for what was done to them, but the statute of limitations on crimes of bodily harm had passed, so the case was shelved. Now the Association is bringing new complaints of crimes against humanity and torture against government officials. The Peruvian government has admitted the eugenic nature of its family planning program and has conceded that over three hundred thousand forced sterilizations took place under the program's directives.[23] Still, there is little chance that the complaints filed by these victims of medical torture and government sterilization will be accepted—and even if they were, a conviction would not serve justice for those who will never again be capable of choosing their own reproductive status.

Often, corporate media coverage of women's issues becomes distorted by an inability to talk about economic inequity because of an uncritical stance on capitalism. Corporate media coverage of female genital mutilation (FGM) generally focuses on the cultural demand for the act and fails to examine how women in the countries that practice

FGM have very little economic freedom, making them dependant upon men and the culturally-held norms of beauty and marriage. By ignoring the economic role in gender/power dynamics, corporate media analysis fails to examine how increased educational and economic opportunities could give women more freedom to choose their own engagement with genital mutilation practices. In the *New York Times* piece "A Rite of Torture for Girls," the focus is on the "what and how" of genital mutilation, with a possible solution being to encourage milder forms of mutilation, or to get religious leaders to speak out against it. "People usually torture those whom they fear or despise. But one of the most common forms of torture in the modern world, incomparably more widespread than water-boarding or electric shock, is inflicted by mothers on daughters they love."[24] What the piece fails to address is why women are being forced into this brutal custom in the first place.

This cultural practice fits within a concept of femininity that is rigidly pure and untouched, making them acceptable for marriage. In contrast, the *Daily Nation* story, "Family Pressure on Young Girls for Genitalia Mutilation Continue in Kenya," addresses the lack of education for young girls, and the threat of being completely ostracized from the community if they do not undergo genital mutilation:

> Many girls have been forced to cut short their studies and are married off at a young age while some of them are still in hiding because their parents would disown them after running away to avoid circumcision. . . . Parents and grandparents in this area tell the young girls they will never get married, and no man would want them if they do not fulfill the rite. Not many women in this region are left to pursue education beyond the age of eight. Young women are told that education was not meant for them because they are supposed to get married and take care of their husbands. Uncircumcised women are generally looked down upon as failed women and discriminated against for not mutilating their genitalia. Because of this, young girls agree to go through with the surgery so that they can be included in the rites of passage so that their community will accept them.[25]

Corporate media do indeed cover the issue of FGM. However, the coverage is scant and framed to avoid any conversation about empowering women through educational and economic opportunities that are denied them. Further, there are no discussions in corporate media about the cultural contexts in which these acts take place, which would broaden the scope of our knowledge on the issue and allow a deeper analysis of the reasons why this tradition has been kept alive, as well as why many oppose it.

Since the United States' invasion of the sovereign state of Iraq in 2003, countless civilians have been murdered by our forces and those fighting against our military. One of the invisible (perceived as incidental) effects of this war has been that many Iraqi women and female children have been left without the male protection that their culture demands. Though Iraqi women hold some legal human rights, they are immeasurably more vulnerable to violence, sexual violence, and abduction without a male head-of-household to stake claim to the safety of their person.

A Women's Commission report from 2008 stated that over 4.5 million Iraqis have been displaced by the war and are living as informal refugees either in Iraq or in neighboring countries, though most have not been granted any formal refugee status or protections. According to the report, over fifty thousand women and children who fled to Syria and Jordan as refugees have found themselves victims of sex traffickers and sexual predators.[26] With no legal refugee status, work visas, or necessary male protectors in these countries, Iraqi women and children are forced into underground economies of sex—often occasional sexual servitude at best and permanent slavery at worst. With no way to report these crimes, women and children can disappear without a trace into these sexual underworlds at any time.

While the United States has taken some responsibility for the situation these women face, it has mostly taken the form of lip service. While our Secretary of State Clinton, an outspoken human rights advocate for women, has been clear that she believes the abuse of Iraqi women and children must end, we have not yet granted them priority refugee status, which would aid in their resettlement and give them protections under UN law.[27] As it stands now, women and children must live and work illegally in Iraq's neighboring countries. If arrested for legal trespass, they may face deportation back to Iraq where they will be criminally prosecuted for their own displacement and negotiated strategies for survival. If an arrest is made for prostitution or other crimes of sexuality, the woman can be legally executed if convicted in Iraq in order to avoid further disgrace to her family and to reinforce the importance of conservative sexual morals to the rest of the populace.[28]

There can be no easy solution to the global problem of human sex trafficking, and the United States certainly does not have a positive record on the prevention of female sexual slavery and trafficking. The US' first antisex trafficking act was the White-Slave Traffic Act of 1910, commonly known as the Mann Act, which was aimed more at restricting the interstate travel of African American men than protecting female sex slaves. While the American culture of sexual voyeurism has brought to life a massive number of television exposés on the subject and realities of women trafficked throughout our own country, our solution has been to enact harsher and evermore intrusive laws, which add to the prison-industrial complex's solvency, and gloss over the multiple causes of female sexual slavery which include gender power inequality, limited economic choices for the poorest of women, and the eroticization of sexual violence through media.

To be clear, the US invasion of Iraq contributed definitively to the displacement, vulnerability, and subsequent sexual enslavement of thousands of Iraqi women and children. Yet, to scapegoat Arab cultures as patriarchal, sexually oppressive, and violent to women without examining the pervasiveness of these characteristics in American culture only furthers the rhetoric of American exceptionalism and the excuse for more extensive military imperialism.

One of the major reasons that corporate media do not cover the news stories reported above is because they are characterized as "women's issues." Though the term may be useful in some cases to acknowledge a common theme that runs through a series of stories, "women's issues" is often a recognition of social injustice within the structures of power. We have reported stories that showcase the global UN initiatives, US military policies, state laws, transnational gender ideologies, and domestic gendered power dynamics that have been denigrated as "women's issues." The subsumption or mischaracterization of these stories by the corporate media structure is purposeful and aimed at silencing the majority of the population that would otherwise be outraged at the global and domestic treatment of others at our hands.

Notes

1. *Global Report on the Status of Women in the News Media*, International Women's Media Foundation, March 24, 2011, http://www.iwmf.org/pdfs/IWMF-Global-Report.pdf.
2. Ibid.
3. Michael Martinez and Moni Basu, "Abortion Battle Rages in State Legislatures," CNN, April 14, 2011, http://articles.cnn.com/2011-04-14/us/abortion.state.laws_1_abortion-providers-abortion-battle-law-that-bans-abortions.
4. Monica Davey, "Nebraska Law Sets Limits on Abortion," *New York Times*, April 13, 2011, http://www.nytimes.com/2010/04/14/us/14abortion.html.
5. Susan Lee, Henry Ralston, Eleanor Drey, John Partridge, and Mark Rosen, "Fetal Pain: A Systematic Multidisciplinary Review of the Evidence," *Journal of the American Medical Association* 294 (2005): 947–54, doi:10.1001/jama.294.8.947.
6. Chet Brokaw, "South Dakota Abortion Bill Signed Into Law by Governor Dennis Daugaard," *Huffington Post*, March 22, 2011, http://www.huffingtonpost.com/2011/03/22/south-dakota-abortion-bil_n_839063.html.
7. Lynda Waddington, "Iowa Bills Open Door for Use of Deadly Force to Protect the Unborn," *Iowa Independent*, February 24, 2011, http://iowaindependent.com/52869/iowa-bills-open-door-for-use-of-deadly-force-to-protect-the-unborn.
8. John Hanna, "Kansas Backs Bill Restricting Abortion Coverage," Associated Press, *Joplin Globe*, May 13, 2011, http://www.joplinglobe.com/local/x1227546545/Kansas-backs-bill-restricting-abortion-coverage.
9. Mary Plummer, "Pregnant Woman Kicked Out of Bar," ABC News, January 12, 2011, http://abcnews.go.com/US/pregnant-lady-turned-illinois-bar/story?id=12600511.
10. Megan O'Rourke, "Breastfeeding Mom Mad at Mall," WDTN, February 14, 2011, http://www.wdtn.com/dpp/news/local/greene_county/wdtn-Breastfeeding-mom-mad-at-mall-mo.
11. Elisabeth Bumiller, "Sexual Assault Reports Rise in Military," *New York Times*, March 16, 2010, http://www.nytimes.com/2010/03/17/us/17assault.html.
12. Anna Mulrine, "Exclusive: 1 in 5 Air Force Women Victim of Sexual Assault, Survey Finds," *Christian Science Monitor*, March 17, 2011, http://www.csmonitor.com/USA/Military/2011/0317/Exclusive-1-in-5-Air-Force-women-victim-of-sexual-assault-survey-finds.
13. Bumiller, "Sexual Assault Reports."
14. David Fahrenthold, "Statistics Show Drop in US Rape Cases," *Washington Post*, June 19, 2006, http://www.washingtonpost.com/wp-dyn/content/article/2006/06/18/AR2006061800610.html.
15. Ibid.
16. "American Women Must Not be Fooled: Smeal Calls for National Reform in Rape Reporting and Investigating," *Ms. Magazine*, September 14, 2010, http://www.msmagazine.com/news/uswirestory.asp?id=12626.
17. Joey L. Mogul, Andrea J. Ritchie, and Kay Whitlock, "Queer Injustice: The Widespread Sexual Abuse LGBT People Face in Prison," AlterNet, March 11, 2011,

http://www.alternet.org/story/149873/queer_injustice%3A_the_widespread_sexual_
abuse_lgbt_people_face_in_prison/.

18. Paul Breer, "With Support From Anti-Gay Foundation, West Virginians Can Sexually Discriminate For Another Year," ThinkProgress, March 14, 2011,
http://wonkroom.thinkprogress.org/2011/03/14/wv-discrimination/.

19. Ibid.

20. "Facts About Discrimination Based on Sexual Orientation," US Equal Opportunity
Employment Commission, modified June 27, 2001, http://www.eeoc.gov/facts/fs-
orientation_parent_marital_political.html.

21. Wendy McElroy, "UN Complicit in Forced Sterilizations," Independent Institute,
December 23, 2002, http://www.independent.org/newsroom/article.asp?id=1417.

22. Ángel Páez, "Women Sterilised Against Their Will Seek Justice, Again," Inter Press
Service, October 15, 2010, http://ipsnews.net/news.asp?idnews=53177.

23. Ibid.

24. Nicholas Kristof, "A Rite of Torture for Girls," New York Times, May 11, 2011,
http://www.nytimes.com/2011/05/12/opinion/12kristof.html.

25. Erick Ngobilo, "Parents Disown Girls for Evading 'the Cut,'" Daily Nation, February
6, 2011, http://www.nation.co.ke/News/Parents%20disown%20girls%20for%20
evading%20the%20cut/-/1056/1102708/-/kdcr7jz/-/index.html.

26. "Women, Children and Youth in the Iraq Crisis: A Fact Sheet," Women's Commission for Refugee Women and Children, January 2008, http://www.rhrc.org/
resources/Iraqi_women_girls_factsheet%20FINAL%20JAn08.pdf.

27. Sebastion Swett and Cameron Webster, "Trafficking of Iraqi Women Rampant
Despite US Commitment To End It," AlterNet, August 25, 2010,
www.alternet.org/news/147962/trafficking_of_iraqi_women_rampant_despite_u.s.
_commitment_to_end_it.

28. Ibid.

Collaboration and Common Good

by Kenn Burrows and Tom Atlee

Censored #22

Participatory Budgeting: A Method to Empower Local Citizens and Communities

Sources:

Daniel Altschuler and Josh Lerner, "Government Can't Solve Budget Battles? Let Citizens Do It," *Christian Science Monitor*, April 5, 2011, http://www.csmonitor.com/Commentary/Opinion/2011/0405/Government-can-t-solve-budget-battles-Let-citizens-do-it.

Nicole Summers, "Chicago's Participatory Budgeting Experiment," *Shareable*, April 6, 2011, http://www.shareable.net/blog/chicagos-participatory-budgeting-experiment.

Student Researcher: Allison Holt (San Francisco State University)

Faculty Evaluator: Kenn Burrows (San Francisco State University)

Censored #23

Worldwide Movement to Ban or Charge Fees for Plastic Bags

Sources:
"Bay vs. The Bag," Save the Bay, March 2011, http://www.savesfbay.org/bay-vs-bag, and http://www.savesfbay.org/about-campaign.
Jim Ries, "Got Plastic?," One More Generation, November 29, 2010, http://onemore-generation.org/2010/11/29/got-plastic.
"L.A. County Approves Plastic Bag Ban," Environment California, Winter 2010–2011, http://www.environmentcalifornia.org/newsletters/winter11/l.a.-county-approves-plastic-bag-ban.
Lisa Davis, "Plastic Rap: Here Are 10 Ways to Reduce Plastics in Your Home," *McClatchy-Tribune News*, January 31, 2010, http://thesouthern.com/lifestyles/leisure/article_2e25cb1c-0e21-11df-8b25-001cc4c002e0.html.
"The Retail Bags Report Maps and Related Detailed Lists," Division of Waste Management, Florida Department of Environmental Protection, January 28, 2011, http://www.dep.state.fl.us/waste/retailbags/pages/mapsandlists.ht.

Student Researcher: Robert Usher (San Francisco State University)

Faculty Evaluator: Kenn Burrows (San Francisco State University)

Related Validated News Stories

Ellen Brown, "A Choice for States: Banks, Not Budget Crises," *Yes! Magazine*, March 25, 2011, http://www.yesmagazine.org/new-economy/a-choice-for-states-banks-not-budget-crises.
"How to Ease the State's Budget Crises: Own a Bank," Public Banking Institute, April 2011, http://publicbankinginstitute.org/advantages.htm.
"Public Banking and Wall Street Bank Analysis," Public Banking Institute, March 2011, http://publicbankinginstitute.org.
Saman Mohammadi, "The Public Banking Movement Comes of Age," OpEdNews, June 3, 2011, http://www.opednews.com/Diary/The-Public-Banking-Movemen-by-Saman-Mohammadi-110603-529.html.
Ellen Brown, "What a Public Bank Could Mean for California," *Yes! Magazine*, May 16, 2011, http://www.yesmagazine.org/new-economy/what-a-public-bank-could-mean-for-california.
Mike Krauss, "It's All About Banking," Philly Blurbs, May 17, 2011, http://www.philly-burbs.com/news/local/courier_times_news/news_columnists/it-s-all-about-banking/article_cf9d9ae4-94b7-51c8-b064-232d02205ad4.html.
Dahr Jamail, "Putting People Over Money," Al Jazeera English, February 15, 2011, english.aljazeera.net/indepth/features/2011/02/2011213174138761638.html.
Marcela Valente, "Thai, Argentine Textile Workers Unite Against Slave Labour," Inter Press Service, May 24, 2010, http://ipsnews.net/news.asp?idnews=51547.
Drake Bennett, "Thorkil Sonne: Recruit Autistics," *Wired*, March 22, 2011, http://www.mediafreedominternational.org/2011/04/17/the-employability-of-autistics/.
Zenifer Khaleel, "Sonne Shines with Company for People with ASD," *Gulf News*, February 13, 2011, http://m.gulfnews.com/life-style/general/sonne-shines-with-company-for-people-with-asd-1.718520.

Student Researchers: Allison Gill (San Francisco State University); Cynthia Solano and Camille Avis (Sonoma State University); Rachel Lounsbury (Indian River State College)

Faculty and Professional Evaluators: Kenn Burrows (San Francisco State University); Lourdes Alvarez (WIC Dietician); Jeffery Baldwin (Sonoma State University); Elliot D. Cohen (Indian River State College); Mickey Huff (Diablo Valley College)

To address human "collaboration and the common good" is to discuss the power of cooperation and community—the social synergy that shows up as people's movements when citizens come together to resolve collective issues. This stands in contrast to the dominant commercial culture that markets fear and worships self-interest. In the market-based culture, the economy is the center story, and problems, obligations, law, and individual achievement are key values. Compare this to a community-based culture, where generosity, empathy, trust, safety, fairness, and the experience of belonging are valued.[1] With community, there is always enough, because sharing is primary. With community, the core question is, "What shall we create together?"[2] This is a different model than the commercial marketplace where competition for scarce resources is primary and the question is, "How will I (we) get what I need?" Both cultures have value and purpose, and they do not have to be separate, as you will see from some of the stories in this cluster.

The bottom line in community and social networking circles is relationship; business is second in priority and is there to serve the common needs of those in the relationship. The essential work is to build a social fabric, both for its own sake, and to gather social power to face common dangers and reach shared goals. The vitality and connectedness of our communities also determines the strength of our democracy. When we as citizens find our capacity to come together, we share in creating a safer, saner world. Building a genuine common life and valuing what we share in common is essential to a healthy future.

Yet, it is clear from looking at the world and our own lives that collaboration is very challenging. Conflict and relational struggle are commonplace. Ways of relating to each other and our world have often been more exploitive and punitive than collaborative.

For centuries, modern industrial societies have been living off the capital of the abundant and underpriced resources of nature and culture. Even with declining resources, increasing populations, and multiple global crises, businesses and nation-states still resist collaborating with each other effectively, to resolve many critical problems that transcend national borders. Our global economic system is now in grave crisis, threatening the entire planet, and most leaders continue to believe that only central governments and markets are capable of meeting global needs. The great folly of the market-state complex is that it leaves nature and society out of the equation. Such an equation is unsustainable and doomed to fail.

We clearly have a lot to learn about the collective dimensions of our lives. It seems we need new forms of social interaction and institutions that can help us, in this stage of human development, to become more socially and ecologically intelligent with each other and able to integrate individual and collective realities. This cluster explores recent news about the power of people's movements and cooperation, and why we find in corporate media relatively little recognition of and support for grassroots democracy building. Chapter 4, Signs of Health & Emerging Culture, also offers a variety of additional news stories and commentary about the emerging collaborative culture.

We face three main challenges to gaining media coverage of common needs and media support for collaborative actions on behalf of the common good:

► Centralized Power and Media

► Escalating Complexity of Interacting Systems: Nature, Culture, and Technology

► Competing Worldviews & Public Engagement

CHALLENGE I: CENTRALIZED POWER AND MEDIA

Concentrated social power can easily be abused and only tends to be benign when it is transparent and balanced by other forms of social power (such as unions balancing management, or the three branches of government balancing each other).[3]

Unless held in check and balanced, power tends to corrupt—concentrating and seeking secrecy and freedom from oversight to maintain and expand itself. Today we can see fear of terrorism, anti-government "freedom" narratives (including "free market" ideology), the equation of profits with jobs, and the fiction of "corporate person-hood" being promoted as primary PR memes to garner public support for the concentration of corporate and elite power which can then be held free of public supervision and accountability. Media ownership, the dynamics of advertising, and the coevolution of corporate and jour-nalistic cultures into closely woven elite mindsets and networks make it increasingly unlikely that elite-supported "mainstream" media will adequately cover any public challenges to elite power or emerging alternatives to the status quo.[4]

Ways that collaborative culture can work to balance concentrated power include 1) funding public, community, and crowd-sourced media; 2) supporting journalistic efforts to report about the positive work of NGOs and grassroots activities; 3) supporting public conver-sations about issues that matter; 4) funding websites that enable people to think and work together to realize shared visions and pre-ferred public policies; and 5) supporting strategic actions and public attention to counter efforts by elite interests to undermine or suppress collaborative actions. Note the following example.

Censored Story: Create a State Bank: Novel Solution to the Budget Crisis

Fourteen states have now introduced bills to form state-owned banks or to study their feasibility. All of these bills were inspired by the Bank of North Dakota (BND), currently the nation's only state-owned bank. While other states are teetering on the edge of bankruptcy, the state of North Dakota continues to report surpluses. On April 20, the BND reported profits for 2010 of $62 million, setting a record for the sev-enth straight year. The BND's profits belong to the citizens and are produced without taxation. The BND partners with local banks in pro-viding much-needed credit for local businesses and homeowners. It also helps with state and local government funding. Now, other states are on track to follow North Dakota's example, moving their state reserves from Wall Street banks to banks owned by their own residents.

Readily available credit made America "the land of opportunity" ever since the days of the American colonists. What transformed this credit system into a Ponzi scheme that must be propped up with bailout money was a shift to private, conglomerate bankers who always require more money back than they create because they charge high interest rates for maximum profits.

Policymakers in Washington have fundamentally altered the landscape of banking and the new landscape is clearly designed for the multinational Wall Street bank. Yet even after the excesses of our biggest banks produced the near collapse of our financial system, federal officials doubled down on the "bigger, riskier" strategy. They guided the largest banks through mega-mergers—Wells Fargo's absorption of Wachovia, JPMorgan Chase's purchase of Bear Stearns and Washington Mutual, Bank of America's deals for Merrill Lynch and Countrywide—then nurtured these fragile conglomerates with billions in taxpayer dollars. The result? The top five banks in the United States in 2010—Bank of America, Wells Fargo, JPMorgan Chase, Citigroup, and PNC—now control more deposits than the next largest forty-five banks combined. Their share of total deposits in the US has more than doubled since 2000, to 40 percent. Their share of assets is even greater—48 percent—up from 26 percent. Today, just one percent of the country's banks have more branches than all of the rest combined. For every big bank executive who has gained from this policy, hundreds of local banks—and the communities that depend on them—have lost out.

Overall, state banks differ from private banks by being mandated to serve the public interest, not shareholders or bank executives seeking personal gain. Both state and private banks receive money from the Federal Reserve Bank at low interest and loan this money plus interest. However, interest rates are typically lower from public banks, saving borrowers and making local investments more likely and more profitable. State banks partner with community banks and credit unions giving them greater liquidity, thus supporting them to make loans to small businesses (vs. the current tightening of credit by most banks).

When the state borrows money from the state bank for public projects, it does not have to pay the higher commercial interest rate charged by private banks—saving on state project costs an average of 30 to 50 percent. These savings are returned to the state, and eventually to the public at large, in terms of lower taxes, more services, etc. State banks are a win-win for virtually everyone—the whole community benefits. Objections are usually based on misconceptions or a lack of information. Get involved and help this "game changer" happen in your state and community.

CHALLENGE II: ESCALATING COMPLEXITY OF INTERACTING SYSTEMS: NATURE, CULTURE, AND TECHNOLOGY

In our current century, technology and global economics are weaving us increasingly into each other's lives, connecting each one of us to more people (most of whom we won't ever know), drawing us into new and expanding streams of information, and rapidly increasing complexity. We find ourselves wrestling with a surreal sense of expanding personal choices combined with collective powerlessness, and all within a context of life being too much, too fast, too confusing.[5]

Our reactions to this are quite understandable; we look for simple things to hold onto and simple things we can deal with, turning away from complexity into at least an illusion of clarity and control.[6] We tune out, let go into distractions, and require entertainment in order to pay attention to anything for very long. So we find a large percentage of the vastly expanding field of human creativity being channeled not into addressing the complex realities that are actually shaping our lives and our future, but into producing oversimplifications, entertainment, and evermore innovative ways to manipulate—rather than inform—the population.

Our world has become so complex and the time allowed for reporting so limited, that there is little room for stories about the interactive, systemic nature of problems, only news about the many discrete symptoms. The public becomes numbed and bewildered by the problems in the news, and increasingly disenchanted with public life.

In such an environment, individuals and families often seek out private solutions, or they narrow their associations to a particular subculture. Meanwhile, the neglected commons become even riper for manipulation by special interests.

When journalism is employed primarily to attract us to advertisements or, worse, to channel our baser desires for enemies and well-targeted certainties, it undermines our ability to muster sufficient collective intelligence to serve our individual and communal benefit.

In fact, journalism becomes part of the system through which we are destroying ourselves and our world.

To serve our ability to function as a democracy by delivering some modicum of wisdom on behalf of a good society, journalism needs to give us insight into the dynamics of the systems that generate the conditions we live in. It needs to help us shift our attention from the presenting problems to their systemic causes, and give us the knowledge to take action where it really makes a difference, rather than flailing at symptoms that return to haunt us over and over.[7]

The rising demand to address these issues is part of the evolution of societies and systems into a global civilization that can survive and thrive at more sophisticated levels of complexity and create a healthier "fit" between humanity, technology, and nature.[8]

Censored Story: Worldwide Movement to Ban or Charge Fees for Plastic Bags

Shoppers worldwide are using five hundred billion to one trillion single-use plastic bags per year and the average use time of these bags is twelve minutes. Plastic bags pollute our waters, smother wetlands, and entangle and kill animals. Plastic is nonbiodegradable and is made from a nonrenewable resource: oil. An estimated three million barrels of oil are required to produce the nineteen billion plastic bags used annually in California. Californians also use 165,000 tons of Styrofoam for take-out food containers. Plastic and Styrofoam pollution not only litters our coast and harms marine life, it also costs California $25 million to cleanup each year.

Most plastic also contains harmful chemicals like Bisphenol A (BPA) and phthalates, which can be unsafe for human consumption or use. These can be avoided by using alternative materials like reusable cloth bags, stainless steel water bottles, and other paper, wooden, glass, and metal substitutes.

In California, people have responded to this problem: thirty-five counties have recently banned the use of plastic bags, nine counties have passed levies and fees on use, twelve counties are considering bans or fees, and twenty-six states in the US have introduced forms of legislation curtailing or banning plastic bag use. Californians are increasingly aware of the dangers associated with plastic. The Environmental Protection Agency (EPA) estimates that plastic bag use in the state has dropped by as much as 33 percent in the last three years.

In response to this public concern and efforts by local governments, the multibillion dollar plastic bag industry has tried consistently to block public proposals that reduce plastic bag use. Now they are suing cities that have voted to ban single-use plastic bags. It's time to support local activists and politicians that stand up to such power tactics and add your efforts to help preserve our environment and reduce plastic use.

CHALLENGE III: COMPETING WORLDVIEWS AND PUBLIC ENGAGEMENT

A startling realization: Our "democratic" society is not institutionalized in ways to get people together who represent different sides of an issue and put them to work collaboratively toward a win-win solution. The only institutionalized procedure that encourages full collaboration or consensus is the jury system. But juries are asked to reach unanimous agreement on yes/no decisions—guilty or not guilty. Juries do not develop win-win solutions; they only pass judgment on prestructured, win-lose outcomes.

We need social processes and methodologies to involve people in effective, collaborative information gathering, problem solving, and decision-making. In all collaborative efforts, community members can also realize the gifts of diversity by reaching beyond traditional left/right factions to include more citizens, bringing new people and cultures together for connection and mutual benefit.

One of the most crippling aspects of our current version of democracy is its intrinsic adversarial nature. Serious dysfunctions arise from the oppositional politics of parties, and the polarization of potentially synergistic views and values into two "sides" that view each other as monolithic enemies, who are blind to nuances, and who cannot imagine alliances with "them" or engaging in cocreative policy development. These dynamics waste immense resources in electoral and lobbying battles, create governmental deadlock when different partisans control different branches of government, feed corruption that arises in such environments, and produce compromises and "deals" that satisfy neither the legitimate interests of the partisans involved nor the real needs of the community being "served."9

In short, we are divided and conquered. A cross-party pioneer, Joseph McCormick remarked: "Those in power are keeping us marching to their drummer—left, right, left, right, left, right—right off a cliff."10 The word "collaborator" takes on a dark meaning in the wartime atmosphere of polarized politics.

Alternative maps and models of the political landscape have been developed to show more complex political realities than left and right, since those polarized formulations simply do not adequately describe the nuanced values and preferences of the population. One simple model divides voters into Republicans, Democrats, and Independents—the latter category rapidly becoming larger than either of the major parties. One simple quadrant model from the transpartisan movement suggests a left-right axis as well as a vertical order-freedom axis, with traditional Democrats in the upper left, traditional Republicans in the upper right, Greens in the lower left and Libertarians in the lower right.11 Twenty years ago, *Utne Reader* issued a map that had two more axes: centralized-decentralized and liberty-equality. More recently, *Utne* described the existence of a massive "radical middle."12

Journalism and activism could both productively step out of the oversimplified and mythic left-right framework, and start enabling and reporting on more efforts by citizens to collaboratively work out the best approaches to our collective challenges among their fully diverse selves.

In chapter 4, Signs of Health & Emerging Culture, we will discuss recent news stories about collaborative success and about emerging social inventions that empower people to get involved and make a real difference in their communities. Here is an example from one of this year's censored stories, about opening up municipal budgets to community stakeholders—getting resources to communities that are often significantly underserved and whose voices often go unheard.

Censored Story: Participatory Budgeting—A Method to Empower Local Citizens and Communities

"Participatory Budgeting" (PB) is a process that allows citizens to decide directly how to allocate all or part of a public budget, typically through a series of meetings, work by community "delegates" or representatives, and ultimately a final vote. It was first implemented in 1990 in the city of Porto Alegre, Brazil, and has since spread. PB has recently taken root in Canadian and US soils. Chicago's 49th Ward, for example, uses this process to distribute $1.3 million of annual discretionary funds. The ward's residents have praised the opportunity to make meaningful decisions, take ownership over the budget process, and win concrete improvements for their neighborhood—from community gardens and sidewalk repairs to street lights and public murals. The initiative proved so popular that the ward's alderman, Joe Moore, credits PB with helping to reverse his political fortunes.

The wave is not stopping in Chicago, either. Elected officials and community leaders elsewhere—from New York City to San Francisco, and from Greensboro, North Carolina, to Springfield, Massachusetts—are considering launching similar initiatives.

Notes

1. Peter Block, *Community: The Structure of Belonging* (San Francisco: Berrett-Kohler, 2008), 29–31.
2. James B. Quilligan, "The Commons and Global Commons Trust," *Kosmos Journal*, Spring 2011, http://www.kosmosjournal.org/_webapp_3957294/The_Commons_and_Global_Commons_Trust.
3. John S. Atlee and Tom Atlee, "Democracy: A Social Power Analysis," Co-Intelligence Institute, http://co-intelligence.org/CIPol_democSocPwrAnal.html.
4. Robert Jensen, "Journalism and Democracy in a Dead Culture: An Interview with Robert Jensen," *Counter Currents*, March 15, 2011, http://www.countercurrents.org/jensen150311.htm. Also see Mark Deuze, "Liquid Journalism," *Political Communication Report* 16, no. 1 (2006): http://frank.mtsu.edu/~pcr/1601_2005_winter/roundtable_Deuze.htm.
5. Tom Atlee, "Learning to BE Evolution," Co-Intelligence Institute, 2003, http://www.co-intelligence.org/Evolution-Learning2BEvol.html.
6. Robert Ornstein and Paul Ehrlich, *New World, New Mind: Changing the Way We Think to Save our Future* (London: Methuen, 1989).
7. Johanna Vehkoo, "What is Quality Journalism and How It Can Be Saved," Reuters Institute for the Study of Journalism, University of Oxford, http://www.scribd.com/doc/44957170/What-is-Quality-Journalism-and-How-Can-It-Be-Saved.
8. Joel De Rosnay, *The Symbiotic Man: A New Understanding of the Organization of Life and a Vision of the Future* (New York: McGraw-Hill, 2000).
9. Tom Atlee, "Exploring the Dynamics of Polarization," Co-Intelligence Institute, July 2004, http://www.co-intelligence.org/polarizationDynamics.html.

10. Joseph McCormick and Tom Atlee in conversation, The Transpartisan Alliance, March 1, 2011, http://network.transpartisan.net.
11. Ibid.
12. Leif Utne, "The Radical Middle," *Utne Reader*, September/October 2004, http://www.utne.com/2004-09-01/the-radical-middle.aspx.

For more information on these and other Censored stories, as well as authors and contributors to this chapter, see http://projectcensored.org.

CHAPTER 2

Déjà Vu
What Happened to Last Year's Top Censored Stories

by Mickey Huff with Project Censored Interns

> We are a democracy, and there is only one way to get a
> democracy on its feet in the matter of its individual, its
> social, its municipal, its state, its national conduct,
> and that is by keeping the public informed about what
> is going on.
> —JOSEPH PULITZER

> 'Tis a lesson you should heed, try, try again. If at first
> you don't succeed, try, try again.
> —Thomas H. Palmer's "Teacher's Manual" from 1840s America

Dr. Carl Jensen, the founder of Project Censored, once wrote, "Weapons may have won the Revolutionary War but it was words that have created the longest lasting democracy in history." The founding fathers recognized the necessity and importance of honest and accurate communication in a democratic society and subsequently sought to protect the institution of the free press with the First Amendment of the United States Constitution. Carefully crafted words underlie the importance of communication—the spreading of ideas in order to educate the public—which greatly influenced the trajectory of America and continues to into the future.

For thirty-five years, Project Censored has contended that if journalism—the protected trade of the free press—is the rough draft of history, then it is crucial that those tasked with recording it get their stories straight the first time. It follows that only an accountable, vibrant, and unfettered free press is capable of supporting a true democracy—one that is functional and can stand the test of time. When the corporate media does not, or will not, cover important stories that matter to the public, then Project Censored will highlight such disparities. In doing so, we beseech the mass media outlets to "try, try again" to keep the public informed. Of course, even if the corporate media outlets do not reform their coverage, we at Project Censored will try and try again, in more ways than ever before, to exemplify free press principles and work to replace a dying system of private and for-profit journalism with one that operates in the public interest.

Each year, Project Censored uses the same criteria to choose our top twenty-five stories for the year, to consider whether the corporate media has reported on, or explored in detail, any of the stories previously mentioned within our yearly sourcebook. We consider if any of these previously underreported stories have become part of the larger public record and, if they have, to what degree and with what biases. Let's take a look at last year's top stories, as well as a few significant stories from years prior, to see if these significant yet underreported stories have gained any ground in mass media coverage—or, to see if Yogi Berra's classic sentiment still holds true: "It's like déjà vu all over again."

Censored 2011 #1

Global Plans to Replace the Dollar

Update by Sy Cowie

Story #1 in *Censored 2011* covered the growing movement to replace the US dollar as the standard international reserve currency. The desire and will of the United States to use its military unilaterally and without the constraint of international law and institutions has created a backlash among nations whose aims are at odds with those of the US. The dominance of the US dollar in the international monetary system allows the US to borrow money on highly advantageous terms. This ability to borrow is an essential part of the economic structure which allows the US to spend more on its military than the rest of the world combined. This massive military machine allows the US to intervene virtually anywhere in the world and for any reason it sees fit. Nations such as Russia, China, Bolivia, Ecuador, and Venezuela, to name a few, are increasingly seeing the dominance of the dollar in international trade as simply a mechanism that gives the US disproportionate economic power. This economic advantage is used by the US to bankroll a militarily aggressive foreign policy which is often not to the benefit of nation-states who do not share US foreign policy goals.

Original Sources: Chris Hedges, "The American Empire Is Bankrupt," *Truthdig*, June 15, 2009, http://www.truthdig.com/report/item/20090614_the_american_empire_is_bankrupt/; Michael Hudson, "De-Dollarization: Dismantling America's Financial-Military Empire: The Yekaterinburg Turning Point," Global Research, June 13, 2009, http://www.globalresearch.ca/PrintArticle.php?articleId=13969; Fred Weir, "Iran and Russia Nip at US Global Dominance" *Christian Science Monitor*, June 16, 2009, http://www.csmonitor.com/2009/0616/p06s12-woeu.html; Lyubov Pronina, "Medvedev Shows Off Sample Coin of New 'World Currency' at G-8," Bloomberg, July 10, 2009, http://www.bloomberg.com/apps/news?pid=20601087 &sid=aeFVNYQpByU4; Edmund Conway, "UN Wants New Global Currency to Replace Dollar," *Telegraph* (UK), September 7, 2009, http://www.telegraph.co.uk/finance/currency/6152204/UN-wants-new-global-currency-to-replace-dollar.html; Jose Arturo Cardenas, "Latin American Leftists Tackle Dollar with New Currency," Agence France-Presse, October 16, 2009, http://www.google.com/hostednews/afp/article/ALeqM5jisHEg79Cz8uRtYfZR6WK4JmWsIg.

Update: The gradual decline of the preeminence of the dollar in the global economic system is widely covered in the global business press, but is rarely discussed in the US corporate media. The US corporate media only reports on the reasons why the dollar cannot be replaced while rarely mentioning movements for its replacement. The concept

that other nations might be reluctant to finance US military adventures by holding US debt and supporting the dollar remains under covered.

The one aspect of this story that has been covered in the US corporate media is the desire of the Russian Federation and China to weaken US global hegemony by undermining the dominance of the dollar. In his Sunday talk show on CNN, Fareed Zakaria claimed Russia and China had "declared war" on the dollar by trading between themselves in their own currencies. Zakaria went on to mention the UN report, calling for the replacement of the dollar as the reserve currency with something "more stable." He noted that if the US dollar was not the reserve currency, US debt "could become much, much worse." This segment of Zakaria's show was titled "What in the World?" It ignored the more complex and controversial issues of US military spending as a major cause of the debt, and its effects on nations like China and Russia. The reporting has silenced the voices of nations who want power to be balanced. Instead, the reporting focuses on what is best to keep the US in control despite the effects this has on other powers.

Sources: Fareed Zakaria, *Fareed Zakaria GPS*, CNN, December 19, 2010, http://archives.cnn.com/TRANSCRIPTS/1012/19/fzgps.01.html; Manmohan Singh, interview by Fareed Zakaria, *Fareed Zakaria GPS*, November 22, 2009, http://archives.cnn.com/TRANSCRIPTS/0911/22/fzgps.01.html.

Censored 2011 #2

US Department of Defense is the Worst Polluter on the Planet

Update by Kira McDonough

The US military is responsible for the most egregious and widespread pollution of the planet, yet this information and accompanying documentation goes almost entirely unreported. In spite of the evidence, the environmental impact of the US military goes largely unaddressed by environmental organizations and was not the focus of any discussions or proposed restrictions at the recent UN Climate Change Conference in Copenhagen. This impact includes uninhibited use of fossil fuels, massive creation of greenhouse gases, and extensive release of radioactive and chemical contaminants into the air, water, and soil.

Original Sources: Sara Flounders, "Add Climate Havoc to War Crimes: Pentagon's Role in Global Catastrophe," International Action Center, December 18, 2009, http://www.iacenter.org/o/world/climatesummit_pentagon121809; Mickey Z., "Can You Identify the Worst Polluter on the Planet? Here's a Hint: Shock and Awe," *Planet Green*, August 10, 2009, http://planetgreen.discovery.com/tech-transport/identify-worst-polluter-planet.html; Julian Aguon, "Guam Residents Organize Against US Plans for $15B Military Buildup on Pacific Island," *Democracy Now!*, October 9, 2009, http://www.democracynow.org/2009/10/9/guam_residents_organize_against_us_plans; Ian Macleod, "US Plots Arctic Push," *Ottawa Citizen*, November 28, 2009, http://www.ottawacitizen.com/technology/navy+plots+Arctic+push/2278324/story.html; Nick Turse, "Vietnam Still in Shambles after American War," *In These Times*, May 2009, http://www.inthesetimes.com/article/4363/casualties_continue_in_vietnam; Jalal Ghazi, "Cancer—The Deadly Legacy of the Invasion of Iraq," *New America Media*, January 6, 2010, http://news.newamericamedia.org/news/view_article.html?article _id=80e260b3839daf2084fdeb0965ad31ab.

Update: Corporate media in the US have not picked up this story, but alternative media continue to report on the widespread and overwhelming pollution created by the US Department of Defense, including oil spills, pesticide contamination, and leftover waste and

ammunition, causing illnesses such as leukemia, cancer, respiratory problems, and skin diseases which have affected the victims exposed—many of whom have died without redress or compensation.

The Department of Defense (DoD), the largest oil consumer in the world, uses 360,000 barrels of oil each day. Twenty-nine million Americans—that's about one in every ten—live within ten miles of a toxic military site, that is, a site that has already been labeled under the Superfund Program as being a top priority for toxic-waste cleanup. There are many, many, more sites that haven't yet been certified. In San Diego alone, the Navy is responsible for creating a hundred toxic sites, and jet fuel has been dumped around the Naval Air Station in Fallon, Nevada, leading to cancer cases as the toxic materials seeped into the ground water. In Denver, tons of asbestos-laced soil left over from the Lowry Air Force Base had to be dug out of the ground before a new housing development could be built. The Air Force refused to pay the $15 million bill for the removal, claiming the risks from asbestos weren't high enough to warrant cleanup.

Agent Orange, rocket fuel, lead, mercury, petroleum, asbestos, and countless other carcinogenic solvents settle into the soil which is used for farming, seep down into the drinking water, and float unseen in the air causing illnesses such as birth defects, cancer, miscarriages, and kidney and thyroid diseases, in many cases, leading to death.

Depleted uranium is only one of a number of aggressive chemicals which may be a cause of "Gulf War Syndrome." About 20 percent of military personnel were affected by chronic tissue damage and a whole array of problems including muscle pains, respiratory problems, memory loss, impaired vision, and motor problems, just to name a few. Likely causes include solvents, insecticides, smoke and other combustion products as well as large doses of immunizations given all at the same time. There is also a suspicion that they may have been exposed to chemical warfare products such as sarin.

Sources: "War Pollution Can Last for Generations," Green Footsteps, http://www.greenfootsteps.com/war-pollution.html; Elizabeth Fiend, "Battlefield Earth, The War on Pollution or Pollution from War" Big Tea Party, http://bigteaparty.com/battlefield-earth-pollution-from-war-by-elizabeth-fiend/; "Military Pollution," Clearwater Revival Company, http://www.toxicspot.com/military/.

Censored 2011 #3

Internet Privacy and Personal Access at Risk

Update by Ryan Shehee

Following in the steps of its predecessor, the Obama administration is expanding mass government surveillance of personal electronic communications. This surveillance, which includes the monitoring of the internet as well as private (nongovernmental) computers, is proceeding with the proposal or passage of new laws granting government agencies increasingly wider latitude in their monitoring activities. At the same time, private companies and even some schools are engaging in surveillance activities that further diminish personal privacy.

Original Corporate Source: Rob Pegoraro, "Copyright Overreach Goes on World Tour," *Washington Post*, November 5, 2009, G01.

Original Sources: Josh Silver, "Deep Packet Inspection: Telecoms Aided Iran Government to Censor Internet, Technology Widely Used in US," *Democracy Now!*, June 23, 2009, http://www.democracynow.org/2009/6/23/deep_packet_inspection_telecoms_aided_iran; David Karvets, "Obama Sides With Bush in Spy Case," *Wired*, January 22, 2009, http://www.wired.com/threatlevel/2009/01/obama-sides-wit/; Kim Zetter, "Deep-Packet Inspection in U.S. Scrutinized Following Iran Surveillance," *Wired*, June 29, 2009, http://www.wired.com/threatlevel/2009/06/deep-packet-inspection; Declan McCullagh, "Bill Would Give President Emergency Control of Internet," CNET News, August 28, 2009, http://news.cnet.com/8301-13578_3-10320096-38.html?tag=mncol; Kevin Bankston, "From EFF's Secret Files: Anatomy of a Bogus Subpoena," Electronic Frontier Foundation, November 9, 2009, http://www.eff.org/wp/anatomy-bogus-subpoena-indymedia; Gwen Hinze, "Leaked ACTA Internet Provisions: Three Strikes and Global DMCA," Electronic Frontier Foundation, November 3, 2009, http://www.eff.org/deeplinks/2009/11/leaked-acta-internet-provisions-three-strikes-and-; Michael Geist, "The ACTA Internet Chapter: Putting the Pieces Together," Michael Geist Blog, November 3, 2009, http://www.michaelgeist.ca/content/view/4510/125; Tim Jones, "In Warrantless Wiretapping Case, Obama DOJ's New Arguments Are Worse Than Bush's," Electronic Frontier Foundation, April 7, 2009, http://www.eff.org/deeplinks/2009/04/obama-worse-than-bush; Steve Aquino, "Should Obama Control the Internet," *Mother Jones*, April 2, 2009, http://motherjones.com/politics/2009/04/should_obama_control_internet; Noah Shachtman, "U.S. Spies Buy Stake in Firm that Monitors Blogs, Twitter," *Wired*, October 19, 2009, http://www.wired.com/dangerroom/2009/10/exclusive-us-spies-buy-stake-in-twitter-blog-monitoring-firm; Noah Shachtman, "CIA Invests in Software Firm Monitoring Blogs, Twitter," *Democracy Now!*, October 22, 2009, http://www.democracynow.org/2009/10/22/cia_invests_in_software_firm_monitoring; Lewis Maltby, "Your Boss Can Secretly Film You in the Bathroom—The Countless Ways You Are Losing Privacy at Work," AlterNet, March 17, 2010, http://www.alternet.org/rights/146047/your_boss_can_secretly_film_you

_in_the_bathroom_—_the_countless_ways_you _are_losing_privacy_at_work; Elliot D. Cohen, *Mass Surveillance and State Control: The Total Information Awareness Project* (New York: Palgrave Macmillan, 2010).

Update: Despite significant, newsworthy events regarding internet privacy, especially Deep Packet Inspection (DPI) and its consequences, the corporate media has failed to recognize the impact of this story. They are not alone; even independent media ignores the extent in which this topic should be covered.

How dire is this situation? In April 2011, the *Journal of Democracy* published a paper by Evgeny Morozov which examines the implication of controlling the internet. Morozov, a Bernard L. Schwartz Senior Fellow at the New America Foundation and a contributing editor of *Foreign Policy*, argues that if we lose our freedoms on the internet, our freedom of expression will also be forfeit, because we will have lost the technologies that enable such liberation. Furthermore, Morozov speculates, internet censorship may be the least of our worries; imprisonment for the freedom of expression afforded by the First Amendment may not be too far behind.

This issue is not something we have the luxury of reflecting on while we wait for it to manifest. The ramifications of these technologies can be seen now. In February 2011, Mediacom, a broadband provider in the United States, apparently implemented DPI technology that facilitates the interception and redirection of certain internet browser requests to its own targeted advertising. Likewise, Canada has found that nearly every one of its major ISPs has admitted to using DPI to throttle traffic, with a focus on peer-to-peer (P2P) protocols used by music and file sharing programs. Now Canada faces three new bills; one that will require customer information disclosure; another requiring mandated, real-time surveillance technologies; and a third that expands police powers grant access to any acquired data. In the past year, the Middle East and other areas of the world have seen revolutions that have been affected both positively and negatively by what Morozov calls "liberation technologies." Although proposed as a benefit for concerned parents, schools, and workplaces, technologies that filter liberation can be used by entire countries, censoring and blocking content while unrest unfolds.

Every day new patents are being secured to make DPI a commonplace reality. To frame this story as one that is interested in "net neu-trality" would be shortsighted. The understanding of DPI and the use of biased routing is a topic that should be on the forefront of everyone's minds because they have a direct influence on our lives and are becoming a significant obstruction in establishing and maintaining a true and free democracy.

Sources: Evgeny Morozov, "Whither Internet Control?" *Journal of Democracy* 22, no. 2 (2011): 62–74; Karl Bode, "Mediacom Injecting Their Ads Into Other Websites Among Other Annoying New DPI Ad Endeavors," *dslreports.com*, http://www.dslreports.com/shownews/ Mediacom-Injecting-Their-Ads-Into-Other-Websites-112918; Lanham, "How Western Companies Help Middle Eastern Governments Censor The Web," Radio Free Europe Documents and Publications, March 29, 2011; Michael Geist, "Lawful Access Bills Would Reshape Internet in Canada," Michael Geist Blog, November 3, 2009, http://www.michaelgeist .ca/content/view/5451/135/; "US Patent Issued to Wisconsin Alumni Research Foundation on June 14 for 'Extended Finite State Automata and Systems and Methods for Recognizing Patterns in a Data Stream Using Extended Finite State Automata' (Wisconsin Inventors)," US Fed News Service, Washington, DC, June 17, 2011.

Censored 2011 #5

Blackwater (Xe): The Secret US War in Pakistan

Update by Kira McDonough

While the United States is not at war in Pakistan and officially is not supposed to have any active military operations in that country, the US private contracting company Blackwater (Xe) is heavily involved in secret operations including planning targeted assassinations of suspected Taliban and al-Qaeda operatives, the gathering of intelligence, and helping to direct secret US military drone bombing campaigns. This information is backed by statements made by Blackwater's founder Erik Prince in a *Vanity Fair* interview.

Original Sources: Jeremy Scahill, "The Secret US War in Pakistan," *Nation*, November 23, 2009, http://www.thenation.com/doc/20091207/scahill; Jeremy Scahill, "Blackwater Wants to Surge Its Armed Force in Afghanistan," Antiwar, January 20, 2010, http://original.antiwar.com/scahill/2010/01/19/blackwater-wants-to-surge; David Edwards and Muriel Kane, "Ex-employees Claim Blackwater Pimped Out Young Iraqi Girls," *Raw Story*, August 7, 2009.

Update: After shooting two men at a crowded traffic stop in Pakistan, in what American officials have described as a botched robbery attempt, American contactor Raymond A. Davis, a retired Special Forces soldier carrying out scouting and other reconnaissance missions as a security officer for a Central Intelligence Agency (CIA) task force of case officers and technical surveillance experts, was arrested and detained in the eastern city of Lahore. The event and subsequent arrest exposed what had previously been a secret war in Pakistan run by the CIA and carried out by contractors of the organization Xe (formerly known as Blackwater). US Ambassador Anne Patterson insisted that "Blackwater is not operating in Pakistan" and claimed that Pakistani journalists were "wildly incorrect," blaming them for compromising the security of US personnel in Pakistan. Secretary of State Hillary Clinton has also dodged questions on the subject.

In a speech at the University of Michigan, Blackwater head Erik Prince was recorded by *The Nation*, acknowledging that his organization does work in Pakistan. In response to the debate on whether armed individuals working for Blackwater could be classified as 'unlawful combatants' ineligible for protection under the Geneva Conventions, Prince said, "You know, people ask me that all the time, 'Aren't you concerned that you folks aren't covered under the Geneva Convention in [operating] in the likes of Iraq or Afghanistan or Pakistan? And I say, 'Absolutely not,' because these people don't know where Geneva is, let alone that there was a convention there."

With the assassination of Osama Bin Laden by the US Navy SEALs, information has resurfaced as to Blackwater's (Xe) presence and role in Pakistan. According to Jeremy Scahill, the Navy SEAL's operate in Pakistan under the Joint Special Operations Command; the same killing team that Blackwater (Xe) operates under in Pakistan that is known for operating with virtually no legal oversight. This story has received quite a bit of coverage, but corporate media outlets still have yet to make it more of a headline story.

Sources: Shahid R. Siddiqi, "How Active is Blackwater in Pakistan?" *Foreign Policy Journal*, August 30, 2010, http://www.foreignpolicyjournal.com/2010/08/30/how-active-is-blackwater-in-pakistan/; Mark Mazzetti et al., "American Held in Pakistan Shootings Worked with the CIA," *Ledger*, February 21, 2011, http://www.theledger.com/article/20110221/NEWS/102215039; Jeremy Scahill, "Secret Erik Prince Tape Exposed," *Nation*, May 3, 2010, http://www.thenation.com/blog/secret-erik-prince-tape-exposed.

Censored 2011 #7

External Capitalist Forces
Wreak Havoc in Africa

Update by Casey Goonan and a special update by authors of the story
"Justice in Nigeria Now"

Since the dawn of Western dominance, Africa has been exploited on a
mass scale for its abundant resources and its primitive appearance to
the Western world. African state sovereignty has been put on the back
burner for numerous exploitations such as slave trades, arms sales,
and the stealing of natural resources—and it is only getting worse.

Recently the new trend of exploitation has been "Land Grabs,"
which are the purchase of vast tracts of land by wealthier nations and
private investors in order to produce crops for export. The recent surge
for agricultural biotechnologies and bio fuels compounded with the
world's most powerful nations' endless (and lawless) search for oil,
creates a new form of colonization which is already presenting an
enormous burden for the African people.

Original Corporate Source: Andrew Rice, "Is There Such a Thing as Agro-Imperialism?" *New York Times*, November 16, 2009, http://www.nytimes.com/2009/ 11/22/
magazine/22land-t.html.

Original Sources: John Vidal, "Food, Water Driving 21st-century African Land Grab,"
Mail & Guardian, March 7, 2010, http://www.mg.co.za/article/2010-03-07-food-water-
driving-21stcentury-african-land-grab; Paula Crossfield, "Food Security in Africa: Will
Obama Let USAID's Genetically Modified Trojan Horse Ride Again?" Civil Eats, August
6, 2009, http://civileats.com/2009/08/06/will-obama-let-the-usaid-genetically-
modified-trojan-horse-ride-again; Thalif Deen, "Land Grabs for Food Production Under
Fire," Inter Press Service, October 23, 2009, http://ipsnews.net/
news.asp?idnews=48979; Stephanie Hanes, "Africa: From Famine to the World's Next
Breadbasket?" *Christian Science Monitor*, December 17, 2009, http://www .csmon-
itor.com/World/Global-Issues/2009/1231/Africa-from-famine-to-the-world-s-next-bread
basket; Amy Goodman and Juan Gonzalez, "Massive Casualties Feared in Nigerian Military Attack on Niger Delta Villages," *Democracy Now!*, May 21, 2009, http://www
.democracynow.org/2009/5/21/nigeria; Justice in Nigeria Now, "Military Attacks Raze
Niger Delta Villages Killing Civilians; Civil Society Groups Call for Immediate Cease-
fire," May 21, 2009, http://uk.oneworld.net/ article/view/162969/1; One World,
"Nigeria Oil Violence Forces Thousands from Homes," One World, May 26, 2009,
http://us.oneworld.net/article/363376-new-outbreak-violence-niger-delta; John "Ahni-

wanika" Schertow, "Stop Killing and Starvation of Samburu People in Kenya," Interconti-
nental Cry, November 20, 2009, http://intercontinentalcry.org/stop-killing-and-starvation-
of-samburu-people-in-kenya; Paula Palmer and Chris Allan, Kenya Human Rights
Research Delegation, "When the Police are the Perpetrators: An Investigation of Human
Rights Violations by Police in Samburu East and Isiolo Districts [Kenya]," Cultural Survival, April 20, 2010, http://www.culturalsurvival.org/files/Samburu%20Report%20Final%205-5-
2010.pdf; Shepard Daniel with Anuradha Mittal, "The Great Land Grab: Rush for World's
Farmland Threatens Food Security for the Poor," Oakland Institute, www.oaklandinsti-
tute.org.

Update: There is little to no corporate media coverage on the topic in
the United States. Coverage on the topic in 2011 has been provided by
United States-based Bloomberg L.P., covering purely economic topics,
and British-based newspaper *The Guardian*, which has produced an
in-depth discussion on the topic. Other coverage has been provided by
local African and Middle Eastern news providers such as an article
from the March 2011 *Pakistan Observer* and a January 2011 article in
the *Tripoli Post* which stated that "Libya plans to provide 60,000
hectares of field for Turkish investors" (sixty thousand hectares is
equivalent to 232 square miles, half the size of New York City).

There is also a growing grassroots movement on the issue of "land
grabs." A variety of blogs and independent journalists are giving their
take on the surging occupation of these communal lands. One of these
grassroots sites is Farmlandgrab.org. The site—created by GRAIN, a
small international NGO—is an open project that encourages readers
to post any articles or media coverage of these massive land grabs, and
has posted research from their October 2008 report titled "Seized: The
2008 Land Grab for Food and Financial Security."

Furthermore, WikiLeaks released a cable explaining investments
and land purchases made by a handful of African leaders, including
investments and plans to develop agricultural projects or tourism
resorts in Ethiopia, and an evasion of a 2007 ban on export of cereals.
Finally, on May 5, 2011, an article was published in *The Economist*
giving a run through of the more recent data about the massive land
grabs in Africa which concluded: "Evidence is piling up against acqui-
sitions of farmland in poor countries."

Sources: William Davison, "Saudi Billionaire's Company Will Invest $2.5 Billion in
Ethiopia Rice Farm," Bloomberg, March 22, 2011, http://www.bloomberg.com/news/2011-
03-23/saudi-billionaire-s-company-will-invest-2-5-billion-in-ethiopia-rice-farm.html;

Madeleine Bunting, "How Land Grabs in Africa Could Herald a New Dystopian Age of Hunger," *Guardian*, Poverty Matters Blog, January 28, 2010, http://www.guardian.co.uk/global-development/poverty-matters/2011/jan/28/africa-land-grabs-food-security; Madeleine Bunting, "Guardian Focus Podcast: Land Grabs in Africa" *Guardian*, Guardian Focus Podcast, produced by Peter Sale, January 28, 2011, http://www.guardian.co.uk/world/audio/2011/jan/28/guardian-focus-podcast-land-grabs; "Libya could Provide 60,000 Hectares of field for Turkish Investors," *Tripoli Post*, January 4, 2011, http://tripolipost.com/articledetail.asp?c=1&i=5285, Staff Reporter; "Australian firms eye investment in food processing sector," *Pakistan Observer*, March 12, 2011, http://pakobserver.net/detail-news.asp?id=80667; "The Surge in Land Deals: When Others Are Grabbing Their Land" *Economist*, May 5, 2011, http://www.economist.com/ node/18648855?story_id=18648855; "Cable 10ADDISABABA247, FOREIGN INVESTORS GRAB UP MORE LAND IN ETHIOPIA," WikiLeaks, released January 28, 2011, http://wikileaks.ch/cable/2010/02/10ADDISABABA247.html.

The following is a special update by Justice in Nigeria Now, which won a Project Censored Award for this particular story last year.

The Niger Delta is unfortunately known worldwide as a region where oil production comes first and human rights a distant second. For well over fifty years, oil operations in the Niger Delta have economically marginalized local villagers, while giving them virtually no control over their own livelihood, land, or resources.

In the spring of 2009 in Nigeria's oil-rich Delta State, oil operations were responsible for a series of brutal attacks perpetrated against thousands of innocent civilians by the military's Joint Task Force (JTF). As Nigerians gathered on May 14th in Oporoza—the region's major town—to celebrate the Gbaramatu Kingdom's hereditary ruler, without warning, the JTF commenced attacks on the festive crowd. JTF helicopter gunships indiscriminately opened fire, targeting children, the elderly, the monarch himself, and anyone else in the crowd. These gunships were quickly followed by ground assault troops, carried by naval warships, in what was obviously a substantial military campaign.

College student Peres Popo noted that "most of the students like me who tried to escape during the deadly incident are dead. Some in the streets, forests . . . they were killed by the bombs. I lost my mother and six of my brothers in the incident. Two of my three sisters are still trapped in the forest. The place is too dangerous for them to come out now. They can't cross with boat and they can't risk swimming. The JTF people have blocked the waterways. One of my sisters has been missing. Nobody seems to know her whereabouts.

"The military people were using their helicopter chopper to destroy everything we have ever had. I saw war with my naked eyes. I saw my mum's dead body. I saw my brothers lying helpless on the ground. Everyone was running without direction. It is a bitter experience. They are wicked people. They are heartless. I don't have any family members as militants. We used to survive with fishing. It was through fishing business that my mum pays our school fees. Why will the [federal government] send military men to kill us, to destroy our community? We don't have anywhere else to go now. No home, no place to go. My OND [school] certificate, my only hope for a better tomorrow has been destroyed."

The JTF stated that they had commenced the ghastly named "Operation Restore Hope" to "root out militants," with the main target being the infamous rebel political leader, Tompolo. Sadly, the devastation in Oporoza turned out to be only the opening salvo in a relentless two-month military campaign by the JTF. On May 18, the Kurutie community was aerially bombed and almost completely destroyed. On May 19, Okerenkoko was bombarded and burnt. On May 20, Oporoza was attacked again, this time with aerial bombing that destroyed the King's palace. On May 23, Benikurukuru was the target of the JTF's illegal aircraft attacks. Bombings, murders, and other depredations were also perpetrated in Kunukunuma, Kokodiagbene, Azama, Ubefan, and many other surrounding communities. Nigerians of all ages and health were chased into the bush and swampy waterways as the JTF became an occupying military force in their homes.

By June 2009, the JTF had moved to neighboring Rivers State, where the destruction continued unabated (and unnoticed) by the world. By the end of June 2009, up to twenty thousand Niger Delta residents had been "internally displaced,"—an inadequate term for losing everything in a single day—forced to flee without their animals or their possessions, losing in that moment their homes and livelihoods. These residents of the Niger Delta were trapped in an unwinnable war between the militants, the JTF, and the international oil companies—who demand keeping the oil and gas flowing, no matter the cost. It was not until August 2009 that the people of the Gharamatu Kingdom were able to safely return to their ruined homes.

The lack of discrimination by the JTF between innocent civilians and armed militants and the JTF's regular use of disproportionate force is a clear violation of human rights law. President Goodluck Jonathan, who comes from neighboring Baylesa State, took some internal and external actions against the JTF. Yet similar attacks by the JTF against Niger Delta civilian communities have continued in 2010 and 2011, with atrocities in Awakormo and elsewhere, leading Niger Delta civil society and traditional leaders to call for the complete disbandment of the JTF.

For a complete account of the JTF attacks in the Niger Delta and links to Delta State eyewitness statements and videos, please visit http://justicein-nigerianow.org/jinn/wp-content/uploads/2010/10/GB-update-final.pdf.

Censored 2011 #9

Human Rights Abuses Continue in Palestine

Update by Salma Habib

The Human Sciences Research Council of South Africa (HSRC) has released a study indicating that Israel is practicing both colonialism and apartheid in the occupied Palestinian territories. The HSRC commissioned an international team of scholars and practitioners of international public law from South Africa, the United Kingdom, Israel, and the West Bank to conduct the study.

Original Sources: Virginia Tilley, Human Sciences Research Council of South Africa, "Occupation, Colonialism, Apartheid," HSRC website, May 2009, http://www.hsrc.ac .za/Media_Release-378.phtml; Jonathan Cook, "Israel Brings Gaza Entry Restrictions to West Bank," *Electronic Intifada*, August 18, 2009, http://electronicintifada.net/ v2/article10718.shtml; "Israel Rations Palestinians to Trickle of Water," Amnesty International, October 27, 2009, http://www.amnesty.org/en/news-and-updates/report/ israel-rations-palestinians-trickle-water-20091027; Rory McCarthy, "Non-Violent Protests Against West Bank Barrier Turn Increasingly Dangerous," *Guardian*, April 27, 2009, http://www.guardian.co.uk/world/2009/apr/27/israel-security-barrier-protests; "Harvard Fellow Calls for Genocidal Measures to Curb Palestinian Births," *Electronic Intifada*, February 22, 2010, http://electronicintifada.net/v2/ article11091.shtml.

Update: Story #9 from Censored 2011 helps further illuminate the growing number of human rights atrocities occurring in the Palestinian region. As many Palestinians are further subjugated by colonial and imperial rule, they continue to be treated like second-class citizens as prejudicial attitudes further relegate them into a subservient role, giving the Israelis larger domain to throw their might around. Instead of shedding light upon the Palestinian struggle, many individuals throughout the community have been seen as the ones antagonizing, rather than being seen as autonomous (and whose plight has been largely overlooked by the international community). The community continues to persist in their fight for communal recognition as they've endured a series of resource redistribution tactics that have rendered this community dependent upon outside aid. To restore a diminished sense of Palestinian self-determination, efforts, though seemingly few, are being made in an act of solidarity to restore the community of their own cultural integrity.

In an attempt to protest Israeli aggression, and as part of the Boycott, Divestment, and Sanctions Movement, students have fired back and responded with their own protest of Sabra, a hummus brand available to most university students at their schools. This Middle Eastern chickpea dip is connected to the Strauss group, an organization that has knowingly funded the Israeli Defense fund. Much of the protest is done in a way to demonstrate that knowingly supporting an organization connected to human rights' abuses is not something that can be done in good conscience. These students have worked in order to draw attention to the international community that disregarding the Palestinian struggle serves to further promote a mentality of apartheid.

While this has been occurring for decades, many that have been infringed upon in the queer community have come to the forefront to speak out about the Palestinian plight. A sense of universal identification has become visibly apparent as many can connect with this sense of alienation and the urgency of knowing that this subjugation need not continue. Muslims throughout the world are seeing this as a struggle not localized by region, but identifiable based on both cultural and human connections. Not only has this become a struggle for one group of people, but cross-culturally people are able to identify with this sense that universal representation and a sense of equality is necessary to recognize Palestinian autonomy as a whole.

As we continue to see a growing trend of harassment, Palestinian women continually face harassment by the Israeli soldiers as they are subjected to rape and are tormented by these grueling acts to demonstrate power and authority. The prisoner rights organization "Women for Support of Women Political Prisoners" has published numerous testimonies illustrating the harassment and detention of women in the "Moscobiya," a detention center in Jerusalem known as the Russian Compound.

Alleged rape and abuse continues to occur as we see a distinctive inequality in treatment toward women as opposed to men, illustrating a whole new range of mistreatment on the part of the Israelis who have demonstrated an attitude of degradation toward objectifying the female form. The plight of Palestinian women is one where there is a necessity for more information on their treatment as well as greater global involvement to promote awareness on the abject treatment of women in this region.

The suffering that has been dealt to Palestinians is one where people have not only heard their calling and their cries, but have risen to the occasion to say that the people have had enough and greater involvement through transnational, global, and humanitarian means is essentially imperative in order to regain a sense of empowerment.

Sources: Boycott, Divestment, and Sanctions Movement, www.bdsmovement.net; C. Hanley, "Students Campaign to Boycott Israeli Aggression," *Washington Report on Middle East Affairs* 30, no. 1 (2011): 58; Laura Pulido Lloyd, "In the Long Shadow of the Settler: On Israeli and US Colonialisms," *American Quarterly* 62, no. 4 (2010): 795–812; *New Statesman* 139 (November 29, 2010): 40; Tim McCaskell, "Queers Against Apartheid," *Canadian Dimension* 44, no. 4 (2010): 14–20; June Edmunds, "Elite' Young Muslims in Britain: From Transnational to Global Politics," *Contemporary Islam* 4, no. 2 (2010): 215; Mia Bloom, "Death Becomes Her: Women, Occupation, and Terrorist Mobilization," *PS, Political Science & Politics* 43, no. 3 (2010): 445–51.

Censored 2011 #10

US Funds and Supports the Taliban

Update by Salma Habib

In a continuous flow of money, American tax dollars end up paying members of the Taliban and funding a volatile environment in

Afghanistan. Private contractors pay insurgents with the hope of attaining the very safety they are contracted to provide. Concurrently, US soldiers pay at checkpoints run by suspected insurgents in order to get safe passage. In some cases, Afghan companies run by former Taliban members, like President Hamid Karzai's cousin, are protecting the passage of American soldiers. The funding of the insurgents, along with rumors of American helicopters ferrying Taliban members in Afghanistan, has led to widespread distrust of American forces. In the meantime, the US taxpayer's dollar continues to fund insurgents to protect American troops so they can fight insurgents.

Original Corporate Source: Andrew Rice, "Is There Such a Thing as Agro-Imperialism?" *New York Times*, November 16, 2009, http://www.nytimes.com/2009/11/22/magazine/22land-t.html.

Original Sources: Aram Roston, "How the US Funds the Taliban," *Nation*, November 20, 2009, http://www.thenation.com/doc/20091130/roston; Ahmad Kawoosh, "Is the US Aiding the Taliban?" *Taiwan News*, October 31, 2009, http://www.etaiwannews.com/etn/news_content.php?id=1095689&lang=eng_news&cate_img=140.jpg&cate_rss=news_Opinion; Ahmad Kawoosh, "Helicopter Rumor Refuses to Die," Institute for War and Peace Reporting, November 2, 2009, http://www.iwpr.net/?p=arr&s=f&o=356886.

Update: The Taliban have made a name for themselves as a resistant group fighting to preserve their control over sovereign territories in Afghanistan. The group has been known to subject citizens and others to heinous forms of torture and to perpetrate great forms of brutality onto citizens of the region. Namely, their treatment of women as second-class citizens through the practice of their imposed authority has placed the Taliban on the global map as an oppressive entity in the public sphere. A concerted effort has been made on the part of the American government to extricate this authority, yet many of the promises made to eliminate their presence have gone unfulfilled. During the period of 2001 to 2009, the US situation in Afghanistan had been growing progressively worse; the Taliban has made a comeback and challenged both the central Karzai government and tribal leaders throughout the region to gain control.

President Obama himself has argued to eliminate the presence of the Taliban, yet what's become most challenging is that most military leaders have failed to present clear and detailed strategies of how they intend on tackling the issue of the Taliban. In the midst of an economy that's recently shelled out roughly $1.5 trillion to save failing companies, it seems questionable why the Obama administration would want to spend billions on financing a war in Afghanistan that could create not only potential casualties, but lead to continued economic fiascos, including funding the Taliban while fighting them at the same time.

This story was reported in alternative media like *The Nation*, but was also picked up, at least marginally, by the corporate media, specifically ABC News and CNN. That said, the story has not been followed up upon, nor has there been any real effort in corporate media to make this a wider issue in the public, especially in matters surrounding the ongoing war in Afghanistan.

Sources: Nick Schifrin, "Report: U.S. Bribes to Protect Convoys Are Funding Taliban Insurgents," *ABC World News with Diane Sawyer*, June 22, 2010, http://abcnews.go .com/WN/Afghanistan/united-states-military-funding-taliban-afghanistan/story?id=10980527; Ed Hornick, "U.S. set to pay Taliban members to switch sides," *CNN*, October 28, 2009, http://articles.cnn.com/2009-10   28/politics/afghanistan.taliban.pay_1_taliban-fighters-taliban-members-afghanistan?_s=PM:POLITICS; James P. Pfiffner, "Decision Making in the Obama White House," *Presidential Studies Quarterly* 41, no. 2 (2011): 244–62; Gary C. Jacobson, "Legislative Success and Political Failure: The Public's Reaction to Barack Obama's Early Presidency," *Presidential Studies Quarterly* 41, no. 2 (2011): 220–43; Richard M. Pious, "Prerogative Power in the Obama Administration: Continuity and Change in the War on Terrorism," *Presidential Studies Quarterly* 41, no. 2 (2011): 263–90; Stephen J. Wayne, "Presidential Character and Judgment: Obama's Afghanistan and Health Care Decisions," *Presidential Studies Quarterly* 41, no. 2 (2011): 291–306.

Censored 2011 #14

Increased Tensions with Unsolved 9/11 Issues

Update by Alexandre Silva

Several contentious issues still plague the US government and their version of the events of September 11, 2001. Those in political power along with corporate media elites would like to see the ongoing grassroots debates surrounding unanswered 9/11 questions and discrepancies disappear, despite the mountains of evidence that suggest that American citizens were told little about the truth of the biggest single-day attack on their homeland in history. Nearly ten years after the events, many unanswered questions still exist: How did

Building 7 fall? What caused the destruction of the twin towers? Who, exactly, was responsible for the attacks and security failures of that day? Where was Osama bin Laden for so long and why are there numerous reports of his death prior to the US declaration of such on May 2, 2011? Are people that question the official story of 9/11 dangerous conspiracy theorists?

Original Sources: PR News Wire, "1,000 Architects & Engineers Call for New 9/11 Investigation: Cite Evidence of Explosive Demolition at Three World Trade Center Towers," February 19, 2009, http://www.prnewswire.com/news-releases/1000-architects—engineers-call-for-new-911-investigation-84768402.html; Shawn Hamilton, "Over 1,000 Architects and Engineers Have Signed Petition to Reinvestigate 9-11 Destruction," *Examiner*, February 23, 2010, http://www.examiner.com/x-36199-Conspiracy-Examiner; Architects & Engineers for 911 Truth, "1,000+ Architects & Engineers Officially Demand New 9/11 Investigation," *Infowars.com*, January 18, 2010, http://www.infowars.com/1000-architects-engineers-officially-demand-new-911-investigation; "1,000 Architects & Engineers Call for a Real 9/11 Investigation," Global Research, January 25, 2010, http://www.globalresearch.ca/index.php?context=va&aid=17507; Sue Reid, "Has Osama bin Laden Been Dead for Seven Years—And Are the US and Britain Covering It Up to Continue War on Terror?" *Daily Mail*, September 1, 2009, http://www.dailymail.co.uk/news/article-1212851/Has-Osama-Bin-Laden-dead-seven-years—U-S-Britain-covering-continue-war-terror.html; Daniel Tencer, "Obama Staffer Wants 'Cognitive Infiltration' of 9/11 Conspiracy Groups," *RawStory*, January 13, 2010, http://rawstory.com/2010/01/obama-staffer-infiltration-911-groups.

Update: Unable to get much recognition from the corporate media regarding the many unresolved 9/11 issues since their launch in 2007, Architects and Engineers for 9/11 Truth assisted in the "Building What?" ad campaign calling for a new investigation regarding the collapse of World Trade Center Building 7 (the forty-seven-story skyscraper that collapsed on 9/11/01, for sometime at freefall speed, into its own footprint, even though it was not hit by a plane). In the ad, which aired in New York City last fall, the families of those who lost loved ones brought attention to the fact that over 1,500 architects and engineers disagree with the official narrative of what occurred to Building 7. Shortly after the launch of the ad campaign, some in the major corporate media took note for the first time.

Geraldo Rivera, who hosts *At Large with Geraldo Rivera* on the Fox News channel, interviewed one of the family members who were present in the ad as well as one of the mechanical engineers calling for a new investigation. In the interview, Rivera was genuinely persuaded that explosives could have been involved in the destruction of Building 7 and went on to state that ". . . if explosives were involved, that would mean that the most obnoxious protestors in recent years are right." Rivera was later a guest on Andrew Napolitano's show (also on Fox) where the two discussed the issue. Both were subsequently attacked by several groups, including the liberal *Media Matters for America* for giving a platform to "Truthers" while never addressing the claims of their reports.

Although the corporate media has not reported on these issues much at all except for a few local and regional cases, this is a breakthrough in covering 9/11 related issues where the message does not conform to the official accounts given by the US government. Further, it demonstrates a more professional journalistic approach to the topic by asking probing questions rather than attacking, labeling, and distorting unfavorable or unpopular views.

Furthermore, prior to May 2, 2011, the location of Osama bin Laden was the focus of several contradictory reports, placing bin Laden in a number of countries since 2001. Since the previous *Censored* yearbook, bin Laden was reported to be in Yemen, Pakistan, Iran, and Sudan, to name a few. The Pakistani Prime Minister had since denied the reports that bin Laden was in Pakistan and others claimed he was in another country (illustrating there were numerous reports, some contradictory).

On May 2, 2011, President Barack Obama declared Osama bin Laden was officially dead. Yet according to international news agencies and foreign dignitaries, it was perhaps the fourth time he has died since 2001. The first was when he allegedly succumbed to a serious kidney complication. The second occurred in 2007, when former Pakistani premier Benazir Bhutto proclaimed he had been assassinated. The third time was in 2009, according to Pakistani President Asif Ali Zardari. The most recent, and now most widely known, was when bin Laden was found in Abbottabad, Pakistan, where he was shot by US Navy SEALs as they invaded his home. However, the true story of what actually happened during this most recent death account will not likely be known, as the body was disposed of into the ocean, the narrative behind what happened has changed multiple times, and no physical evidence of the death has been verified and provided. Although the corporate media have focused extensively on this most recent death, little to no coverage has been allowed for the others in context of the recent declarations of bin Laden's demise. In terms of the corporate media in the US, this was largely celebrated, even though it was likely against international law and if the Navy SEALs did find him in Pakistan, it was reported he was unarmed, which means they could have detained him and tried him for the crimes of 9/11 (which bin Laden claimed he did not plan, nor did the FBI hold him as wanted for that crime due to lack of evidence—all of these were precious Project Censored stories). Regardless, the death of bin Laden has not marked an end to the 9/11 wars which rage on despite this finale, even though the original goal of the War on Terror has now been achieved.

Corporate Sources: Scherer, "Locating Osama bin laden," *USA Today Magazine* 139, no. 2788 (2011): 22–25; "Report: Bin Laden Already Dead," FoxNews.com, December 26, 2011, http://www.foxnews.com/story/0,2933,41576,00.html; Nate Jones, "The 'Official Story' of bin Laden's Death: A Timeline," *Metro*, May 5, 2011, http://www.metro.us/newyork/international/article/851858—the-official-story-of-bin-laden-s-death-a-timeline.

Sources: "9/11 Family Group Releases TV Ad Calling for World Trade Center Building 7 Investigation," PR Newswire, November 2, 2010, http://www.prnewswire.com/news-releases/911-family-group-releases-tv-ad-calling-for-world-trade-center-building-7-investigation-106506548.html; Manal Alafrangi, "Gulf News: Expert points to strong evidence of Bin Laden presence in country," *Gulf News*, November 3, 2010, http://gulfnews.com/news/gulf/yemen/expert-points-to-strong-evidence-of-bin-laden-presence-in-country-1.705680; "US: Have no information about Osama's hideout," *Economic Times*, October 20, 2010, http://articles.economictimes.indiatimes.com/2010-10-19/news/27595119_1_zawahiri-top-al-qaeda-leaders-al-qaeda; Rob Crilly, "Bin Laden living in comfort in Pakistan: NATO," October 19, 2010, *Edmonton Journal*, A16; "Pakistan denies presence of bin Laden," *McClatchy—Tribune Business News*, October 18, 2010; "FBI Raids Homes of Antiwar and Pro-Palestinian Activists in Chicago and Minneapolis," *Democracy Now!*, September 27, 2010, http://www.democracynow.org/2010/9/27/fbi_raids_homes_of_anti_war; "'BuildingWhat?' on Geraldo At Large," *BuildingWhat.org*, 2010, http://buildingwhat.org/buildingwhat-appears-on-geraldo-at-large-on-fox-news/; Alex Jones, "Benazir Bhutto said Osama bin Laden was dead," Infowars, December 28, 2007, http://www.infowars.com/articles/world/pakistan_bhutto_said_osama_bin_laden_was_dead.htm; "Osama Bin Laden Believed Dead By Pak Intel," People's Voice, April 29, 2009, http://www.thepeoplesvoice.org/TPV3/Voices.php/2009/04/29/osama-bin-laden-believed-dead-by-pak-int; Eric Hananoki, "Fox host Napolitano is a 9-11 Truther: 'It couldn't possibly have been done the way the government told us,'" Media Matters for America, November 24, 2010, http://mediamatters.org/mobile/blog/201011240019; for an in-depth account on the controversies surrounding bin Laden and his many reported deaths, see David Ray Griffin, *Osama bin Laden: Dead or Alive?* (Northampton, MA: Olive Branch Press, 2009), 1–17.

Censored 2011 #17

Nanotech Particles Pose Serious DNA Risks to Humans and the Environment

Update by Alexandre Silva

Personal products you may use daily and think are harmless—cosmetics, suntan lotion, socks, and sports clothes—may all contain atom-sized nanotech particles, some of which have been shown to sicken and kill workers in plants using nanotechnology. Known human health risks include severe and permanent lung damage, and cell studies indicate genetic DNA damage. Extremely toxic to aquatic wildlife, nanoparticles pose clear risks to many species and threaten the global food chain.

Original Sources: Carole Bass, "Tiny Troubles: Nanoparticles are Changing Everything From our Sunscreen to our Supplements," *E Magazine*, June 30, 2009, http://www.emagazine.com/archive/4723; Janet Raloff, "Nanoparticles' Indirect Threat to DNA," *Science News*, November 5, 2009, http://www.sciencenews.org/view/generic/id/49191/title/Science_+_the%20_Public__Nanoparticles_indirect_threat_to_DNA; L. Geranio, M. Heuberger, and B. Nowack, "The Behavior of Silver Nanotextiles During Washing," *Environmental Science & Technology* 43, no. 21 (2009): 8113–18; Paul Eugib, DVM, and Wendy Hessler, "Silver Migrates From Treated Fabrics," *Environmental Health News*, January 7, 2010, http://www.environmentalhealthnews.org/ehs/newscience/silver-migrates-from-nanoparticle-treated-fabrics; David Rejeski, "Nanotech-enabled Consumer Products Top the 1,000 Mark," *Project on Emerging Nanotechnologies*, August 25, 2009, http://www.nanotechproject.org/news/archive/8277/; Y. Song, X. Li, and X. Du, "Exposure to Nanoparticles Is Related to Pleural Effusion, Pulmonary Fibrosis and Granuloma," *European Respiratory Journal* 34, no. 3: 559–567; "Health Risks of Nanotechnology: How Nanoparticles Can Cause Lung Damage, and How the Damage Can Be Blocked," *Science Daily*, June 11, 2009, http://www.sciencedaily.com/releases/ 2009/06/090610192431.htm; "Nanotechnologies and Food, House of Lords Media Notice," Science and Technology Committee, January 8, 2010, http://www.parliament.uk/business/committees/committees-archive/lords-press-notices/pn080110st/; Ian Sample, "Attack of the Tiny Nano Particles—Be Slightly Afraid," Organic Consumers Association, November 15, 2008, http://www.organic-consumers.org/articles/ article_15621.cfm; George John, "Silver Nanoparticles Deadly to Bacteria," Physorg, March 10, 2008, http://www.physorg.com/news124376552.html; Nanowerk Spotlight, "Problematic New Findings Regarding Toxicity of Silver Nanoparticles," Nanowerk, June 6, 2008, http://www.nanowerk.com/spotlight/spotid=5966.php; R. J. Aitken et al., "Nanoparticles: An Occupational Hygiene Review," Institute of Occupational Medicine, Health and Safety Executive (Edinburgh), March 2, 2004, www.hse.gov.uk/research/rrpdf/rr274.pdf.

Update: The corporate mainstream press have not widely covered the health risk that nanoparticles present to the human race, but there have been plenty of new findings in data released from recent research. In a study by the State University of New York, Stony Brook, they have found that gold nanoparticles from products that are known to contain them penetrate human cells. Although it is not precisely clear as to the amount of damage the gold nanoparticles present to human cells, it is known that gold enters the human cell and can remain there for a long period of time. According to another study by the National Institute for Public Health and the Environment, they found that silver nanoparticles, once injected in rats, quickly distribute themselves throughout the major organs of the subject's body. Given that rats have the same basic biological constitution that humans have, there is a high probability that silver nanoparticles also enter the human body.

A recent report found that printers, via the toners, produce an aerosol form of carbon based nanoparticles that can be inhaled and pose severe respiratory health risks. This adds to a growing list of problems with nanoparticles, a list which includes permanent lung damage, debilitating skin effects, and long term genetic damage.

Sources: "Studies from National Institute for Public Health and the Environment provide new data on nanoparticles," *Drug Week*, 2010; "Findings from State University of New York in apoptosis reported," *Obesity, Fitness & Wellness Week*, September 25, 2010; "Researchers from University Hospital, Institute of Pathology Report on Findings in Nanotechnology—Nanoparticles," *Women's Health Weekly*, February 3, 2011, 2023.

Censored 2011 #18

The True Cost of Chevron

Update by Sy Cowie

Story #18 in *Censored 2011* covered, with specific reference to the Chevron corporation, the ongoing and unadvertised costs of oil extraction to the environment, economic needs, politics, and health of the world's population. The story covered the effects of Chevron's operations in places such as Nigeria, Angola, Ecuador, Chad, Cameroon, and Myanmar. The importance of this story concerned the hidden costs of the maintenance of the North American standard of living.

Original Source: Antonia Juhasz, "The True Cost of Chevron: An Alternative Annual Report," True Cost of Chevron, May 27, 2009, http://truecostofchevron.com/report.html.

Update: The coverage of the costs to local populations in the areas where resource extraction occurs continues to be lacking in the corporate media in the US. Coverage of issues surrounding resource extraction often appears only in the business press. The stories covered in these venues are consistently framed to fit the perspective of the business interests who are the typical consumers of information from these sources. Occasionally the consequences for local populations of major resource extraction projects do find their way into the corporate media. The set of court cases involving Chevron and local populations residing in the area of former Texaco extraction operations in Ecuador is one such occasion (Texaco was acquired by Chevron in 2001).

The legal, political, and public relations battles over who is responsible for environmental damage caused by oil extraction in the formerly Texaco-operated fields in the Oriente region of Ecuador took what might seem to be an odd turn when Chevron filed a civil RICO suit against the legal team and hired consultants of the plaintiffs in the case. The purpose of this suit is to call into question the validity of the ruling of the Ecuadoran courts in the eyes of the US court system. The Ecuadoran courts must rely on the US court system to enforce the settlement because Chevron has no assets in Ecuador. Among the allegations included in the RICO lawsuit are charges that the lawyers for the plaintiffs conspired to falsify environmental impact reports and intimidate the presiding judge. It is Chevron's position that the legal proceedings in Ecuador have been tainted from the beginning of the process and the RICO suit is the legal reflection of that position.

What this fight over liability for environmental damage in Ecuador fails to address are the larger issues of energy consumption in the developed world and the frontier settlement policy in the developing world. Resource extraction companies exist as a result of a materialist culture that every year consumes greater and greater quantities of energy and resources. That Petroecuador, Texaco, and a variety of other European, Chinese, North and South American resource extraction companies are responsible for pollution in the Ecuadoran Amazon is not a matter for honest dispute. However, it is a lifestyle that hundreds of millions of people choose to live which is ultimately responsible for the excesses of the extraction industry and its effects on local populations. The true cost of Chevron is, in reality, the true cost of the excesses of the so-called "western" lifestyle.

Corporate Source: Lawrence Hurley, "Chevron's RICO Lawsuit in Pollution Case Part of Wider Legal Strategy," *New York Times*, February 2, 2011, http://www.nytimes.com/gwire/2011/02/02/02greenwire-chevrons-rico-lawsuit-in-pollution-case-part-0-68778.html.

Sources: Martha Niel, "Chevron Shifts Gears, Files Civil RICO Suit Against Plaintiffs," *ABA Journal*, February 3, 2011, http://www.abajournal.com/news/article/chevron_rico _suit_says_plaintiffs_law_firm_falsified_expert_reports/; Maria Kielmas, "All Could Lose in Ecuadorian Judgement Against Chevron," Suit101, February 16, 2011, http://www .suite101.com/content/all-could-lose-in-ecuadorian-judgement-against-chevron -a348321.

Censored 2011 #20

Obama's Charter School Policies Spread Segregation and Undermine Unions

Update by Kelli Baumgartner

Charter schools continue to stratify students by race, class, and sometimes language, and are more racially isolated than traditional public schools in virtually every state and large metropolitan area in the country. Charter schools are often marketed as incubators of educational innovation, and they form a key feature of the Obama administration's school reform agenda. But in some urban communities, they may be fueling *de facto* school segregation and undermining public education.

Original Sources: E. Frankenberg, G. Siegel-Hawley, and J. Wang, "Choice without Equity: Charter School Segregation and the Need for Civil Rights Standards," Civil Rights Project/Proyecto Derechos Civiles, University of California, Los Angeles, http://www.civil-rightsproject.ucla.edu/news/pressreleases/pressrelease20100204-report.html; Danny Weil, "Obama and Duncan's Education Policy: Like Bush's, Only Worse," *CounterPunch*, August 24, 2009, http://counterpunch.org/weil08242009.html; Michelle Chen, "Equity and Access in Charter School Systems," *Race Wire*, August 19, 2009, http://www.racewire .org/archives/2009/08/special_education_equity_and_a_1 .html; Paul Abowd, "Teacher Reformers Prepare for Battle Over Public Education," *Labor Notes*, October 13, 2009, http://www.labornotes.org/node/2472.

Update: While there has been some coverage on segregation in charter schools in independent sources, there has been very little coverage throughout the corporate media. *Newsweek* had an article regarding charter schools featured in their June 2010 magazine. The article starts by praising charter schools for comprising fifteen out of the top one hundred public high schools while the population of charter schools is only at 4 percent of all public schools. A study was conducted by Stanford University's Center for Research on Educational Outcomes which found that "37 percent of charter schools produce academic results that are worse than public schools, while only 17 percent perform significantly better. Arne Duncan, Secretary of Education, made a priority of opening new charters in the $4 billion Race to the Top competition for federal funding." The *Newsweek* article suggests that there is a problem in the academic role of charter schools; however, it fails to address the additional problem of segregation in charter schools.

Unlike the corporate media, independent news sources did cover the issue of segregation rather than only addressing academic performance. As reported in the Washington, DC–based *US Fed News Service* in February 2011, Erica Frankenberg, the assistant professor of educational leadership in Penn State's College of Education, found that "in 15 states, nearly 70 percent of the black students in charter schools are attending hyper segregated schools, which are defined as having at least a 90 percent minority population." Likewise, the Civil Rights Project at UCLA shows that the majority of charter school students are either low-income or minority students. Frankenberg says, "Little state or federal direct action has been taken to change or correct racial isolation in charter schools despite numerous past reports by The Civil Rights Project and others highlighting this persistent and growing problem."

Although many news sources have suggested this problem with charter schools, some dispute this conclusion despite statistics showing otherwise. An alternate opinion has been presented in *Times Union* in an article titled "Charter Schools Don't Segregate." Their main argument is that charter schools have appealed more to minority families who seek a better education for their children. Their subsequent conclusion is that charter schools may wrongly be characterized as "segregated . . . simply because minority head counts are a bit higher than for the school system as a whole." People may hold different opinions regarding why charter schools are segregated, but either way it is an important issue that was hardly covered by the corporate media even though charter schools and public schools have oft been a point of contention for other reasons.

Sources: Evan Thomas and Pat Wingert, "Understanding Charter Schools," *Newsweek*, June 13, 2010, http://www.newsweek.com/2010/06/13/understanding-charter-schools.html; "Research Shows Segregation in Charter Schools," US Fed News Service, February 17, 2011; Robert Holland, "Charter Schools Don't Segregate," *Times Union*, September 13, 2010, http://www.timesunion.com/opinion/article/Charter-schools-dont-segregate-655727.php.

Censored 2011 #25

Prisoners Still Brutalized at Gitmo

Update by Kira McDonough

In Guantánamo, the notorious but seldom-discussed thug squad, officially known as the Immediate Reaction Force (IRF), deployed by the US military remains very much active. Inside the walls of Guantánamo, the prisoners know the squad as the Extreme Repression Force.

Original Sources: Jeremy Scahill, "Little Known Military Thug Squad Still Brutalizing Prisoners at Gitmo Under Obama," AlterNet, May 15, 2009, http://www.alternet.org/story/140022; Andrew Wander, "Guantánamo Conditions 'Deteriorate,'" Al Jazeera English, November 10, 2009, http://www.commondreams.org/headline/2009/11/10-0.

Update: In April 2011, WikiLeaks released numerous documents revealing the continued torture and brutality at Guantánamo Bay Prison. The documents detailed the imprisonment and brutal treatment of over seven hundred prisoners that, even in the eyes of the US military/intelligence, there was no evidence connecting the vast majority to any form of terrorism, let alone terrorist threats against the United States and US citizens. Many prisoners were held for months or years after interrogators cleared them of having any connection to terrorism. At least a hundred prisoners were diagnosed with psychiatric disorders, including psychosis, depression, and bipolarity. Those incarcerated at Guantánamo range in age from fourteen (thought to know some local Taliban leaders—a description that would apply to most youth in the east and south of Afghanistan), to an eighty-nine-year-old suffering from senile dementia, cancer, and other serious illnesses. Many people have been sold into custody and imprisonment.

The Obama administration issued an executive order on March 7, 2011, allowing detainees who the administration claims are too dangerous to release but is unwilling to prosecute, the ability to challenge their detention before a new Periodic Review Board. Detainees will be able to submit documentary evidence every six months, but will only go before the full panel once every three years and will be assigned a "representative" by the military but are able to be represented by counsel of their choice at no cost to the government. This order still falls short of basic due process under international law.

Source: "US: Indefinite Detention Authorized but Restricted," Human Rights Watch, March 7, 2011, http://www.hrw.org/en/news/2011/03/07/us-indefinite-detention-authorized-restricted.

Censored 2011 Runner-up

America's Secret Afghan Prisons: Investigation Unearths New US Torture Site, Abuse Allegations in Afghanistan

Update by Kira McDonough

US secret prisons in Afghanistan continue to exist under the Obama administration according to interviewed Afghans who were detained and abused at several disclosed and undisclosed sites at US and Afghan military bases across the country. They also reveal the existence of another secret prison on Bagram Air Base that even the Red Cross does not have access to. It is dubbed the "Black Jail" and is reportedly run by US Special Forces.

Original Source: "'America's Secret Afghan Prisons': Investigation Unearths New US Torture Site, Abuse Allegations in Afghanistan," *Democracy Now!*, February 2, 2010, http://www.democracynow.org/2010/2/2/americas_secret_afghan_prisons_investigation_unearths.

Update: The US military has denied that it runs secret prisons in

Afghanistan, and has said it does not mistreat the prisoners it holds in the known prisons, insisting that conditions are compliant with both the Geneva Convention's and the US military's own guidelines. But a report released by the US-based Open Society Foundation—an organization placing high priority on protecting and improving the lives of people in marginalized communities—details the testimony of eighteen detainees held at the Tor Prison who say they were mistreated there. The testimony includes repeated claims that their cells were kept uncomfortably cold so they were unable to sleep, that they were given inedible food, and that bright lights were kept on in windowless cells twenty-four hours a day. Such treatment would not only fall short of international standards for the treatment of prisoners, but also would run counter to US military's own guidelines on the issue, which says prisoners should not be exposed to "excessive or inadequate heat, light, or ventilation."

Source: Andrew Wander, "Afghan Detainees Claim US Abuse," Al Jazeera English, October 15, 2010, http://english.aljazeera.net/news/asia/2010/10/2010101514217930443.html.

Censored 2010 #3

Toxic Waste Behind Somali Pirates

Update by Ryan Shehee

The international community has come out in force to condemn and declare war on the Somali fishermen pirates, while discreetly protecting the illegal, unreported, and unregulated (IUU) fleets from around the world that have been poaching and dumping toxic waste in Somali waters since the fall of the Somali government eighteen years ago.

According to the High Seas Task Force (HSTF), there were over eight hundred IUU fishing vessels in Somali waters at one time in 2005, taking advantage of Somalia's inability to police and control its own waters and fishing grounds. The IUUs poach an estimated $450 million in seafood from Somali waters annually. In so doing, they steal an invaluable protein source from some of the world's poorest people and ruin the livelihoods of legitimate fishermen.

Original Sources: Najad Abdullahi, "'Toxic Waste' Behind Somali Piracy," Al Jazeera English, October 11, 2008, http://english.aljazeera.net/news/africa/2008/10/2008109174223218644.html; Johann Hari, "You are Being Lied to about Pirates," *Huffington Post*, January 4, 2009, http://www.huffingtonpost.com/johann-hari/you-are-being-lied-to-abo_b_155147.html; Nicholas Kralev, "Multinational Policing Curbs Piracy off Somalia," *Washington Times*, February 19, 2010, http://www.washingtontimes.com/news/2010/feb/19/ multinational-policing-curbs-piracy-off-somalia/; Firoz Osman, "For Many Somalis, These 'Pirates' are Marine Police," *Star* (South Africa), June 30, 2009; Mohamed Abshir Waldo, "The Two Piracies in Somalia: Why the World Ignores the Other," *Wardheer News*, January 8, 2009, http://wardheernews.com/ Articles_09/Jan/Waldo/08_The_two_piracies_in_Somalia.html.

Update: This story originally appeared as story #3 in *Censored 2010* and was revisited in the Déjà Vu chapter of last year's *Censored 2011*. Although this year has seen a change in the corporate media's degree of attention to this story, they have continued to ignore the issues behind it, promoting only an erroneous, one-sided classification of the Somali people.

In September 2010, the *New York Times* investigated the role of piracy in the conflict between Somalia's dysfunctional government and Islamist insurgents. However, the article frames the Somalis as "famous opportunists," and claims any necessary interactions with them as the lesser of two evils. This article came shortly after the June 2010 premiere of

US Navy: Pirate Hunters on the American cable television channel Spike—a channel whose demographic is men ages eighteen to thirty-four, providing an opportunity to use the show as a recruiting tool according to Navy spokesman Commander Robert K. Anderson. In the first episode, suspects are referred to as pirates who are "terrorizing the open seas" before they have ever reached trial. When, in the course of the constructed narrative, they are found with weapons on their boats, the purpose behind such arms while navigating dangerous waters is not questioned. Ultimately, the suspected pirates are left without a voice in the broadcast, unable to explain their side of the conflict.

Meanwhile, in neighboring Kenya, the views on piracy are not so black-and-white. While some Kenyans agree, claiming the pirates block aid and justify military protection of an integral waterway in the world's oil supply and economy, others view their neighbors as protectors of Somalia's natural resources and sovereignty, and defenders against illegal actions by foreign nations. Furthermore, the line may not be so clear here in the United States. On November 24, 2010, three months after receiving a conflicting ruling by a previous judge, five Somalis were sentenced to the mandatory life sentence plus eighty years for piracy against the USS Nicholas. The first conviction of piracy by an American jury in two centuries, this precedence was set after only sixteen days of trial and deliberation.

Somalia has not had a functional government for two decades, and is facing a humanitarian crisis according to Jerry Rawlings, the former president of the Republic of Ghana and the African Union High Representative for Somalia. Rawlings is calling on donor nations for aid in Somalia. Although significant international funding is currently finding its way to Somalia, it is not in the form of an immediate emergency trust as Rawlings has urged. Instead, alarmingly, millions of dollars in capital comes from unidentified donors for an ultimate purpose which is unknown. What is known is that these funds involve Erik Prince, founder of Xe Services LLC (formerly Blackwater Worldwide), who is ostensibly charged with forming an anti-pirate task force—a project that may violate the arms embargo imposed by the United Nations nearly twenty years ago.

Corporate Sources: Jeffrey Gettleman, "In Somali Civil War, Both Sides Embrace Pirates," *New York Times*, September 2, 2010, A1; David Bauder, "Show to Tail Pirate

Hunters," Associated Press, April 14, 2009; "Kenya's Somali Service Radio Audience Divided Over Piracy," *BBC Monitoring Africa*, May 8, 2010; "Callers to Kenyan State Radio's Somali Talk Show Give Mixed Views on Piracy," *BBC Monitoring Africa*, May 30, 2010; "Somali Foreign Minister Views Situation in Country, Notes Need for Arab Support," *BBC Monitoring Africa*, July 17, 2010; Tim McGlone, "Federal Judges in Norfolk Wrestle Over Definition of Piracy," *Virginian-Pilot*, November 8, 2010; "Five Somalis Sentenced to Life Plus 80 Years in Prison for Piracy Against USS Nicholas Press Release," United States Attorney's Office for the Eastern District of Virginia, March 14, 2011; "Ex-Ghanaian president calls for renewed commitment to peace in Somalia," *BBC Monitoring Africa*, April 21, 2011.

Source: Jason Ditz, "Blackwater Founder Trains Somali 'anti-Pirate' Militia," Antiwar, January 20, 2011, http://news.antiwar.com/2011/01/20/blackwater-founder-trains-somali-anti-pirate-militia.

Conclusion: Uncensoring Déjà Vu Stories One Tweet at a Time

Some of the aforementioned stories received corporate mainstream coverage since they originally appeared on the Censored Top 25, though many others still languish in obscurity despite their continued significance. It is difficult for people to recall or identify something they have never seen; censorship, by its very nature, suppresses and restricts information. Yet, even in instances where there has been some amount of coverage of these stories, the public at large seems unable to focus on them for long. Certainly, no person should be expected to pay attention to every newsworthy event—we all have to meet basic, physiological needs. However, in our society, we are often overwhelmed with information possibilities, and many people do not know whom to trust. Some are so inundated with the tabloidization of news that they tune out. Still, other factors may be responsible for this seeming malaise.

Bill Keller, the executive editor of the *New York Times*, contends in a May 18, 2011 article titled "The Twitter Trap," that our memory is being negatively affected by our current reliance on Wikipedia and social media like Twitter and Facebook. While Keller argues that we as people are losing some of our humanity, perhaps in exchange for productivity, it would seem there are other significant factors left unaddressed. For example, these technologies equip us with the ability to spread the news as situations develop. Further, social media can be used as part of public record and as a reminder of what events transpired and how, including all of the complexities that occur while events unfold. The glossing over or distortion of a story might even become impossible in a culture that embraces new social networking technologies, if it does so under the guise of free press principles—making the right to know paramount among public concerns. The Oscar Grant shooting in Oakland, California, is an example of how citizen journalism and social network technology built a more complete accounting of that tragic event which led to the conviction of the police officer that shot Grant, despite the many cover up attempts by various officials and the inadequate coverage by the traditional corporate media.

Erasing and distorting history in an attempt to conform to present agendas could become harder as well. The revolutions ongoing in the Middle East made their way to the internet via vernacular participants before they made their way to the official views propounded by the corporate media. This is media democracy in action, a positive trend related to our current technological achievements. Even failed coups, stolen elections, and potential false flag events can be uncovered if we look beyond the corporate media and pay more attention to independent reporting based on transparently sourced and factual information. And while technology can be used as an instrument of distraction and propaganda by those in power, We the People can also use technology to educate each other about newsworthy events in our society and how best to move forward as a human community.

As George Santayana once said, "Those who cannot remember the past are condemned to repeat it." Remembering the past is one thing, but remembering it in full, factual, uncensored context is another. Making this distinction is imperative if we are to break the déjà vu cycle of ongoing censored news. With the rise of new technologies, history is no longer being written, recorded, and read, solely by the victors, but by all of us. The media revolution cannot be censored, and our words will continue to be our greatest weapon since the Revolutionary War. It is our only hope in the quest to achieve a truly egalitarian and democratic culture.

MICKEY HUFF is the director of Project Censored, an associate professor of history at Diablo Valley College, and a member of the board of directors of the Media Freedom Foundation.

KELLI BAUMGARTNER, SY COWIE, CASEY GOONAN, SALMA HABIB, NOLAN HIGDON, KIRA MCDONOUGH, YARI OJEDA-SANDEL, RYAN SHEHEE, and ALEXANDRE SILVA are interns with Project Censored.

CARL JENSEN is the founder of Project Censored.

CHAPTER 3

Framing the Messengers
Junk Food News and News Abuse for Dummies

by Mickey Huff and Adam Bessie, with contributions by Abby Martin, Nolan Higdon, and Clifton Roy Damiens

> *We are awash in electronic hallucinations. The worse it gets, the more we retreat into those hallucinations. Dying cultures always sever themselves from reality, because reality becomes so difficult to face, and we're no exception to that.*
> —CHRIS HEDGES, interview with MediaRoots.org

INTRODUCTION: THE EVER-BLURRING LINES OF NEWS AND ENTERTAINMENT . . . THAT'S INFOTAINMENT!

Since Project Censored founder Dr. Carl Jensen coined the term "Junk Food News" in 1983 in an interview with *Penthouse* magazine, many serious studies on the "tabloidization" of news in the US have been conducted. From scholars such as Neil Postman and Mark Crispin Miller to journalists and commentators like Barbara Ehrenreich and Chris Hedges, the problem of infotainment—the blurring of lines of entertainment and information while favoring the trivial and inane over the substantive and germane—has been deconstructed, analyzed, and accordingly derided by free press proponents. Prescriptions for rectifying these infectious and distracting tendencies have been put forth and will be reiterated throughout this chapter. Despite this, Junk Food News (and its younger sibling, News Abuse—the framing or distortion of information for propagandistic purposes) have essentially taken over much of the televised news media and a substantial portion of the print press as well, arguably due to the massive extent of commercial control over major media institutions by corporations.

At Project Censored, we write about the growing problem of Junk Food News in our publication every year, and we do so again this year, though not with pleasure. The pejorative subtitle of this chapter alludes to a growing "when are we in America going to get it?" level of frustration. Our media landscape is addled with Junk Food News, what Jensen called akin to "Twinkies for the brain." This is hardly a secret. But what are we going to do about it? Comedy Central's Jon Stewart and other late-night television court jesters get in on the act of criticizing and lampooning the failures of the US news media on a regular basis. In fact, it is a key component of many of these nightly "infotainment" programs (especially given that these shows are the most watched "news" sources by those under twenty-five in the US). Is it supposed to be funny that our information systems are so dysfunctional? Perhaps we are truly severed from reality in a nervous last gasp response given the severity of the situation, "awash in electronic hallucinations," as Chris Hedges believes.[1]

As a study from the Pew Research Center for People and the Press revealed a few years ago, many are turning to these comedy shows for information because they are not only entertaining, but are often factually correct, at least insofar as what they air. Nonetheless, viewers should remember that the purpose of this type of late-night programming is humor, not news reporting. However, that so many people are tuning away from traditional news broadcasts is also an indicator of increasing lack of public trust in the Fourth Estate.[2] Regardless, we are in dire straits, as pointed out by media scholars Robert W. McChesney and John Nichols in their recent book, *The Death and Life of American Journalism.* The authors rightly point out, "Our nation faces the absurd and untenable prospect of attempting what James Madison characterized as impossible: to be a self governing constitutional republic without a functioning news media."[3] We should consider ourselves forewarned, for as our press is reduced to parody, so is democracy itself.

Junk Food News has become such a phenomenon, one that poses a serious threat to the democratic function of the Fourth Estate, that entire books have been devoted to the topic, including journalist Tom Fenton's *Junk News: The Failure of the Media in the 21st Century,* published in 2009. Again, this illustrates the increased attention the problem is receiving, but the Junk keeps coming. Project Censored has been covering this troublesome trend ever since some news editors took umbrage at Carl Jensen's critiques of the failures of the mainstream press dating back to 1976. They claimed his cries of censorship were too harsh, that they had to use news judgment when deciding what was reported and what was not.

Jensen thought that might be a fair response. So, by the early 1980s, he focused more on what the media *were* covering, not just what they weren't. What he discovered was vindicating, though sad, for his initial views that the news media were in fact systematically failing to report important stories to the public turned out to be true in more ways than he had originally thought, and the Junk Food News analysis by Project Censored was born.

In *Censored 1994*, Jensen wrote:

> Our annual Junk Food News effort evolved from criticism by news editors and directors that the real issue isn't censorship, but rather a difference of opinion as to what information is important to publish or broadcast. Editors point out that there is a finite amount of time and space for news delivery—about 23 minutes for a half-hour network television evening news program—and that it's their responsibility to determine which stories are most critical for the public to know.
>
> This appeared to be legitimate criticism, so I decided to review the stories that editors and news directors consider to be most important and worthy enough to fill their valuable news time and space. The critics said I wasn't exploring media censorship but rather was just another frustrated academic criticizing editorial news judgment. In the course of this research project, I haven't found an abundance of hard-hitting investigative journalism. Quite the contrary. Indeed, what has become evident is the journalistic phenomenon I call Junk Food News, which in essence represents the flip side of the 'Best Censored Stories.'[4]

Jensen laid out several major categories of Junk Food News that continue to be useful to this day, as demonstrated by cursory yet current examples from this past year, some of which will be expanded upon in this chapter:[5]

▶ Brand Name News: Celebrity branding, where the name says it all, as in Brangelina, Donald Trump, Charlie Sheen, Sarah Palin and her family's reality show, the anniversary of Michael Jackson's death; anything with these people is somehow "news"

▶ Sex News: Weinergate, John Edwards's affair and its aftermath, Tiger Woods (from last year's list of Junk Food News), Hollywood trysts and breakups—there is never a shortage in this category

▶ Yo-Yo News: Economy is up or down, employment rates are up or down, the stock market is up and down, various candidates may or may not run for president (Trump, Palin, Gingrich), which candidate raised the most money last week, who is ahead in the horse race polls in election years

▶ Crazed News: The craze or fad of the day, the Birthers, the Tea Partiers, Angry Townhall meeting crashers, Rapture fever and the End of Days for 2012, the Angry Birds game, and other commercial fads, fashion styles, and so on

▶ Showbiz News: Charlie Sheen's goddesses, Sheen's Tiger Blood meltdown, Lindsay Lohan's ongoing exploits, Lady Gaga's shocking antics, Donald Trump's show, Sarah Palin's daughter on *Dancing with the Stars*, the final season of (insert show here)

▶ Sports News: It isn't just Super Bowls, March Madness, and stats; it's also about life on and off the field, with Tiger Woods (on and off the course), Bret Farve's sexy phone messages, Big Ben's marriage after scandal, and the buildup to big championship events that oft do not really impact the lives of many people

▶ Political News: Endless candidate campaign promises, horse race polls, fundraisers and photo ops, plus the cult of personality, (e.g. Trump, Palin, or America's political dynasties from the Kennedys to the Bushes to the Clintons)

Over fifteen years after Jensen compiled these Junk Food News categories, they sadly not only continue, but also intertwine: notice how there is significant overlap between the recent examples—political news overlaps with sex news, crazed news, brand name news, and so on. The Junk Food News matrix has grown out of control, with entertainment thriving and substantive news withering. And when real news *is* covered in the mass media, it is covered with a concerning lack of substance called News Abuse, the phenomenon where a story may have a newsworthy component to it, but the coverage of it veers off into the trivial and inconsequential, which includes framing and omission as a major part of media propaganda.

With the advent of round-the-clock news coverage of daily world events, the time to cover important stories has maxed out, but coverage has in fact dropped precipitously in terms of corporate media coverage of relevant stories. Several media scholars and journalists, along with Project Censored, have argued that the news has become more Junk-addled and Abused than ever. In 1994, Jensen said, "We're suffering from news inflation—there seems to be more of it than ever before—and it isn't worth as much as it used to be."[6] Sadly, that seems even truer today than ever. There is almost an inverse correlation between media time on the 24/7 news outlets and actual news coverage as much of the "news" is now more opinion journalism, News Abuse, or just Junk Food News, and much of it is simply repeated around the clock. Further, it is not just that there is a plethora of Junk Food News across the airwaves and cyber optic cables, it is that this steady diet of trash crowds out what independent journalists are covering (i.e. what's really going on in the world yet is not widely broadcast to the public).

Our news cycle has become not unlike a 7-11: open for business 24/7, aisles overflowing with empty calories. Here are some of the lowlights of this past year's Junk Food News alongside what the corporate media could have been serving viewers if they were exercising sound news judgment and providing the public with information necessary for a healthy democracy.

I. JUNK FOOD NEWS FROM 2010–2011:
SHEEN TRUMPS PALIN: DON'T TOUCH
MY JUNK FOOD NEWS!

If you touch my junk . . . I'll have you arrested.
—John Tyner, US citizen protesting TSA screening techniques
at a San Diego, CA airport, which became a viral news
story that dominated the corporate media

Given that Junk Food News is now more ubiquitous than ever, we at Project Censored no longer rank "The Top Ten Junk Food Stories of the Year." The ranking, while amusing, is no longer a way to mark how far off course corporate news media have gone. Instead, we highlight some of the more egregious examples, oft in thematic fashion and sometimes tongue-in-cheek, to show our contempt for those in corporate media that still claim censorship doesn't happen and rather that news judgment is what determines coverage. Given the proliferation of Junk Food News and the sheer escalation of its coverage, it is clear that news judgment has gone horribly awry. Below are some of the past year's top stories Americans couldn't ignore if they tried, despite their complete inanity, and what corporate media could have been covering instead.

America's severance from reality is abetted by the corporate media's inundation of sensationalized trivialities, which grossly distort the context and relevance of many issues in the mainstream political discourse. Here are a few significant examples from the past year that could be summed up under the headline "Vicarious Anger Mismanagement: Insane is the New Fame."

Of Tiger Blood and Birthers

During the first four days of the corporate media's fanatical coverage of actor Charlie Sheen's drug-addled, tiger-blooded neurosis, four more US soldiers were killed in combat in Afghanistan. Yet, CNN only took notice[7] after a Facebook campaign initiated by a fellow soldier went viral, which pitted the coverage of fallen heroes against the celebrity addict. The campaign galvanized tens of thousands of people to write the following on their Facebook pages:

Charlie Sheen is all over the news because he's a celebrity drug addict, while Andrew Wilfahrt, 31; Brian Tabada, 21; Rudolph Hizon, 22; and Chauncy Mays, 25, are soldiers who gave their lives this week with no media mention. Please honor them by posting this as your status update.

In addition to nonstop updates about Charlie Sheen's "winning" streak, ABC's 20/20[8] and CNN's Piers Morgan[9] cleared hour-long time slots for Sheen to rant about his wild escapades and delusions of grandeur. *Good Morning America* also dedicated an entire show to broadcast live from Sheen's Hollywood home for a revelation not to be missed: his urine drug test results. MSNBC ran and reran a "documentary" of Sheen over several weekends.[10]

Showbiz veteran Charlie Sheen and his gaggle of euphemisms became quintessential brand name news, virally marketed by frothing media outlets worldwide. The public platform given to his breakdown resulted in his gaining a record-breaking 1 million Twitter followers in just one day, a feat which begat another onslaught of corporate news coverage.[11]

Meanwhile, less than two weeks later, the devastating earthquake and nuclear disaster in Fukushima caused a brief switch in coverage to focus on the tragedy. This was not to last long, though: once Donald Trump, billionaire real estate mogul and reality TV star, announced his presidential run and reignited the distracting "Birther" controversy about President Barack Obama's birth certificate, the corporate media unquestioningly followed suit, propelling the non-issue to the forefront of political discourse.[12] There were few discussions about the global implications of Fukushima's nuclear meltdown and the importance of pursuing sustainable energy alternatives. Instead of focusing on the dangers of the twenty-three nuclear reactors in the US designed almost identically to those in Fukushima,[13] the corporate media irresponsibly dwelled on Trump's crazed news "Birther" claims. Although the Fukushima crisis still loomed heavily, the media's focus shifted again, along with the American public's attention span.

As Charlie Sheen's downward spiral and Trump's "Birther" campaign reigned supreme in the corporate press, the US government continued its controversial bombing campaign against Libya unabated,[14] potentially in violation of international law—something the nation's media should likely address instead of the latest Sheen or Trump distractions. The obsession over such superficialities dilutes rational debate on American foreign policy, like the feasibility of spending forty million dollars a month in Libya[15] when our country is already racked with debt, or the sheer contradiction of bombing other countries for "humanitarian" reasons.

Palin Saturation Bomb

When the popular reality television show "Dancing With the Stars" approached its season finale, the airwaves became saturated with the devastating news that Bristol Palin's winning streak on the show might have been rigged by Tea Party enthusiasts. This meaningless topic wasn't just hot on *Entertainment Tonight* or TMZ, but was extensively covered in *Time*,[16] CNN,[17] the *Washington Post*,[18] NPR,[19] and a slew of other corporate media outlets, which seemed far more engrossed in the potential fraud than in the documented national election irregularities of the past decade. The cultural fixation on the Palin family's crazy antics—from Sarah Palin's misquotes of important facts of American history to Bristol's plastic surgery and pregnancy out of wedlock—props up the notion in the mainstream that the more insane one acts, the more fame one is awarded.

Thanks to the corporate media's crazed and yo-yo "news" coverage of everything Palin, she has turned into one of the most titillating household showbiz names in the US despite her potentially making a mockery of the political process in her quest for celebrity. Yet, her role in the establishment is an enigma—one day she's a politician, the next she's starring in a reality TV-show about her "down home" Alaskan lifestyle. The lines are blurred by the corporate news media, and the public becomes slack-jawed and Palinized as a result of this incessant matrix of Junk Food News and News Abuse.[20]

The week prior to the earth-shattering revelation that Bristol Palin might not be worthy of the "Dancing with the Stars" trophy, two important stories cycled through the corporate media with very little discussion about their political and societal repercussions. Robert Mueller, Director of the FBI, met with Google and Facebook[21] to coordinate an intensified push to expand online government wiretapping.

These extensions of online surveillance could effectively create a "chilling effect" among internet users, who might suppress or monitor their speech more carefully in fear of being penalized by the government.

Another story overshadowed by Palin melodrama was that of US Army Sergeant Chuck Luther.[22] Sergeant Luther gave heart-wrenching congressional testimony describing his experience of being tortured at the hands of fellow US Army officials. He was confined to a small closet and deprived of sleep for a month until he signed documents that made him ineligible to receive health benefits for wounds incurred during combat. This story could have exposed a systemic problem of abuse and censorship all the way up the military chain of command if it were properly covered and investigated.

The establishment press's version of political news exploits the personal lives of political players like Trump and Palin, instead of dissecting their stances on domestic or foreign policy. By sensationalizing inane trivialities and underreporting the real news, Junk Food News coverage grossly distorts the context and relevance of important issues in the political discourse. Whatever topics the corporate press deems worthy enough to cover at length will invariably skew the public's perception away from the issues that should be most relevant to their lives: food, water, shelter, jobs, and education in relation to so-called defense spending—not sex scandals, drug abuse, or "reality" television.

X-Rated Headlines: Junk Men Trash the Newshole

Weiner in general is overplayed, in every sense and phrase of the word.
—Jenn Strenger, a model to whom NFL player
Brett Favre texted X-rated photos[23]

Before 2010, the word "junk" mostly referred to "trash," or "something of little meaning, worth, or significance," according to family-friendly dictionaries. After everyman Jon Tyner recorded his confrontation with agents of Transportation Security Administration (TSA) at San Diego Airport over refusing to submit to a groin check, the word "junk" took on a new meaning, quite literally.[24] "Touch my junk, and I'll have you arrested," Tyner told TSA agents over a thirty-minute cell-phone recording which earned Tyner fifteen minutes of fame, as his story was featured on the *Huffington Post* and retold across the corporate media.[25] Tyner became a celebrity known as "The Junk Man," and was elevated by conservative columnist Charles Krauthammer to the level of a "folk hero," singing the "anthem of the modern man, the Tea Party Patriot, the late-life libertarian, the midterm-election voter," one fighting against "Obamacare" and other big government imposi-tions.[26] While "The Junk Man" provoked a newsworthy discussion about the invasiveness of TSA's security procedures, which included full-body scans and pat-downs for those who "opt-out," the coverage quickly veered into a circus of double entendre highlighting the fad of the catchphrase.[27] "So much for hiding your junk: now it's out of the closet, and on mouse pads and panties," reported CNN's Jeanne Moo, referencing a segment devoted to the catchphrase, which highlighted products and parodies inspired by it.[28] Moo's narration—filled with puns playing on the new definition of junk—was itself a parody of news: the report focused not on the security procedures, but on the efforts to cash in on the catchphrase and turn it into panties and other mass-manufactured junk (literally).

While Tyner may have made "junk" a household word, quarterback Brett Favre and New York State Representative Anthony Weiner made news for purportedly texting theirs to women. Much like Tiger Woods the year before,[29] superstar Favre found himself in hot water when the sports website *Deadspin* posted a video with recordings and an e-mail message which they claim were sent by Favre to model Jenn Sterger, culminating with an image of his penis. The post was viewed over five million times, shared on Facebook over thirty-two thousand times, and was covered in the corporate media by the Associated Press (AP), *USA Today*, and CNN, among others.[30] The *Huffington Post* posted a poll asking readers if they believed it was really Favre's "junk" (60 percent believed so).[31] The incident not only made Sterger famous, much like the women in the Tiger Woods scandal, but also pushed MTV to run a Public Service Announcement to discourage "teens from sending naughty photos."[32] Apparently, New York Representative Anthony Weiner did not watch MTV's PSAs on the dangers of sexting, as he was caught—like Favre—sharing illicit photos with women online.

"Weinergate" became the dubious title of the corporate news media's fascination with Weiner's exchange of messages and photos with various women online. According to Pew's Project for Excellence in Journalism, Weiner was "easily the top newsmaker" for the week of June 6 to 12, 2011, more than doubling the number of stories focused on President Barack Obama.[33] Pew called it "the scandal that launched a thousand puns," such as the *Philadelphia Daily News* front-page headline "Weiner Bares All."[34] Even Favre's "sexting victim" Sterger believed the coverage of Weiner was excessive, calling it "overplayed."

Tyner, Favre, and Weiner were turned into "Junk Men" by the corporate media, who couldn't get enough of their junk as news. Tyner's real gripe with the TSA became a punch line not only on comedy shows, but in real news coverage: Favre and Weiner's "sext scandals" turned the front page into the gossip page, turning headlines into punch lines themselves. "News outlets apparently could not resist relying on double entendres to describe the episode and some of the coverage had an inevitably giggling quality to it," Pew reported, showing readers that the news had become entertainment—literally. And in this way, valuable national airtime was degraded into the traditional meaning of junk: "something of little worth, meaning, or significance."

Weiner—the most overexposed "Junk Man" of the bunch—not only titillated the public, but in doing so, distracted them from serious news. Journalist Anne Landman highlighted the problem at the heart of the coverage, explaining that it "diverted attention from a huge number of truly important domestic and global issues, for example that the US is spending two billion dollars a week in Afghanistan while cutting desperately-needed programs and services here at home."[35] As the irrelevant tale played out, Americans were treated to less or no coverage of stories such as the Global Commission on Drug Policy declaring the war on drugs a failure,[36] 90 percent of Petraeus's captured "Taliban" turning out to be civilians,[37] outgoing CIA director Leon Panetta's claim that US troops will be asked to stay in Iraq after the 2011 deadline,[38] ThinkProgress's report on the $2.5 trillion that the Bush era tax cuts have cost the country,[39] or that one in four US hackers work for the FBI.[40] In short, "Weinergate"—and the rest of the Junk Men stories—have been a distraction offering nothing useful to people's lives while undermining the democratic process.

Forbes blogger Susannah Breslin claimed that the popularity of junk—in every sense of the word—is the fault of the American people. She argued that it is our sublimated urge to cheat on our own spouses that is to blame for the intense media coverage of sex scandals. "Americans are fascinated by political sex scandals because the politician is doing what Americans are doing but won't admit, or what they wish they were doing but won't say, and Americans, rather than confess their natural tendencies or sexual fantasies, would rather criticize those political figures who there, but for the grace of God, are doing what Americans wish they were doing."[41] Breslin might be right. In the age of Networked News, Americans are certainly complicit in sharing these stories on social media, helping to hype and promote gossip. At the same time, it is the establishment media's responsibility not to confuse gossip with news, or entertainment with information. But as we've said before at Project Censored, that's infotainment.

II. NEWS ABUSE AS PROPAGANDA: FRAMING THE MESSENGERS

The print media is dying—is anemic. Television no longer makes any serious attempt to report news in the sense that a traditional journalist would understand it. We are diverted by trivia, gossip, celebrity scandal, whether that is revolved around a lunatic fringe figure that wants to burn Korans, or Tiger Woods's sexual escapades, or John Edwards's meltdown. There are these constant narratives that dominate the news cycles and make it impossible for those of us who care about actually reporting news and investigating serious issues to even find a place any more.
—Journalist Chris Hedges, in an interview with *OpEd News*'s Rob Kall

News Abuse is a category created by former Project Censored director, Dr. Peter Phillips. Phillips noticed that there wasn't only Junk as news, but that serious news stories often took a turn into a trivial, even titillating direction that took away from the significance of a particular story. News Abuse, like most propaganda, often has some truth to it, and the information contained within may even be true. However, the story may not be as significant as the corporate media hypes it to be. In the process, the news media can lose sight of what a given story is really about, and can miss important facts along the way that may alter the entire meaning of the story. Lost in the moment, these News Abusers seldom go back to contextualize or add to previously reported stories which then linger in the public mind, albeit in a confused, distorted, or even outright erroneous way.[42]

Here are a few examples of some of the more important and lingering News Abuse stories of this past year, followed by an in-depth analysis and case study of News Abuse as propaganda concerning the public debate and framed news coverage of education reform.

The Sherrod Charade
The resignation of Shirley Sherrod over alleged racist comments made while addressing the NAACP

On July 19, 2010, Tea Party activist and conservative pundit and blogger, Andrew Breitbart, posted on his BigGovernment.com website an excerpt of a speech given to the NAACP by Georgia State Director of Rural Development for the United States Department of Agriculture, Shirley Sherrod.[43] The heavily edited video clip of the speech, in which comments made by Sherrod could be construed as racist, was picked up by FoxNews.com and spread across the blogosphere before airing on *The O'Reilly Factor* that same evening where host Bill O'Reilly called for her resignation. The story was picked up by all the major media outlets provoking condemnation from government officials, media pundits from the left and right, and even the president of the NAACP. Sherrod, who resigned that same day, was later exonerated when the video of the entire speech was vetted, resulting in apologies from many people involved, including President Obama. The mishandling of the story was so egregious that, in a rare mea culpa, even Bill O'Reilly of Fox News offered an apology to Ms. Sherrod for "not doing my homework."[44] In his apology, O'Reilly admitted that he depended upon Breitbart for "facts" without bothering to confirm them. This was an astounding confession given that Breitbart had been exposed as a dubious source.

In 2009, Breitbart demonstrated that he was a conservative political strategist operating in the blogosphere. That year he published propaganda videos against Democrat-supported ACORN.[45] A year later the attorney general's office in both California and Massachusetts discovered the videos to be "heavily" falsified and edited.[46] However, as in Sherrod's case, the lies behind the ACORN videos were uncovered after the damage had been done. O'Reilly and other complicit media figures clearly ignored Breitbart's standing as a right wing propagandist when they used his work in the Sherrod scandal.

In 2011, Breitbart demonstrated that he was not just a propagandist, but also addicted to airtime. On June 6, 2011, Anthony Weiner provided a teary-eyed apology for the sexual indiscretions Breitbart helped expose. Breitbart appeared at the event providing multiple interviews and speeches for reporters "before, after and during" Weiner's admission. He claimed he had been at a hotel nearby and showed up "to watch myself be vindicated."[47] Breitbart's comments insinuate that he was the one experiencing character assassination under unfair scrutiny from the Sherrod charade. However, he was anything but scrutinized as he smiled and glowed while the press treated him like a journalist instead of the political operative and propagandist that he is, based on the Sherrod and ACORN incidents, among others, discussed later in this chapter.

Ground Zero Intolerance
Major coverage of protests over the building of the "Ground Zero" mosque which was neither at "Ground Zero" nor strictly a mosque

In May 2010, the so-called "Ground Zero Mosque" set off a firestorm around the nation. The would-be controversy was started by conservative bloggers Pamela Geller and Robert Spencer. Both Geller and Spencer, founders of Stop Islamization of America, were given a platform on Andrew Breitbart's website.[48] Geller and Spencer spoke out against proposed plans for the building of an Islamic community center in downtown Manhattan. The center was to be built in an abandoned Burlington Coat Factory building, blocks from the former site of the World Trade Center towers.[49] Despite the building site being neither a mosque nor located at Ground Zero, Geller and Spencer dubbed the project the "Ground Zero Mosque."[50]

The corporate media ran with this title unquestioningly and intro-duced the issue as a controversial one, claiming that real debate needed to take place about what amounted to the right of a group or individual to buy or lease private property. Corporate media figures continued to claim that the so-called mosque was going up "at Ground Zero" despite its actually being two blocks away. *The Boston Globe* claimed "an Islamic center so close to Ground Zero is, not surpris-ingly, controversial"[51] while the *New York Post* reported, "A mosque rises over Ground Zero"[52] and Fox News reported on the rallies against the "proposed mosque *near* ground zero."[53] Defenders of the project fed into the negative discourse by constantly repeating the phrase "Ground Zero Mosque."[54]

This memetic fodder worked in favor of politicians looking to crit-icize President Obama, who had erroneously been characterized as a Muslim previously by many in the corporate press. In an egalitarian society like America, one that purports to have freedom of religion and respect for all people, whether or not one is a Muslim should have no bearing on public debate on private property development. Yet, the issue ignited controversy that was exploited for potential political gain. Leading up to the midterm elections, conservatives and Tea Party activists heavily promoted the "Ground Zero Mosque" meme, pro-voking several protests against plans for similar projects across the nation. Fox News demonstrated its keen bias in reporting when it reported on Obama's support for the mosque.[55] Obama did support the construction of the center, but FOX vilified him while censoring a key piece of information about its own parent company: that the second largest shareholder in News Corporation was Saudi Prince Al-Waleed bin Talal, who was helping to fund the Islamic Center.[56] His interest in the project would have been bad for the network's ratings so the focus remained on Obama, Democrats, and the effects of the "mosque" on the upcoming election.

This story demonstrates the danger that the current corporate media structure not only allows, but increasingly relies upon. The term "Ground Zero Mosque" was created by bloggers with a racist and xenophobic political agenda. The facts were falsified in their assess-ment since the "Ground Zero Mosque" lacked a mosque and was not at Ground Zero. The major media outlets, rather than do investigative work to uncover these distortions and report the facts, picked up the story and terms and reported them out of context, and as fact. Thus, Fox and other networks were able to use the story as a public opinion weapon against political rivals. They only told part of the story, one that benefited their interests and ignored the rest. The reporting was aimed to deceive, not inform the populace; it was propaganda. Unless people demand more from their media and shut off those who engage in manipulation, this News Abuse will likely continue.

Shooting the Messenger
WikiLeaks hysteria and Julian Assange as arch villain

On April 5, 2010, WikiLeaks released a classified US military video of Iraqi civilians and two Reuters news staff being gunned down by a US Apache helicopter in the suburb of New Baghdad.[57] This led to an outburst among US journalists and political figures, not necessarily about the content of the story, but about the leak itself. The corporate media talking heads focused on the legality of the release rather than question the legality of what the video and other WikiLeaks releases revealed about US policy and actions around the globe. It became a classic case of shoot the messenger.

Almost immediately, the media was calling for the death and/or trial of WikiLeaks head Julian Assange (he was even accused of treason by some even though he is not a citizen of the US).[58] A debate continues over whether the documents are innocuous or a national security threat. In March 2010, Pentagon officials claimed the cables were a threat, but in December 2010, they claimed they did not rise to the level of national security breaches.[59] Government officials are also divided over whether Assange's involvement was in fact illegal. Texas Congressman Ron Paul argued that Assange has the same protections as the media,[60] while Kentucky Senator Mitch McConnell and Vice President Joe Biden called Assange a "high tech terrorist."[61]

The corporate media did not oft investigate the WikiLeaks releases as a topic for debate. Instead, WikiLeaks itself and Assange were the focus, and were portrayed as criminals or worse. The content of the cables went mostly undiscussed during the assault on Assange. In December 2010, the corporate media reported on the sexual misconduct charges against Assange and neglected to mention inaccuracies of the report. However, Stockholm police reported that the whole scandal was nonsense; both women involved in the case stated that the sex was consensual, and the charges amounted to having sex without a condom. It should also be noted that Assange's chief accuser has ties to possible CIA funded anti-Castro front groups so it wasn't just some random person with whom he had been involved (and the accuser's background should raise other questions the corporate media did not ask).[62] Without mentioning these important details, the media continued to focus on Assange and the dubious charges against him while ignoring the content of WikiLeaks cables.

The case against WikiLeaks exemplifies the US government's vulnerability to exposure of wrongdoing by brave and hardworking investigative journalists. The corporate media are not those people. Instead, they sided with most government officials and took dubious police reports at face value because doing so was easier than researching the cables' content and assessing their impact. They tried to lynch Assange instead of assail potential wrongdoings exposed in the WikiLeaks documents. The treatment of WikiLeaks exhibits the media's dissidence with the concept of investigative journalism. WikiLeaks, which provides actual documentation of government behavior and abuse, has been vilified, while Andrew Breitbart and others who peddle smut and lies are hailed as examples of good journalism by the corporate media.

As chapter 1 of this volume explained, the US government has been pushing for internet surveillance and censorship. The WikiLeaks issue, when reported on erroneously, or only partially, provides a justification for internet censorship in the name of silencing whistleblowers to protect national security. This ignores the advancements to the democratic process that whistleblowers have historically provided. Daniel Ellsberg and the Pentagon Papers, which exposed the lies concerning US policy in Vietnam in the 1960s, exemplify this contribution.

In June 2011, as the Pentagon Papers were officially released by the government, Ellsberg explained, "What we need released this month are the Pentagon Papers of Iraq and Afghanistan (and Pakistan, Yemen, and Libya)."[63] With the possibilities for free speech available on the internet, it is becoming increasingly harder for the US government to operate in the shadows. This vulnerability has propelled the

Obama administration to prosecute more whistleblowers than all other presidents combined. He and those around him can only get away with prosecuting whistleblowers like Assange (as Nixon tried to do with Ellsberg, but failed) if the people are complicit. The media-driven game of shooting the messenger is an underhanded attempt to sway public opinion against Assange while the facts and details of the WikiLeaks cables go largely unprobed. The fact that the so-called news media in the US are more interested in shooting the messenger than in protecting whistleblowers shows clearly that the Fourth Estate is merely a propaganda arm of the state.

III. CASE STUDY OF NEWS ABUSE: FRAMING, PROPAGANDA, AND CENSORSHIP

Private Enemy #1: Public Workers

"Educator and scholar Adam Bessie made clear just how devoid of thought are claims that schools should be protected from responsible belt-tightening," writes American Enterprise Institute (AEI) resident education scholar Frederick Hess. Hess was writing in reference to the coauthor of this chapter, specifically a piece he wrote for the *Daily Censored* blog.[64] Hess, an intellectual leader in the corporate education reform movement,[65] personally attacked Bessie in direct reply to a critique he wrote of a cover story in the *Oakland Tribune*. The story used Hess as an authoritative, non-partisan source, without explaining that AEI is a neoconservative organization that claims, "The government's authority to tax and regulate represents a growing encroachment on the private sector."[66] Bessie quoted this line in his blog and argued that Hess's association with AEI should be fully revealed so readers would know his ideological orientation. Bessie wrote, "I am not saying that Hess, nor the AEI should be avoided, but rather the reporter should report to us what their background is—for complete disclosure."[67] In response to a call for transparency, Hess—who received $500,000 in grant money from the Bill and Melinda Gates Foundation for AEI's advocacy[68]—dubbed Bessie, a community college English instructor, a "vapid champion of the status quo."

Hess's ad hominem attack on Bessie, however, has become the "status quo" of political rhetoric in the last year, particularly in the debates on public education, but also across the policy spectrum in the corporate media. Public workers—teachers, firefighters, police officers, and especially their unions—have been depicted as enemies of prosperity and public welfare, feeding greedily on benefits while the "rest of us" starve. This was illustrated quite literally in a popular cartoon showing a gigantic pig with "UNION" emblazoned across its chest telling a skeletal taxpayer to "tighten his belt."[69]

More concerning is that public workers have been cast as villains in the wake of economic collapse, not only by conservative think tanks and political cartoonists, but by the corporate (so-called) mainstream media in a broader sense. Even public supported radio KQED, of San Francisco, ran an op-ed lambasting lazy Department of Motor Vehicles (DMV) employees.[70] In early August 2010, the *New York Times*'s Ron Lieber accurately predicted, "There's a class war coming to the world of government pensions."[71] And sure enough, as a new class of Republicans began their term in January 2011, public workers—and their supposedly excessive benefits—gained considerable coverage. The once vague term "public employee" burst into the public consciousness as a new pejorative, while the fiscal conservative buzzword "austerity" was billed as the only solution to economic woes. The latter term was the number one most searched word on Merriam-Webster online last year.[72]

In corporate media coverage over the past year, public workers lost the class war that Lieber predicted, and became victims of persistent and systemic factual distortion and villainizing. Out of all public workers, however, teachers and their unions have fared the worst in the last year. They have been subject to relentless mythmaking, largely underwritten or influenced by billionaires such as Bill Gates, that falsely portrays the educational system as irreparably broken, with bad teachers as the primary cause and the free-market as the only viable solution, and ignoring, misrepresenting, maligning, or explicitly censoring alternative perspectives and dissent. So while the worthy topic of public education earned a great deal of coverage in the corporate media, it clearly qualifies as News Abuse because the issue itself is distorted—framed and cast as propaganda for free-market ideologues under a rubric of open debate in a supposed free press.

The Recurring Myth of the Welfare Queen

In 1976, on a failed campaign to the White House, Ronald Reagan coined one of his enduring linguistic legacies: the "Welfare Queen," a mythical inner-city resident who wastes the public's hard-earned money on "welfare Cadillacs" and other luxuries she can't afford and doesn't deserve. The misleading term suggests the false notion that welfare abuse is rampant, that money spent on social services is going to luxuries rather than necessities. While nearly thirty-five years old, the image of the Welfare Queen remains as strong as ever and Reagan's battle against her lives on.[73] However, now she has traded her Cadillac for a fire engine, a "Cadillac" health care plan, and a pension, as Jonathan Cohn presciently pointed out in "Why Public Employees Are the New Welfare Queens" in the *New Republic*, shortly after Lieber's *New York Times* article.[74] In the same way that Reagan characterized those on welfare as cheating the taxpayers out of their hard-earned money, so have public employees been framed, accused of receiving excessively generous handouts from the public. In several cases where some academics at public institutions fought against these attacks, they were targeted by conservative media activists and the Republican Party.

The mythmaking success of Reagan's Welfare Queen is critical to understanding how public workers have been portrayed as "public enemies in some way," as an AP story claimed "some people" saw it.[75] The Welfare Queen—a Chicago black woman cheating the social service system—"was a symbol of everything that was supposedly wrong with welfare," explained University of California, Berkeley, cognitive linguist George Lakoff in an analysis of the term. While this example symbolized the evils of the welfare state, the actual Welfare Queen, whom Reagan claimed "has eighty names, thirty addresses, twelve Social Security cards," did not exist; even though the "media dutifully tried to find her . . . there never was such a person." Even though Reagan never explicitly called the Welfare Queen black, he nonetheless invented a powerful stereotype that played the political race/class card, exploiting a fictional denizen of Chicago who "came to stand for a whole category of welfare recipients." Reagan's Welfare Queen worked because it fit existing cultural stereotypes—or frames—

about those on welfare. Lakoff further argues that Reagan presented his made-up example as a typical case, and because it received so much press, the Welfare Queen became very real to the public, even if she did not really exist. As a matter of fact, "the majority of welfare recipients are white and few own vehicles of any kind." This fact didn't matter, as Reagan's Welfare Queen furthered the myth that most people on welfare are black and cheating the system.[76]

Public employees have now become mythologized in the same way Welfare Queens were almost three decades ago. In the last year, "public employee" has become a bad word, a symbol of greed and undeserved excess, one that is responsible for our crumbling budgets, and thus, our own struggling economy. An NPR listener shares in a "Perspectives" segment on San Francisco's public radio station KQED an anecdote of lazy DMV workers which, like the Welfare Queen, is supposed to be typical of all public workers. "There is only one person serving a long line of customers. As I wait, I watch her coworkers, who should be helping me, eat birthday cake. . . . It seems in the eyes of public employees, my needs come second—after cake." Just like the Welfare Queen, this single instance of nameless and anecdotally related bad service becomes a stand-in for how public employees are lazy and disinterested in serving the public, and are receiving benefits they don't deserve while thumbing their noses at the public in true let-them-eat-cake fashion.

Like the Welfare Queen, the term public employee allows negative stereotypes of public workers to flourish. The perfectly ambiguous term sounds more like a faceless, heartless bureaucrat than a public servant risking her or his life for the common good, as is the case with firefighters or police. The term strips away the humanity and the nobility of a public worker, replacing it with an uninspiring, and certainly unrespectable, blandness. Further, by using the term "employee," rather than "worker," or even specific job descriptions like "firefighter," any associations with work or labor are eliminated; it's much easier to visualize a lazy employee than a lazy worker or an undeserving firefighter. And thus, with the vague term "public employee," the NPR "Perspectives" segment is able to use the fallacy of overgeneralization via a couple of DMV workers as a symbol of all government workers, implying that this one instance (which may or may not be real) symbolizes the work that firefighters, police, and teachers perform across the system. And this is aired on public broadcasting, not only in the corporate media.[77]

Media coverage also tends to add to the perception that public workers are somehow welfare cases that the rest of the taxpayers support (even though public workers clearly pay taxes). "The media have repeatedly targeted public employees by suggesting that the public dislikes their supposed generous pay and benefits," though numerous polls demonstrate that the public tends to side with employees, as the liberal group *Media Matters for America* illustrated with a thorough review of corporate media coverage.[78] A popular 2011 article in the Associated Press, cited in the *Media Matters* analysis, vividly shows the mischaracterization of public workers. The following passage, in particular, reinforces distorted notions of public workers' compensation. "At its heart, the issue is this: Some public workers get a sweet deal compared to other workers. And it's taxpayers who pay for it. That's set off resentment in a time when economic doldrums have left practically everyone *tightening their belts*."[79] While the reporter uses the phrase "public worker," he also uses fiscally conservative language nearly identical to the political cartoon mocking unions when he references "belt-tightening." Further, while the reporter acknowledges that polls show two in five Americans are not on the employees' side, it is nonetheless the focus of the report, titled "Anger brews over government workers benefits." The title—and the article itself—all but ignores the two-thirds who are not angry, implying that the anger is far more widespread than it actually is. This is called framing, and this particular form, propagandistic in its nature, is a form of News Abuse.

The aforementioned AP story reinforces this distorting frame by giving disproportionate coverage to studies and scholars that claim public workers are compensated on a greater scale than private sector workers.[80] For instance, while the reporter interviewed locals in Wisconsin, he did not refer to an April 2010 study conducted by two University of Wisconsin economics professors, which found that the opposite is in fact true: that state and local workers make less, overall, than those in the private sector. "This recession calls for equal sacrifice, but long-term patterns indicate that the average compensation of state and local employees is not excessive," the authors conclude.

"Indeed, if the goal is to compensate public and private workforces in a comparable manner, then the data do not call for reductions in average state and local wages and benefits."[81] Additionally, two weeks before the AP story, the Economic Policy Institute released a study that "indicates that state and local government employees in Wisconsin are not overpaid."[82] Neither of these studies was mentioned by AP, nor any study that contradicts the majority of the interview subjects who state, as undisputed fact, that public worker benefits are excessively generous in comparison to private sector worker benefits.

Professors Get a Lesson in "Advanced Thuggery"

President of the National Historical Association William Cronon was personally targeted for critiquing Governor Scott Walker's attempt to end public employee collective bargaining rights. Cronon, a distinguished professor of history, geography, and environmental studies at the University of Wisconsin, Madison, posted a blog and published an op-ed in the *New York Times* in which he placed Gov. Walker's effort to diminish public union rights in a greater historical context of the rise of conservative thinking since the late 1960s.[83] In his blog, Cronon attributes this success to the well-funded conservative intellectual infrastructure, especially the American Legislative Exchange Council (ALEC), a free-market organization that drafts "model" bills which conservative legislatures use around the country. "Each year, close to 1,000 bills, based at least in part on ALEC Model Legislation, are introduced in the states. Of these, an average of 20 percent become law," ALEC's website claims, a fact Cronon also pointed out.[84]

Following his blog and *New York Times* essay, the Wisconsin Republican Party filed an Open Records Request to access his e-mails, requesting "copies of all e-mails into and out of Prof. William Cronon's state e-mail account" which referenced terms like "Republican, Scott Walker, collective bargaining . . . rally, [and] union." The search also asked for names of Republican legislators. [85] Further, The Mackinac Center, a Michigan based conservative think tank born of the GOP political turnaround Cronon describes, filed a similar Freedom of Information Act request for the labor studies departments at Wayne State University, University of Michigan, and Michigan State University.[86] "Legally, Republicans may be within their right," *New York Times* columnist Paul Krugman observed. "But there's a clear chilling effect when scholars know that they may face witch hunts whenever they say things the GOP doesn't like." And while Cronon will be able to withstand the assault, he claims that "less eminent and established researchers won't just become reluctant to act as concerned citizens, weighing in on current debates; they'll be deterred from even doing research on topics that might get them in trouble."[87]

This "chilling effect" goes against the principles of academic freedom, part of the bedrock of a vibrant democracy, like a free press. Also, this First Amendment intimidation came far sooner than Krugman might have predicted. Around the same time as the Cronon controversy, two labor studies professors at the University of Missouri, St. Louis, and the University of Missouri, Kansas City, were targeted by Andrew Breitbart's conservative *Big Government* blog. "We're going to take on teachers next, we're going to go after the teachers, the union organizers," Breitbart told Sean Hannity on Fox News.[88] Shortly thereafter, Breitbart released videos of the professors purportedly promoting violence, which he titled "advanced thuggery."[89] Much like with Shirley Sherrod (discussed earlier in this chapter), it turned out that Breitbart's video of her speech was edited to take parts of it out of context. Sherrod was made to appear to be saying the opposite of what she really was, just as the professors were made to look like they were supporting the use of violence in protests, which is not at all what they were advocating. Gail Hackett, provost of the Kansas City campus, released a statement denouncing the videos: "From the review completed to date, it is clear that edited videos posted on the internet depict statements from the instructors in an inaccurate and distorted manner by taking their statements out of context and reordering the sequence in which those statements were actually made so as to change their meaning."[90] In other words, the Breitbart videos were doctored—they were propaganda passed on as news and just another form of News Abuse.

Despite the fact that the film was factually inaccurate, adjunct professor Don Giljum resigned under what he claimed was pressure from his Dean, who in turn had been told by "higher ups" to get his resignation—much like the Sherrod incident in the federal government. Gilgum, in an interview with *Inside Higher Education*, described the chilling effect of Breitbart's attack: "Teachers here are no longer going to be able to express comments, theories or counter-positions or make statements to force students to push back and critically challenge the comments and statements of the teacher."[91] In that type of educational climate, it seems critical thinking will be impossible to teach, and free speech will be difficult to encourage inside the classroom where it is supposed to be modeled as a great American virtue.

The Myth of the Bad Teacher

In the 2011 Columbia Pictures film *Bad Teacher*, Cameron Diaz is the titular awful instructor, slouched behind her desk with dark glasses covering her sleeping eyes, who "doesn't give an 'F,'" according to the tagline. In the preview, she gets motivated to teach only when she can get a bonus for test scores so that she can buy breast implants to impress the new substitute teacher played by Justin Timberlake.[92] Diaz's Bad Teacher is much like the Welfare Queen or the Public Employee: it is no one specifically, but rather a sort of free-floating, ill-defined stereotype, one who is an inept, uncaring, and self-interested bureaucrat waiting for an oversized pension—one not only disinterested in students, but actively engaged in standing in the way of student achievement, rather than encouraging it. Comedy Central's *The Daily Show* captured the bad teacher stereotype hilariously, as faux-reporter Samantha Bee showed off the "luxurious" apartments of middle-class public school teachers.[93] Following the 2010 release of the education documentary *Waiting for Superman,* however, this bad teacher and her protector, the Evil Union, were no laughing matter. These lazy, self-interested, poorly trained, and overpaid public workers appeared to be endemic, and primarily responsible for the state of ruin in public schools—at least according to persistent and consistently misleading coverage in the corporate (and even some independent) media.

Waiting for Superman (WFS) promotes the myth of the Bad Teacher, the Broken School, and the Evil Union most vividly and forcefully. The promotional poster for *WFS* looks like the set for the zombie TV series *The Walking Dead,* as an innocent, uniformed child sits attentively at her desk amidst a bombed-out wasteland, the undead surely waiting just outside the frame, hungry for her youthful brain. This apocalyptic imagery is reinforced by the dire title—Superman, after all, is only called in to save the world from crashing asteroids or malevolent plots by arch-nemesis Lex Luthor. And to make this end-times comic book real, disaster documentarian Davis Guggenheim, famous for the global warming documentary *An Inconvenient Truth*, was tapped to direct the film. Just as *An Inconvenient Truth* highlighted the emergency of global warming, so did *WFS* seek to highlight the disaster happening in American public schools. AEI's Hess wrote that *WFS* "chronicl[ed] the travails of five students seeking spots in heavily oversubscribed charter schools."[94] The "superheroes" of the film are charter school advocates like Geoffrey Canada, and "teacher's unions are big screen villains," as a review in the conservative *Weekly Standard* observed.[95] The head of the American Federation of Teachers, Randi Weingarten, is painted not just as a villain, but as "something of a foaming satanic beast," a reviewer from *Variety* magazine noted.[96] A conservative blogger's post on Weingarten depicts a devil, and added "teacher union leaders have approximately the same level of credibility on education reform as tobacco executives have on cancer research."[97] *WFS*, in short, pits Bad Teachers and Evil Unions against education reformers and engaged parents trying to save innocent children, in an epic battle worthy of an action-packed comic book. The script for this comic book version of education reform comes straight from the pages of neoconservative educational philosophy.

Hess observes that *WFS* has been powerful in calling attention to the free-market reforms he advocates at AEI: "[*WFS*] drew rave reviews, star-studded premières, and breathless talk of a new era of reform. While the American Federation of Teachers and a handful of liberal publications tut-tutted the film's critical portrayal of teacher's unions, its clarion call for change has been embraced by opinion leaders across the political spectrum."[98] President Obama had the children from *WFS* visit the White House,[99] Roger Ebert initially gave it a thumbs up,[100] and former sitcom star Alyssa Milano tweeted the film's greatness to all of her 1.5 million followers.[101]

Despite the powerful emotional pull of the film, scholars on both sides of the political spectrum have serious concerns about some of its questionable factual content. Diane Ravitch, the Secretary of Education under President George H. W. Bush, former supporter of President

George W. Bush's "No Child Left Behind" policy, and author of the best-selling book *The Death and Life of the Great American School System*, calls *WFS* "propagandistic" in an extensive review of the film. The film, she argues, maligns public schools and places charter schools on a pedestal through selective reporting of facts. The children—and the charter schools they try to attend—are supposed to present a typical view of American students, and America's public and charter schools. Yet, "No successful public school teacher or principal or superintendent appears in the film; indeed there is no mention of any successful public school, only the incessant drumbeat on the theme of public school failure," Ravitch observes. Further, she claims that the film oversells the success of charter schools. *WFS* "quietly acknowledges" a study that finds only one in five get "amazing" results, which means performance superior to public schools; yet, it doesn't acknowledge that in the very same study, 37 percent of charter schools are considered worse than their public counterparts. Further, *WFS* paints the charter schools portrayed in the film in a more flattering light than the evidence suggests: even though Canada's school purports to have "amazing results," the film neglects to note that in its 2010 tests, "60 percent of fourth-grade students in one of his charter schools were not proficient in reading, nor were 50 percent in another." The film also neglected to point out that "Canada kicked out his entire first class of middle school students when they didn't get good enough test scores to satisfy his board of trustees." Finally, even as the film maligns unions as an impediment to school reform, it applauds Finland as a country "the US should emulate." Yet the documentary neglects to tell viewers that Finland has a "completely unionized workforce."[102] Even Hess—who would no doubt disagree with Ravitch on many of these points—agrees that the film has created a "goopy groupthink symbiosis with the Paramount marketing operation," which left him feeling that "large doses of cynicism are in order."[103]

Still, despite the fact that two influential scholars on the left and right of the education debate called for further exploration of the claims made in the film, *WFS* met with almost no criticism in the corporate or so-called liberal media, as a result of an enormous, exceptionally well funded and strategized marketing campaign. Thus, *WFS* was able to perpetuate negative stereotypes about public schools and their teachers, and to pave over any dissenting opinions.

WFS was more than a film: it was a corporate media movement heavily cross-promoted across highly influential platforms on the air, in print, and online. *WFS's* end-times vision of education was brought to life on *Oprah* in a TV segment cross-promoting "The Shocking State of Our Schools,"[104] in which Oprah Winfrey interviewed Guggenheim, then Washington, DC, superintendent and icon of the free-market reform movement Michelle Rhee, and billionaire Bill Gates, whose Bill and Melinda Gates Foundation gave Paramount a two million dollar grant to market the film, and has spent hundreds of millions focused on the reforms it documented.[105] In the program, Oprah claims that the students featured in the film are "eager to get an education," but have to fight their way through a "system riddled with ineffective teachers." NBC stalwart Tom Brokaw echoed Oprah in a report for *NBC Nightly News*. Promoting the NBC Special Program *Education Nation*, Brokaw broadened the bad teacher motif to more of a systematic educational conspiracy that ensured students wouldn't learn.[106] Brokaw asked a new teacher if she had met resistance from "the teacher establishment," authoritatively confirming to any naysayers that a) there is one, and b) it consists of "unions" and "veteran teachers." Brokaw, echoing *WFS*, stated as fact that unions were impeding students and contributing to problems in education.[107] According to the *Education Nation* press release, the program was promoted for an entire week on NBC programs *Meet the Press, Nightly News, Today, Your Business*, as well as on network affiliate stations MSNBC (partially controlled by Bill Gates's Microsoft), CNBC, Telemundo, MSNBC.com, and NBCLearn.com.

It is not surprising that *WFS* gained such mass attention while providing a platform for free-market education reform as it was heavily financed by billionaires invested in the very reforms applauded in the film.[108] In an e-mail conversation with coauthor of this chapter Adam Bessie, Ravitch explained the complex web of interests of those who financed the film, which included several free market think tanks and organizations, but also, and perhaps especially, Microsoft's Bill Gates. Gates seems to have exerted the most influence in pushing the national dialogue toward focusing on bad teachers and broken schools. The Bill and Melinda Gates Foundation helped subsidize *Education Nation*, which Gates appeared in. Brokaw interviewed Gates but did not challenge the corporate reform ideas or present any opposing views.[109] Similarly, a *Time* magazine editorial promoting the film, "'Waiting for Superman': Education Reform Isn't Easy," was written by an educational policy analyst whose blog is underwritten in part by The Bill and Melinda Gates Foundation.[110]

Gates's and other billionaires' PR investment in *WFS* has paid off, as the myth of the Bad Teacher, the Broken School, and the Evil Union blanket the corporate and even so-called liberal media—CNN, the *Huffington Post*, *The Colbert Report*, *Oprah*, and *Real Time with Bill Maher*—have all uncritically repeated the claims made in *WFS*, as *Daily Censored* blogger, veteran teacher, and education professor Paul Thomas points out in his numerous essays analyzing media coverage on education.[111] Thomas observes that Rhee and other *WFS* and *Education Nation* supporters made a "celebrity tour" of the corporate media, where promoted the claims from the film without serious analysis.[112] Even NPR, which Republicans routinely attempt to defund for being too liberal, "offered Rhee an unchallenged forum for spouting common sense without a shred of evidence."[113]

WFS, in conjunction with heavy promotional support, created a largely uncritical media circus that ended up promoting stereotypes about public school teachers, unions, the education system, and even charter schools themselves. In his satiric review of the film, AEI's Hess snidely jokes, "Happily, my earlier skepticism is gone. Much like Winston in *1984*, I now feel pleasantly persuaded. You see, the peer pressure finally got to me and, just hours ago, I walked out of the theater with my eyes, finally, wide open."[114] And as the "goopy groupthink" faded, as the "celebrity tour" ended, and critical reviews of the film's factually distorted arguments by scholars like Diane Ravitch and others began to come out, film critic Roger Ebert—who had originally given the film a "thumbs up," took back his review, writing on Twitter: "Why maybe 'Waiting for Superman' wasn't all that it seemed. If I'd known, my review would have been different."[115]

Corporate Deformatory School:
The New Rhetoric of "Productivity"

Sitting alongside Hess at an AEI session entitled "The New Normal:

Doing More With Less," Secretary of Education Arne Duncan gave a speech on how to make public education work in tight budgetary times. During the course of the speech, Duncan said "productivity" seventeen times and "learning" five times.[116] Indeed, Duncan's speech at a neoconservative think tank reveals a "New Normal," where the language and policies of the corporate world and the free-market are being proposed as the only solutions to what ails education. Duncan's corporate pose is unsurprising, as his boss President Obama has been applauding the corporate reform message, according to Hess. "Interviewed in October on the *Today Show*, President Obama seemed to be channeling a generation of conservative education analysts in stating bluntly that more money absent reform won't do much to improve public schools."[117] And the "corporative takeover of American schools," as Paul Thomas calls it,[118] has gone all but unchallenged in most media, as a result of powerful advocacy not only from the Obama administration but three billionaire venture philanthropists.[119]

In the last year, education reform has become a euphemism for a very specific philosophy: a free-market one, which Fred Hiatt of the *Washington Post* called "the Obama-Duncan-Gates-Rhee philosophy of education reform."[120] As Joanne Barkan observes in a comprehensive investigative report on private spending in education policies, reform has come to mean "choice, competition, deregulation, accountability, and data-based decision-making."[121] In other words, this means supporting policies that either privatize public education, or turn public education into a simulation of the private sector. This includes, as Barkan shows, "charter schools, high-stakes standardized testing for students, merit pay for teachers whose students improve their test scores, firing teachers and closing schools when scores don't rise adequately, and longitudinal data collection on the performance of every student and teacher."[122] In other words, the "Obama-Duncan-Gates-Rhee" education reform movement means pushing public schools from a model of cooperation to one of competition, as Ravitch points out, "turning schools into a marketplace where the consumer is king."[123]

The "Big Three"—the Bill and Melinda Gates Foundation, the Walton Family Foundation, and the Eli and Edythe Broad Foundation—have invested billions in trying to turn schools into a marketplace, and tens of millions in advocacy to influence national policy, according to

Barkan.[124] The editors of the Hoover Institution's education journal *Education Next* agree: "Prodded by Bill Gates, Eli Broad, and other veteran private-sector reformers, the Obama administration has lent unexpectedly forceful support to such causes as common standards, better assessments, charter schools, merit pay, refurbished teacher preparation, and the removal of ineffective instructors."[125] In her research, Barkan found that Gates and Broad joined forces, "funding a $60 million campaign to get both political parties to address the foundations' version of education reform." In their annual report, the Broad Foundation claimed that "the stars have aligned" with the election of President Obama and Secretary Duncan. And according to Barkan, the foundations got a return on their investment, as the Obama administration's education plan titled "Race to the Top," "came straight from the foundations' playbook, including testing-based accountability and charter schools."[126] This should not be surprising, as Duncan, before coming to the White House, referred to his work with Gates in the Chicago school system as a "partnership."[127]

In much the same way, "The Billionaire Boys Club" (as Ravitch has called them), has heavily invested in public advocacy, working to sway media coverage toward corporate education reform, often covertly. According to the *New York Times*, the Gates Foundation has spent seventy-eight million dollars on education advocacy, which includes a vast intellectual and communication infrastructure. "It's easier to name which groups Gates doesn't support than to list all of those they do, because it's just so overwhelming," noted a graduate student who had studied the Gates Foundation's advocacy in the article.[128] This funding has gone to support research, the major education publication *Education Week*, proxy bloggers, and has gone to develop a Koch Brother's-style Astroturf organization called Teach Plus, which, according to its website, supports teachers in writing op-eds, and creating and influencing policy.[129] In one striking example covered by the *New York Times*, Teach Plus members spoke against tenure, describing "themselves simply as local teachers who favored school reform," without mentioning their affiliation or training. Teach Plus, which has received over four million dollars in grants from the Gates Foundation claims that "none of Teach Plus work in Indianapolis is supported by Gates funding."[130] (Within days, this statement disappeared from its website). As the *New York Times* article reports, "Few policy makers, reporters, or members of the public who encounter advocates like Teach Plus or pundits like Frederick Hess of the American Enterprise Institute realize they are underwritten by the foundation."[131]

Hess—a recipient of a half million dollars from the Gates Foundation—also acknowledges how the influence of educational venture philanthropists like Gates works to dull or silence criticism. Both Barkan and Ravitch cite Hess's book *With the Best of Intentions: How Philanthropy is Reshaping K-12 Education,* in which he finds that "[A]cademics, activists, and the policy community live in a world where philanthropists are royalty—where philanthropic support is often the ticket to tackling big projects, making a difference, and maintaining one's livelihood."[132] Because academics can only take on projects with money, Hess contends, they are hesitant to bite the hand that may feed them. "Not a single book has been published that has questioned their education strategies," Ravitch paraphrases Hess.[133] Further, Hess found that the corporate media also avoided criticism of the "Big Three's" educational advocacy: in a study from 1995 to 2005 of the *New York Times,* the *Los Angeles Times,* the *Washington Post,* the *Chicago Tribune, Newsweek,* and Associated Press, Hess found that there were "thirteen positive articles for every critical account."[134] Hess himself acknowledges that he feels "constrained" by taking money from Gates: "There can be an exquisite carefulness about how we're going to say anything that could reflect badly on a foundation." Hess concludes in the *New York Times* article that "everyone is implicated" in what he called, in *The Best of Intentions,* an "amiable conspiracy of silence."[135]

Diane Ravitch and the "Conspiracy of Silence"

"Diane Ravitch is in denial and she is insulting all of the hardworking teachers, principals and students all across the country who are proving her wrong every day," Secretary of Education Duncan told *Newsweek* senior editor Jonathan Alter. The interview, in an editorial blog which attempted to debunk Ravitch, was titled "Don't Believe the Critics: Education Reform Works."[136] Alter published the blog for Bloomberg News, a media organization owned by billionaire New York Mayor Michael Bloomberg, who instituted "the Obama-Duncan-Gates-Rhee philosophy of education reform" in New York City. In the blog—and another *Newsweek* editorial—Alter applauded the reforms made in New York, the very same reforms Ravitch spends a chapter critiquing in *The Life and Death of the Great American School System*.[137] This coordinated attack on Ravitch illustrates what happened when she broke the "conspiracy of silence," around the free market education reform movement. In the last year, Ravitch was ignored, censored, and when given a voice, publicly flogged for critiquing the policies heralded in *WFS*.

Ravitch's *The Life and Death of the Great American School System* is the product of what she calls an "intellectual crisis."[138] An education historian who studied trends in American education over the last hundred years, Ravitch was a fierce advocate of free-market reforms, worked for George H. W. Bush as Secretary of Education, promoted George W. Bush's "No Child Left Behind" (NCLB) policy, and helped found the Koret Task Force at the Hoover Institution. "Like many others . . . I was attracted to the idea that the market would unleash innovation and bring greater efficiencies to education," she says.[139] Ravitch had her "epiphany around NCLB in November 2006" at an AEI conference focused on NCLB: "I went to a meeting . . . to hear a series of studies of how NCLB was working. . . . They were not, and at the end of the day, I concluded (and said publicly) that NCLB was not working."[140] She began to see the free-market movement she supported as another one of the ill-fated education fads that she had studied throughout her career, and found, "I had drunk too deeply of the elixir that promised a quick fix to intracticable [sic] problems. I too had jumped aboard a bandwagon."[141]

With *The Life and Death* she jumped off the bandwagon, and was consequently no longer welcome on the national stage. In *Education Nation*, "she was represented in a thirty-second-long clip, and otherwise completely blocked from participating. *Waiting For Superman* director Davis Guggenheim refused to share the stage with her on any program," Anthony Cody, a veteran urban public school teacher observed in his blog for *Education Week*.[142] Pop musician John Legend played a far more prominent role in the program on education reform than did Ravitch, as did the CEO of Netflix.[143]

Further, in an e-mail conversation with coauthor Bessie, Ravitch claimed that she was censored from debating free-market reformers in the corporate media. Ravitch claimed, "My book publisher has tried repeatedly, but I can't get onto any of the national TV shows to challenge Gates, Rhee, et al."[144] Further, Ravitch noted: "I have published many, many op-eds in the *New York Times*, but for the past year, my editor rejected every idea, proposal, suggestion. So I stopped offering, realizing that the door was closed."[145]

Months after the PR blitz of *WFS*, Ravitch broke through the corporate media blockade with an appearance on *The Daily Show*, NPR, and finally the *New York Times*.[146] In her op-ed, "Waiting for a Miracle School," Ravitch claimed that both President Obama and New York Mayor Bloomberg inflated the results of the studies they cited[147] in order to better promote the success of their free-market reforms. Ravitch went on to discuss the studies in more detail, providing readers with a more complete picture of the research. Arne Duncan and Jonathan Alter made scathing critiques immediately following Ravitch's op-ed. Both attempted to discredit Ravitch's work and her personally. Alter claimed, "She's the education world's very own Whittaker Chambers, the famous communist turned strident anti-communist of the 1940s," and accused her of using "phony empiricism." Yet, just two weeks before, Ravitch was awarded the Daniel Patrick Moynihan Prize of the American Academy of Political and Social Science. The Board of Directors includes esteemed social scientists from Harvard and Yale and the award is given to those "who champion the use of informed judgment to advance the public good . . . while contributing to the civility of public discourse and pursuing a bipartisan approach to society's most pressing problems."[148] And while AEI's Hess thinks Ravitch is misguided in her analysis, he nonetheless appears to agree with her concerns that proponents of corporate reform—like Duncan—may be "overpromising" on the results of these education policies.[149] In a 2010 essay, Hess even foreshadows Ravitch's 2011 *New York Times* essay by suggesting that reform proponents, when faced with criticism, may "oversell ideas as miracle cures."[150]

In the last year, when the vital issue of public education finally came to the forefront of the corporate media, Ravitch, a respected voice with a relevant, award-winning work of scholarship, was effectively censored from the corporate media for making a research-based critique of the Obama administration's educational program—one supported by the vast financial interests described herein. As a result, the public was deprived of a valuable dissenting perspective on an issue of national interest, and was left with an education discussion that resembled an advertisement for free-market education policies rather than an authentic and complex debate. Indeed, the treatment of Ravitch—and of public education and public workers in general—is an example of News Abuse in its most virulent form.

WHERE DO WE GO FROM HERE?

Listen to me: Television is not the truth! Television is a God-damned amusement park! Television is a circus, a carnival, a traveling troupe of acrobats, storytellers, dancers, singers, jugglers, side-show freaks, lion tamers, and football players. We're in the boredom-killing business! So if you want the truth. . . . Go to God! Go to your gurus! Go to yourselves! Because that's the only place you're ever going to find any real truth.
—Howard Beale, from the 1976 film *Network*

Given that so much attention has been paid to the topic of Junk Food News, News Abuse seems to be a more under-covered, yet very problematic and increasingly ubiquitous category that merits additional serious attention in terms of the efficacy of proffered solutions for big news media failures. In fact, News Abuse is propaganda, and should be seen and understood as such. In more contemporary parlance, it is more specifically framing and spin. These issues in particular, along with attacking, the use of labels, distortion, overgeneralization, and the straw person fallacy all work to create a faux news landscape that must be called out. New models of independent journalism must be based on accountability, transparency, and full factual reporting if we are to be serious about being our own governors. This is what the American people need as the failures of the news media mount and Junk Food News exponentially expands, depriving the body politic of the fact-based, substantive discussion it needs to be healthy and to survive. Unless we embrace the positive possibilities of grassroots, democratic, independent journalism, including the use of new communications technologies, time just might be running out for real change to unfold and we may be severed not only from reality, lost in "electronic hallucination," but from the promises of our country's founders to future generations of Americans.

Carl Jensen prescribed a possible way to cure the press of their Junk Food habits almost twenty years ago that goes unfulfilled, but which still stands as sage advice worth considering. Jensen wrote, "The corporate media owners should start to earn their unique First Amendment privileges. Editors should rethink their news judgment. Journalists should persevere in going after the hard stories. Journalism professors should emphasize ethics and critical analysis and turn out more muckrakers and fewer buckrakers. The judicial system should defend the freedom-of-the-press provision of the First Amendment with far more vigor. And the public should show the media it is more concerned with the high crimes and misdemeanors of its political and corporate leaders than it is with dinosaurs, sluts, and adulterers."[151] Or with Tiger's Blood and Birthers. At Project Censored, we strongly believe that Jensen's prescription is still one worth fulfilling, and is necessary for maintaining a vibrant and functional democracy.

MICKEY HUFF is the director of Project Censored, an associate professor of history at Diablo Valley College, and a member of the board of directors of the Media Freedom Foundation.

ADAM BESSIE is an assistant professor of English at Diablo Valley College, and he cowrote "Manufacturing Distraction: Junk Food News and News Abuse" in *Censored 2011*. Last year, Bessie analyzed media coverage on education reform for *Daily Censored* and *Truthout*, on which much of the case study in this chapter is based. His scholarship on metaphor and framing was published in the academic journal *Inside English*, and cited extensively in 2011 peer-reviewed article featured in the *Journal of Psychoanalytic Inquiry* written by a former president of the International Psychoanalytic Association. He thanks his wife and public school history teacher, Corin Greenberg, for her tireless support and inspiration.

ABBY MARTIN holds a BA in political science from San Diego State University. She has years of experience working as a news correspondent, editor, and producer for internet television, and now writes investigative reports for multiple publications. Abby pioneered the creation of Media Roots, a grassroots citizen journalism project, to help inform and connect the conscious community. She is a member of the board of directors of the Media Freedom Foundation. You can check out her media organization at www.mediaroots.org, her art at www.abbymartin.org or follow her on Twitter: twitter.com/AbbyMartin.

CLIFTON ROY DAMIENS is a junior at the University of California, Berkeley, and NOLAN IIIGDON is a graduate student in history at San Diego State University. Both are Project Censored interns.

Special thanks to the Diablo Valley College "Critical Reasoning in History" classes, Spring 2011, and thanks to Ryan Shehee and Meg Huff for additional edits and proofing.

Notes

1. This alludes to the epigraph for this chapter, an interview with journalist Chris Hedges by Media Roots, online at http://www.mediaroots.org/media-roots-tv-interview-with-chris-hedges.php. For more on the subject of Junk Food News and News Abuse, see previous Project Censored chapters with full citations: Mickey Huff and Frances A. Capell, "Infotainment Society: Junk Food News and News Abuse for 2008/2009," *Censored 2010: The Top 25 Ccensored Stories of 2008–09* (New York: Seven Stories Press. 2009), 147–174; and Mickey Huff, Frances A. Capell, and Adam Bessie, "Manufacturing Distraction: Junk Food News and News Abuse on a Feed to Know Basis," *Censored 2011: The Top 25 Censored Stories of 2009–10* (New York: Seven Stories Press, 2010), 159–191.
2. Katie Stapleton-Paff, "College Students Prefer 'The Daily Show' to Real News," *The Daily*, May 21, 2007, http://dailyuw.com/blog/2007/05/21/college-students-prefer-the-daily-show-to-real-ne/; see the study by PEW, "How Young People View Their Lives, Futures and Politics: A PORTRAIT OF 'GENERATION NEXT,'" January 9, 2007, http://people-press.org/http://people-press.org/files/legacy-pdf/300.pdf; and another study from Indiana University by Professor Julie R. Fox titled, "No Joke: A Comparison of Substance in *The Daily Show* with Jon Stewart and Broadcast Network Television Coverage of the 2004 Presidential Election Campaign," discussed online at http://newsinfo.iu.edu/web/page/normal/4159.html and published in the *Journal of Broadcast and Electronic Media*, summer 2007. While these studies are dated, they show a trajectory of the trends described as they have been in the making for some time.
3. Robert W. McChesney and John Nichols, *The Death and Life of American Journalism: The Media Revolution that will Begin the World Again* (New York: Nation Books, 2010), 3.
4. Carl Jensen and Project Censored, *Censored 1994* (New York: Four Walls Eight Windows, 1994), 142–143; further, Jensen added to this sentiment in "Junk Food News 1877–2000," as chapter 5 of *Censored 2001* (New York: Seven Stories Press, 2001), 251–264.
5. Jensen, *Censored 1994*, 143.
6. Ibid.
7. Wayne Drash, "Viral Post Pits Coverage of Sheen Fallen Soldiers," CNN, March 2011, http://afghanistan.blogs.cnn.com/2011/03/10/viral-post-pits-coverage-of-sheen-fallen-soldiers/.
8. Andrea Canning, "Charlie Sheen, ABC News Interview on 20/20 Special Edition," *ABC News*, February 26, 2011, http://abcnews.go.com/Entertainment/charlie-sheen-interview-special-edition-2020/story?id=13008140.
9. Glynnis MacNicol, "Watch Charlie Sheen's Last Minute Live Hour Long Interview With Piers Morgan," *Business Insider*, February 28, 2011, http://www.businessinsider.com/charlie-sheen-piers-morgan-video-2011-2.

10. Dylan Howard, "Sheen Drug Test Revealed Live—Video," *ABC News*, February 28, 2011, http://abcnews.go.com/GMA/video/sheen-drug-test-results-revealed-live-13017942.

11. Tiffany Hsu, "Charlie Sheen's Twitter Account Breaks More Records," *Los Angeles Times*, March 9, 2011, http://latimesblogs.latimes.com/technology/2011/03/charlie-sheens-twitter-account-breaks-more-records.html. See also Benny Evangelista, "Charlie Sheen Sets New Twitter Record? Zero to One Million in 24 Hours," *SF Gate*, March 2, 2011, http://www.sfgate.com/cgi-bin/blogs/techchron/detail?entry_id=84205.

12. Alexander Mooney, "Trump Says He Has Doubts About Obama's Birth Place," CNN Political Ticker, March 17, 2011, http://politicalticker.blogs.cnn.com/2011/03/17/trump-says-he-has-doubts-about-obama%E2%80%99s-birth-place/.

13. Bill Dedman, "General Electric Designed Reactors in Fukushima Have 23 Sisters in US," MSNBC, March 13, 2011, http://openchannel.msnbc.msn.com/_news/2011/03/13/6256121-general-electric-designed-reactors-in-fukushima-have-23-sisters-in-us.

14. Matthew Rothschild, "Obama's Libya War: Unconstitutional, Naïve, Hypocrytical," *Progressive*, March 19, 2011, http://www.progressive.org/wx031911.html.

15. "Cost of Libya War Soaring For US," *Press TV*, June 10, 2011, http://www.presstv.ir/detail/184023.html.

16. James Poniewozik, "Bristol Palin and the Future of Democracy," *Time*, November 11, 2010, http://tunedin.blogs.time.com/2010/11/22/bristol-palin-and-the-future-of-democracy/.

17. List of the Latest Stories on Bristol Palin, CNN, November 2010 - May 2011, http://topics.cnn.com/topics/bristol_palin.

18. Lisa De Moraes, "Bristol Palin Gets Viewers Heated Up On 'Dancing With The Stars,'" *Washington Post*, November 16, 2010, http://voices.washingtonpost.com/tvblog/2010/11/bristol-palin-gets-viewers-hea.html.

19. Linda Holmes, "The Non-Scandal of Bristol Palin's 'Dancing With The Stars' Success," National Public Radio, November 22, 2010, http://www.npr.org/blogs/monkeysee/2010/11/22/131508417/the-non-scandal-of-bristol-palin-s-dancing-with-the-stars-success.

20. Nancy Franklin, "Mush! Sarah Palin Take Us For a Ride," *New Yorker*, November 15, 2010.

21. Charlie Savage, "FBI Seeks Wider Wiretap Law For Web," *New York Times*, November 16, 2010, http://www.nytimes.com/2010/11/17/technology/17wiretap.html?_r=1.

22. Joshua Kors, "Video of Torture Hearing Released," *Huffington Post*, November 11, 2010, http://www.huffingtonpost.com/joshua-kors/video-of-torture-hearing_b_781993.html.

23. Alyson Shortnell, "Jenn Sterger: Sexts, Start-Ups, and Single Life," *Business Insider*, June 10, 2011, http://www.businessinsider.com/exclusive-jenn-sterger-interview-single-brett-favre-sext-startup-tv-personality-host#ixzz1PGneqkF7.

24. Robert Hawkins, "Oceanside man ejected from airport for refusing security check," *Sign On San Diego*, November 14, 2010, http://www.signonsandiego.com/news/2010/nov/14/tsa-ejects-oceanside-man-airport-refusing-security/.

25. Jesse Holcomb, "PEJ News Coverage Index: November 15–21, 2010," PEW Research Center's Project for Excellence in Journalism, http://www.journalism.org/index_report/pej_news_coverage_index_november_1521_2010.

26. Charles Krauthammer, "Don't Touch My Junk," *Washington Post*, November 18, 2010, http://www.washingtonpost.com/wp-dyn/content/article/2010/11/18/AR2010111804494 .html.

27. "Social Media Deride TSA Security Measures," PEW Research Center's Project for Excellence in Journalism, December 2, 2010, http://pewresearch.org/pubs/ 1816/social-media-tsa-security-pat-downs.

28. "The Story Behind 'Don't Touch My Junk,'" CNN, November 15, 2010, http://www.youtube.com/watch?v=9reOs70_iMw.

29. Mickey Huff et al., "Manufacturing Distraction: Junk Food News and News Abuse on the Feed to Know Basis," *Censored 2011: The Top 25 Censored Stories of 2009–10* (New York: Seven Stories Press, 2010), 159–191.

30. A. J. Daulerio, "Brett Favre's Cell Phone Seduction of Jennifer Sterger," *Deadspin*, October 7, 2010, http://deadspin.com/5658206/brett-favres-cellphone-seduction-of-jenn-sterger; "AP: NFL, Brett Favre meet about texts, photos," *USA Today*, October 19, 2010, http://www.usatoday.com/sports/football/nfl/vikings/2010-10-19-brett-favre-meeting_N.htm; "Sterger retains legal counsel in Favre case," CNN, October 20, 2010, http://edition.cnn.com/2010/SPORT/football/10/20/favre.sterger.lawyer/index.html.

31. "Brett Favre NAKED pictures? Alleged Penis Photos Surface," *Huffington Post*, October 17, 2010, http://www.huffingtonpost.com/2010/10/07/brett-favre-naked-pictures-photos_n_754490.html.

32. "Jenn Sterger: Sexts, Start-Ups, and Single Life."

33. Mark Jurkowitz, "PEJ News Coverage Index: June 6–12, 2011," PEW Research Center's Project for Excellence in Journalism, www.journalism.org/index_report/ news_coverage_index_june_612_2011.

34. Ibid.

35. Anne Landman, "Twitter the Winner in Weinergate," PR Watch, June 8, 2011, http://www.prwatch.org/node/10801.

36. Bernd Debusmann, "Failed: The War on Drugs and a Milestone Critique by Bernd Debusmann," Reuters, June 3, 2011, http://blogs.reuters.com/bernddebus-mann/2011/06/03/the-war-on-drugs-and-a-milestone-critique/.

37. Gareth Porter, "Ninety Percent of Petraeus's Captured 'Taliban' Were Civilians," Inter Press Service, June 12, 2011, http://ipsnews.net/news.asp.

38. "Iraq Will Ask US Troops to Stay Post-2011, says Panetta," BBC, June 10, 2011, http://www.bbc.co.uk/news/world-middle-east-13722786.

39. Zaid Jilani, "The $2.5 Trillion Tragedy: What America Has Given Up For 10 Years Of Bush Tax Cuts . . . and Counting," Think Progress, June 7, 2011, http://thinkprogress .org/economy/2011/06/07/237560/10-years-bush-tax-cuts/.

40. Ed Pilkington, "One in Four US Hackers is an FBI Informer," *Guardian*, June 6, 2011, http://www.guardian.co.uk/technology/2011/jun/06/us-hackers-fbi-informer.

41. Susannah Breslin,"Weinergate Offers a Window Into America's Faux-Prudery," *Forbes*, June 3, 2011, http://blogs.forbes.com/susannahbreslin/2011/06/03/wein-ergate-offers-a-window-into-americas-faux-prudery/.

42. For the original and more detailed definition and explanation of News Abuse, see Peter Phillips, ed., *Censored 2003* (New York: Seven Stories Press, 2004), 196.

43. Andrew Breitbart, "Video Proof: The NAACP Awards Racism—2010," *Big Government*, July 19, 2010, http://biggovernment.com/abreitbart/2010/07/19/video-proof-the-naacp-awards-racism2010/.

44. Matea Gold, "Bill O'Reilly apologizes to Shirley Sherrod for 'not doing my homework,'" *Los Angeles Times*, July 21, 2010, http://latimesblogs.latimes.com/showtracker/2010/07/bill-oreilly-apologizes-to-shirley-sherrod-for-not-doing-my-homework.html.

45. Andrew Breitbart, "Shock Undercover Video Shows ACORN Workers Advising 'Pimp' & 'Prostitute' to Avoid Law," http://www.breitbart.tv/shock-undercover-video-shows-acorn-workers-advising-pimp-prostitute-to-avoid-law/.

46. Frank James, "Shock Undercover Video Shows ACORN Workers Advising 'Pimp' & 'Prostitute' to Avoid Law,' National News, NPR, December 7, 2009, http://www.npr.org/blogs/thetwo-way/2009/12/acorn_workers_cleared_of_illeg.html; California Department of Justice Office of The Attorney General, Report of The Attorney General on The Activities of ACORN in California, April 1, 2010, http://ag.ca.gov/cms_attachments/press/pdfs/n1888_acorn_report.pdf.

47. Matt Sledge and Jack Mirkinson, "Andrew Breitbart Takes Over Anthony Weiner's Press Conference (VIDEO)," *Huffington Post*, June 6, 2011, http://www.huffingtonpost.com/2011/06/06/andrew-breitbart-hijacks-_n_872066.html.

48. Pamela Geller and Robert Spencer, "The 9/11 Mosque's Peace Charade," *Big Government*, May 18, 2010, http://biggovernment.com/pgeller/2010/05/18/the-911-mosques-peace-charade/; also see Geller and Spencer's website for Stop Islamization of America at http://sioaonline.com/.

49. Ajay Singh Chaundary, "The 'Mosque Affair,' or, Far and Away the Country's Most Ridiculous Controversy," *Huffington Post*, August 17, 2010, http://www.huffingtonpost.com/ajay-singh-chaudhary/the-mosque-affair-or-far-_b_684141.html.

50. Geller and Spencer, "The 9/11 Mosque's Peace Charade," *Big Government*, May 18, 2010, http://biggovernment.com/pgeller/2010/05/18/the-911-mosques-peace-charade/.

51. Jeff Jacoby, "A mosque at ground zero?" *Boston Globe*, June 6, 2010, http://www.boston.com/bostonglobe/editorial_opinion/oped/articles/2010/06/06/a_mosque_at_ground_zero/.

52. Andrea Peyser, "Mosque madness at Ground Zero," *New York Post*, May 13, 2010, http://www.nypost.com/p/news/national/mosque_madness_at_ground_zero_OQ34EBoMWSolXuAnQau5uL#ixzz1PODqLbP5.

53. "Rallies Over Ground Zero Mosque Get Heated," FoxNews.com, August 23, 2010, http://www.foxnews.com/us/2010/08/22/supporters-opponents-ground-zero-mosque-hold-dueling-rallies/#ixzz1POEOWw6B.

54. Pamela Geller and Robert Spencer, "The 9/11 Mosque's Peace Charade," *Big Government*, May 18, 2010, http://biggovernment.com/pgeller/2010/05/18/the-911-mosques-peace-charade/.

55. "Under Fire, Obama Clarifies Support for Ground Zero Mosque," FoxNews.com, August 14, 2010, http://www.foxnews.com/politics/2010/08/14/obamas-support-ground-zero-mosque-draws/#ixzz1POFEhAuB.

56. "Fox News shareholder funded 'Ground Zero mosque' imam: report," *Raw Story*, August 21, 2010, http://www.rawstory.com/rs/2010/08/21/fox-shareholder-funded-mosque-imam/.

57. WikiLeaks, "Collateral Murder," WikiLeaks, April 5, 2010, http://www.collateralmurder.com/. With the closing of WikiLeaks original site, the link above is to one of their many mirror sites.

58. Natalie Chandler, "WikiLeaks sister site names and shames public figures calling for its founder's death," *Australian Anthill*, January 17, 2011, http://anthillonline

.com/wikileaks-sister-site-names-and-shames-public-figures-calling-for-its-founder%E2%80%99s-death/.

59. Justin Elliot, "Pentagon says WikiLeaks war logs do NOT harm national security; Neocons disagree," *Salon*, July 26, 2010, http://www.veteranstoday.com/2010/07/26/pentagon-says-wikileaks-war-logs-do-not-harm-national-security-neocons-disagree/; Tom Leonard, "Pentagon deems Wikileaks a national security threat," *Telegraph*, March 18, 2010, http://www.telegraph.co.uk/technology/7475050/Pentagon-deems-Wikileaks-a-national-security-threat.html.

60. Andy Barr, "Ron Paul stands up for Julian Assange," *Politico*, December 3, 2010, http://www.politico.com/news/stories/1210/45930.html.

61. Ryan Witt, "Senator Mitch McConnell calls WikiLeaks chief Assange a 'high tech terrorist,'" *Political Buzz Examiner*, December 5, 2010, http://www.examiner.com/political-buzz-in-national/senator-mitch-mcconnell-calls-wikileaks-chief-assange-a-high-tech-terrorist.

62. Nick Davies, "10 days in Sweden: the full allegations of Julian Assange," *Guardian*, December 17, 2010, http://www.guardian.co.uk/media/2010/dec/17/julian-assange-sweden. Also see Kirk James Murphy, "Assange Accuser Worked with US-Funded, CIA-Tied Anti-Castro Group," *Firedoglake*, December 4, 2010, http://my.firedoglake.com/kirkmurphy/2010/12/04/assanges-chief-accuser-has-her-own-history-with-us-funded-anti-castro-groups-one-of-which-has-cia-ties/. Murphy states, "Julian Assange's chief accuser in Sweden has a significant history of work with anti-Castro groups, at least one of which is US funded and openly supported by a former CIA agent convicted in the mass murder of seventy-three Cubans on an airliner he was involved in blowing up," For more background see barrister James D. Catlin, "When it comes to Assange rape case, the Swedes are making it up as they go along," *Crikey*, December 2, 2010, http://www.crikey.com.au/2010/12/02/when-it-comes-to-assange-r-pe-case-the-swedes-are-making-it-up-as-they-go-along/.

63. Daniel Ellsberg, "Why the Pentagon Papers matter now: While we go on waging unwinnable wars on false premises, the Pentagon papers tell us we must not wait 40 years for the truth," *Guardian*, June 13, 2011, http://www.guardian.co.uk/commentisfree/cifamerica/2011/jun/13/pentagon-papers-daniel-ellsberg.

64. Frederick Hess, "Why Debate Education Facts When You Can Wax Conspiratorial?" *The American: The Journal of the American Enterprise Institute*, August 2, 2010, http://blog.american.com/why-debate-education-facts-when-you-can-wax-conspiratorial/.

65. "Biography: Frederick Hess," American Enterprise Institute for Public Policy Research Scholars and Fellows, http://www.aei.org/scholar/30.

66. "Corporations," American Enterprise Institute for Public Policy Research, http://www.aei.org/supportCorporations. Please note that the original quote from above was changed in the last few months: "The growth in the size and scope of the federal government represents a direct threat to the values AEI shares with the private sector—the engine of America's freedom and prosperity." For further information on AEI, see SourceWatch: http://www.sourcewatch.org/index.php?title=American_Enterprise_Institute.

67. Adam Bessie, "Public Education Under Attack By Bay Area Media," *Daily Censored*, August 1, 2010, http://dailycensored.com/2010/08/01/public-education-under-attack-by-the-san-jose-mercury-news/. For a further discussion of this issue, see Bessie,

"American Enterprise Institute Critiques Daily Censored on Education: 'Conspiratorial,'" *Daily Censored*, August 2, 2010, http://dailycensored.com/2010/ 08/02/american-enterprise-institute-critiques-daily-censored-on-education-"conspiratorial"/.

68. Sam Dillon, "Behind Grass-Roots Advocacy, Bill Gates," *New York Times*, May 21, 2011, http://www.nytimes.com/2011/05/22/education/22gates.html?_r=2&ref=todayspaper. According to NYT, many journalists turn to Hess for commentary, and "[The Bill and Melinda Gates Foundation] is his biggest single funder," Mr. Hess said.

69. Sean Delonas is a cartoonist for the *New York Post*, and illustrates covers for the conservative magazine the *Weekly Standard*. For the widely syndicated image, see Steven Malanga, "The Beholden State," *City Journal* 2, no. 20 (2010): http://www.city-journal.org/2010/20_2_california-unions.html.

70. "Perspectives," KQED Radio. Listener Susan Hare shared a two-minute segment "Let Them Eat Cake: Susan Hare believes public employee unions breed shoddy service and contempt for taxpayers," March 9, 2011, http://www.kqed.org/a/perspectives/R201103090735.

71. Ron Lieber, "Battle Looms Over Huge Cost of Public Pensions," *New York Times*, August 6, 2010, http://www.nytimes.com/2010/08/07/your-money/07money.html?hp.

72. "Word of the Year 2010," Merriam-Webster.com, December 20, 2010, http://www.merriam-webster.com/info/10words.htm. "Pragmatic" and "moratorium" came in second and third place, respectively, beating out "socialism." For a discussion of how conservative budget language has dominated the media in the last year, see Bessie. "In the Battle of the Budget, A Fog of Words," *Truthout*, May 26, 2011, http://www.truthout.org/battle-budget-fog-words/1306429453.

73. Paul Krugman, "Republicans and Race," *New York Times*, November 17, 2007, http://www.nytimes.com/2007/11/19/opinion/19krugman.html?_r=2.

74. Jonathan Cohn, "Why Public Employees are the New Welfare Queens," *New Republic*, August 8, 2010, http://www.tnr.com/blog/jonathan-cohn/76884/why-your-fireman-has-better-pension-you. Also, refer to Adam Bessie, "Public Teachers: America's New Welfare Queens," *Truthout*, http://www.truthout.com/public-teachers-americas-new-welfare-queens68208.

75. Geoff Mulvihill, "Anger Brews Over Government Workers' Benefits," Associated Press, March 8, 2011, http://abcnews.go.com/Business/wireStory?id=13083008.

76. George Lakoff, "Confronting Stereotypes: Sons of the Welfare Queen," *The Political Mind* (New York: Penguin, 2008), 159-162.

77. Adam Bessie, "Let's Not 'Reform' Public Education," *Truthout*, January 22, 2011, http://archive.truthout.org/lets-not-reform-public-education67006.

78. "Media Baselessly Suggest Americans View Public Employees as 'Public Enemies in Some Ways,'" *Media Matters*, March 8, 2011, http://mediamatters.org/research/201103080043. For further polling information on attitudes toward public worker unions see: Scott Keeter, "Who's Winning the Fight Over Public Employee Unions?" PEW Research Center Publications, March 7, 2011, http://pewresearch.org/pubs/1915/polls-winning-losing-fight-over-public-employee-unions-wisconsin.

79. Mulvihill, "Anger brews over government worker benefits." Emphasis added.

80. For a more thorough discussion of both sets of evidence on public worker benefits and compensation, see Jonathan Cohn, "Do Wisconsin's Workers Make Too Much?" *New Republic*, February 21, 2011, http://www.tnr.com/blog/jonathan-cohn/83884/wisconsin-walker-public-worker-salary-benefit. Also see Keith Bender and John Heywood, "Out of Balance? Comparing Public and Private Sector Com-

pensation Over 20 Years," National Institute on Retirement Security, April 2010, http://www.slge.org/vertical/Sites/%7BA260E1DF-5AEE-459D-84C4-876EFE1E4032%7D/uploads/%7B03E820E8-F0F9-472F-98E2-F0AE1166D116%7D.PDF.

81. Jeffrey Keefe, "Are Wisconsin Employees Overcompensated?" Economic Policy Institute Briefing Paper 290, February 10, 2011, http://epi.3cdn.net/9e237c56096a8e4904_rkm6b9hn1.pdf.

82. William Cronon, "Who's Really Behind Recent Republican Legislation in Wisconsin and Elsewhere? (Hint: It Didn't Start Here)," *Scholar as Citizen*, March 15, 2011, http://scholarcitizen.williamcronon.net/2011/03/15/alec/.

83. William Cronon, "Wisconsin's Radical Break," *New York Times*, March 21, 2011, www.nytimes.com/2011/03/22/opinion/22cronon.html.

84. "History," *American Legislative Exchange Council*. http://www.alec.org/AM/Template.cfm?Section=Home. For more information see SourceWatch, http://www.sourcewatch.org/index.php?title=American_Legislative_Exchange_Council. Note that the Koch Brothers—who financed some of the Tea Party's Astroturf efforts—are donors.

85. William Cronon, "Abusing Open Records to Attack Academic Freedom," *Scholar as Citizen*, http://scholarcitizen.williamcronon.net/2011/03/24/open-records-attack-on-academic-freedom/.

86. Ken Braun, "The Public Purpose of Our 'Professors' Email' FOIA Request," Mackinac Center for Public Policy, April 4, 2011, http://www.mackinac.org/14863. Learn more about the Mackinac Center at SourceWatch, http://www.sourcewatch.org/index.php?title=Mackinac_Center_for_Public_Policy. Also, see Jason Deparle, "Right-of-Center Guru Goes Wide With the Gospel of Small Government," *New York Times*, November 17, 2006, http://www.nytimes.com/2006/11/17/us/politics/17thinktank.html?ei=5090&en=3b6af3fbfa4ffo1e&ex=1321419600&partner=rssuserland&emc=rss&pagewanted=all.

87. Paul Krugman, "American Thought Police," *New York Times*, March 27, 2011, http://www.nytimes.com/2011/03/28/opinion/28krugman.html?src=ISMR_AP_LO_MST_FB.

88. "Breitbart Announces His Next Big Move: 'Go After the Teachers,'" *Media Matters*, http://mediamatters.org/mmtv/201104180045.

89. Ned Resnikoff, "Breitbart Starts Big Push to 'Go After Teachers' With His Trademark Deception," *Media Matters*, April 29, 2011, http://mediamatters.org/blog/201104290017.

90. Scott Jaschik, "The Shirley Sherrods of Academe," *Inside Higher Education*, April 29, 2011, http://www.insidehighered.com/news/2011/04/29/fallout_from_videos_of_labor_course_at_university_of_missouri.

91. Ibid.

92. "Bad Teacher" promotional website, Columbia Pictures, http://areyouabadteacher.com/?hs308=BTR6186.

93. "Cribs: Teacher's Edition," *The Daily Show with Jon Stewart*, March 10, 2011, http://www.thesddailyshow.com/watch/thu-march-10-2011/crisis-in-dairyland—apocalypse-cow.

94. Frederick Hess, Martin West, and Michael Petrelli, "Pyrrhic Victories," *Education Next: A Journal of Opinion and Research* 11, no. 2 (2011): http://educationnext.org/pyrrhic-victories/.

95. Sonny Bunch, "Bright Lights, Bad Schoolhouses: Teachers' Unions as Big Screen Villians," *Weekly Standard*, July 26, 2010, http://www.weeklystandard.com/articles/bright-lights-bad-schoolhouses.

96. John Anderson, "Review: *Waiting for Superman*," *Variety*, January 23, 2010, http://www.variety.com/review/VE1117941947?refcatid=2471. See also Lloyd Grove, "*Superman's* Villain Fights Back," *Daily Beast*, September 17, 2010, http://www.thedailybeast.com/blogs-and-stories/2010-09-17/waiting-for-superman-randi-weingarten-education-films-villain/#.

97. Matthew Ladner, "Randi Weingarten Endorses Florida K-12 Jebolution," *Jay P. Greene's Blog*, May 6, 2011, http://jaypgreene.com/tag/randi-weingarten/.

98. Hess, "Pyrrhic Victories."

99. "President Obama Hosts 'Waiting for Superman' Children At The White House," *The Huffington Post*, October 10, 2010, http://www.huffingtonpost.com/2010/10/11/president-obama-hosts-waiting-for-superman-children_n_758549.html.

100. Roger Ebert, "Review: *Waiting for Superman*," *Chicago Sun-Times*, September 29, 2010, http://rogerebert.suntimes.com/apps/pbcs.dll/article?AID=/20100929/REVIEWS/100929981/1023.

101. On January 4, Alyssa Milano tweeted, "I'm watching 'Waiting for Superman.' Wow. Everyone should see this documentary," with the link attached: http://twitter.com/#!/alyssa_milano.

102. Diane Ravitch, "The Myth of Charter Schools," *New York Review of Books*, November 11, 2010, http://www.nybooks.com/articles/archives/2010/nov/11/myth-charter-schools/.

103. Rick Hess, "Waiting for Superman: My Conversion Experience," *Education Week*, September 22, 2010, http://blogs.edweek.org/edweek/rick_hess_straight_up/2010/09/waiting_for_superman_my_conversion_experience.html.

104. "The Shocking State of Our Schools," *The Oprah Winfrey Show*, September 20, 2010, http://www.oprah.com/oprahshow/The-Shocking-State-of-Our-Schools.

105. The Bill & Melinda Gates Foundation provided Participant LLC a one-year grant of $2 million to "execute a social action campaign that will complement Paramount's marketing campaign of Waiting for Superman." See http://www.gatesfoundation.org/Grants-2010/Pages/Participant-Media-LLC-OPP1019819.aspx.

106. "Bill Gates: Excellence in Teaching is Measurable," *NBC Nightly News*, September 28, 2010, http://www.educationnation.com/index.cfm?objectid=A98ABB66-CB5E-11DF-8853000C296BA163.

107. Adam Bessie, "The Myth of the Bad Teacher," *Truthout*, October 10, 2010, http://archive.truthout.org/the-myth-bad-teacher64223.

108. NBC Education Nation Press Release, September 13, 2010.

109. The Bill & Melinda Gates Foundation, http://www.educationnation.com/index.cfm?objectid=8579D07E-6A91-11E0-B646000C296BA16.

110. Andrew Rotherham, "'Waiting for Superman': Education Reform Isn't Easy," *Time*, October 7, 2010, http://www.time.com/time/nation/article/0,8599,2023953,00.html. Also, see Rotherham's blog, *Eduwonk*, which "is funded by support provided, in part, by the Bill & Melinda Gates Foundation for the purpose of creating an educational forum for sharing research, ideas, and opinions regarding issues related to P-20 education systems . . . the Bill & Melinda Gates Foundation take[s] no positions regarding any legislation discussed in the Blog," http://www.eduwonk.com/2004/04/about-eduwonk.html.

111. Paul Thomas has written a number of essays on this topic over the last year, which will be collected in the forthcoming book *Ignoring Poverty in the US: The Corporate Takeover of Public Education* (North Carolina: Information Age Press, 2011).

112. Thomas, "The Education Celebrity Tour: Legend of the Fall, Part II," *Daily Censored*, December 2, 2010, http://dailycensored.com/2010/12/02/the-education-celebrity-tour-legend-of-the-fall-pt-ii/.

113. Thomas, "Celebrity 'Common Sense' Reform for Education: Legend of the Fall, Part VI," *Daily Censored*, February 27, 2011, http://dailycensored.com/2011/02/27/celebrity-common-sense-reform-for-education-legend-of-the-fall-pt-vi/.

114. Rick Hess, "Waiting For Superman: My Conversion Experience," *Education Week*, http://blogs.edweek.org/edweek/rick_hess_straight_up/2010/09/waiting_for_superman_my_conversion_experience.html.

115. Valerie Strauss, "Film critic Ebert rescinds positive 'Superman' Review," *Washington Post*, January 28, 2011, http://voices.washingtonpost.com/answer-sheet/school-turnaroundsreform/film-critic-ebert-rescinds-pos.html.

116. Arne Duncan, "The New Normal: Doing More With Less," presented at the American Enterprise Institute panel "Bang for the Buck in Schooling," November 17, 2010, http://www.aei.org/docLib/20101117-Arne-Duncan-Remarks.pdf.

117. Hess, "Pyrrhic Victories."

118. Paul Thomas, "The corporate takeover of American schools," *Guardian*, November 16, 2010, http://www.guardian.co.uk/commentisfree/cifamerica/2010/nov/15/education-schools.

119. Scholar and *Daily Censored* blogger Danny Weil has researched and written extensively on efforts to privatize public education. In "Charter school capital projects: cashing in on kids" (*Daily Censored*, June 12, 2011). Weil shows how the trend extends far beyond the "Big Three": even tennis great Andre Agassi has invested "hundreds of millions" in the privatization of public education: http://dailycensored.com/2011/06/12/charter-school-capital-projects-canyon-capital-realty-advisors-intel-citigroup-and-other-venture-wall-street-capitalists-team-up-with-andre-agassi-to-cash-in-on-kids/.

120. Fred Hiatt, "How Bill Gates Would Repair Our Schools," *Washington Post*, March 30, 2009, http://www.washingtonpost.com/wp-dyn/content/article/2009/03/29/AR2009032901353.html. For further commentary, see Diane Ravitch, *The Death and Life of the Great American School System* (New York: Basic Books, 2010), 219.

121. Joanne Barkan, "Got Dough? How Billionaires Rule Our Schools," *Dissent Magazine*, Winter 2011, http://www.dissentmagazine.org/article/?article=3781.

122. Ibid.

123. Ravitch, *Death and Life*, 221.

124. Barkan, "Got Dough?"

125. Paul E. Peterson, Marci Kanstoroom, and Chester E. Finn, Jr., "A Battle Begun, Not Won," *Education Next: A Journal of Opinion and Research* 11, no. 2 (2011): http://educationnext.org/a-battle-begun-not-won/.

126. Barkan, "Got Dough?"

127. Erik Robelen, "Gates Learns to Think Big," *Education Week*, October 10, 2006. See also Ravitch, *Death and Life*, 210.

128. Sam Dillon, "Behind Grass-Roots School Advocacy, Bill Gates," *New York Times*, May 21, 2011, http://www.nytimes.com/2011/05/22/education/22gates.html?pagewanted=all.

129. "Impact," *Teach Plus*, http://www.teachplus.org/page/policy-13.html.

130. For more information on Teach Plus financing from the Gates Foundation grant page see http://www.gatesfoundation.org/Grants-2009/Pages/Teach-Plus-Incorporated-OPP1003735.aspx.

131. Dillon, "Behind Grass-Roots School Advocacy."

132. Barkan. "Got Dough?" For the original source, see Frederick Hess, ed., *With the Best of Intentions: How Philanthropy is Reshaping K-12 Education* (Massachusetts: Harvard Educational Publication Group, 2005).

133. Ravitch, *Death and Life*, 201.

134. Barkan, "Got Dough?"

135. Ravitch, *Death and Life*, 201.

136. Jonathan Alter, "Don't Believe Critics: Education Reform Works," Bloomberg, Opinion, June 3, 2011, http://www.bloomberg.com/news/2011-06-03/don-t-believe-critics-education-reform-works-jonathan-alter.html.

137. Ravitch, "The Business Model in New York City," 69–92.

138. Ibid., 1.

139. Ibid., 10.

140. Anthony Cody, "Diane Ravitch: Organized, We Will Be Heard," Living in Dialogue at Education Week, http://blogs.edweek.org/teachers/living-in-dialogue/2010/03/when_i_first_heard_about.html.

141. Ravitch, "The Business Model," 3.

142. Anthony Cody, "An Unlikely Hero Breaks Through the Blackout: Diane Ravitch," Living in Dialogue at Education Week, February 27, 2011, http://blogs.edweek.org/teachers/living-in-dialogue/2011/02/an_unlikely_hero_for_teachers.html.

143. NBC Education Nation Press Release.

144. Diane Ravitch, e-mail message to Adam Bessie, January 22, 2011.

145. Diane Ravitch, e-mail message to Adam Bessie, June 1, 2011.

146. "Op-Ed: Rage Simmering Among American Teachers," NPR's *Talk of the Nation*, http://www.npr.org/2011/02/28/134134735/Op-Ed-Rage-Simmering-Among-American-Teachers.

147. Diane Ravitch, "Waiting for the Miracle School," *New York Times*, May 3, 2011, http://www.nytimes.com/2011/06/01/opinion/01ravitch.html.

148. "About the Moynihan Prize," American Academy of Political and Social Science, http://www.aapss.org/the-moynihan-prize/about-the-moynihan-prize.

149. Frederick Hess, "Ravitch's Consistent Confusion," *Review Online*, March 25, 2010, http://www.frederickhess.org/7110/diane-ravitch-consistent-confusion.

150. Frederick Hess, "Solve school problems, but do not oversell," *Washington Examiner*, November 30, 2010, http://washingtonexaminer.com/opinion/columnists/2010/11/frederick-m-hess-solve-school-problems-do-not-oversell.

151. Jensen, *Censored 1994*, 148.

CHAPTER 4

Signs of Health and Emerging Culture
Stories of Hope and Creative Change from 2010 and 2011

by Kenn Burrows

> *Live out of your imagination, not your history.*
> —STEPHEN COVEY

This is a chapter about "good news" . . . yet I must warn you, we first have to explore some bad news: Business as usual is not working—for people or the planet. We are facing a fundamental revision of human culture.

Expect a lot of change in the coming years, changes on a bigger scale and happening more quickly than before, due in part to the explosion in digital technology and to necessary adjustments in global economics and society. Our times are increasingly complex with instant sharing of information and an infinite range of opinion. If you're feeling overwhelmed these days, you're not alone. We seem to have lost our ability to collectively solve the important problems facing us as a human family. Multiple crises seem to proliferate, and we seem powerless to do much about it.

From a sociobiological perspective the primary cause of our global crises is the accelerating complexity of human society, *and* the limitations of the human thought processes that evolved to give priority to short term (here and now) threats—threats that are obvious, immediate, sudden, personal, and dramatic. We are therefore poorly equipped to attend to what is invisible, tasteless, long-term, theoretical, and vast. Crises like overpopulation, overfishing, invisible toxins, climate change, economic instability and disparity, militarization, climate change, commercialization of everything, and the erosion of soil, aquifers, and democracy—to say nothing of people working well together in communities, groups, and organizations—do not incite the same attention and engagement as the latest crimes, police actions, or personal tragedies.[1]

In addition, studies of perceptual blindness show how human brains are hard-wired to exclude (ignore or discredit) information that does not fit into their current system of meaning.[2]

When overwhelmed it is common to start making false correlations and substitute beliefs for facts. Our minds are fundamentally out of step with the needs of our times. This is to say that all our ecological and social crises reflect a single crisis, a "crisis of perception." To face and shift this internal crisis, we need to explore and expand the limiting worldviews inhabiting our minds and driving our culture. To change our world, we have to change our worldview.[3]

To a great degree our cultural worldview is embodied by market and money systems, and by the material achievements of science. The market-state externalizes human problems primarily as resource issues to be managed through technology and investment, corporate production and government support. This materialist approach leaves nature and society (you and I) and alternative views out of the equation, and we all pay a big price for this exclusion—a separation and existential loss of meaningful association, shared purpose, and sense of place.[4]

Let's take a moment to step back and give perspective to our predicament. As we approach seven billion people on the planet, and growing reports of ecological and social crises, we naturally tend to see the negative impacts of the modern world. Yet, let's also acknowledge the benefits as well. The strengths of modern culture—both from a scientific and technical perspective, and a commercial perspective—have yielded many gifts; a few key examples, comparing today to a century ago: increased life expectancy, vastly improved healthcare (antibiotics, dentistry, prosthetics, etc.), the computer, personal phone and global information systems, great advancements in transportation, and new economic growth for many and greater economic interconnectivity throughout the world.

With these advances, globalization offers some promising trends. In particular, the flow of information across cultures has led to more connections and sharing than ever before. History's greatest theme has been the trading of goods and ideas. If we maintain the open exchange of information and the social media that the internet provides, we will have a rich field of possibility. The interaction of more people and more ideas invites new thinking and new possibilities and a deepening of our collective intelligence. In this way of thinking, the more we share, the more we have. This co-creativity is the hope of the future, and together we are inventing a new global era.[5]

To solve the massive problems the human family is facing, the world needs lots of new and workable ideas. The future is calling for innovators, people who can see and think in new creative ways. Innovators are collaborators—creativity feeds off social interaction and loves novelty and diversity; it is, by nature, inclusive and integrative. Collaboration with others can be challenging, but it is rich in rewards if you are willing to be inclusive in your thinking.

Innovators are also "knowledge workers," people comfortable with ideas or knowledge as part of the currency of social exchange. Knowledge workers learn how to hold multiple points of view and think comprehensively; they are drawn to the challenges of complexity. Knowledge workers wear different hats: designers, programmers, architects, writers, educators, managers, etc. Their worldview is holistic, informed by systems of thinking, and they don't normally get stuck in false dichotomies—such as liberal versus conservative politics, or public versus private sectors. Knowledge workers are outliers; they get their ideas from anywhere. They don't have their identity wrapped up in any single ideology or group, but will associate with many.[6] They honor the worldview of those they are with, being aware that every view has value and perspective to offer. Good knowledge workers learn how to swim in the paradoxes inherent in human existence and constantly look to "pattern recognition" for what is emerging out of relationship with others.

Innovators know that problems are natural to living, and that creative attention to problems is the first step in the change process. Problems are necessary catalysts that drive all evolution. And doomsayers are usually overstating the risks and understating the power of collaboration and innovation—that we always have the choice of being a victim or an innovator. *Victims* tend to focus on what they don't want or what isn't working (problem focus) and fear more of it. People feel victimized by the economy, not having enough time, circumstances like an illness, a bad childhood, etc. *Innovators* focus on what they want and reach for a shift in thinking (and identity) that is life-changing. Focusing on what you want begins the shift.[7]

Collaborators know when problems are clearly identified and people see a way to help, they will. Rebecca Solnit stated it this way: "Most of the real work on this planet is not done for profit: it's done at home, for each other, for affection, out of idealism. . . . Behind the [capitalist] system we all know, is a shadow system of kindness, the other invisible hand. Much of its work now lies in simply undoing the depredations of the official system. Its achievements are often hard to see or grasp."[8]

This chapter is a call to repair and evolve the modern worldview by finding our way back to the relational world of body, nature, and community, joining with others who are taking the future into their own hands and living lives of meaning and purpose. The news stories in this chapter are examples of people doing just that—making good news—becoming more collaborative, innovative and building the future. There are six good news clusters—each an essential area of need and innovation. The stories are informative and inspiring signs of the emerging culture.

Final thoughts for your journey for this coming year of change:

▶ Humor, compassion, and positive emotions are great tools to help meet the challenges of complexity and support creative social change. Studies of effective traffic safety ads show the use of humor and empowerment (appealing to positive emotions) work much better than fear-based ads.[9] This is something to remember for daily life and for our activism.

▶ A reminder: There is great goodness in the world of which you are a part—a "fierce affection and determination [that] pushes back everywhere at the forces of destruction."[10] Find yourself a community and feel and gain support from those associations.

▶ The Institute of Noetic Sciences published studies about their Worldview Literacy Project which describes five developmental levels of social consciousness and an educational curriculum to facilitate worldview development. Their studies show success in training young people to shift their world-view by cultivating social-emotional intelligence and new states of mind that help them navigate complexity.[11] These are the skills and capacities for the knowledge workers of the twenty-first century. This is good news!

▶ If you ask, "Where should I begin?" there are many resources in this chapter to help you get oriented. Ultimately, that is up to you. Find an important question and listen to yourself—your heart will answer! We are ecosystems and nature knows what to do.

Good News Sources

Good: Good News daily, videos, infographics, projects, slideshows. http://www.good.is.

Happy News: Compelling stories, news, and activities. http://www.happynews.com.

OdeWire: Tired of hearing bad news daily? Calling all intelligent optimists! Get your daily dose of what's going right in our complex world by turning to OdeWire, a new 24/7 outlet for optimistic/solution-oriented news harvested from multiple news sources. http://odewire.com/.

COMMUNITY AND COLLABORATION

These news stories are about the power of sharing and community. Community is about people coming together out of common need to build a circle of trust and association—a social fabric that provides meaning, justice, shared resources, and social support.

The Antidote to Apathy: Redesigning Public Communication

Perhaps apathy is not some kind of internal symptom, but a complex web of cultural obstacles that reinforces disengagement. If we can identify those obstacles and work together to remove them, things could get quite exciting!

Source: Dave Meslin, "The Antidote to Apathy," video, TED, filmed October 2010, 7:05, posted April 2011, http://www.ted.com/talks/dave_meslin_the_antidote_to_apathy.html.

Neighbors for Common Security

Communities around the country are coming together to support each other in hard times. Known as "Common Security Clubs," "Resilience Circles," or by other names, these are places for neighbors to face a tough economy together by learning the root causes of the economic crisis, forming bartering and sharing cooperatives, creating locally rooted support networks, etc.

Sources: Sarah Byrnes, "Can Small Group Organizing Save the Country?" *Yes! Magazine*, November 5, 2010, http://www.yesmagazine.org/blogs/common-security-clubs/can-small-group-organizing-save-the-country; Sarah Byrnes, "Writing Our Own Economic Future," *Yes! Magazine*, April 20, 2011, http://www.yesmagazine.org/blogs/common-security-clubs/dont-get-fooled-again-writing-our-own-economic-future.

Reclaiming Public Space

People are working to reclaim streets as public spaces by partnering with residents and local businesses to create a renewed sense of community. Claim a small space and make it beautiful and inviting with art, plants, and seating areas, or clean and create common space. Putting the public space back where it's supposed to be has a profound effect on the social culture.

Sources: Erika Kosina, "Reclaim Your Streets," *Yes! Magazine*, September 22, 2010, http://www.yesmagazine.org/planet/reclaim-your-streets-how-to-create-safe-and-social-pedestrian-plazas; Brooke Jarvis, "Building the World We Want," *Yes! Magazine*, May 12, 2010, http://www.yesmagazine.org/happiness/building-the-world-we-want-interview-with-mark-lakeman.

Twenty Easy Ways to Share and Spark Your Life

Take a leap into the expansive world of sharing and explore creative ways to make sharing a meaningful part of your life with this great list of ways to share (tool-sharing, bartering, yard-sharing, "freecycling," co-working, etc.), which shows that a complete lifestyle based on sharing is possible and can be very rewarding. There is always food and time to share.

Source: Kelly McCartney, "Top 20 How-To-Share Posts," *Shareable*, January 9, 2011, http://www.shareable.net/blog/shareables-top-20-how-to-share-posts; http://shareable.net/how-to-share.

The Power of Conversation to Change the World

Conversation shifts our thinking and deepens social connections. It is essential for sharing resources and for mutual understanding that leads to co-creating and caring for our world. It enables communities to connect, find common ground, and pursue common action.

Source: Melinda Blau, "Art of Conversation Is Key to Sharing," *Shareable*, April 18, 2011, http://www.shareable.net/blog/why-the-art-of-conversation-is-key-to-sharing; The National Coalition for Dialogue & Deliberation (NCDD): http://ncdd.org.

Unexpected Benefits from Disaster in Japan

The disaster in Japan has caused people in the city of Sendai to come together and become a strongly knit, supportive community. The recent events have brought a lot of people who were once strangers together, many showing compassionate acts to help one another through times of distress. Instead of stepping on one another for survival people are lending helping hands, reaffirming the positive side of human nature and community bonds.

Source: Anne Thomas, "A Letter From Sendai," *Ode*, March 14, 2011, http://www.odemagazine.com/blogs/readers_blog/24755/a_letter_from_sendai.

Happiness Not Linked to Material Wealth

In a worldwide survey, people in poorer countries reported greater happiness than people in many of the world's wealthier nations. Research suggests this is due to the strong link between national and personal satisfaction among poor people, and among those with strong cultural and regional ties.

Source: Mike Morrison et al., "Subjective Well-Being and National Satisfaction," *Psychological Science* 22, no. 2 (2011): 166–71.

Co-ops Support Community

Co-ops create equitable and stable economies, build strong communities that promote education, and merge economic growth with social goals. Co-ops exist to serve people's needs, not to maximize profits for shareholders.

Source: Steven Van Yoder, "Fixing the Free Market," *Ode*, October 2010, http://www.odemagazine.com/doc/73/fixing-the-free-market/all.

Three Ways to Bring People Together in Your Neighborhood

Great ways to connect your community: set up a "gift circle" for neighbors to meet each others' needs by sharing what they have; throw a community swap meet where people come together with food, music, and all kinds of creative exchanges; or start a neighborhood work group that pools local talent for meaningful collaboration on community projects.

Sources: Charles Eisenstein, "A Circle of Gifts," *Shareable*, November 1, 2010, http://www.shareable.net/blog/charles-eisenstein-gift-economy-gift-circles; Shira Golding, "How to Throw a Community Swap Meet," *Shareable*, January 24, 2010, http://shareable.net/blog/how-to-throw-your-own-community-swap-meet; Emily Doskow, "How to Start a Neighborhood Work Group," *Shareable*, March 1, 2010, http://shareable.net/blog/how-to-start-a-neighborhood-work-group.

Couchsurfing: Offer Your Couch, Make New Friends

The gift economy is alive and global among an improbable network of "Couchsurfers." Since its launch in 2003, Couchsurfing.org has become an international phenomenon. It has attracted 1,930,000 registered Couchsurfers from around the world and facilitated 2,086,778 successful surf and host experiences. Couches are offered in 230 countries and 73,339 cities.

Source: David Bollier, "When Couches Become Communities," *Yes! Magazine*, July 29, 2010, http://www.yesmagazine.org/new-economy/when-couches-become-communities.

More Friends, Bigger Brain

Research shows that the amygdala—a small, almond-shaped region located deep inside our brain—is linked to the size of our social networks.

Source: Sian Beilock, Greater Good Science Center, March 3, 2011, http://greatergood.berkeley.edu/article/item/more_friends_bigger_brain/.

ECONOMY AND FAIR EXCHANGE

It is increasingly clear that our entire economic system needs major reform. A "New Economy" movement is emerging that seeks a shift away from the current money system and the financial bottom line toward a community-based, partnership economy. The new economy redefines wealth to emphasize sharing and access over ownership. It recognizes and promotes three types of wealth production: the gift economy (family, close friends, and intimates), community-exchange systems (time banks, co-ops, gift circles, community currencies, etc.), and federal money. In this third area, the focus is on the use of public/partnership banks that serve the community and return any profits to the residents. The news stories below explore these innovative options.

The New Economy Movement

The emergence of the term "new economy" in public discourse in recent decades may be a sign that support for status quo capitalism is wavering. A growing movement of people accepts the idea that the entire economic system must be radically restructured for critical social and environmental goals to be met. They call for institutions with more egalitarian priorities than the narrow corporate focus on profits and growth. As the economy continues to falter, this movement is working to define a viable path toward long-term systemic change.

Source: Gar Alperovitz, "The New-Economy Movement," *Nation*, May 25, 2011, http://www.thenation .com/article/160949/new-economy-movement.

How to Get Free from Wall Street: Redefine Wealth and Create New Systems of Exchange

Economist David Korten proposes that we create real wealth through increased political participation; by basing value on living systems rather than on the money system; by shifting power from global financial markets to local, community-controlled economies; and by expanding the areas of our lives that are based on gift economies, barter, mutual aid, and caring for the greater good.

Source: Doug Pibel, "Get Free from Wall Street: An Interview with David Korten," *Yes!* *Magazine*, October 1, 2010, http://www.yesmagazine.org/ issues/a-resilient-community/get-free-from-wall-street.

State Banking Takes Off: With Profits for Public vs. Private Gain

Fourteen states have introduced bills to form state-owned banks or are studying their feasibility. All of these bills were inspired by the Bank of North Dakota (BND), the nation's only state-owned bank. While other states are teetering on the edge of bankruptcy, North Dakota continues to report surpluses. On April 20, BND reported profits of $62 million for 2010, setting a record for the seventh straight year. These profits belong to the citizens and are produced without taxation. BND partners with local banks to provide credit for local businesses and homeowners. It also helps with state and local government funding. Now other states are on track to follow North Dakota's example, moving their state reserves from Wall Street banks to a bank owned by their residents.

Sources: John David, "Reviving Main Street: A Call for Public Banks," *Shareable*, May 16, 2011, http://www.shareable.net/blog/reviving-main-street-a-call-for-public-banks; Ellen Brown, "Washington State Joins the Movement for Public Banking," *Yes! Magazine*, January 24, 2011, http://www.yesmagazine.org/new-economy/washington-state-joins-movement-for-public-banking; Public Banking Institute: http://publicbankinginstitute.org.

Time Banks Swap Skills, Not Dollars

Modern forms of time exchange, called Time Banks and Local Employment Trading Systems (LETS), have been around since the 1980s.

They are based on the hour as a unit of account, and everyone's hour could either be exchanged for another hour of service or for the equivalent in goods. Now, with more than one in ten Americans unemployed (likely twice that, given recording problems), time exchanges are making a comeback in communities across the United States. The network TimeBanks USA alone includes more than 120 Time Banks. Every community determines its own rules, but the idea is to allow people to purchase the services that they need without toiling endlessly to meet high prices in the market economy. It is a way to help the underprivileged and for the underserved to help each other through an organized system of reciprocity. In the process, people get to know and trust their neighbors, establishing caring relationships that can help reweave the fabric of our communities and replace our culture's over-reliance on individual financial security.

Sources: Mira Luna, "How to Share Time," *Yes! Magazine*, July 8, 2010, http://www.yesmagazine.org/new-economy/how-to-share-time; Mira Luna, "How to Share Time Through Timebanking," *Shareable*, January 27, 2010, http://www.shareable.net/blog/how-to-share-time-through-timebanking.

Ways Our World Is Becoming More Shareable

There are countless examples of how our world is becoming more shareable: carsharing, bikesharing, ridesharing, yardsharing, co-working, co-housing, tool libraries, open space, world café, public transit, urban agriculture, civic engagement, bike lanes, social enterprises, nonprofit groups, microfinance, the internet, social media, cooperatives, employee-owned firms, community land trusts, resident-owned communities, and much more.

Sources: Neal Gorenflo, "10 Ways Our World is Becoming More Shareable," *Shareable*, March 8, 2010, http://shareable.net/blog/10-ways-our-world-is-becoming-more-shareable; Neal Gorenflo, "Top 10 Tips for Starting a Campus Food Coop," *Shareable*, March 20, 2011, http://www.shareable.net/blog/top-10-tips-for-starting-a-campus-food-coop.

Americans Buying More Locally

There are now more than 5,274 active farmers markets in the US; nearly half of them started within the last decade. Food co-ops and neighborhood greengrocers are likewise on the rise. Local business alliances have now formed in over 130 cities and collectively count some thirty thousand businesses as members. These alliances are making a compelling case that choosing independent businesses and locally produced goods is critical for rebuilding prosperity, averting environmental catastrophe, and ensuring that we are not smothered by corporate uniformity.

Sources: Stacy Mitchell, "A New Deal for Local Economies," *Yes! Magazine*, April 29, 2010, http://www.yesmagazine.org/new-economy/a-new-deal-for-local-economies; Jeff Milchen, "5 Ways to Help Your Community Go Local," *Yes! Magazine*, February 3, 2011, http://www.yesmagazine.org/new-economy/5-ways-to-help-your-community-go-local.

Homemade Prosperity: The Reemergence of Home Economics

By reducing expenses in creative ways (preserving the harvest from local farms, repurposing used clothing, etc.), Americans are transforming their homes from units of consumption into units of production. Now, instead of the family working to support the household, the household works to support the family. Members of this growing home economics movement enjoy time with family and a greatly reduced ecological footprint.

Source: Shannon Hayes, "Homemade Prosperity," *Yes! Magazine*, December 10, 2010, http://www.yesmagazine.org/issues/what-happy-families-know/homemade-prosperity.

MEDIA AND EDUCATION

We've entered the digital age and the media explosion is impacting everything. Journalism is struggling to reinvent itself and local newspapers (those still standing) are trying to find a new commercial model that will allow them to survive. What about public accountability in this era? Media freedom? Education will never be the same, nor perhaps should it be. Yet where is this all going? The following independent news stories point toward trends and possibilities.

Social Media Isn't Changing the World, It's Creating a New One

Social media is a great tool for spreading information and connecting people from all over the world. Ninety-six percent of Generation Y has joined a social network. It is estimated that Google, Facebook, and Twitter connect two billion people worldwide—a third of the planet's population! More video was uploaded to YouTube in six months than was produced by the three major TV networks in sixty years. Wikipedia has over thirteen million articles, all written by volunteers. Through social media, a radically new order based on open access, decentralized creativity, collaborative intelligence, and easy sharing is emerging.

Source: Neal Gorenflo, "Social Media isn't Changing the World, It's Creating a New One," *Shareable*, October 12, 2010, http://shareable.net/blog/social-media-isnt-changing-the-world-its-creating-a-new-one.

National Conference for Media Reform 2011: Change the Media, Change the World

Enjoy audio and video archives of this historic conference with presentations on: Journalism and Public Media, Social Justice and Movement Building, Policy and Politics, Technology and Innovation, Media Makers, and Culture and the Arts.

Source: National Conference for Media Reform archives, April 8–10, 2011, http://conference.freepress.net/archive.

Changing the Educational Paradigm

Shifting from educational factories to creative, twenty-first century education.

Source: "RSA Animate—Changing Education Paradigms," video, YouTube, 11:41, posted by theRSAorg, October 14, 2010, http://www.youtube.com/watch?v=zDZFcDGpL4U.

Let's Use Video to Reinvent Education

Media-led learning enables children of various learning abilities to learn at their own pace, helping shift the education paradigm to a more self-directed and effective learning experience.

Source: "Salam Khan: Let's Use Video to Reinvent Education," video, TED, 20:27, March 2011, http://www.ted.com/talks/salman_khan_let_s_use_video_to_reinvent_education.html.

Virtual Reality and Inner Space: Technology's New Frontier?

Virtual reality is immersive and interactive—and it's changing people's lives, tapping into individuals' potential to transform themselves and their world. Coming Home, for example, is a program that uses virtual reality to help veterans struggling with mental health issues.

Source: Matthew Gilbert, "Inner Space—Technology's New Frontier?" Institute of Noetic Sciences, November 16, 2010, http://www.noetic.org/blog/inner-space-technologys-new-frontier/.

Transformative Films Educate and Awaken as Well as Entertain

Transformative movies are deeply impacting twenty-first century audiences. What differentiates these films from others is their explicit intention to either affirm a positive vision of the world or to actually change people—to challenge personal or cultural conditioning or beliefs.

Source: Matthew Gilbert, "Transformational Films: A Genre on the Threshold," Institute of Noetic Sciences, February 2011, http://www.noetic.org/noetic/issue-7-february/transformational-films-a-genre-on-the-threshold/.

The Greatest TED Talk Ever Sold

Using humor, transparency, and bold parody of PR industry reps to explore the underlying dynamics of branding and marketing hype.

Source: "Morgan Spurlock: The Greatest TED Talk Ever Told," video, TED, 19:28, February 2011, http://www.ted.com/talks/morgan_spurlock_the_greatest_ted_talk_ever_sold.html.

INNOVATIONS IN JOURNALISM AND NEWS

Community-Funded Reporting: A New Model for Journalism

Through Spot.Us the public can commission and participate with journalists to do reporting on important and overlooked topics. Contributions are tax deductible and Spot.Us partners with news organizations to distribute content under appropriate licenses: http://spot.us.

Journalism That Matters: Lively Interaction Between Journalists and Community

Journalism That Matters supports journalists and leaders who are shaping the news and information ecology so that journalism serves the needs of people to be self-governing. JTM focuses on cultivating "healthy journalists" and informative interaction between journalists, educators, reformers, and community members. They support renewing the inner life of the journalist, and embrace all forms of media engagement: http://journalismthatmatters.org.

Real Talk Express: Hip-Hop and Street News

Jasiri X's groundbreaking hip-hop news series: http://www.realtalkxpress.com.

WikiLeaks: Pentagon Papers 2.0?

The website WikiLeaks has released hundreds of thousands of classified intelligence reports, military logs, diplomatic cables, and other material related to US foreign policy, including the ongoing wars in Iraq and Afghanistan. The documents have brought the misdeeds of war into the sunlight of public attention, fueling today's antiwar movement in much the same way the Pentagon Papers once galvanized those protesting the Vietnam War.

Source: Phyllis Bennis, "WikiLeaks: Pentagon Papers 2.0?" *Yes! Magazine*, July 27, 2010, http://www.yesmagazine.org/peace-justice/pentagon-papers-2.0-afghanistan.

MIND AND CONSCIOUSNESS

The news stories that follow report recent studies of consciousness on two levels: personal and psychosocial. These studies emphasize how our worldviews and habits of thought shape and limit our perspective, and how, when we open our minds and hearts, everything else seems to change as well: our health, our capacity to create, and our ability to relate and succeed.

PTSD Treatment Success Using MDMA-Assisted Psychotherapy

Clinical research studies showed psychotherapy assisted by the drug MDMA significantly outperformed the pharmaceutical industry in effective PTSD treatment. A recent pilot study showed the rate of clinical response for the active treatment group was 83 percent, with 30 percent of treatment-group participants no longer meeting criteria for PTSD just two months after the study and no evidence of impaired cognitive functioning. These results are especially significant considering the chronic and resistant nature of PTSD. To do this research, scientists have had to overcome greatly exaggerated estimates of the risks of MDMA put forth by anti-drug authorities seeking to block research into the beneficial uses of MDMA and other psychedelic medicines. *Note: MDMA is not Ecstasy. Substances sold on the street under the name Ecstasy often contain MDMA, but also may contain ketamine, caffeine, BZP, and other narcotics or stimulants. In laboratory studies, pure MDMA has been proven sufficiently safe for human consumption when taken a limited number of times in moderate doses.*

Sources: Michael C. Mithoefer et al., "The Safety and Efficacy of MDMA-Assisted Psychotherapy in Subjects with Chronic, Treatment-Resistant PTSD," *Journal of Psychopharmacology* 0, no. 0: 1–14; Jessica Winter, "Can a Single Pill Change Your Life?" *O, The Oprah Magazine*, February 15, 2011, http://www.oprah.com/health/PTSD-and-MDMA-Therapy-Medical-Uses-of-Ecstasy; "Harvard Study Published in Addiction Shows Ecstasy Not Associated with Cognitive Decline," PR Newswire, February 15, 2011, http://www.prnewswire.com/news-releases/harvard-study-published-in-addiction-shows-ecstasy-not-associated-with-cognitive-decline-116226594.html; "MDMA to Treat Post Traumatic Stress Disorder—Unnecessary Risk?" PTSD Trauma Treatment, November 26, 2010, http://www.ptsdtraumatreatment.org/ptsd-treatment/mdma-to-treat-post-traumatic-stress-disorder-%E2%80%93-unnecessary-risk/.

Precognition: Evidence That People Can Sense and Predict Future Events

The term "psi" denotes anomalous processes of information or energy transfer that are currently unexplained in terms of known physical or biological mechanisms. A paper by Cornell psychology professor Daryl Bem shows that a significant number of people are able to sense and predict future events. Resistance to this idea quickly surfaced, and scientists are in the throes of a heated debate about how to interpret the data. Human potential is poised for redefinition, warranting a closer look at all psi phenomena.

Sources: Daryl J. Bem, "Feeling the Future: Experimental Evidence for Anomalous Retroactive Influences on Cognition and Affect," *Journal of Personality and Social Psychology*, March 2011, http://www.dbem.ws/FeelingFuture.pdf; Cassandra Vieten, "It's About Time: The Scientific Evidence for Psi Experiences," *Huffington Post*, December 17, 2010, http://www.huffingtonpost.com/cassandra-vieten/esp-evidence_b_795366.html; Jonah Lehrer, "Feeling The Future: Is Precognition Possible?" *Wired*, November 15, 2010, http://www.wired.com/wiredscience/2010/11/feeling-the-future-is-precognition-possible; "Psi and Psychology: the Recent Debate," video, YouTube, 1:55:44, posted by "zooharvard," April 25, 2011, http://www.youtube.com/watch?v=oTdiu5kwjKs.

Meditation and Brain-Mind Changes

Meditation can ease the symptoms of depression and anxiety disorders and improve quality of life for people with chronic diseases. A recent study shows that even novice meditators were able to significantly increase gray brain matter density after practicing for only thirty minutes each day over an eight-week period.

Sources: Mary Desmond Pinkowish, "The Muse in The Moment," *Ode*, Spring 2011, http://www.odemagazine.com/doc/74/muse-in-the-moment/; Jason Marsh, "A Little Meditation Goes a Long Way," Greater Good Science Center, February 9, 2011, http://greatergood.berkeley.edu/article/item/a_little_meditation_goes_a_long_way.

Grief, Fear, and Despair: Essential for a Healthy Mind

As the multitude of twenty-first century threats to the planet grow more ominous, positive psychology has risen to the top of the pop psych chart. But there are times when "staying positive" hits a wall, and adversity calls on us to attend to the darker realities we'd prefer to avoid, ignore, or deny. But that only masks our hidden sorrows, allowing them to grow and consume us. As a culture, we perceive our darker realities as signs of impairment, but perhaps the only thing that's impaired is our perception.

Source: Miriam Greenspan, "How the Light Gets In," *Ode,* Spring 2011, http://www.odemagazine.com/doc/74/how-the-light-gets-in/.

Coherence and Chaos: Why We Need Both

On every level of living systems, there exists evidence of the value of both chaos and coherence; healthy function is dependent on their coexistence. Each is important in different situations. When we exclusively reify one over the other, we pay a price. For example, a lack of healthy variability in neural activity is associated with depression. Conversely, a lack of coherence in brain wave patterns is characteristic of schizophrenia. Context matters.

Source: Larry Dossey, "Coherence, Chaos, and the Coincidentia Oppositorum," *Explore: The Journal of Science & Healing* 6, no. 6: 339–45.

Tasting the Universe: What Synesthesia Suggests about the Nature of Consciousness

Synesthesia can be simply understood as a blending of senses (tasting colors, seeing music, etc.). It may sound unbelievable, but exacting brain scans can show locations of intense brain activity when synesthesia is stimulated. Many see synesthesia as a disorder, but some believe that it may be a kind of quantum consciousness and should be further studied for its possible implications for human consciousness.

Source: Maureen Seaberg, "Tasting the Universe: What Synesthesia Suggests about the nature of Consciousness," Institute of Noetic Sciences, May 2011, http://www.noetic.org/noetic/issue-ten-may/tasting-the-universe/.

Primates are Not Genetically Predisposed to Violence

It has long been thought that our primate cousins, the chimpanzees, have genetic predispositions toward violence, suggesting that violence is a natural part of human nature. However, new evidence suggests that this is not necessarily true. In the Gombe National Park in Tanzania, Jane Goodall studied the primates for decades and reported little aggressive interactions during the first fourteen years. But patterns of aggression changed among the troop in later years. Some suggest this was due to human interactions. Human feeding of the chimpanzees, with its restrictions and control, deeply affected the behavior and culture of the animals.

Source: Darcia Narvaez, "Male Chimps and Humans Genetically Violent—NOT!" *Psychology Today*, March 29, 2011, http://www.psychologytoday.com/blog/moral-landscapes/201103/male-chimps-and-humans-are-genetically-violent-not.

Early Societies Suggest Humans are Naturally Collaborative, Not Self-Serving

Humans are not born to be competitive, self-serving, and violent (as many believe) but rather collaborative. The human genus spent 99 percent of its existence in small-band, hunter-gatherer societies. These societies were fiercely egalitarian and didn't have an organized hierarchy or leader. It wasn't until societies began cultivating crops and became sedentary that political hierarchy and, therefore, violence appeared. But when we believe hierarchy to be a part of human nature, we are more likely to tolerate inequality.

Source: Darcia Narvaez, "What You Think About Evolution and Human Nature May Be Wrong," *Psychology Today*, April 17, 2011, http://www.psychologytoday.com/blog/moral-landscapes/201104/what-you-think-about-evolution-and-human-nature-may-be-wrong.

Studies Indicate Humans are Wired for Empathy

Scientists recently discovered mirror neurons in all primates. Mirror neurons enable us to experience another's plight as if we were experiencing it ourselves. Several studies suggest we are not soft-wired for aggression, violence, and self-interest but for collaboration and companionship. As humans, our main drive is to belong. Our secondary drives of narcissism, materialism, and violence emerge when our homo-empathicus nature is repressed by today's parenting, educational systems, business practices, and governments. Consciousness has changed throughout history. As we evolve, we extend our empathetic ties. Our hunter-gatherer ancestors only had empathy for those in their bloodline, the people they interacted with on a daily basis. Any other humans they encountered were considered a threat. Today's technology allows people around the globe to interact, furthering our potential for empathetic connection.

Source: "RSA Animate: The Empathic Civilisation," video, YouTube, 10:40, posted by theR-SAorg, May 6, 2010, http://www.youtube.com/watch?v=l7AWnfFRc7g&feature=relmfu.

Mindfulness and Parenting

Practice mindfulness to reduce stress during pregnancy, childbirth, and early parenting. Staying centered and present with children will foster a strong bond between parent and child and help kids feel safe, secure, and loved. Furthermore, children who are well attended to grow up to be mindful and compassionate themselves, creating a more peaceful future for all.

Source: Cassandra Vieten, "Riding the Rollercoaster of Pregnancy and Early Parenthood," *Psychology Today*, May 3, 2010, http://www.psychologytoday.com/blog/mindful-mother-hood/201005/riding-the-roller-coaster-pregnancy-and-early-parenthood.

Does Sharing Come Naturally to Kids?

A study on collaboration found that young children naturally share rewards when they are successful at completing a task together.

Source: Jason Marsh, "Does Sharing Come Naturally to Kids?" Greater Good Science Center, February 24, 2011, http://greatergood.berkeley.edu/article/item/does_sharing _come_naturally_to_kids.

The Power of Positive Perspectives on Race and Diversity

Journalist Joe Klein said, "Diversity has been written into the DNA of American life; any institution that lacks a rainbow array has come to seem diminished, if not diseased." Indeed, research has demonstrated that some surprising victims of racism are racists themselves. When racists encounter someone different from them they experience an immediate surge in stress hormones. Over time this response can lead to numerous chronic problems such as heart disease, cancer, and diabetes. Interracial interactions are not inherently stressful. Studies show that people who have a positive attitude when exposed to different ethnicities are more successful academically, occupationally, and socially. A diverse array of perspectives creates better communicators and problem solvers. Expecting kids to act colorblind is illogical. However, research has shown that talking about race and racism helps counteract prejudice.

Source: Rodolfo Mendoza-Denton, "Should We Talk to Young Children about Race?" Greater Good Science Center, May 5, 2011, http://greatergood.berkeley.edu/article/item/should_we_talk_to_young_children_about_race; Elizabeth Page-Gould, "Warning: Racism Is Bad for Your Health," Greater Good Science Center, August 3, 2010, http://greatergood.berkeley.edu/article/item/why_racism_is_bad_for_your_health; Darcia Narvaez and Patrick L. Hill, "The Relation of Multicultural Experiences to Moral Judgment and Mindsets," *Journal of Diversity in Higher Education*, March 2010, http://psycnet.apa.org/journals/dhe/3/1/43/.

The Health Benefits of Gratitude

The world's leading expert on gratitude finds that people who regularly cultivate gratitude report a host of physical, psychological, and social benefits. Gratitude celebrates the present, blocks negative emotions, and affirms goodness by recognizing external, greater-than-self factors. People who are grateful have a higher sense of self worth because they are continually aware that others are looking out for them.

Source: Robert A. Emmons, "Why Gratitude is Good," Greater Good Science Center, November 16, 2010, http://greatergood.berkeley.edu/article/item/why_gratitude_is_good/.

Giving is Getting: The Benefits of Altruism

Research indicates that altruistic behavior is good for you mentally, emotionally, and physically. In a survey of 4,500 American adults, 73 percent agreed that "volunteering lowered my stress levels," 89 percent reported that "volunteering has improved my sense of well-being," and 92 percent agreed that volunteering enriched their sense of purpose in life. The benefits of altruism may be especially helpful when one is in the midst of a crisis.

Source: Stephen G. Post, "Six Ways to Boost Your 'Habits of Helping,'" Greater Good Science Center, March 15, 2011, http://greatergood.berkeley.edu/article/item/six_ways _to_become_more_altruistic.

NATURE AND TECHNOLOGY

Our fates and that of nature are one and the same. Here are news stories of efforts to align human culture with nature, including strategies to reduce environmental degradation caused by human activity, restore ecosystems, and create the health, beauty, and abundance we all seek.

Green Design for a Healthier World: At the Tipping Point for Renewable Energy

We face many environmental challenges. But imagination and creativity provide the means to transform those challenges into opportunities for meeting human needs while healing and regenerating the world around us—the global commons that is our shared heritage. Through creative design and the use of technology, we can better integrate human and natural systems. With time, as we learn ways to enhance the environments that sustain and enrich us, our collective ecological "footprint" may become one that nourishes rather than diminishes the planet.

With a growing list of innovations to combat climate change, the capacity of green power could soon exceed that of fossil fuel stations worldwide. If we account for the full economic, environmental, and health costs of coal and nuclear energy, non-fossil fuels such as wind and solar power are economically competitive with their environmentally unfriendly counterparts. Other ideas to limit or adjust our consumption of energy and resources include a machine that will turn plastic back into oil; recycling plastics from complex waste products— requiring less than 10 percent of the energy needed to produce virgin plastics; the "artificial leaf," a small solar cell that mimics photosynthesis, can split water into its two components and uses those gases to produce electricity; a battery that "uses the contrast in salinity between fresh and seawater to produce an electric current"—a technology with the potential to meet 13 percent of the world's current consumption of electricity; turning windows into solar panels; and utilizing the decomposing characteristic of fungi to restore ecosystems, control pests, filter farm waste, and treat disease. While some of these ideas seem out of reach for individuals, innovations such as a water faucet that cuts water flow by more than 90 percent are available for use in households worldwide.

Sources: Brooke Jarvis, *Yes! Magazine*, "A Tipping Point for Renewable Energy," July 28, 2010, http://www.yesmagazine.org/blogs/brooke-jarvis/2010-a-tipping-point-for-renewable-energy; Paul R. Epstein et al., "Full Cost Accounting for the Life Cycle of Coal," *Annals of the New York Academy of Sciences*, February 2011, http://onlinelibrary.wiley.com/doi/10.1111/j.1749-6632.2010.05890.x/pdf; "True Cost Accounting for Nuclear Power," Living on Earth, March 25, 2011, http://www.loe.org/shows/segments.html?programID=11-P13-00012&segmentID=2; Robert Costanza et al., "Can Nuclear Power Be Part of the Solution?" *Solutions*, April 5, 2011, http://www.thesolutionsjournal.com/node/918; Carol Smith, "Plastic To Oil Fantastic," Our World 2.0, August 27, 2010, http://ourworld.unu.edu/en/plastic-to-oil-fantastic/; Mark van Baal, "Every Little Dripp Counts," *Ode*, Spring 2011, http://www.odemagazine.com/doc/74/dripp-faucet/; Mira Stauffacher, "Biology Professor Leads Student in 'Fuel from Aquatic Biomass' Project," *Sonoma State Star*, September 15, 2010, http://www.sonomastatestar.com/news/biology-professor-leads-students-in-fuel-from-aquatic-biomass-project-1.1598867; Nicole Casal Moore, "'We've All Been Taught That This Doesn't Happen,'" *Michigan Today*, April 13, 2011, http://michigantoday.umich.edu/2011/04/story.php?id=7980&tr=y&auid=8154157; "Solar 'Artificial Leaf' Is Unveiled by MIT Researchers," *e360 Digest*, March 28, 2011, http://e360.yale.edu/digest/first_practical_solar_leaf_converts_water_and_sunlight_into_electricity/2870/; "New Battery Uses Seawater and Freshwater to Produce Electricity," *e360 Digest*, March 30, 2011, http://e360.yale.edu/digest/new_battery_uses_seawater_and_freshwater_to_produce_electricity/2875/; "*The Economist* Announces the First of the 2010 Innovation Award Winners," press release, *The Economist*, September 19, 2010, http://www.economistconferences.co.uk/press-release/economist-announces-first-2010-innovation-award-winners; James Trimarco, "Can Mushrooms Rescue the Gulf?" *Yes! Magazine*, October 1, 2010, http://www.yesmagazine.org/issues/a-resilient-community/can-mushrooms-rescue-the-gulf.

Sustainability Means Resilient Communities

Our most powerful way forward lies in people working with the environment, not against it, to build a healthy and secure foundation upon which all members of the human family and all life on Earth can thrive. With nature as model, mentor, and co-creator with humans, we can establish a permanent culture that's about regeneration, connectivity, synergy, and abundance. In the process, we will need to collaborate with one another and redefine our relationships with the environment, rethinking everything from the way we design settlements to how we use resources and get energy. People around the world have been joining together to support the environment and the resources it provides. Those who have been impacted the most by our changing world have led the defense; for example, the poorer communities in Bolivia, have called for "rights for nature"; the Dutch have incorporated bicycling into everyday transportation by educating children about riding and providing bike-only boulevards for safer, efficient, and emission-free travel; and organizations like the Goldman Environmental Prize have encouraged those working against terrible odds to be leaders in their communities to protect the environment.

Fortunately, creativity is an unlimited resource. The following are inspired examples of ways in which communities and visionaries are building resilience, adaptability, and ingenuity into their plans for a sustainable future.

The Transition Town Movement
"Transition" is an approach to embracing and preparing for a post-carbon future. Closely aligned with the principles of permaculture, the Transition movement fosters resilience and local self-reliance through network-building, reduced energy consumption, and eco-farming.

Integrative Settlement Design Through Nature-Inspired Technologies
The Sahara Forest Project will use Seawater Greenhouses and concentrated solar power to generate fresh water and abundant energy while producing zero-carbon food and reversing desertification. Radical, closed-loop efficiencies mimic those of natural ecosystems.

Radically Sustainable Homes Built from Recycled Materials
"Earthships" are permanent structures that provide their own energy, water, and food and are made from locally sourced recycled materials. Hundreds dot the globe, some now in Haiti.

Sources: Mason Inman, "Skill Up, Party Down," *Yes! Magazine*, September 17, 2010, http://www.yesmagazine.org/issues/a-resilient-community/party-down; "Using Nature's Genius in Architecture," video, TED, November 2010, http://www.ted.com/talks/lang/eng/michael_pawlyn_using_nature_s_genius_in_architecture.html; "Haiti Earthship Project: Overview," video, YouTube, 14:47, posted by earthship, March 21, 2011, http://www.youtube.com/watch?v=h7jAkwhTq4c.

How Food Impacts Every Aspect of Our Lives

Food issues are political, social, emotional, psychological, ecological, and economic. The following are stories about how the ways we produce and transport food are changing to support the ever-growing population in sustainable ways.

Research Shows That Eco-Farming, Not Big Ag, Is the Key to Feeding the World

The dominant narrative on the issue of food security and quality is that only industrial-scale corporate agriculture can feed the growing human population; ecology-based and organic farming are mere luxuries. According to this myth, growing enough food will require expanding the current agribusiness model of production, which is fossil fuel-, petrochemical-, water-, and capital-intensive, and based largely on plantation-style monocultures of genetically modified crops. Yet recent scientific evidence demonstrates that farms designed to emulate natural ecosystems not only protect and restore natural resources, but are more productive than industrial farms—and much more resilient to climate change.

The Permaculture Design Movement

Permaculture is the conscious design and maintenance of agriculturally productive systems which have the diversity, stability, and resilience of natural ecosystems. It is the harmonious integration of landscape and people—providing their food, energy, shelter, and other material and nonmaterial needs in a sustainable way—working with, rather than against, nature. This permanent agriculture also provides the possibility of a stable order.

The New Food Manifesto

From hundred-mile diets to green markets and organics, from obesity to genetically modified organisms, food is always in the news. The new food movement is an act of popular resistance against a system as harmful to life as military conflict. Food isn't just something we need to shovel down each day to survive. It's far more potent: it's the means, more than any other, by which we humans shape our planet and ourselves. We need a new food manifesto outlining how our food choices can shape a better world. Bring friends together to enjoy good food, and talk about where your food came from—and about your food choices.

Sources: Tom Levitt, "Agroecological Farming 'Can Double Food Production in Africa over Next 10 Years,'" *Ecologist*, March 8, 2011, http://www.theecologist .org/News/news _round_up/802483/agroecological_farming_can_double_food_production_in_africa_o ver_next_10_years.html; Nidhi Prakash, "World Hunger Best Cured by Small-Scale Agriculture," *Guardian*, January 13, 2011, http://www.guardian.co.uk/environment/ 2011/jan/13/world-hunger-small-scale-agriculture; Tom Philpott, "Debunking the Stubborn Myth That Only Industrial Ag Can 'Feed the World,'" *Grist*, March 10, 2011, http://www .grist.org/industrial-agriculture/2011-03-10-debunking-myth-that-only-industrial- agri- culture-can-feed-world; "UMass Permaculture Documentary Series (Part 1/3)," video, YouTube, 5:54, posted by UMassPermaculture, February 4, 2011, http://www .youtube.com/watch?v=XWHSzGDItBA; Carolyn Steel, "A New Food Manifesto," *Ode*, Spring 2011, http://www.odemagazine.com/doc/74/new-food-manifesto/.

More Sources on Aligning Ourselves with Nature

Sustainable World Sourcebook: The go-to guide for getting engaged. Get up to speed fast on the critical issues—and on solutions and actions to take. http://swcoalition.org/index.php.

Resource Directory: http://swcoalition.org/media/pdf/sourcebook _resources.pdf.

Bioneers: The solutions to most of our environmental and social crises already exist. "Bioneers" are innovators looking to nature to uncover those solutions. http://www.bioneers.org/.

POLITICS AND PEOPLE POWER

The political and social consciousness of the world is shifting before our eyes. There is a growing realization that true power resides in "the people," not in governments or politicians. When people unite and are organized and determined, they are likely to succeed. In the United States, polarized politics, the corrupting influence of corporate money, and the disintegration of democratic values have elicited some pushback. Yet broad movements have yet to gel. The stories below reflect public concerns and actions, both in the US and around the world.

Arab Spring Topples Dictators

In December, following a vegetable seller named Mohammed Bouazizi, the people of Tunisia rose up in an unarmed insurrection to overthrow the regime of dictator Ben Ali. Their success prompted a popular uprising against President Hosni Mubarak of Egypt, which, after weeks of unprecedented protests, succeeded in ousting him. Soon, the grassroots struggles for democracy spread, with protests taking place throughout the Middle East and North Africa. Though protests in some nations were violently suppressed, movements of the Arab Spring have dramatically altered the way many view prospects for democratization in the Middle East.

Sources: Steven Zunes, "Egypt: Lessons In Democracy," *Yes! Magazine*, February 1, 2011, http://www.yesmagazine.org/peace-justice/egypt-lessons-in-democracy; Bruno Giussani, "TED: After the Tunisian Revolution, Imagining the Way Forward," TED, March 24, 2011, http://blog.ted.com/2011/03/24/tedxcarthage-notebook-after-the-tunisian-revolution-imagining-the-way-forward; Ruaridh Arrow, "Gene Sharp: Author of the Nonviolent Revolution Rulebook," *BBC*, February 21, 2011, http://www.bbc.co.uk/news/world-middle-east-12522848.

Arizona Awakens the "21st Century Civil Rights Movement"

After Arizona passed SB 1070, a controversial measure also known as the "Show-me-your-papers" law, the public response in opposition to the bill was swift, large, and diverse. Hundreds of thousands of people protested against the law in at least seventy US cities. Sports stars denounced it. Boycotts, including by other US cities, dogged the state for months. Though copycat bills were introduced in many other states, popular pressure kept most from gaining traction; a year later, only Georgia's bill had passed. The mobilization of Latino communities and their supporters has remained high, influencing the debate on federal immigration reform legislation. As Dr. Warren Stewart, a Phoenix pastor, told supporters of the law: "You have awakened the 21st century civil rights movement."

Sources: Kety Esquivel, "The 21st Century Civil Rights Movement," *Yes! Magazine*, May 18, 2010, http://www.yesmagazine.org/people-power/the-21st-century-civil-rights-movement; Jordan Flaherty, "In Arizona, A Human Rights Summer," *Yes! Magazine*, July 30, 2010, http://www.yesmagazine.org/people-power/in-arizona-a-human-rights-summer.

Boycott, Divestment, Sanctions: Fighting the Israeli Occupation

Increasingly, people and organizations across the United States are standing up to say no to US support for Israeli policies of occupation and apartheid in Palestinian territories. In the first days and weeks after Israel attacked a humanitarian flotilla bringing aid to Gaza, sympathetic actions occurred across the US. In California, hundreds of activists formed a picket line at dawn at the Port of Oakland, where an Israeli cargo ship waited, and urged dockworkers not to unload the ship in protest of the flotilla assault. Workers of the International Longshore and Warehouse Union (ILWU) refused to cross the picket line, a labor arbitrator upheld their right to refuse to unload the ship, and the shipping company abandoned the effort. Workers in Sweden, South Africa, Norway, and Malaysia, have all announced their refusal to unload Israeli ships.

Source: Phyllis Bennis, "Waging Peace from Afar: Divestment and Israeli Occupation," *Yes! Magazine*, August 20, 2010, http://www.yesmagazine.org/peace-justice/waging-peace-from-afar-divestment-and-israeli-occupation.

A Realistic Vision for World Peace

Nobel Peace Laureate Jody Williams says peace is only possible with justice and equality: we all need access to enough resources to live dignified lives; access to education and healthcare; freedom from want and fear; hard work and creativity; collaboration and collective struggle. What's your definition of peace?

Source: "Jody Williams: A Realistic Vision for World Peace," video, TED, posted by TEDWomen, December 2010, http://www.ted.com/talks/lang/eng/jody_williams_a _realistic_vision_for_world_peace.html.

Making Peace Possible: Everyday Acts of Resistance and Positive Change

Monumental change is always a result of smaller acts. Whether it be rejecting fiction-based television news, refusing to cooperate with an unjust system, whistle-blowing, or defying military orders when you know something is wrong, ordinary people are dropping their fears and finding creative ways to challenge leaders who abuse the power given them.

Source: Steve Crawshaw and John Jackson, "10 Everyday Acts of Resistance That Changed the World," *Yes! Magazine*, April 1, 2011, http://www.yesmagazine.org/people-power/10-everyday-acts-of-resistance-that-changed-the-world.

Wisconsin: First Stop in an American Uprising?

Thousands of citizens filled the streets of Madison and the State Capitol in protest of a bill reducing the rights and benefits of workers. Though the bill passed, it was later defeated in the courts. But the Wisconsin union movement didn't die; their ardor inspired people across the country and sparked direct actions in all fifty states.

Sources: Sarah van Gelder, "Wisonsin: The First Stop in an American Uprising?" *Yes! Magazine*, February 18, 2011, http://www .yesmagazine.org/blogs/wisconsin-the-first-stop-in-an-american-uprising; Micah Uetricht, "Bigger than Unions, Bigger than Wisconsin," *Yes! Magazine*, February 25, 2011, http://www.yesmagazine.org/people-power/bigger-than-unions-bigger-than-wisconsin.

Pushing Back Against Corporate Spending in Elections

Bipartisan citizens' groups have been mobilizing to curb corporate spending in a variety of ways, such as amending the Constitution to declare that corporations do not have the same right to free speech as people; requiring shareholders to approve companies' political spending; passing legislation to require fuller disclosure of where political money originates; and working to expand publicly financed elections.

Sources: Brooke Jarvis, "After the Campaign Cash, the Backlash," *Yes! Magazine*, November 4, 2010, http://www.yesmagazine.org/blogs/brooke-jarvis/after-the-campaign-cash-the-backlash; Gwen Stowe and Jeff Clements, "Give Us Our Law Back: Montana Fights to Stop Corporate Corruption," *Yes! Magazine*, May 24, 2011, http://www.yesmagazine.org/people-power/give-us-our-law-back-montana-fights-to-stop-corporate-corruption.

Oregon Senate Approves Citizens' Initiative Review Bill

The Oregon Senate passed legislation to establish the Citizens' Initiative Review as a permanent feature of Oregon's initiative process. The bill, HB 2634, establishes a new state commission to administer future Citizens' Initiative Reviews (CIRs). The funding for the program will be provided by foundations and private donations—at no additional cost to the state.

Source: "Oregon Senate Approves Citizens' Initiative Review Bill," press release, Healthy Democracy Oregon, June 1, 2011, http://www.healthydemocracyoregon.org/blog/2011/06/01/news-release-oregon-senate-approves-citizens%25E2%2580%2599-initiative-review-bill.

Participatory Budgeting Comes to the US

Through the first "participatory budgeting" experiment in the US, residents of Chicago's 49th Ward spent a year deciding how to spend $1.3 million in taxpayer dollars. Over 1,600 community members stepped up to decide on improvements for their neighborhoods, showing how participatory budgeting can pave the way for a new kind of grassroots democracy, in Chicago and beyond.

Source: Josh Lerner and Megan Wade Antieau, "Chicago's $1.3 Million Experiment in Democracy," Yes! Magazine, April 20, 2010, http://www.yesmagazine.org/people-power/chicagos-1.3-million-experiment-in-democracy.

A Push for Civility in Politics

"I may disagree with you, but I'm pretty sure you're not Hitler," read one sign at the Rally to Restore Sanity, organized by comedian Jon Stewart. In an increasingly emotional political climate, hundreds of thousands of people came out to celebrate reasonableness and respect in political debates instead of hatred, violence, and division.

Sources: "Signs of Sanity (and/or Fear)," Yes! Magazine, November 1, 2010, http://www.yesmagazine.org/people-power/rally-to-restore-sanity-and-or-fear-1; Sarah van Gelder and Brooke Jarvis, "Words Matter: How Media Can Build Civility or Destroy It," Yes! Magazine, January 12, 2011, http://www.yesmagazine.org/people-power/words-matter-how-media-can-build-civility-or-destroy-it.

Acknowledgments

Thanks to San Francisco State University students who helped in preparing and editing this chapter: Ally Gill, Robert Usher, Celeste Richmond, and Aaron Peacock. And big thanks to: Laralyn Yee, University of California, Berkeley.

A special thanks to Brooke Jarvis, Sarah van Gelder, and Fran Korten, of *Yes! Magazine*, for contributing many of the stories, and happy fifteenth anniversary to *Yes!*, an award-winning, ad-free, non-profit publication that supports people's active engagement in building a just and abundant world.

Thanks also to Tom Atlee, of the Co-Intelligence Institute, and Neal Gorenflo, Shareable magazine—both of you for your clear thinking and caring counsel. And appreciation to Brad Burge, Multidisciplinary Association for Psychedelic Studies; Jason Marsh of the Greater Good Science Center, University of California, Berkeley; Marilyn Schlitz, Jenny Mathews, and Mathew Gilbert of the Institute of Noetic Sciences; and Mira Luna, from Bay Area Community Exchange and Trust is the Only Currency. Thank you all for your stories and your good work in the world.

To continue your exploration of creativity, integrative thinking, and an expanded definition of health and activism, visit the Holistic Health Learning Center, San Francisco State University, online, where you'll find an extensive set of links and emerging ideas: www.sfsu.edu/~holistic.

KENN BURROWS has been an educator and consultant for over thirty years, teaching Holistic Health Studies at San Francisco State University since 1991. He is founder and director of the Holistic Health Learning Center, a unique library and community action center staffed by student volunteers. He is also the producer of the biennial conference "The Future of Health Care." Prior to coming to SF State, he taught at Foothill Community College for twelve years and operated Stress-Care, a corporate training and consulting company. For the last sixteen years, he has taught the popular course "Holistic Health: Human Nature & Global Perspectives." He also serves as faculty evaluator to three different campus student organizations, including Project Censored—SF State Affiliate, and he is a member of the board of the Media Freedom Foundation.

Notes

1. Rebecca Costa, *The Watchman's Rattle—Thinking Our Way out of Extinction*, (New York: Vanguard Press, 2010).
2. D. J. Simons and C. F. Chabris, "Gorillas In Our Midst: Sustained Inattentional Blindness For Dynamic Events," *Perception* 28, 1059–74.
3. Costa, *The Watchman's Rattle*.

4. James B. Quilligan, "Making the Great Adjustment: Coalition for the Global Commons," *Kosmos*, Spring–Summer 2008, http://www.kosmosjournal.org/CustomContentRetrieve.aspx?ID=3846791.
5. John Tierney, "Doomsayers Beware, a Bright Future Beckons," *New York Times*, May 17, 2010, www.nytimes.com/2010/05/18/science/18tier.html?ref=science.
6. Neal Gorenflo, "Knowledge Workers & The Commons: A Reflection," *Shareable*, January 19, 2011, http://www.shareable.net/blog/knowledge-workers-and-the-commons-a-reflection.
7. David Emerald, *The Power of TED* (*The Empowerment Dynamic)*, 2009, http://www.powerofted.com.
8. Rebecca Solnit, "Iceberg Economies & Shadow Selves: Further Adventures in the Territories of Hope," *Common Dreams*, December 22, 2010, http://www.commondreams.org/view/2010/12/22.
9. "Public Service Announcements," Dutch Institute for Road Safety, 2010.
10. Solnit, "Iceberg Economies & Shadow Selves."
11. Marilyn M. Schlitz, Cassandra Vieten, and Elizabeth Miller, "Worldview Transformation and the Development of Social Consciousness," *Journal of Consciousness Studies* 17, no. 7–8, 18–36.

CHAPTER 5

Media Democracy in Action

by Mickey Huff with contributions by Abby Martin, Tracy Rosenberg, Jeff Cohen, Lisa Graves, Josh Wolf, Khalil Bendib, Emma
Cape, Logan Price, Nolan Higdon, and Ryan Shehee

> As Jefferson and Madison put it, unless all citizens
> have easy access to the same caliber of information as
> society's wealthy and privileged, self-government cannot
> succeed.
> —ROBERT MCCHESNEY

In past editions of *Censored,* we occasionally included highlights of the
many groups and individuals that dedicate their lives to media freedom,
and help create and protect a vibrant free press in maintenance of
democracy. In 2003, then Project Censored director Dr. Peter Phillips
compiled the *Project Censored Guide to Independent Media and Activism,*
which was released by our publishers at Seven Stories Press. We have
partnered with many in this broad and diverse community over the
years and hope to continue building solidarity with those who, like
Project Censored, strongly believe that we are on the verge of a media
revolution that can revitalize our democratic institutions and restore
hope to hundreds of millions that self-government can work, but only
if the people have access to highly accurate and factual information.

This year, we highlight some of the shining lights, some newcomers,
some veterans. The following truly represent media democracy in action
and they bring updates from the frontlines of the media revolution.

MEDIA ROOTS
by Abby Martin

The root system of a tree is five times more extensive than the tree
itself, reaching far underground to form a solid base for growth and
nourishment. Just as this root system is integral to the survival of a

tree, media is integral to the foundation and survival of a democracy. However, the corporate consolidation and top-down control of America's current media system undermines democracy by stifling and diluting the discourse crucial to maintaining a critical and informed public.

The mainstream media establishment has conceded its journalistic integrity time and time again by catering to corporate and political interests. The people can no longer wait on Congress and the Federal Communications Commission (FCC) to eke out miniscule reforms to the dysfunctional system in which they are embedded. Instead, the people must create alternative methods to freely communicate and exchange information.

In the San Francisco Bay Area, such an organization has been formed. Media Roots is a grassroots, independent citizen journalism project that reports the news from outside of party lines, while providing a collaborative space of open dialogue for conscious citizens, artists, and activists.

The website, MediaRoots.org, aggregates a variety of critical and fascinating underreported news on various subjects: local and world news; political and corporate corruption; food and health; and science and philosophy.

In conjunction with providing an ever-expanding archival base of crucial information, Media Roots also conducts original reporting on an array of important local, national, and global issues. The organization produces a regular radio talk show, original video content, and extensive interviews with artists, activists, journalists, and inspiring Bay Area locals.

The merit of citizen reporting is increasingly recognized as corporate journalism continues to fail in its intended role as the watchdogs against corruption. Many people find that their voice isn't represented in the political dialogue and are seeking alternative media sources reporting raw, unfiltered, and truthful information.

Media Roots is a valuable tool for people to begin revolutionizing the media dialogue. The organization's aim is to build community through collaboration and participation, and its openness to feature submissions of all kinds encourages others to take an active role in the field of media. Everyone has the ability to be a citizen journalist, and Media Roots, while maintaining strong principles of integrity that require all content to be based on sound research, provides an important outlet for others to explore their ideas and share their skills.

Since the inception of the project, Media Roots has motivated multiple people worldwide to directly engage with their communities, whether by interviewing inspirational figures or by conducting investigatory research on a range of issues. Furthermore, the organization has provided a voice for multiple active duty soldiers to speak out anonymously about their political beliefs.

Many people who get their news from the corporate media have a highly skewed perspective on what issues should be of concern to their health, family, and communities. The mainstream political discourse truncates issues into oversimplified talking points that pit one political party against another, causing a deep divide in the American citizenry. Media Roots holds no party bias, and reports from the bigger picture by analyzing issues through a broad historical lens.

As a completely independent organization, Media Roots will never cater toward corporate sponsors or censor credible information. Because it exists outside the rigid corporate model that capitalistic societies are accustomed to, it has a unique and unrestricted ability to spontaneously grow and flourish. Instead of competing monetarily with other independent media outlets with similar goals, Media Roots simply seeks to coexist as an organic beacon of information in the emerging renaissance of grassroots journalism happening worldwide.

Like a tree's widespread root system, grassroots networks of communication in all fields of media must extend far beyond the top-down institutional structures created for us. The Media Roots model is not mechanized, and will continue to naturally evolve as more people participate in and contribute to the project.

People must create the alternative they wish to see from the bottom up. Media Roots is paving an important path that is driven by a shared passion for media justice and the core belief that unfettered access to information is a human right.

Find out more about Media Roots at www.MediaRoots.org and its founder Abby Martin at her website www.AbbyMartin.org.

MEDIA ALLIANCE

by Tracy Rosenberg

Founded in 1976, at the pinnacle of idealism about what journalism could accomplish by speaking truth to power, the Bay Area–based non-profit organization has followed the same winding path as the profession it follows. Over the past thirty-five years, it has bird-dogged the mainstream media for accountability to communities, called foul on faux-objectivity as the measure of good journalism, fought for the survival of independent media, and re-imagined itself as the regional voice in the media policy battles that will determine the playing field for generations to come.

In 2011–2012, Media Alliance has identified the following priorities as the key battlegrounds for an independent communications future:

▶ Establishing an open internet as standard operating policy (network neutrality).

▶ Delivering on the promise of the passage of Local Community Radio Act with hundreds of new, locally based low-power radio stations to deliver unique news, information, and culture to their neighborhoods.

▶ Stopping the merger of AT&T with T-Mobile, a corporate power grab that will consolidate the emerging wireless market in a consumer-unfriendly duopoly.

▶ Preserving the public access system, a hard-fought concession from the cable companies, that delivers coverage of local government, educational opportunities, and public programming via the television dial.

▶ Working to develop sustainable and ethical funding streams for local independent media that retain editorial freedom and the ability to cover controversial material.

▶ Fighting noncommercial radio consolidation by preserving the independent Pacifica Network as well as college radio stations under threat of sale due to the privatization of higher education.

If we can make progress on these six goals in the next two years, then *Censored 2014* will be a lot thinner than *Censored 2011*. If you'd like to join us in solution-based advocacy for a vital media landscape that delivers information instead of censoring it, in the interests of vigorous truth-based dialogue and meaningful democracy, here are some places to go for more information:

Website: www.media-alliance.org
Huffington Post column: www.huffingtonpost.com/tracy-rosenberg
The Media Action Grassroots Network: www.mag-net.org
The Media and Democracy Coalition: www.media-democracy.net

PARK CENTER FOR INDEPENDENT MEDIA: SPOTLIGHTING TODAY'S JOURNALISTIC HEROES

by Jeff Cohen

With United States mainstream politics and media growing ever more corporatized and dumbed down, one of the few bright spots in our society is the growth of smart, independent media.

Decades ago, if aggressive journalism had pushed a deceptive member of the president's cabinet to resign, credit would likely go to a big outlet like the *New York Times*. But corporate outlets have shrunk their newsrooms. Nowadays, it's bloggers at *Talking Points Memo* who force an attorney general to resign. When Vice President Dick Cheney's top aide was indicted, the reporter-of-record at the trial was a blogger for Firedoglake.com.

Nowadays, when a momentous movement for democracy erupts in Egypt, informed Americans rush for continuous on-the-scene coverage to outlets like *Democracy Now!* and Al Jazeera English. American TV networks (now lacking foreign bureaus) got to the story late and covered it by parachuting their star anchors into the country, with little knowledge of the language, culture, or history.

When unbridled Wall Street greed tanked the global economy, US corporate media largely offered surface coverage while the full story of bipartisan corruption got told in-depth by independent journalists like Matt Taibbi, filmmaker Danny Schechter, *Truthdig*'s Robert Scheer and by documentaries like *Inside Job*.

As the failures of corporate media keep mounting—from the run-up to the Iraq invasion to Wall Street crime to the current debt crisis—independent media gain audience and credibility. Launched out of a broom closet in 1996, *Democracy Now!* has grown into a powerful global newscast with resources and personnel. A solo "blogger in his pajamas" in 2000, Josh Marshall has built Talking Points Memo into an aggressive news operation with over a dozen reporters.

The Park Center for Independent Media (PCIM) was established at Ithaca College in 2008 to track these exciting developments in independent media, and to point communications students toward career paths in independent media. Ithaca students have interned in recent summers at dozens of media organizations, large and small, including Brave New Films, The Real News Network, Free Speech TV, GRITtv with Laura Flanders, *Democracy Now!*, Common Dreams, Prometheus Radio, City Limits, and the *Nation*.

To spotlight "outstanding achievement in independent media," the center gives out the annual Izzy Award, named after legendary independent journalist I. F. "Izzy" Stone. In 2009, the inaugural Izzy Award was shared by blogger Glenn Greenwald and Amy Goodman of *Democracy Now!* In 2010, the Izzy was awarded to investigative journalist Jeremy Scahill, whose reporting in independent outlets had pushed the issue of abuse by war contactors into mainstream discussion. In 2011, the award was shared by the unique New York City investigative outlet "City Limits" and by *Truthdig* cofounder Robert Scheer. (An editor of *Ramparts* in the 1960s, Scheer sees today's internet-driven independent media as "*Ramparts* on speed.")

Besides the Izzy winners, PCIM's speakers series has brought many shining lights of independent media to Ithaca to inspire and motivate students, including authors Naomi Klein and Matt Taibbi, television and radio hosts Laura Flanders and Farai Chidaya, cartoonist Tom Tomorrow, and *Talking Points Memo*'s Josh Marshall.

The recent growth in independent media is exciting—as is the wave of college students hungry to work in independent media and think outside the corporate box.

JEFF COHEN, who founded the media watch group Fairness & Accuracy In Reporting (FAIR) in 1986, became the founding director of Park Center for Independent Media in 2008. www.ithaca.edu/indy.

PR WATCH: THE CENTER FOR MEDIA AND DEMOCRACY CONTINUES ITS CRUCIAL MISSION

by Lisa Graves

Almost two years ago, I took the baton to lead the Center for Media and Democracy from John Stauber. John, a visionary activist who had been fighting Monsanto, founded the Center in 1993 to fight corporate public relations (PR) spin and government propaganda. The first book he coauthored was the breakthrough *Toxic Sludge Is Good for You.* It documented many PR scams, including the sewage sludge industry's effort to rename the toxic soup of industrial and human waste "biosolids" for "use" on forests and land, despite all the heavy metals and other contaminants in it.

This past year, John spent some of his "retirement" working as an activist against the latest version of this scam by helping the Center establish the "Food Rights Network" to fight sludge peddlers who are now labeling it as the "organic" compost or "soil" amendment. The Center believes you have a right to know if your fruits and vegetables are being grown in heavy metals, flame retardants, and other toxics in sludge. Sadly, this scam was even covered up by "green" Democrats in San Francisco, who had been giving this junk away to local residents as "organic compost." We helped stop this practice.

The Center has dramatically expanded its PR-busting in the past two years, with new exposés on the Koch brothers and their radical agenda and on the corporate creation of a new right-wing vanguard like radical governor Scott Walker and his efforts to crush workers' rights. While the corporate media was initially ignoring the dramatic labor uprising in Wisconsin and then turning minimal coverage into some sort of he said, she said dispute, on PRWatch.org we were breaking the real story about the inspiring unity of protestors from every walk of life coming together to fight this radical agenda. We documented "tractor-cades" of farmers marching together with other laborers, students, and people from all walks of life, hundreds of thousands of Americans marching in the freezing Wisconsin winter, being discounted numerically and dismissed substantively by the mainstream press (except at night on MSNBC). We have a real day-by-day account of breakthroughs, setbacks, and victories that you won't find anywhere else. You certainly will not find it on Fox's propaganda machine or its echo on CNN and the Associated Press, whose wire stories feed local papers with few reporters.

We also launched BanksterUSA.org to get you the truth about the Goldman Sachs "alumni" pulling the strings in Washington regardless of who wins the White House. With veteran trade activist Mary Bottari at the helm, we helped push for the first ever public audit of the Federal Reserve, backed Elizabeth Warren's appointment to get the Consumer Financial Protection Bureau off the ground along with needed reforms, and documented the true cost of the bailout of Wall Street—beyond just the TARP funds. We are now helping to support a move-your-money campaign, spearheaded by firefighters getting their funds out of banks that back anti-union politicians.

In the summer of 2009, Mary joined me at the Center along with Wendell Potter, the former CIGNA health insurance PR exec turned whistleblower, who sought us out to fight the insurance industry's spin machine on health reform. Wendell has testified before Congress and written a new book, *Deadly Spin*, that documents the untold story of the industry's spin doctors. Wendell is continuing to fight the PR campaign corporations that have mounted to undo the progress made in the compromise passed last year.

Also, I have brought my expertise in battling national security surveillance policies—such as the PATRIOT Act, warrantless wiretapping, the FBI Joint Terrorism Task Force's spying on peace activists and other Americans, and expanded powers of the Department of Homeland Security—to the Center's agenda. I have also devoted substantial effort to fighting back against the US Supreme Court's deplorable decision to expand the power of corporations to corrupt politicians through spending unlimited money to influence elections. The Center is one of the leading voices in the national effort to repeal this decision, which unfortunately is going to result in the most expensive and deceptive election cycle in US history in 2012. Our team will be in overdrive for the next eighteen months exposing corporate front groups, busting spin, and debunking lies being peddled by "special" interests. We will be relying heavily on our specialized wiki, SourceWatch.org, to document these deceptive groups with their innocent, patriotic sounding names that are really advancing a corporate agenda at odds with the real interests of ordinary people. Americans don't need a faked out Wall Street economy built on shipping US jobs overseas while cutting social services, job security, and environmental protection at home. We need a real economy with good secure jobs that helps the American dream be possible, a safety net that protects our health and lives when illness comes and aging takes its toll, and healthier food and a more sustainable planet for our families and our children's children.

In the past two years, we've made some big changes at the Center, cutting overhead while expanding and deepening our investigative work. This past year we produced more original articles than in the past two years combined. Our team is proud to be part of the Center for Media and Democracy's second chapter, devoted to exposing corporate spin and propaganda in order to protect our health, our planet, our economy, and the power of the people in our democracy. We are also proud to support Project Censored's work getting important stories out that are overlooked by the mainstream media. We are honored to be part of that muckraker tradition. We know that knowledge is power in a democracy, and we at the Center are working to help arm you with the truth, compellingly told. So, we hope you will check out the Center for Media and Democracy version 2.0 on our sites—PRWatch.org, SourceWatch.org, BanksterUSA.org, and on Facebook as well as on Twitter (please follow and share our work under "PRWatch").

LISA GRAVES is the executive director of the Center for Media and Democracy, which exposes corporate PR and government propaganda and which publishes PRWatch.org, SourceWatch.org, and BanksterUSA.org. She previously served as a senior advisor in all three branches of the federal government, as a leading strategist on civil liberties advocacy, and as an adjunct law professor at one of the top law schools in the country, after joining the US Department of Justice through the attorney general's Honor Program following a clerkship with a federal judge and graduation with honors from Cornell Law School.

FIRST AMENDMENT FORGOTTEN AT BIRTHPLACE OF FREE SPEECH MOVEMENT: WHAT THEY DON'T TEACH AT JOURNALISM SCHOOL

by Josh Wolf

The First Amendment of the United States Constitution makes it clear that the rights of journalists are to be respected, but it offers few clues on how the free press should be protected. It's generally understood that reporters are not given extra rights, and they certainly don't have a pass to break the law. But journalists often have legitimate reasons to venture into areas they otherwise wouldn't and to talk to people engaged in suspicious activities.

In November 2010, I followed a group of students into a lecture hall at the University of California, Berkeley. I filmed them as they barricaded themselves inside and held fast onto doors as dozens of police tried to get inside.

Despite my presence as a journalist (I was a student at the Graduate School of Journalism at the time), a conduct panel found me responsible for violating the student code of conduct. The panel found that since there is no exception carved into the code for the student press, I should be held responsible for being inside.

My punishment? To research and develop a proposal that would protect the rights of journalists who may find themselves ensnared by the Office of Student Conduct for simply reporting about activities on campus.

Very few schools have codes that explicitly address the rights of the press. The University of Louisville seems to be one of the sole exceptions. Section Eight of the Code of Student Rights and Responsibilities states:

A. The student press is free to deal openly, fearlessly, and responsibly with issues of interest and importance to the academic community. There shall be no prior approval of student press content by the University.

B. The student press is responsible for adhering to the canons of responsible journalism and for complying with the law. Student publications and broadcasts shall not publish libelous or slanderous matter, or any other content that violates the law.

C. All student publications and broadcasts shall explicitly state that the opinions expressed are not necessarily those of the University or its student body.

D. Students may not be disciplined by the University for their participation with the student press except for violations of University rules that are not inconsistent with the guarantees contained herein.

Although this Code is not ideal, it does provide a good starting point, and I was unable to find a better model at any other university in my research. Although this code might provide enough protection for students who work for the school newspaper, it contains a limited definition for student press that includes only a "student publication or a student broadcast." It defines a "student publication" as one published by a student organization and a "student broadcast" as pertaining to a "student operated radio or television station."

Under the Louisville Code, students' blogs and even their freelance work for mainstream media outlets appear to be outside the protections offered.

But as anyone can be a blogger, the people in charge of creating these codes will probably have reservations about extending the above protections to the entire student body.

The code also requires that students adhere to "the canons of responsible journalism," but since there is no licensing body for journalists, there is not always a clear answer as to what constitutes "responsible journalism." We can look to the Code of Ethics by the Society of Professional Journalists for guidance, but its advice is not absolute.

At UC Berkeley, a disciplinary panel is made up of at least one student, a non-academic employee, and a faculty member who serves as chair. These panels are in no position to decide if a student's behavior is within "the canons of responsible journalism."

For example, in my hearing the panel found that I violated journalistic ethics because I spent part of my time inside the building working on a different reporting assignment that I was writing at the time for class.

"During the downtime while the batteries [were] being charged, a journalist covering the Wheeler Hall occupation would have resorted to other means of reporting the protest. Mr. Wolf could have interviewed the other student protestors by other means including pen and paper if necessary. Instead of continuing in the role of a journalist, Mr. Wolf (sic) he turned on his laptop and began to work on a writing assignment for one of his courses. At this point, Mr. Wolf transitioned from the role of a journalist to that of a student, and in this case, a student in protest within Wheeler Hall," said optometry professor Robert DiMartino in his report.

The panel also found that I violated my journalistic responsibilities when I waved to a classmate through an open window as a crowd gathered below to listen to the protestors.

"He, in fact, by virtue of these actions, became a participant in the story, and as such, a student protestor. He was no longer detached and

objective, but allowed himself to become a part of the story he intended to cover," said the report.

While objectively covering a story from a detached perspective might be the professor's definition of responsible journalism, it is clearly not the only one.

In light of these weaknesses in the Louisville Code, I am writing to propose that the University of California Office of the President direct the Chancellor at each of its ten campuses to amend their respective Codes of Conduct in order to help ensure that the First Amendment rights of student journalists are protected, by adding the following language:

A. The University may not restrict students from freely publishing material in a lawful manner. While the University has a legitimate interest in reviewing academic work before it is published, this interest does not allow the University to exercise prior restraint over student media or prevent students from publishing their work independently.

B. Students are free to deal openly, fearlessly, and responsibly in reporting issues of interest and importance to the university community. Although student journalists are not given any special rights under the Code, it is understood that their reporting may take them to places and situations where they otherwise wouldn't go. And while no student is allowed to violate trespassing rules or regulations, the Office of Student Conduct shall exercise reasonable discretion in pursuing cases where a student journalist's alleged violation occurred while engaged in news gathering activities.

C. Students are responsible for complying with the law and should strive to adhere to the canons of responsible journalism. No student shall publish or broadcast libelous or slanderous matter, or any other content that violates the law. While the SPJ Code of Ethics may function as a baseline guide for responsible journalism practices, the Office of Student Conduct shall at no time make any determinations whether a student's conduct was responsible journalism.

Their review should be limited to determining only if the student's own actions violated the University Code of Conduct.

D. Students may not be disciplined by the University for their participation in journalistic activities except for violations of University rules that are not inconsistent with the guarantees contained herein.

E. In any cases the Office of Student Conduct elects to pursue in which a student has made an affirmative defense to the charges as a journalist, the Office will appoint a faculty member from either the Graduate School of Journalism or a faculty member from the Berkeley Law School with experience in First Amendment Law. In the event that a hearing is pursued, the Office of Student Conduct will appoint at least one student from either the Graduate School of Journalism or a member of the *Daily Californian* staff to also serve on the panel.

F. All proceedings under the auspices of the Office of Student Conduct shall be governed by the provisions of the California Shield Law and under the common-law "reporter's privilege" as recognized by the courts of this state.

My case is not the first time in which the rights of student journalists have clashed with university administrators, and it certainly won't be the last. But by implementing these changes to the code of conduct, the University of California and other institutions around the country can demonstrate their commitment to preserving the First Amendment's rights guaranteed under the Constitution and a good faith effort in creating an atmosphere on campus that actively encourages a free and vibrant press.

JOSH WOLF is a journalist, filmmaker, and a First Amendment activist. He spent 226 days in prison after he invoked the reporter's privilege and refused to cooperate with a Federal Grand Jury's investigation into a protest he reported on in 2005. After his release Wolf worked in print, radio, and television before attending the UC Berkeley Graduate School of Journalism where he focused on documentary film production. His thesis film *Police Tape*, which examines the hotly contested intersection between cops and cameras, was awarded the Reva and David Logan Prize for Excellence in Investigative Reporting. Wolf graduated in May 2011 and is now working as a freelance journalist and documentary filmmaker.

VOICES OF THE MIDDLE EAST AND NORTH AFRICA KPFA FREE SPEECH RADIO PROGRAM
by Khalil Bendib

Voices of the Middle East and North Africa is a nine-year-old radio program produced by a diverse group of individuals from various lands in West Asia and North Africa. Several essential features that distinguish this program from other Middle East-themed programs in North America are its scope, its authenticity, and its perspective.

An Alternative Perspective
Voices of the Middle East and North Africa brings informed and authentic voices that take listeners beyond the headlines into the diverse and fascinating world of culture and politics of the Middle East and North Africa, exploring the complex web of class, gender, ethnic, religious, and regional differences distinguishing the ways of life, and political and ideological perspectives of people in that part of the world. Most importantly, thanks to the support of free speech radio KPFA, it does all this in a completely uncensored way, taking to task the myriad taboos that have seriously hampered any serious understanding of the Islamic world.

Through the lens of academic scholarship, grassroots activism, and artistic and intellectual expression, our radio program goes beyond the reductive stereotypes of the sword and the veil, and oil and war to help create a fuller understanding of that crucial region, deconstructing the artificial duality of the so-called "clash of civilizations" and bridging the chasm of misperceptions that exists between East and West.

It is our belief that humanizing and understanding others is essential to understanding ourselves, that factual information and education are indispensable in a democracy and that a truly informed public is our best defense against war and tyranny. Our nation's increasing involvement in the Middle East and its dramatic consequences for all have made it plain that we, the people, can no longer afford the luxury of indifference or ignorance in matters Middle Eastern.

Scope

A handful of other radio shows across the country focuses on the Middle East, but precious few are those that seriously cover the countries of North Africa as well, which are typically lumped into the broad category of "Middle East" and are not covered on a consistent basis. For the past nine years, our show has featured regular stories on the history of French colonialism in the Maghreb (Algeria, Morocco, and Tunisia) and how that history has prefigured today's Arab Awakening in Tunisia, Egypt, and neighboring countries. We are also the one radio program in the country to delve into the fascinating culture and history of the native Berber (Amazigh) people of the Maghreb, as well as the rich and long history of Jewish culture in the Middle East and North Africa, the Armenian genocide, and other important topics such as labor struggles and queer rights in those countries, among other topics.

Authenticity

Ours is a program which systematically gives a platform to native voices (thus the program's title—*Voices of the Middle East and North Africa*) whether they are based within the countries themselves or from within the international diaspora. Our hosts and producers are all immigrants from the Middle East and North Africa (Iran, Kurdistan, Algeria, Morocco, Palestine, Iraq, Lebanon, and Egypt) and the overwhelming majority of our guests are scholars, activists, writers, poets, musicians, and artists with roots in the lands of the Middle East and North Africa. It is also our policy to always be inclusive and representative in terms of gender in each and every one of our programs.

Weekly Magazine Format

Ours is an attractively produced and packaged, entertaining one-hour weekly program produced in the studios of Pacifica's original station, KPFA 94.1 FM in Berkeley, the first ever listener-sponsored community radio station in the country. Another unique feature of our show is that it highlights, every single week, both the political and the cultural side by side, combining a public affair segment (politics, history,

and analysis) of approximately thirty minutes with an art and literature segment (cinema, theater, etc.) of approximately twenty-two
minutes, complemented with short commentaries and a weekly community calendar of events. We strive to maintain a good geographic
balance in every single program (if the public affairs is on Iran, for
example, the arts and literature might be on Morocco, and so on),
showcase the wide cultural diversity of the region, and appeal to a wide
range of listeners from different backgrounds. This balance has been
key to our success and popularity with the Northern California and
Western Florida (Tampa) listening audiences.

Where else in North America can you hear, on a regular basis,
about issues of feminism, labor, grassroots democracy, environment,
and gender as they pertain to the lives of Middle Easterners and North
Africans and their diaspora communities? By going in depth into such
varied and largely under-the-radar issues, we strive to demystify the
Arab, Iranian, Turk, or Berber as the "Other," furthering the cause of
mutual understanding, world peace, and justice.

WIKILEAKS, BRADLEY MANNING, AND THE ONGOING BATTLE OVER GOVERNMENT TRANSPARENCY

by Emma Cape, and edited by Logan Price, both of Courage to Resist

The year 2010 was one that marked the beginning of the largest leak
of classified documents in US history. The information contained
within the material known as the Collateral Murder video, the Afghan
War Diary, the Iraq War Logs, and the US Diplomatic Cables (which
includes the Guantanamo Files) collectively covers an astonishing
breadth of issues. The leaks allegedly come from a single source—US
Army private Bradley Manning—but nearly one-half of all *New York
Times* editions published so far in 2011 have cited one or more of these
documents.

The leaks enable ordinary citizens to better understand the
interworking of international diplomacy and our government's
aggressive military policies. The documents include such details as
the true number and cause of civilian casualties in Iraq and

Afghanistan, and the processes by which the US State Department negotiates with foreign governments over economic policies and human rights abuses.

Altogether, they paint a picture of a world in which national economic self-interest consistently takes priority over any other publicly stated ideals, and even democratically elected governments deliberately mislead their citizens with regularity. US officials are not necessarily more or less guilty of this than those from other nations. However, the documents also disclose that the US State Department habitually interferes with the executive and judicial processes of other countries to protect US corporate interests and US government officials who have run afoul of international law—made possible no doubt by the enormity of our international bargaining power.

A twenty-four-country Reuters News poll published in April found that of people who knew of WikiLeaks, overall 79 percent supported the organization's mission to make public secret government and corporate documents. In making their case against the organization's actions, high-ranking government officials, including President Obama, have suggested that the leaks pose a threat to national security, an argument often-repeated by major news sources.

The extent to which national security is actually endangered by any of the leaks has been called into question by a number of prominent experts. In December 2010, the House of Representatives convened a Judicial Committee Hearing on the Espionage Act and the Legal and Constitutional Issues Raised by WikiLeaks. The purpose of the hearing was to determine whether it should be illegal to distribute classified material after the material had been leaked, thus making it possible to prosecute WikiLeaks. The committee experts deemed such an act unconstitutional, and furthermore, agreed that documents are often classified unnecessarily. One committee member, Ralph Nader, stated that, "The suppression of information has led to far more loss of life, jeopardization of American security, and all the other consequences now being attributed to WikiLeaks and Julian Assange," using the buildup to the Iraq War—which was based on faulty pretenses—as an example.

Thus far no evidence has been provided of anyone being killed as a direct result of the leaks. It seems that in the post-9/11 world, a "threat to national security" may be invoked much like the specter of communism during the Cold War. Lacking a distinct source (or sources) and difficult to quantify, yet demanding immediate action, these ideas have been used to build support for a variety of otherwise controversial policies throughout both Republican and Democratic administrations.

While the suppression of information under the Bush administration is now widely acknowledged, the mainstream media has, in general, failed to comprehend or convey the continuation of this pattern under the Obama administration. For example, the current administration has so far used the obscure and harsh Espionage Act of 1917 to prosecute five individuals who released classified documents. Previously only two people had been prosecuted under the law since the year of its adoption.

Alleged WikiLeaks source, Bradley Manning, is the first person in US history to be charged with "aiding the enemy" for making information public. Furthermore, he was held in solitary confinement for the first ten months of his detention. In April, the UN Rapporteur on Torture issued a reprimand, stating that the United States repeatedly denied his requests for an official meeting with Manning—required protocol for his office.

US voters have never had as much insight or control with regards to US foreign policies as they have with domestic policies. However, it is also true that the US Executive Branch has never had as much power relative to Congress as it does today, a fact made clear when President Obama casually bypassed the War Powers Act of 1973 to invade Libya. A new groundswell of organizations like WikiLeaks offer new means by which citizens can better understand their own governments' actions, thus enabling more democratic control. In an online chat attributed to Bradley Manning by the FBI, before his arrest, he stated, "I want people to know the truth, no matter who they are . . . because without information, you cannot make informed decisions as a public." The question Americans need to ask themselves now is: if those acting with these ideals are our "enemies," what type of nation does that make us?

See more at http://www.couragetoresist.org/.

Notes

Caitlin Dickson, "Nearly Half of *New York Times* 2011 Issues Rely on Wikileaks," *Atlantic Wire*, April 25, 2011, http://www.theatlanticwire.com/global/2011/04/over-half-2011s-new-york-times-issues-use-wikileaks/37009/.

"Espionage Act and the Legal and Constitutional Issues Raised by Wikileaks," Committee on the Judiciary House of Representatives, December 16, 2010, http://judiciary .house.gov/hearings/printers/111th/111-160_63081.PDF.

Jay Kernis, "Daniel Ellsberg: All the Crimes Richard Nixon Committed Against Me are Now Legal," CNN, June 7, 2011, http://inthearena.blogs.cnn.com/2011/06/07/daniel-ellsberg-all-the-crimes-richard-nixon-committed-against-me-are-now-legal/.

"Merged Manning-Lamo Chat Logs," *Firedoglake*, http://firedoglake.com/merged-manning-lamo-chat-logs/.

Michelle Nichols, "Wikileaks Assange is Not a Criminal—Global Poll," Reuters, April 26, 2011, http://www.reuters.com/article/2011/04/26/usa-wikileaks-assange-idUSN2629178720110426.

Rania Khalek, "5 WikiLeaks Hits of 2011 That Are Turning the World on Its Head—And That the Media Are Ignoring," AlterNet, June 7, 2011, http://www.alternet .org/world/151232/5_wikileaks_hits_of_2011_that_are_turning_the_world_on_its_head_—_and_that_the_media_are_ignoring/.

Sibel Edmonds and Coleen Rowley, "Rescind President Obama's 'Transparency Award' Now," *Guardian*, June 14, 2011, http://www.guardian.co.uk/commentisfree/cifamerica/2011/jun/14/rescind-barack-obama-obama-transparency-award.

MEDIA DEMOCRACY IN ACTION
A brief listing compiled by Project Censored interns
Nolan Higdon and Ryan Shehee

Various groups from across the political spectrum call for media democracy in action. The following is a non-comprehensive list of groups, in alphabetical order, which advocate these ideals. For a more extensive list, see http://www.projectcensored.org/news-sources/.

Action Coalition for Media Education / acmecoalition.org
ACME is a group aimed at democratizing information and reforming the media.

Adbusters: A Magazine of Media and Environmental Strategies / adbusters.org
Adbusters is a foundation with the goal of changing the way society and the mass media interact.

American Library Association / ala.org/bbooks
ALA's mission is "to provide leadership for the development, promo-

tion, and improvement of library and information services and the profession of librarianship in order to enhance learning and ensure access to information for all." ALA is famous for their annual Banned Books Week, an event celebrating the freedom to read and the importance of the First Amendment.

Anonymous

Anonymous endorses the use of "hacktivism," a marriage of activism and the hacker subculture that calls for civil disobedience in cyberspace. By definition, this group calls for internet privacy while promoting free speech and information transparency in maintenance of democracy.

Censored News / censorednews.org

Daily Independent News Feeds from over twenty of the most trusted news sites as determined by the Media Freedom Foundation and Project Censored.

Center for Digital Democracy / democraticmedia.org

CDD's project works to keep the public informed and the online ad industry accountable.

Center for Media and Democracy / prwatch.org

A wiki-based investigative journalism collaborative focused on the public relations industry and whistle-blowing manipulative or misleading practices.

Center for Public Integrity / iwatchnews.org

The mission of the Center for Public Integrity and iWatch News is to produce original investigative journalism about significant public issues to make institutional power more transparent and accountable.

Centre for Research on Globalisation / globalresearch.ca

CRG is a Canadian independent research and media organization that publishes and supports humanitarian projects and crucial economic and geopolitical issues.

Center for War, Peace, and the News Media / bu.edu/globalbeat/budget-brief.html
Based at the Department of Journalism at Boston University, the Center is a nonprofit, nonpartisan organization supporting journalists and news organizations in their efforts to sustain an informed and engaged citizenry.

Civic Media Center / civicmediacenter.org
CMC provides views alternative to those of talking heads in the US mainstream media.

Communications Consortium / ccmc.org
CCMC is a public interest media center dedicated to helping nonprofit organizations use media and new technologies as tools for public education and policy change.

Daily Censored / dailycensored.org
Daily Censored delivers underreported news and commentary, working closely with the Media Freedom Foundation and Project Censored.

Electronic Frontier Foundation / eff.org
A donor-funded nonprofit group, EFF focuses on defending civil liberties of consumers and the general public in the digital arena, and accomplishes this through policy analysis, activism, and litigation.

Electronic Privacy Information Center / epic.org
EPIC is a public interest research center established to focus public attention on civil liberties in the information age: the research and protection of privacy, public education and activism, and publication and litigation.

Fairness & Accuracy In Reporting / fair.org
FAIR is a national media watchdog group advocating independence and criticism in journalism.

Free Press / freepress.net
Free Press believes that media reform is crucial not just for creating better news and entertainment, but also for advancing every issue you care about.

Flashpoints Radio / flashpoints.net
Flashpoints is a daily, national investigative news magazine based out of KPFA-FM in Berkeley, California. They broadcast Monday through Friday live at 5pm PST.

Gay and Lesbian Alliance Against Defamation / glaad.org
GLAAD amplifies the voice of the lesbian, gay, bisexual, and transgender (LGBT) community by empowering real people to share their stories, holding the media accountable for the words and images they present, and helping grassroots organizations communicate effectively.

The Government Attic / governmentattic.org
The Government Attic provides electronic copies of hundreds of interesting federal government documents obtained under the Freedom of Information Act.

Institute for Public Accuracy (IPA) / accuracy.org
IPA allows numerous policy analysts, scholars, and other independent researchers to be heard in mass media, while boosting many progressive grassroots groups with scant resources for media outreach.

International News Net World Report / innworldreport.net
INN takes on difficult, underreported but crucial issues that are rarely broadcast on corporate news. They bring viewers/listeners more than one hundred original news stories each week.

Labor Video Project / laborvideo.org
The Labor Video Project supports the use of labor computer networks and helps distribute labor videos from around the world.

Map Light / maplight.org
Map Light is a nonprofit, nonpartisan research organization that provides citizens and journalists the transparency tools to shine a light on the influence of money on politics. They currently track money and influence in the US Congress and the California legislature, with more states to come.

Media Alliance / media-alliance.org
Media Alliance dedicates itself to fostering a genuine diversity of media voices and perspectives, holding the media accountable for their impact on society and protecting freedom of speech.

Media Education Foundation / mediaed.org
Media Education Foundation produces and distributes documentary films and other educational resources to inspire critical reflection on the social, political, and cultural impact of American mass media.

Media Freedom International / mediafreedominternational.org
Media Freedom International is a source of Validated Independent News from colleges and universities worldwide.

Media Matters for America / mediamatters.org
Founded by David Brock, Media Matters for America is a nonprofit progressive research and information center dedicated to comprehensively monitoring, analyzing, and correcting conservative misinformation in the US media.

Media Monitors Network / usa.mediamonitors.net
Media Monitors Network is a grassroots media watchdog that seeks to

uncover journalistic and media bias and provide contrary information and opinions.

Media Roots / mediaroots.org
Media Roots is a citizen journalism project that reports the news from outside party lines while providing a collaborative forum for conscious citizens, artists, and activists to unite.

Media Watch / mediawatch.com
Media Watch focuses on media literacy and challenging stereotypes commonly found in the media.

National Coalition Against Censorship / ncac.org
The National Coalition Against Censorship, an alliance of fifty-two participating organizations, is dedicated to protecting free expression and access to information.

New America Media / newamericamedia.org
New America Media is the country's first and largest national collaboration and advocate of 2000 ethnic news organizations. Over 57 million ethnic adults connect to each other, to home countries, and to America through 3000+ ethnic media, the fastest growing sector of American journalism.

News Hounds / newshounds.us
News Hounds is a volunteer watchdog group focused on Fox News.

News Dissector / newsdissector.com/blog
News Dissector is the blog of journalist and media critic Danny Schechter, of MediaChannel.org.

News From Underground / markcrispinmiller.com
Selected underreported news and commentary from NYU scholar Mark Crispin Miller.

NewsTrust / newstrust.net
NewsTrust is a social network that aims to help people identify quality journalism.

On the Media / onthemedia.org
The On the Media website accompanies the weekly, one-hour National Public Radio program devoted to media criticism and analysis.

PEN American Center / pen.org
PEN American Center is the US branch of the world's oldest international literary and human rights organization.

Project Censored / projectcensored.org
Project Censored is the longest-running media research organization in the US. The Project surveys top censored stories each year dating back to 1976 and publishes an annual book on corporate managed news and the international Truth Emergency.

ProPublica / propublica.org
ProPublica is an independent, nonprofit newsroom that produces investigative journalism in the public interest.

PR Watch / prwatch.org
PR Watch provides investigative reporting on the practices of public relations and public affairs industry, from the Center for Media and Democracy.

SourceWatch / sourcewatch.org
SourceWatch provides documented information about the corporations, industries, and people trying to sway public opinion. Their goal is to expose the truth about the most powerful interests in society—not just relating their self-serving press releases or letting real facts be bleached away by spin.

Spot.Us / spot.us
Spot.Us is an open source project to pioneer "community powered reporting."

The Women's Media Center / womensmediacenter.com
Women's Media Center makes women visible and powerful in the media.

Who What Why / whowhatwhy.com
Independent journalist Russ Baker's site relies on an approach of skepticism toward power and credentialed expertise; a determination to unearth the facts interested parties want to keep hidden; and an unflinching commitment to follow the trail wherever it leads: "truth seeking—not quote seeking."

Women in Media and News / wimnonline.org
WIMN is a media analysis, education, and advocacy group that works to increase women's presence and power in the public debate.

Women's Institute for Freedom of the Press / wifp.org
WIFP is a nonprofit, tax-exempt research, education, and publishing organization. Their goal is to increase communication among women and inform the public of their experience, perspectives, and opinions.

WikiLeaks / wikileaks.org
WikiLeaks is a nonprofit organization that provides a secure and anonymous method for providing journalists with independent sources that focus on ethical, political, or historical significance, providing a way to reveal censored and otherwise suppressed information.

Truth Emergency
Understanding Propaganda in Theory and Practice
INTRODUCTION BY MICKEY HUFF

The conscious and intelligent manipulation of the organized habits and opinions of the masses is an important element in democratic society. Those who manipulate this unseen mechanism of society constitute an invisible government which is the true ruling power of our country.
—Edward Bernays, *Propaganda*, 1928

Political language—and with variations this is true of all political parties, from Conservatives to Anarchists—is designed to make lies sound truthful and murder respectable, and to give an appearance of solidity to pure wind.
—George Orwell, "Politics and the English Language," 1946

The twentieth century has been characterized by three developments of great political importance: the growth of democracy, the growth of corporate power, and the growth of corporate propaganda as a means of protecting corporate power against democracy.
—Alex Carey (1922–88), social psychologist, in *Taking the Risk Out of Democracy: Corporate Propaganda Versus Freedom and Liberty*, 1997

We face a Truth Emergency in the United States, largely as a result of dominant, top-down, managed news agencies of information control. Both the US government and the corporate media essentially have a duopoly on manipulating the public mind for political or commercial gain. Leading the public to one view or another is the name of the game, rather than reporting all the facts and letting the chips fall where they may. In America, consumers of corporate news broadcasts are the most likely to be confused about the facts of what is really going on in the world,[1] and those who follow political discourse among elected officials, are likely to come away equally confused based on the increasing ideological nature and partiality of these exchanges.

This ongoing Truth Emergency is created by a lack of purity in news (transparency and accurate sourcing), a lack of full factual reporting by the press, and a lack of critical thinking by journalists and the public at large. In this climate, propaganda thrives, as it generates a society based on hyperreality and illusions—one unable to discern fact from opinion, one incapable of deconstructing dissembling demagogues. This clearly represents a crisis for democracy; the truth of major issues remains illusive to the public. The antidote lies not only in exposing the charlatans of the establishment order as propagandists, but also in providing a broader understanding of how propaganda works, what it looks like and how to detect it, and what the public can do about it. Namely, the solution is to create an independent free press, one not beholden to moneyed interests, but rather one that tells people the truth about all matters, regardless of which powerful parties may be exposed for their possible state crimes against democracy.[2]

The Truth Emergency section of this year's *Censored* volume is dedicated to exposing propaganda in our culture and offering better ways to understand it, to deconstruct it, and to create alternatives to the deception we call "the news." Included in this section are some of the brightest voices in the important area of Propaganda Studies. The first four contributors are professors of philosophy. Randal Marlin's chapter gives a brief though mandatory primer on the history of propaganda, creating an anchor for the section as a whole. Without history, we lack context, which makes us easier prey for the propagandist. Jacob Van Vleet offers a significant theoretical framework through which to understand propaganda and its dangers by looking at the influential scholar Jacques Ellul. Robert Abele analyzes the structural framework of propaganda in a concise seven-point argument, and Elliot D. Cohen looks at the issue of net neutrality as a vehicle for informing the public and explains why It Is under attack by establishment politicians and media moguls alike. Communications scholar Anthony DiMaggio concludes our Truth Emergency section this year, giving us a case study in propaganda by looking at Astroturfing and the mass media–generated phenomenon of the Tea Party. All of these subjects are worthy of book-length treatments and, indeed, many already have been published as such (or will be soon).

Walter Lippmann, the twentieth-century journalist known for his work in support of elite management of information, warned about the dangers of propaganda after the First World War, where its use was widespread especially in the US under the Committee on Public Information. Lippmann wrote in *Liberty and the News*, "Without protection against propaganda, without standards of evidence, without criteria of emphasis, the living substance of all popular decision is exposed to every prejudice and to infinite exploitation.... The quack, the charlatan, the jingo, and the terrorist, can flourish only where the audience is deprived of independent access to information."[3] Understanding this is one antidote to the current Truth Emergency.

Even more critically, two generations later, Jacques Ellul, the subject of Professor Van Vleet's chapter, wrote, "Propaganda feeds, develops, and spreads the system of false claims—lies aimed at the complete transformation of minds, judgments, values, and actions (and constituting a frame of reference for systematic falsification). When the eyeglasses are out of focus, everything one sees through them is distorted."[4] It is for these very reasons that the public must not only have access to accurate information, but also understand and combat propaganda along the path to forming a better, more democratic free press structure. Ultimately, this helps to create a more informed, more thoughtfully engaged citizenry, one no longer susceptible to propaganda. This is a crucial step toward the restoration of our republic, a major component of the media revolution.

Notes

1. "Jon Stewart Says Those Who Watch Fox News Are the 'Most Consistently Misinformed Media Viewers,'" Politifact.com, project of the *St. Petersburg Times*, June 20, 2011, http://www.politifact.com/truth-o-meter/statements/2011/jun/20/jon-stewart/jon-stewart-says-those-who-watch-fox-news-are-most/.

A remark by late-night television host Jon Stewart about misinformed viewers of Fox News reignited debate about this topic, which in turn brought up previous studies that suggested corporate news viewers in general were quite misinformed about key issues of the day, not merely viewers of Fox. The article contained several studies confirming the broad misinformation from corporate media sources over the past eight years from Pew Research Center for the People and the Press (http://pewresearch.org/) and the Program on International Policy Attitudes at the University of Maryland (http://worldpublicopinion.org/).

2. For more on the Truth Emergency, see Peter Phillips, Mickey Huff, et al., "Truth Emergency Meets Media Reform," in Peter Phillips and Andrew Roth, eds., *Censored 2009: The Top 25 Censored Stories of 2007–08* (New York: Seven Stories Press, 2008), 281–95; Peter Phillips and Mickey Huff, "Truth Emergency: Inside the Military Industrial Media Empire," in Peter Phillips and Mickey Huff, eds., *Censored 2010: The Top 25 Censored Stories of 2008–09*, (New York: Seven Stories Press, 2009), 197–220; and "Truth Emergency," sec. 2, in Mickey Huff and Peter Phillips, eds., *Censored 2011: The Top 25 Censored Stories of 2009–10*, (New York: Seven Stories Press, 2010), 221–352. Also see the 2008 Truth Emergency conference website, http://truthemergency.us.

    For more on the concept of hyperreality, see Andrew Hobbs and Peter Phillips, "The Hyperreality of a Failing Corporate Media System," in Phillips and Huff, eds., *Censored 2010*, 251–59. And for more detail on this concept, see Jean Baudrillard, "The Procession of Simulacra," in *The Norton Anthology of Theory and Criticism*, eds. Vincent B. Leitch et al. (New York: Norton, 2001), 1729–41.

    For more on State Crimes Against Democracy (SCADs), which were a major focus of the Truth Emergency section in *Censored 2011*, see Lance deHaven-Smith, "Beyond Conspiracy Theory: Patterns of High Crime in American Government," in Huff and Phillips, eds., *Censored 2011*, 231–66; and Peter Phillips and Mickey Huff, "New Academic Research on State Crimes Against Democracy," Global Research, March 4, 2010, http://www.globalresearch.ca/index.php?context=va&aid=17922.

3. Walter Lippmann, *Liberty and the News* (Princeton, NJ: Princeton University Press, 2008, originally published in 1920).

4. Jacques Ellul, *Propaganda: The Formation of Men's Attitudes* (New York: Knopf, 1968), 61.

CHAPTER 6

A Brief History of Propaganda

by Randal Marlin

Propaganda is in some ways a very modern phenomenon, linked to a highly mediated, technology-dominated environment. But there are enough similarities to past persuasive practices so as to make a historical review valuable in order to understand the phenomenon. Though a universalist perspective incorporating Asian, African, and other historical dimensions would be ideal, we will here be limiting this historical treatment mainly to the development of propaganda, both theory and practice, in the European tradition, starting with ancient Athens and Rome. The goal here is to provide insight into propaganda, not history of propaganda for the sake of such a history. The aim is not to provide a comprehensive catalog of propaganda occurrences through history, but to choose some salient examples that will illustrate the development of the practice through the millennia.

A specialized historical treatment of anything must start by defining its subject matter. The term "propaganda," as the gerundive of the Latin word *propagare*, meaning "to propagate," etymologically means things that are to be propagated. The idea is linked to that of dissemination, or "spreading the word." In that sense, propaganda is morally neutral, since one can disseminate good or bad ideas or messages. However, anyone attuned to customary speech practices in the English language will recognize that the word carries negative connotations. This may reach back to the time the Roman Catholic Church instituted a committee of cardinals and others to form the counter-reformation body known as the *Congregatio de Propaganda Fide*, or Congregation for the Propagation of the Faith. For Catholics such "propaganda" would appear good, for Protestants the reverse. Widespread use of propaganda in World War I, followed by revelations about the deceptions used to support the war, gave the word "propaganda" a very bad connotation. People are likely to think of propaganda in negative terms—as lies, deceptions, evasions, false suggestions, and other means of bamboozling audiences. In this history, we will be focusing on "propaganda" as a negative term, but the existence of a positive or neutral connotation should be borne in mind, as the etymological meaning still plays a role in contemporary discourse.

Propaganda, negatively construed, involves the conscious use of communication to manipulate audiences. Lying is one way of doing this, but lies are risky because exposure will discredit the liar. To avoid this unwanted outcome, a propagandist will employ many other ways of deceiving audiences. A time-tested one has the Latin labels *suppressio veri* and *suggestio falsi*: here you say things that are true, but you select your truths while suppressing other truths in such a way that a false impression is created. Back in 1909, the British writer G. K. Chesterton put the matter in a rhetorically emphatic way when he wrote that the blackest of all lies is that which is an entire truth, but so selected as to give a false impression.[1] Suppression of key facts, and of historical background, has been the basis of a great deal of propaganda through the ages. In this way, propaganda is very closely related to censorship. Thus, exposure of censorship can tell us a lot about the propaganda motives of the censors.

Suppression of truth is but one among a number of different propaganda strategies, and in the following historical account we will be encountering others, including use of distraction, emotional manipulation, and other means of persuasion. For convenience, we will adopt this working definition of propaganda: "The attempt to shape the thoughts, beliefs, and actions of target audiences in ways that fit ulterior goals of the communicator and can be seen as manipulative because the means used violate proper standards of truthful communication." Besides lies, unsupported statements recklessly publicized, innuendo, deceptive imagery, a sinister and misleading soundtrack, and many other devices can all fit this definition. The noted French propaganda theorist Jacques Ellul has given a somewhat different, but useful, definition of propaganda as manipulative communication used for the purpose of gaining or maintaining power over others.[2]

ANCIENT ATHENS AND ROME

One of the earliest reported uses of propaganda technique was by Pisistratus (sixth century BCE), who faked an attack on himself and convinced Athenians to provide him with bodyguards whom he then used to acquire power, eventually becoming tyrant of Athens. The use of staged attacks to support aggression has been repeated in modern times. Before Adolf Hitler attacked Poland in 1939, he staged an attack on Germany, supposedly by Polish soldiers, and claimed his attack was merely a response to Polish aggression. The United States went to war against Vietnam with the adoption of the Gulf of Tonkin Resolution in 1964, in response to alleged unprovoked attacks on two US naval vessels in the area, though the evidence in support of this claim was later discredited. In 2000, a document known as "Operation Northwoods" came to light. Submitted to US Secretary of Defense Robert Macnamara, on March 13, 1962, by the US chairman of the Joint Chiefs of Staff General Lyman Lemnitzer, it proposed different, sometimes elaborate, false flag scenarios, such as sinking a ship with "real or simulated passengers," blaming Cuba, and using the incident as a reason to go to war.[3] The term "victim hegemony" has been used to describe the parlaying of sympathy for one's status as victim into a power grab, though it can apply to genuine as well as simulated victimization.

Pisistratus was expelled from Athens when his enemies united against him, but he later returned with a beautiful, tall woman, dressed in armor, who he presented as the goddess Athena. He successfully regained power while pioneering a long-standing device for gaining allegiance: namely, the suggestion that the leader has support from a deity. During the First and Second World Wars, each side claimed to have the Christian God on its side, with expressions such as "*Gott mit uns*," "*Dieu est avec nous*," or "God is on our side."

Oratory played was influential in the ancient world, and Pericles had a reputation as an outstanding speaker. His funeral oration on the occasion of the Peloponnesian War in 431 BCE was a model of civic fervor, celebrating the superiority of Athenians over its rivals. In honoring those who gave their lives for Athens, he encouraged others to take up their cause. Funerals, as occasions of great emotion, have continued to be harnessed by political leaders for persuasive effect: in much the same spirit as Pericles, Abraham Lincoln proclaimed, in his Gettysburg Address, that the living should be dedicated to the unfinished work left behind by the noble people who died for their cause. Honoring the dead tells the living that they too will be greatly honored if they follow a similar path of noble self-sacrifice.

Ancient Greek philosophers thought deeply about techniques of persuasion found mainly in rhetoric, and about the ethical implications of using some of these techniques. Plato understood two important things about rhetorical persuasion. One is that the speaker needs to appeal to preexisting beliefs among a targeted audience. All too often this meant pandering to prejudice, something that Plato decried when it was practiced by the Sophists, who were successful at winning over crowds, but at the cost of reinforcing the ignorance fostered by prejudices. By contrast, Plato's model Socrates engaged in challenging the prejudices of his interlocutors, and at his trial provoked his juror-judges into calling for his execution. Plato's description of the trial famously casts Socrates in the role of a martyr for speaking truth to power.[4]

Plato's second observation about rhetoric is that one can deceive people by leading them to accept slightly different wordings for the same thing, and, through a succession of different ostensible equivalences, bring them to a point where they appear to accept the opposite of what they initially believed.

Aristotle's *Rhetoric* includes a valuable statement of principles of persuasion, as well as some particular tricks to use in debate. Though his observations are transferable to other forms of persuasion besides speech making, given his time—fourth century BCE—his focus was mainly on the verbal. Persuasion, he said, is based on three different things: *ethos*, the character of the speaker; *pathos*, the emotional impact of the speech; and *logos*, the cogency of the argument. As a philosopher, he might have been expected to emphasize the third, but in fact he places greater stress on *ethos*. The speaker wants to be believed, but audiences need to have confidence that the speaker is trustworthy, honest, and knowledgeable. At election time, audiences want to know that the candidate shares their interests and values. The speaker needs to come across as a friend, not as someone aloof and arrogant. In today's world, efforts are made to discredit opponents by bringing up some misdeed or unpopular vote from the past, or by publicizing pictures suggestive of shadiness or frivolity. Aristotle counseled that negative character observations should come from someone other than the candidate, who needs to avoid appearing mean.

Aristotle realized that moving people to action requires more than a theoretical statement of things that would be desirable. A speaker needs to engage an audience, and this means paying attention to *pathos*, appealing to appropriate emotions. Among the powerful emotions he cited, fear and anger are at the top of the list. To make people fearful you have to do more than provoke generalized worry; you must persuade them that a particular worrisome thing will happen at a particular time in a particular way. Persuading some group that others are likely to use weapons of mass destruction against them is one way of exciting fear, as was seen in 2002–2003 with the buildup of support for the US-led war against Iraq in 2003. People tend to hate those who show contempt for them, so the orator who wants to harness and instill hate needs merely to portray the targeted person or group as showing such contempt, perhaps with historical reminders of harms they have inflicted in the past. George Orwell's book *1984* satirically illustrates the use of hatred by political rulers to manipulate subjects with the institution of "Two Minutes Hate," during which time some object of scorn is presented to the people on a big telescreen.

Finally, in the matter of *logos*, Aristotle advised the rhetorician to tailor the arguments to the audience's capacity to receive and understand them, counseling against the use of lengthy syllogisms, suggesting simplification and repetition, and, importantly, emphasizing the use of example, especially when it grips the imagination—a tip still true to a large extent today. A recent vivid crime or accident can be exploited rhetorically in order to strengthen police forces or enact safety measures, or to elect politicians whose platforms support those things. Though statistics are more rationally relevant, they may often be defeated in rhetorical force by a well-chosen example. Aristotle also cautioned the speaker to be thoroughly versed in the facts of the matter under discussion. To be exposed as ignorant on some matter, even a minor one, could undermine credibility and cast doubt in an audience's mind about all the other claims one has made. Conversely, if an opponent makes a factual error, even a minor one, it may be worth calling attention to it to undermine the opponent's credibility. In today's world, the stakes are higher in some ways because errors can be recorded digitally and replayed to the discredit of the speaker long after the mistake was made. In keeping with these principles, Aristotle offered the following practical advice to orators: know your audience; know your subject matter; simplify, to ensure understanding; repeat, so people will remember; maintain attention, maybe by raising one's voice or gesturing appropriately; get people in the right emotive frame of mind; maintain credibility; emphasize one's own strong points and downplay one's weak points, while doing the opposite to the opponent.

Today's communicative environment is replete with opportunities to illustrate Aristotle's principles by applying them to media not available in his time. Where Aristotle could talk about the inflection of a speaker's voice for emotive effect, today video productions can include background music affecting an audience's mood, sometimes without the latter being conscious of this effect. One can evoke hatred by having eerie or discordant music to accompany portrayal of an enemy. Photographs can be taken out of context for good or bad effect. Facebook users who post silly pictures of themselves to entertain friends may need to consider possible adverse use of such imagery by opponents.

Rhetoric was not the only means of winning people over in the ancient world, nor is it today. Political power could also be enhanced by prestige, or by the demonstrated ability to get things of value done in the people's interest. Quintus Cicero, brother of the famous orator Marcus Tullius Cicero, successfully advised the latter on how to win the consulship in 63 BCE. Apart from dirty tricks, such as spreading rumors (true or false) about opponents' vices, he emphasized cultivating some powerful people to give his campaign credibility. He stressed the importance of never giving out-and-out refusals when asked to promise to do something, even though it may seem impossible. The good person will be upfront about such matters, but the good politician will not want to burn bridges to potential supporters, he said. In the spirit of "one never knows" it is better to equivocate than to definitely refuse a request for help.

Augustus Caesar, formerly known as Octavian, had a kind of genius for propaganda. Like his great-uncle, Julius Caesar, he understood the power of victory and spoils for winning Roman allegiance. But he also knew how to avoid antagonizing senators and how to reward poets, who burnished his image in their writings. Coins with his portrait on the obverse proclaimed his victories on the reverse side, thus disseminating important messages at a time when the means of communication were much more limited than today. In addition to supplying spectacular games, he gained respect with his construction of monuments to deities. Julius Caesar had adopted Augustus as his son in his will, so that when Julius came to be regarded as divine, it allowed Augustus to promote himself as "son of a God." Augustus ensured that knowledge of his many benefactions would survive his death by constructing elaborate monuments around the Roman Empire, with extensive inscriptions proclaiming his good deeds. He proclaimed himself *Pater Patriae* ("Father of his Country"), having brought unity to Rome following the divisiveness that occurred in the wake of Julius's assassination. These no doubt contributed to the durability of the Roman Empire itself, with this constant reminder of the benefits of empire.

Concurrently with Augustus's rule and that of his successor Tiberius, Jesus Christ grafted onto the Judaic monotheistic religion a universalism based on love and the willingness of God, in the person of Jesus, to identify with the lowliest among the people, to the point of enduring the pain and humiliation of crucifixion, a punishment allotted to rebellious slaves. This religion spread to Rome, rivaling established polytheistic beliefs. Early emperors persecuted followers of Christianity, but later ones were converted and Christianity spread through the empire, surviving its fall. To call this spread of religion "propaganda" requires careful attention to the meaning of that word. Under Ellul's definition, sincere followers of Christianity, anxious to spread the word to benefit others, would not be engaging in propaganda, as their aim was to benefit others rather than gain power over them. On the other hand, at the time of the Crusades, there were undoubtedly those who harnessed the Christian faith for their own aims, to seek power. Atrocity stories encouraged militancy against Muslims in the Holy Land. The involvement of the Church in temporal affairs increased starting from the eighth century, after the supposed will of the Emperor Constantine (274–337 CE)—the "Donation of Constantine"—bequeathed the western part of the Roman Empire to the Catholic Church, though the document was later determined to be a forgery.

Among the notable techniques assisting the spread of Christianity was Saint Paul's practice of becoming "all things to all men," by adapting his speech so as to be accessible to his audiences. He gained access to the Athenians by venturing to speak about "the unknown god," who figured in the Athenian Pantheon. Christianity was also spread with the assistance of memorable symbols, such as the fish, which in Greek is *ichthys*. The letters of *ichthys* can be taken as an acronym for Jesus Christ, of God, Son, Saviour (*Iesous Christos, Theos, Yios, Soter*). The Emperor Constantine reportedly experienced a heavenly vision in which the symbol of the Christogram, made up of the Greek letters *chi* and *rho*, appeared to him along with the words "*in hoc signo vinces*" ("with this sign you will conquer"). This symbol was widely reproduced.

BEYOND THE MIDDLE AGES

Following the twelfth century, Anglo-Norman princes promoted monarchical power, helped by favorably written history, the political songs of wandering minstrels, the recitation by pilgrims of heroic poems, and visual works such as the Bayeux Tapestry, which gave an account of William the Conqueror's victory at the Battle of Hastings in 1066, told from a Norman viewpoint. Legal philosophers called legists made their appearance in universities, promoting the new centralized monarchy. Adept both in canon and feudal law they were able to combat both the church and the lords. They made use of slogans, such as "The king is above the law," or the French "*Que veut le roi, si veut la loi*" ("What the king wills is law"). Kings and queens in turn founded colleges at universities and paid attention to communications, including dramatic presentations, to maintain, as we would say today, a favorable image. Writers and playwrights who negatively portrayed the monarchy paid with their lives.

The invention of the printing press in the mid-1400s provided opportunities for large-scale print propaganda, both in support of or in opposition to the Reformation, and so royalty asserted its power by restricting publication through licensing requirements. John Milton's famous tract against licensing, *Areopagitica*, was addressed to Parliament in 1644 as a protest against reinstitution of the practice. To counteract the influence of heterodox teaching on the faithful, the

Catholic Church developed an index of prohibited books and imposed the death penalty on influential figures that persisted in heretical teaching during the Inquisition.

In France, King Louis XIV (1638–1715) made use of the propaganda of prestige with the splendid buildings at Versailles. Court etiquette was elaborate and provided a way of distinguishing between the favored and the disfavored. He made use of gazetteers, who brought messages from the king to the public, and who also sounded out reactions from the people. In that way he could get early warnings of dissent and act to prevent them from turning into revolt.

With the French Revolution came the uprooting of established order and a corresponding search for meaning to replace that which had been previously provided by church, king, family, and community. Voltaire, Jean-Jacques Rousseau, and other writers of the Enlightenment cast doubt on some of the beliefs underpinning the old order. The example of successful revolution in the United States, based on John Locke's idea of individual rights, and Rousseau's rhetorically powerful statement, "Man is born free, but everywhere he is in chains," contributed to the hope and energy to bring about a more just world. The governing ideas of the revolution—of *"patrie"* (fatherland); of liberty, equality, and fraternity—were reinforced everywhere by all manner of different media: festivals, pamphlets, posters, medallions, playing cards, engravings, dress, ribbons, songs, crockery, and more. The liberty cap, the liberty tree, and the pikestaff took on symbolic importance. Trousers (*sans-culottes*) replaced knee breeches. The cock (*gallus* in Latin) symbolized France by virtue of the connection with *Gallus* (a Gaul). Clubs such as the Jacobin Club served as instruments of propaganda, spreading the message around the country. Where the Romans had the crucifixion to keep the lower orders in check, the revolutionaries terrorized leaders of the old order by use of the guillotine, at the same time creating a bond among those looking for justice or revenge.

Napoleon Bonaparte (1769–1821) knew how to capitalize on the need for a sense of identity, promoting himself, with the help of artist Jacques-Louis David, as a glorious, heroic leader of the French, destined to spread the values of the Enlightenment around the world. Like Augustus Caesar, he influenced people with impressive military victories and, more importantly, with how his activities were reported.

He provided employment with the army and with public works such as the Arc de Triomphe. He showed concern for health and education, instituting elite schools and encouraging free vaccination for all citizens. He gave prizes to authors and pensions to actors. By decree he drastically reduced the number of newspapers and theaters in Paris, subjecting the remainder to controls. "Truth is not half so important as what people think to be true," was part of his guiding philosophy. He gave the appearance of being faithful to the Catholic Church, but for symbolic reasons took the crown of emperor from the Pope and put it on his own head at his coronation. School catechisms proclaimed: "To honor and serve our Emperor is . . . to honor and serve God himself."

The growth of mass-circulation newspapers in the next century, then, subsequently, other mass communication media of the twentieth century—notably radio, film, and later television—added to the potential for totalitarian rule. German nationalism grew in reaction to Napoleon's conquest. Carl von Clausewitz (1781–1831), director of the Berlin Military Academy, recognized that the new warfare required the support of the people and hence saw the importance of propaganda to encourage one's own side while undermining the morale of one's enemies, and also to win over the support of neutral nations. Soldiers who risk their lives need to believe that their cause is just if they are to fight with passion.

In the latter half of the nineteenth century a powerful form of imperial ideology took root in Britain and France, an ideology that was not altogether new. Already, the poet Edmund Spenser (1552–1599) had written about the state of Ireland as one that was primitive and lawless beyond the Pale (a fortified area around Dublin where the British ruled more effectively). Ideas of nationalist superiority were combined with neo-Darwinian racial beliefs and enhanced symbolism of the monarchy under Queen Victoria, in order to give new impetus to military conquest of other parts of the world deemed to be in need of civilizing influence. Invaders were rewarded with gold, diamonds, and other valuable resources. Rudyard Kipling's expression, "White Man's Burden," captured the belief that imperialism was in line with Victorian ideas of moral duty and self-sacrifice. The push for imperialism best fits Ellul's observations of "pre-propaganda" or "sociological propaganda," whereby individuals' outlooks are transformed by myths about the Nation, the Hero, the Race, Progress, the Leader, and the like, without necessarily emanating from a specific, identifiable source.[5] Rather, they arise from situations where certain ideas and feelings are generated with a measure of spontaneity and find a responsive and reinforcing chord among the general public. The ugly side of British imperialism—such as the internment of the Boers' wives and children in deadly, disease-ridden concentration camps—was inadequately reported to the public; the *Times* instead gave glowing reports of the heroism of people like Colonel Robert Baden-Powell. Cecil Rhodes, along with two partners, acquired a controlling interest in influential South African newspapers, which furnished anti-Boer atrocity stories passed on by the *Times* as truth, inciting the British to supply troops for war. J. A. Hobson, the South African correspondent for the *Manchester Guardian*, termed the Rhodes-controlled press "an elaborate factory of detailed mendacity for the purpose of stimulating British action."[6]

French and German nationalisms developed in a collision course in the nineteenth century, each reacting against the other. The Franco-Prussian War of 1870, where an increasingly united Germany defeated its former conquerors, set the stage for renewed militarism in France and the later outbreak of World War I. Schools in both countries indoctrinated youth on the need to preserve the honor of their nation against its rivals. A poignant scene in the classic antiwar movie, *All Quiet on the Western Front*, shows the German Gymnasium (an elite college) classics professor linking Roman history to the duty of the young to serve in their country's armed forces, it being fitting and proper to die for one's country.

MODERN PROPAGANDA AND THE TWENTIETH CENTURY

World War I gave rise to propaganda on an unprecedented scale. The British engaged in worldwide propaganda, developing a highly articulated apparatus for influencing world opinion. The main source of propaganda was Wellington House, Britain's War Propaganda Bureau, named after the building where operations were located. From the beginning, in August 1939, it organized an extensive network of well-known writers, speakers, and communicators under the direction of C. F. M. Masterman, publishing books, pamphlets, picture magazines, speeches, articles, and other materials for circulation around the world. The aim was to reinforce support for the war among Commonwealth nations and to win over the support of neutral countries, especially the United States of America. In general, Wellington House publications concealed the fact that the government was paying to have the materials circulated, so as to hide the propaganda aspect and improve their receptivity. A separate branch of propaganda distribution took place in the foreign office, which was concerned with telegraphing relevant news items with the greatest speed to news outlets around the world so that these outlets would receive the British viewpoint first, on the assumption that this would color the reception of later accounts. The British pioneered and took special pride in the method of personal contact. Leading journalists, magnates, and politicians would be brought to England and France to see and hear the British war effort firsthand. They would then return to their countries and be credible spokespeople reflecting the views of their hosts. Another propaganda operation, located at Crewe House, dealt with propaganda directed at the enemy, including the dropping of leaflets from planes and balloons.

The Germans were first to use movies as propaganda with two companies, *Eiko-Woche* and *Messter-Woche*, producing newsreels distributed both domestically and among neutral countries.[7] The Germans also exercised censorship control over films imported and exported. Starting in 1916 the British made a big impact with films such as *Britain Prepared*, and *The Battle of Arras*. In *The Battle of the Somme*, the viewer sees British troops going off to war amid much camaraderie, with no indication of the impending deaths of hundreds of thousands. A graphical representation of British arms production gave the impression that victory was assured. The British pioneered what they called the "film-tag," short messages attached to news résumés shown to home audiences. These would be seen by ten million people, and might urge them to "Save Coal" or "Buy War Loans."

Britain had the advantage of controlling the cable between Germany and the US, enabling it to decode a message sent by the Foreign Secretary of the German Empire, Arthur Zimmermann, on January

16, 1917, to the German ambassador in Washington, DC, Johann von Bernstorff, who forwarded the telegram to the German ambassador in Mexico, Heinrich von Eckardt. The telegram revealed that Germany was conspiring with Mexico against the US, and tipped the scales in favor of the US going to war against Germany.

British propaganda included themes of numerical superiority over Germany, with forces drawn from all over the Commonwealth. The most extensively exploited theme was that of German barbarity, reinforced by numerous atrocity stories, both real and unfounded. These included the stories collected and published by The Bryce Report—The Report of the Committee on Alleged German Outrages—headed by Viscount James Bryce, former British ambassador to the US. This report was widely circulated by Wellington House, which added its own editorial commentary: "It is the duty of every single Englishman who reads these records, and who is fit, to take his place in the King's army, to fight with all the resolution and courage he may, that the stain, of which the following pages are only a slight record, may be wiped out, and the blood of innocent women and children avenged." Much was made of the barbaric sinking of the Cunard liner *Lusitania* in May 1915, though it carried war materials and the German ambassador had issued a warning that it might be sunk.

Perhaps the most notorious atrocity story was invented and disseminated worldwide by the Northcliffe press (mainly the *Times* and the *Daily Mail*), with the help of Belgian émigré writers and publishers of the London-based *Indépendance belge* (a daily French-language newspaper). This was the story about the Corpse Utilization Plant, which, according to the press, is where the Germans boiled down their own dead soldiers to extract useful chemicals and bone meal for pig food and fertilizer. The desecration of their dead in this way was presented as proof positive that the Germans were subhumans, ghouls, a throwback to barbarism that the world would have to defeat if civilization were to survive. Rumors of the existence of such factories are easy to explain. The Germans did indeed have installations for boiling down horse carcasses, and as horses were widely used for transportation of artillery and other war materials during World War I, many of these animals were brought to these factories upon their death. The Northcliffe press cleverly made use of a report in an official German newspaper to make it appear that the Germans were admitting to boiling down their own soldiers. They did this with a mistranslation of a report from the French front, where the writer, Karl Rosner, made a passing remark on the smell emanating from a *Kadaverververtunganstalt* (Corpse Utilization Plant) and explained that this is where the chemicals are extracted from carcasses (using the word "Kadaver," for carcass) observing, "Nothing must go to waste." The word was mistranslated as "corpse" and the German word *Leim*, "glue," was mistranslated as "lime," both mistranslations giving the impression that human bodies were involved, as quicklime was used as a disinfectant. On April 17, 1917, the Northcliffe press juxtaposed this mistranslation with another detailed eyewitness account by an actual observer who supposedly witnessed corpses being processed. Published in the free Belgian press in London it was a gruesome account, stimulating the imagination with vivid descriptions, but short on details to answer obvious problems about its authenticity, including the question of how the observer could have gained access to what was described as a heavily guarded and concealed plant. The impression that the Belgian and German accounts were describing the same factory was bolstered by the fact that both Belgian and German newspapers carried the same date of publication: April 17, 1917.

The British officially repudiated the story in 1925, but the intricate role of the Northcliffe press was effectively concealed in the different versions of how the story came into being. The irony of this story is that it hindered belief in reports, during World War II, that Germans were incinerating Jews, as people recalled the earlier invented corpse factory story.[8]

For the most pervasive, thorough, and effective propaganda in the twentieth century, we can turn to the machine invented by Adolf Hitler and Josef Goebbels, beginning in the early 1920s with the founding of the German Nazi Party. Hitler studied propaganda carefully and laid out his observations in his book, *Mein Kampf* ("My Struggle"), in which he wrote that the masses have a short memory, and so messages must be repeated endlessly to convert them. The party would have to consist of a small number of active members who would secure and inspire a much larger number of passive members. With small numbers, they needed to attract attention, which they did through violence. Whereas the Communists disseminated the doctrine of class struggle, the Nazis chose to focus on a doctrine of racial purity, locating social problems in alleged racial contamination. The Nazis made use of party newspapers, posters, theater, and film. Nazi leaders were assigned areas, or *Gaus*, where they were to organize party membership and activities. They would concentrate their forces in small areas where they could easily win elections and give the impression of victory. When Hitler was banned for speeches inciting violence, he was championed on the basis of free speech principles, with posters showing a gagged Hitler. The burning of the Reichstag (Parliament) in February 1933 helped to bring the Nazis to power the following month. The Nazis instituted extensive censorship, requiring party membership among those holding positions of cultural influence, all while excluding Jews. Cheap radio sets were sold on a large scale, thus providing a medium through which to receive Nazi propaganda. Goebbels knew that propaganda had to be entertaining, and so Wagnerian music and myths were widely utilized to convey the Nazi ideology. Hitler made use of powerful extended metaphors by speaking of filth, rubbish, and disease connected with unsanitary living, by discussing "degenerate art" to invoke the desired emotions among his audience. Through these metaphors he fostered the idea that human beings responsible for the "spiritual death" of Aryans (Hitler's favored racial group) should be exterminated in the same way as rodents who spread disease causing physical death. From the beginning, propaganda of fear dominated the Nazi route to power, as they made it clear that constitutional niceties would not hamper the elimination of those who would attempt to thwart their aims. The 1936 Summer Olympics in Berlin were used to showcase German power and alleged peaceful intentions while downplaying anti-semitism, but with the outbreak of war in 1939, a strategy of terror was used to dissuade the United States from joining the Allies. Hitler offered the threat of war while holding out the prospect of peace, but a peace on (unacceptable) Nazi terms. The image of the Führer as a man of god-like features was carefully cultivated, as in *Triumph of the Will*, Leni Riefenstahl's film about the 1934 Nuremberg Nazi Party rally, where Hitler arrives by airplane, majestically descending from the clouds with appropriate accompanying music from Wagner's opera *Die Meistersinger von Nürnberg*. The film shows Hitler responding to adoring crowds, greeting mothers and their children with mutual warmth and encouragement. Nazi propagandists were sensitive to the need for credible spokespeople and used fluent and witty French speakers to address the French and a sharp-tongued Anglo-Irish speaker, William Joyce, to communicate with the British.

Allied propaganda against the Axis and Japan followed a similar pattern to that of World War I in the matter of demonizing the enemies. One stereotype showed a monocled German in uniform threatening torture: "Ve haf our vays!" A "Jap" would often be shown in the form of a snake with buckteeth.

The initial British propaganda of victory fell flat when Hitler's Blitzkrieg sent British and French forces reeling in 1940, but a new propaganda of Dunkirk heroism emerged. In the United States many films showed the heroism of US fighting forces, encouraging recruitment and war bond sales. A widely viewed Hollywood film, *The Fighting Sullivans*, was about a mother who lost five sons when a naval ship sank, making the loss of one son seem more bearable by comparison. Well-known actors such as John Wayne often played roles in war movies where their characters would give the impression that the US could not lose. Canadians would feel similarly about Canadian actor Lorne Greene, who had a deep, booming, and thoroughly confident voice reporting war news on radio.

The arrival of the Cold War and the struggle for ascendancy between the United States and the Soviet Union led to numerous proxy wars and deception on both sides. In the context of the Cold War one needs to talk about propagandas in the plural. Propaganda depicting the Soviet Union as an aggressor seeking world domination served to arouse fear in the United States. This fear helped to sustain a large military capability, which in turn sparked fear among the Soviets. In this way the arms race began and has continued today with the help of lobbyists and public relations experts, and with a largely compliant mass media that is reluctant to question the wisdom of a war backed by powerful government and corporate interests. George Orwell's depiction of the need for external enemies to justify extensive government powers in *1984* has been largely borne out since the book's appearance in 1948. US President Dwight Eisenhower warned the world about the dangers of what he called the "Military-Industrial

Complex," which he feared would dominate US policy if unchecked, running the US in its interests rather than those of the population as a whole. Voices such as those of I. F. Stone in the 1950s, '60s and '70s, and Noam Chomsky today have exposed many of the propaganda ruses used to promote the military-industrial interests. Daniel Ellsberg leaked to the press important documents, known as the Pentagon Papers, compiled by the Pentagon during the Vietnam War that showed the strength of the opposing forces to be much greater than the military was revealing to the public, with General William Westmoreland regularly promising "light at the end of the tunnel." Senator J. William Fulbright showed in a 1970 book, *The Pentagon Propaganda Machine*, how the Pentagon used PR techniques, such as co-opting citizen group leaders, to overcome resistance to the deployment of missiles in various sites across the country.

Celebrating war heroes is good for recruitment, but the Pentagon's initial attempts to lionize soldiers Pat Tillman in Afghanistan and Jessica Lynch in Iraq were thwarted when it came to light that the former had been killed by "friendly fire" and the latter, by her own account, had been in no condition to fight back, contrary to stories about her bravely taking on the enemy in an exchange of gunfire. Both Lynch and Tillman's family resented the deceit and the false honors bestowed on them by the military for its own purposes.

Modern propaganda is largely shaped in democracies by a public relations industry that has grown by leaps and bounds in the last fifty years. Hill & Knowlton, a public affairs and public relations consultancy, helped US President George H. W. Bush get support for the war against Iraq in 1991, following the invented story that Iraqi soldiers took over three hundred babies from incubators in Kuwait, leaving them to die while taking the incubators to Baghdad. A tearful young woman, identified only as Nayirah testified that she saw an instance where this happened, and her moving testimony was widely broadcast. Only later was she revealed to be the daughter of Kuwaiti Ambassador Saud Nasir al-Sabah, who obviously had an interest in helping the US go to war. The official story to justify a second, US-led attack on Iraq in 2003 was that Iraqi leader Saddam Hussein had weapons of mass destruction that he was ready and able to deliver and that Iraq would soon have a nuclear capability. Further, it was said that he had been in collusion with al-Qaeda and bore some responsibility for events of 9/11. Undeniably, Hussein had at one time used gas to poison Kurds and had supported payment to relatives of terrorists, but the other claims did not stand up to later investigation.

Those who doubt official stories used to promote war or shift blame are often branded conspiracy theorists. Yet the document "Operation Northwoods," mentioned earlier in connection with Pisitratus, should be convincing evidence that Pentagon planners are capable of thinking up outrageous and intricate deceptions for propaganda purposes.

One of the pioneers of public relations early in the twentieth century was Ivy Lee, who wrote about the ethics of this activity. He had one rule for ethical public relations: do not misrepresent the source of your information; if someone has paid you to disseminate a message in his or her interests, you should not conceal that source. The current propaganda scene is awash with misrepresentations breaking this rule, one example being the use of "video news releases." These appear to be genuine news broadcasts, using bona fide journalists, but they are often scripted and filmed by a corporation or government department to get its message across, knowing that free, well-produced footage will be welcomed by television stations, saving them the cost. When the stations don't acknowledge the source, the viewer loses an important item of information affecting the credibility of the message.

Similarly, the phenomenon of "Astroturf" creates a deception. For example, industrialist David Koch funds "grassroots" organizations that agitate on his behalf to benefit his interests. If the same messages came from him they would be viewed suspiciously, but by funding a front group, say, against climate change theories, the message becomes more easily accepted in the public consciousness. PR Watch is a public-interest group that has exposed these kinds of deceptions online for many years, and with books by John Stauber and Sheldon Rampton.

More recently, on April 20, 2008, the *New York Times* brought attention to high-ranking retired military officers and how they often speak out in support of Pentagon initiatives. The fact of their being retired might seem to enhance their detachment, but revelation of lucrative contracts with military-allied groups belies that detachment. In all of this, the mass media would do the public a service by seeking to expose the source of news items, including relevant funding, rather than referring to anonymous sources or officials who speak "on condition they not be named." Sometimes anonymity must be respected, but an editor could insist that short of revealing the identity of an informant, the possible motivations for speaking should be revealed.

CONCLUSION

The main hope for countering propaganda lies in exposing it. In the past, leaks helped to expose deceptions perpetrated by the tobacco industry, and the pharmaceutical industry has had whistle-blowers calling attention to unpublicized harmful side effects found by researchers. Today, the arrival of WikiLeaks, the organization founded by Julian Assange with the purpose of guaranteeing anonymity to those who would leak important information, brings a whole new dimension to the risks and strategies of propaganda operations. With Twitter, Facebook, and other means of internet connection, messages can reach huge populations in a very short time, providing speedy and timely counter-propaganda. Financial institutions that tried to cut off Assange's access to their services were bombarded with computer-generated messages sent by a group called "Anonymous," effectively jamming their operations.

Propaganda has always run the risk of a boomerang event, in the event it is exposed. But whereas in earlier times it might take too long to counter falsehoods spread just before an election, today false allegations might be swiftly and successfully rebutted, especially if they spark public indignation. The problem for the general public will be to decide who gives reliable news reports and who does not. This will involve some investment of time, but responsible citizenship will require a measure of this involvement, beginning with the study of videos like *Outfoxed*, which shows the bias in Fox News and the power of the latter-day Lord Northcliffe, Rupert Murdoch.

RANDAL MARLIN, AB Princeton, MA McGill, PhD Toronto, is adjunct professor of philosophy at Carleton University in Ottawa, Canada. He is the author of *Propaganda and the Ethics of Persuasion* (Broadview, 2002) and guest editor of the December 2010 issue of the Canadian edition of *Global Media Journal*, an issue devoted to Propaganda, Ethics and Media.

Notes

1. G. K. Chesterton, "Distortions in the Press," *Illustrated London News,* November 6, 1909.
2. For a fuller account of the problems of definition and numerous suggested definitions see Randal Marlin, *Propaganda and the Ethics of Persuasion* (Peterborough, Ontario: Broadview Press, 2002). The same text discusses Ellul's ideas in greater detail.
3. The reader may question the authenticity of this document, readily available through a Google search. An inquiry directed at the curator of the National Security Archives at George Washington University (nsarchiv@gwu.edu) produced the following e-mail response Thursday, July 8, 2010: "The documents we have posted on our website concerning 'Operation Northwoods' are genuine declassified US Government documents. National Security Archive Senior Analyst Peter Kornbluh is our expert on Cuba and he is the scholar responsible for our postings on Operation Northwoods. . . . Thank you for your interest in the work of the National Security Archive. Mary Curry, PhD, Public Service Coordinator and Research Associate."
4. For citations relating to most of the historical claims made in this article, see Marlin, *Propaganda and the Ethics of Persuasion.*
5. Ellul's ideas on this are found in Jacques Ellul, "The Characteristics of Propaganda," chapter 1 in *Propaganda: The Formation of Men's Attitudes* (New York: Vintage Books, 1973).
6. This account is derived partly from an "Open Letter to the Duke of Devonshire," sent to the *Times* of London January 7, 1900, by Charles Boissevain, editor of the influential Dutch newspaper, the *Algemeen Handelsblad.* The letter, widely circulated in Britain by Labour Leader Keir Hardie, was published in a book of Boissevain's newspaper writings titled *Van Dag tot Dag* (Amsterdam: Jacob van Campen, 1925). It gives as references J. A. Hobson's articles in then-current issues of the *Speaker;* Other material in this account is derived from Phillip Knightley, *The First Casualty* (London: André Deutsch, 1975).
7. On German World War I propaganda generally, see David Welch, *Germany, Propaganda and Total War, 1914–1918* (New Brunswick, NJ: Rutgers University Press, 2000). The specific reference to newsreel film is on page 49ff.
8. Sources supporting this account are found in *Propaganda and the Ethics of Persuasion,* but new material has been added and can be found in Joachim Neander and Randal Marlin, "Media and Propaganda: The Northcliffe Press and the Corpse Factory Story of World War I," *Global Media Journal,* Canadian ed., 3, no. 2 (2010): 67–82, http://www.gmj.uottawa.ca/1002/v3i2_neander%20and%20marlin_e.html.

CHAPTER 7

A Theoretical Approach to Mass Psychological Manipulation
Jacques Ellul's Analysis of Modern Propaganda

by Jacob Van Vleet

> *Propaganda cannot be satisfied with partial successes,*
> *for it does not tolerate discussion; by its very nature it*
> *excludes contradiction and discussion.*
> —JACQUES ELLUL[1]

INTRODUCTION

French sociologist Jacques Ellul (1912–1994) authored more than fifty books and hundreds of scholarly essays, and was professor of the History and Sociology of Institutions at the University of Bordeaux. His work influenced a number of prominent intellectuals including Paul Ricoeur, Marshall McLuhan, Thomas Merton, and Paul Virilio. In 1962 Ellul published *Propaganda: The Formation of Men's Attitudes*.[2] In it, he described and detailed various characteristics, methods, and types of propaganda in primarily contemporary Western societies. Ellul hoped to inform and educate the public of the true nature of modern propaganda and to awaken them to its disastrous social, psychological, and spiritual costs. He concluded that propaganda is inextricably linked to technological development, consumerism, and the rise of global capitalism.

In order to challenge propaganda, Ellul argued that we must first recognize its many forms and its entangled relationship to other systems of power, be they political, educational, or religious institutions. Ultimately, Ellul wanted to change these systems, which enable propaganda to exist and thrive. He was a true believer in freedom in all forms—freedom of speech, religion, politics, and more. In fact, Ellul argued that freedom was precisely what propaganda was destroying. This quest for authentic individual and collective freedom was the reason for his work.[3]

By elucidating Ellul's central theoretical ideas, this essay will give the reader a deeper knowledge of the foundations of modern propaganda, and will provide the analytical tools needed to confront and critique today's mass psychological manipulation.

PROPAGANDA AS METHOD

Ellul defined propaganda as ". . . a set of methods employed by an organized group that wants to bring about the active or passive participation in its actions of a mass of individuals, psychologically unified through psychological manipulations and incorporated into an organization."[4] Expanding this definition, Ellul maintained that, in its broadest sense, propaganda often involves one or more of the four following methods.

First, there is *psychological action,* a method through which the propagandist seeks to manipulate and modify public opinion using psychological means.[5] Appeals to fear, pity, guilt, sexual desire, and the like are employed in order to unconsciously sway the audience. This technique is clearly seen in advertisements that use scantily clad men and women in provocative sexual positions to sell various commodities. One can also observe this approach in political and military campaigns that rely primarily on fear tactics. The influential propagandist Edward Bernays recognized the effectiveness of this type of methodology and recommended it to the corporations and politicians he advised.[6] Psychological action appeals to people's unconscious with very effective results.

Secondly, propaganda can involve what Ellul called the method of *psychological warfare.*[7] This occurs when the propagandist tries to "break down" the public's self-confidence in their decision-making abilities. In other words, the propagandist conveys the message that he/she/it knows better than the individual and the public. Often part of a select group of people working for a corporation or institution, the propagandist wants people to trust the corporation's or institution's message rather than listening to their own intuitions or opinions. This is often done by appealing to "experts" (or "technicians" as Ellul referred to them) and by manipulating or fabricating statistical data. This psychological warfare ends up creating a society deeply dependent upon the corporate media and other social institutions. Furthermore, most people cease to think critically and analytically about the messages they are receiving; they simply allow the propagandist to spoon-feed them the "truth."

An example of the consequences of this technique is found in the fact that millions rely solely on mainstream media for their news. Many of these people have no idea that the "experts" who frame, present, and analyze the current news are often ideologically driven, have little in-depth knowledge, or simply lack the basic qualifications to intelligently comment on the topic at hand.

Thirdly, according to Ellul, propaganda often involves what he called *re-education* or *brainwashing*. This occurs when sources of public information are limited or edited in order to further a dominant ideology. Two recent examples illustrate this method. First, in March 2010, the Texas Board of Education voted to alter textbooks used in public institutions. These changes included challenging the Darwinian theory of evolution, emphasizing capitalism over other forms of economic systems, and leaving out discussion of the secular influences upon the Founding Fathers.[8] This is an irrefutable example of an ideologically motivated "re-education."

A second example is the British Petroleum (BP) purchase of key search words from Google and Yahoo search engines after the Gulf oil disaster that BP had caused.[9] By drastically limiting public information, thus revealing only select answers and impressions about the oil spill, BP demonstrated attempts at what Ellul called the "brainwashing" of modern society.

Finally, in its broadest sense, propaganda often utilizes *public relations*. Institutions and corporations are always concerned with their relationship to the public and with the public's perception of them. Thus, these entities frequently rely on a group of public relations experts to sell their products or services. According to Ellul, the sphere of public relations always involves a distortion of truth and a misrepresentation of the institutions in order that they might appear more palatable to the masses. Furthermore, public relations technicians often use a myriad of manipulative and deceptive means to sway the public.

The key to understanding these four types of propaganda is to recognize that each of them is a *method*.[10] The first two employ psychological techniques and the last two employ the limiting and/or manipulation of information. All four, according to Ellul, are based on the propagandist's knowledge of basic psychological and sociological principles. He states:

> . . . the propagandist builds his techniques on the basis of his knowledge of man, his tendencies, his desires, his needs, his psychic mechanisms, his conditioning—and as much on social psychology as on depth psychology. He shapes his procedures on the basis of our knowledge of groups and their laws of formation and dissolution, of mass influences, and of environmental limitations. Without the scientific research of modern psychology and sociology there would be no propaganda . . .[11]

Public relations experts, advertisers, and marketers use these principles to achieve a calculated outcome. Propaganda, therefore, has become a highly specialized technique that is generally not discussed in the public realm. Furthermore, even though it is all around us, propaganda often remains opaque. This is because many propagandists are skilled in camouflaging their work with a myriad of effective techniques, including those previously discussed.

An important aspect of this discussion is that modern propaganda is not simply a trick, a gimmick, or a dissemination of lies. To assume this is to be in a dangerous position. For example, many believe that they are quite capable of discerning truth from falsehood, and are thus able to recognize propaganda and readily dismiss it. However, in reality, propagandists often use a combination of true and false statements in their appeals. They also commonly rely on a few truthful propositions in their petitions, while omitting other relevant and factual information. This creates an illusion of objectivity when in fact only one side of the issue at hand is being presented. In its portrayal

of partially true—or true but partially distorted—information, propaganda proves to be more complicated than sheer lies that are easily
detectable. Indeed, propaganda involves incredibly complex and multifaceted methods. It is created by experts who specialize in
psychological, sociological, and cultural knowledge. The average
person is usually unaware of the propagandist's involved techniques
and methodology, making propaganda all the more diabolical.

POLITICAL AND SOCIAL PROPAGANDA

According to Ellul, these methods—psychological action, psychological
warfare, re-education/brainwashing, and public relations—are employed
by two primary overarching categories of propaganda: *political* and
social.[12] Political propaganda is primarily concerned with three goals:
convincing the public to place their trust in politicians, manipulating the
public into believing that politicians have the interest of the people at
heart, and making military acts acceptable to the public.[13] These are
essential to maintaining political hierarchies of control and order.

Social propaganda, according to Ellul, is a form of propaganda that
aims to influence society's "style of life."[14] This propaganda appeals to
and reinforces common societal assumptions. Examples in the United
States include the conviction that forty hours constitute a workweek,
the notion that more money equals a better job, the reinforcement of
traditional gender roles, and the emphasis on Western democracy's
supremacy over other political systems. These assumptions lead individuals to believe that their society—including their government,
educational, and economic systems—holds the best way of life. It follows from this reasoning that other societies and cultures are inferior
or inadequate at best, and evil or loathsome at worst. Examples range
from the use of pejorative references, such as calling others "un-Amer-
ican" or "anti-Christian," to feeling justified in going to war in an
"inferior" or "backwards" country.

One of the key dangers of both political and social propaganda is
that each propagates a particular ideology. Ellul, who was deeply influenced by the theories of Karl Marx, believed that ideology (or "false
consciousness" as Marx called it) served to increase the numbers of
unthinking, inactive masses, with the ultimate purpose of integrating

the individual into the political and social system. Once this occurs, the system can continue to develop, grow, and dominate.

PRE-PROPAGANDA: CONDITIONED
REFLEX AND MYTH

Ellul maintained that, before social and political propaganda could be effective, the public had to be conditioned to accept various types of psychological manipulation. Ellul referred to this conditioning as "pre-propaganda," which he distinguished from the "active propaganda" discussed thus far in this chapter. The goal of pre-propaganda is to lock individuals into the current ideological system, to prepare them to act in a certain way.[15] Ellul stated:

> [P]re-propaganda does not have a precise ideological objective; it has nothing to do with an opinion, an idea, a doctrine. It proceeds by psychological manipulations, by character modifications, by the creation of feelings or stereotypes useful when the time comes.[16]

In other words, in order to prepare one for orthopraxy (i.e., "correct" behavior), one must first be conditioned. One needs to see the world through a predetermined lens, to think in certain categories, and to truly believe that one's social and political decisions are necessary and efficacious.

Pre-propaganda involves two methods, according to Ellul: *conditioned reflex* and *myth*.

First, propagandists condition reflexes by training the public to respond in specific ways to certain signs, symbols, images, and authority figures. By doing this, the propagandist can predict a given response with a high degree of accuracy. For example, since the 1970s, many fast food restaurants have been giving children toys with their meals. This creates an image in the child's mind, as well as a specific response: the child goes on to associate the establishment with not only food, but also new toys, and is thus magnetized by this restaurant above others. Even adults can now get specialized movie or sports paraphernalia at fast food restaurants with their meals. One imagines these adults being conditioned as children to associate a particular restaurant with a toy and therefore buying into the same tactic today. Whether or not this is the case, the adult customer is as lured by the restaurant's free gift as is a child.

Another example of a conditioned reflex is found in the strong reactions evoked by the American flag. From a young age, those of us who grew up in the United States have been programmed to unquestioningly respect and honor this symbol. Reciting the Pledge of Allegiance with hands over hearts in elementary school, standing to sing "The Star-Spangled Banner" at sporting events, and watching presidential debates with the flag prominently displayed in the background all add to this pre-propaganda. The flag symbol evokes in many a deep sense of pride, patriotism, and even awe. Furthermore, people are unconsciously conditioned to assume that anyone disrespecting the flag must be disrespecting the United States and all of its good qualities. Ellul explained:

> Each person's psychology is shaped by that culture. He is conditioned by the symbols of that culture, and is also a transmitter of that culture; each time its symbols are changed he is deeply affected. Thus, one can change him by changing these symbols. The propagandist will act on this [knowledge] . . .[17]

As the second method of pre-propaganda, *myth* creates a worldview that is rarely questioned. According to Ellul, propagandists are highly skilled at creating myths: narratives and images reliant on symbols, which shape the individual's consciousness.[18] Some examples include idealized stories about the "discovery" of the Americas; fairy-tale wedding, marriage, and family traditions; and sentimental rags-to-riches legends that purport the divine superiority of capitalism. These myths can lead to a blind faith in the message of the propagandist, creating both the illusion that buying into its industry or customs is morally right, and the assumption that one's culture and way of life are legitimate, beneficial, and superior to all others. In turn, a firm foundation of pre-propaganda is created, preparing the individual to be further psychologically manipulated by social and political propaganda. Ellul described:

Eventually the myth takes possession of a man's mind so completely that his life is consecrated to it. But that effect can only be created by slow, patient work by all the methods of propaganda, not by any immediate operation. Only when conditioned reflexes have been created in man and he lives in a collective myth can he be readily mobilized.[19]

CONCLUSION

Propaganda's reliance on brainwashing, conditioned reflexes, and myth make it increasingly difficult to detect without a solid theoretical framework. This is precisely why only knowledge of the various methods and forms of propaganda can free us from the layers of persuasion with which we are faced on a daily basis.

Ellul's sociological work concerning modern propaganda offers a clear and accurate description of mass psychological manipulation. He calls us to challenge the systems of power and to encourage one another to discover the truth without relying solely on mass media, politicians, educational systems, and other institutions. In order to do this, we need to distinguish among the sources, consequences, and complications of propaganda. Only when we can make these distinctions will we be able to fight and resist. Ellul concludes *Propaganda* with the following:

> The only truly serious attitude—serious because the danger of man's destruction by propaganda is serious, serious because no other attitude is truly responsible and serious— is to show people the extreme effectiveness of the weapon used against them, to rouse them to defend themselves. . . . [I]n this game, propaganda is undoubtedly the most formidable power, acting in only one direction (toward the destruction of truth and freedom), no matter what the good intentions or the good will may be of those who manipulate it.[20]

Ellul's work can give us the theoretical tools needed to arm ourselves against propaganda. And once armed, we can authentically adopt the serious attitude Ellul encourages us to take, to work toward a greater dissemination of truth and, ultimately, freedom.

RECOMMENDED READING

1. *Propaganda: The Formation of Men's Attitudes* by Jacques Ellul (New York: Knopf, 1968).
First published in France in 1962, this work is primarily a sociological analysis of methods of propaganda in the modern Western world. Ellul conclusively demonstrates the inextricable relationship between the rise of propaganda and political and corporate systems of control.

2. *Propaganda and the Ethics of Persuasion* by Randal Marlin (New York: Broadview, 2002).
Marlin, a former student of Jacques Ellul, presents a brief but excellent overview of the history of propaganda, and gives insightful examples of propaganda in contemporary society. Marlin is particularly perceptive in his analysis of the consequences of propaganda and in his discussion of its intersection with ethics.

3. *Age of Propaganda: The Everyday Use and Abuse of Persuasion* by Anthony Pratkanis and Elliot Aronson (New York: Henry Holt and Co., 2002). Social psychologists Pratkanis and Aronson focus specifically on propaganda's connection to human emotions, unconscious desires, and fears. This book, originally published in 1992, is of particular interest for those concerned with the psychological dimension of propaganda.

4. *Manufacturing Consent: The Political Economy of the Mass Media* by Edward S. Herman and Noam Chomsky (New York: Pantheon, 2002). Now a classic work in the field of propaganda studies, the authors outline their theoretical "propaganda model" via various case studies, demonstrating that corporate-dominated media is profoundly ideologically biased and undemocratic.

5. *Mass Media, Mass Propaganda: Examining American News in the "War on Terror"* by Anthony R. DiMaggio (Lanham, MD: Lexington,

2008). A scholarly analysis of propaganda techniques used in the corporate media's coverage of September 11 and the invasion of Iraq and Afghanistan. An engaging work full of clear and insightful examples proving that propaganda is more ubiquitous in the West than ever.

6. *Public Opinion* by Walter Lippmann (New York: Free Press, 1997). First published in 1922, celebrated journalist Lippmann argues that, due to the complexity of modern society and the ignorance of the masses, a special class of elite individuals should "manufacture consent" in order to persuade and control public opinion. Although it is blatantly pro-propaganda, this work is certainly recommended for those seeking a deeper understanding of the theoretical foundations of modern psychological manipulation from the propagandist's perspective.

7. *Propaganda* by Edward Bernays (New York: IG Publishing, 2005). Originally published in 1928, Bernays, known as the "father of Public Relations," argues that various methods of propaganda are efficacious in politics, business, education, science, and nearly every other social sphere. Influenced by Lippmann, Bernays unapologetically endorses propaganda that relies primarily on knowledge of Freudian psychoanalysis. On Bernays's work, Noam Chomsky states: "Bernays's honest and practical manual provides much insight into some of the most powerful and influential institutions of contemporary industrial-state capitalist democracies."

JACOB VAN VLEET teaches philosophy at Diablo Valley College in the San Francisco Bay Area. He is a member of the International Jacques Ellul Society and a contributor to *The Ellul Forum: The International Journal of Jacques Ellul Studies*. He lives in Berkeley with his wife, Moriah.

Notes
1. Jacques Ellul, *Propaganda: The Formation of Men's Attitudes*. (New York: Knopf, 1968), 11.
2. Originally published as *Propagandes* by Librarie Armand Colin in 1962. English version translated by Konrad Kellen and published in 1965 by Alfred A. Knopf Inc. This work has since become a classic text in the field of propaganda studies, but is little known outside academia.
3. Ellul's primary work on freedom, *The Ethics of Freedom* (1976), is primarily theo-

logical in nature, but relies to a great extent on his earlier sociological works, such as *Propaganda* (1965) and *The Technological Society* (1954).

4. *Propaganda*, 61.
5. Ibid., xiii.
6. For examples of Bernays's techniques, see Larry Tye, *The Father of Spin: Edward L. Bernays and the Birth of Public Relations* (New York: Holt, 1998). Also, Bernays's own book give insight into his methodology. See Edward L. Bernays, *Propaganda* (New York: Ig Publishing, 2005).
7. *Propaganda*, xiii.
8. See James C. McKinley Jr., "Texas Conservatives Win Curriculum Change," *New York Times*, March 12, 2010.
9. See Matthew Shaer, "Gulf Oil Spill: To Control Message, BP Buys Search Terms from Google," *Christian Science Monitor*, June 9, 2010.
10. We should remember that Ellul is primarily a sociologist and his work is often descriptive rather than definitional. It is helpful to think of Ellul as a phenomenologist similar to G. W. F. Hegel. Like Hegel, Ellul often works to carefully describe a large system of thought—including all of its components, corollaries, and entailments—rather than simply offering definitions.
11. *Propaganda*, 4.
12. Ibid., 62–70.
13. Ibid., 63.
14. Ibid., 62.
15. Ibid., 30. Ellul also refers to pre-propaganda and sub-propaganda.
16. Ibid., 31.
17. Ibid., 34.
18. Ibid., 31.
19. Ibid., 31–32.
20. Ibid., 257.

CHAPTER 8

Drawing Back the Veil on the US Propaganda Machine[1]

by Dr. Robert Abele

Even to the casual observer, the last thirty years has witnessed a revolution in American media. No longer fulfilling the valued democratic function of "the Fourth Estate," the media complex has co-opted itself simultaneously into both mega corporations and government megaphone.[2] The result is a government-corporate media complex, whose function is to profit those who run them and use them. It is the point of the following analysis to elucidate the existence, structure, and values of this mega-complex. The ensuing seven-part argument is intended to produce in the reader the commitment to become the media, since there is currently no Fourth Estate in the US.

1. METHODOLOGY: STRUCTURAL ANALYSIS OF INSTITUTIONS

The structural analysis I have in mind parallels the method of Noam Chomsky in *Aspects of the Theory of Syntax*, in which Chomsky sees syntax as providing meaning to semantics.[3] In this case, the structure of institutions reveals their meaning, in terms of their functions and values. It is derived more directly from Herman and Chomsky's *Manufacturing Consent*, where such an institutional analysis is actually performed on mainstream American media, and additionally from other authors who contributed to this analysis after Chomsky and Herman published their groundbreaking work.

The primary assumption guiding this analysis is that the more pervasive, complex, and powerful the institutional structure is, the more authoritarian it will be—or will become. The reason for this is that the degree to which these structures embody these traits is the degree to which they have a tendency to become removed from the people they are designed to serve, and to become *sui generis*—i.e. not only take on a life of their own, but whose functionaries maintain and increase those institutional power structures.

The key indicators of this structural isolation from the people include the constant expansion of state powers, combined with the increased threat to civil liberties. As a primary example, one need only review the main issues of the USA PATRIOT Act, passed in October 2001. [4] Regarding the issues of probable cause, privacy, checks and balances, due process, and free speech, the federal government's power grabs through PATRIOT demonstrate institutional distance from the persons it is designed to serve.

2. DEFINING PROPAGANDA

The Oxford English Dictionary defines propaganda as: "Any association, systematic scheme, or concerted movement for the propagation of a particular doctrine or practice."[5] The nephew of Sigmund Freud and the watershed for advancing propaganda in a distinct direction favoring political and economic elites, Edward Bernays interpreted propaganda in narrow terms: democracy will only work if the mass of people is guided by an enlightened elite class that is imperceptible to the masses in its crafting of public opinion. This understanding comes from his intellectual mentor, Walter Lippmann, who said that the people "are incapable of lucid thought and clear perception, and are driven instead by the herd instinct, raw emotions, and pure prejudice."[6]

What we may take from this is that propaganda is a form of coercion—the verbal manipulation of the people to whom it is directed by the cloaking of the message in terms with which no one can disagree (e.g. euphemisms such as "American *x*," "USA PATRIOT Act," "Support our troops," "Fighting to bring democracy," etc.), thereby creating the illusion in people that they are in control of their lives and their institutional structures, as well as the illusion of having free choice in such matters, while allowing the perpetrator of it to have his way.[7]

3. THE ELITES BEHIND THE PROPAGANDA

For the propagandist and the elites behind the propaganda, the function of propaganda is to create ideological conformity by limiting the range of "acceptable" dissent. Lippmann, for example, argues that "the democratic El Dorado" is impossible in America because the populace is incapable of lucid thought and clear perception, and is driven instead by the herd instinct, raw emotions, and pure prejudice, and thus could not make rational and informed decisions.[8]

Noam Chomsky interprets Lippmann as maintaining that "the practice of democracy" must be "the manufacture of consent," based on the position that the opinion of the masses could not be trusted. There are two political roles that are to be clearly distinguished: the role of the specialized class, the "insiders," who have access to information and understanding, and "the task of the public" which "acts only by aligning itself as the partisan of someone in a position to act executively."[9]

4. STRUCTURAL ANALYSIS OF THE AMERICAN MEDIA

When one examines how this process of "manufacturing consent" works, one finds the following structure.[10] The first structural dynamic leads us to see that there are elite media, such as the *New York Times*, the *Washington Post*, CBS, NBC, etc., that set the news agenda that others use in their coverage of world and national news. Second, there are five filters the elite media use in determining the news:

i. The size: concentrated ownership; owner wealth; profit orientation of the dominant mass media firms;
ii. Advertising as the primary income source of the mass media;
iii. Reliance of the media on information provided by government, business, and "experts" funded and approved by these primary sources and agents of power;
iv. "Flak" as a means of disciplining the media;
v. The "national religion" and control mechanism of news: once "anticommunism," now changed, in the words of Ronald Reagan, to "the miracle of the market."[11]

This structure of the media is what media analysts refer to today as "the mainstream media." According to many analysts, its function is to divert attention away from the important issues and into side issues, leaving the elite to determine solutions to the main issues. For example, in the run-up to the US-led Iraq invasion in 2003, the mainstream media focused on issues of the threat of Iraq's alleged weapons of mass destruction, and also stated, without critical review, the Bush administration's claims that Saddam Hussein was connected to the attacks on the US on September 11, 2001. Both these tactics inspired fear and bloodlust in the US population. If the structural dimensions of the media had been different, instead of asking such "sideshow" questions, the questions would have been more along the lines of verifying such assertions, and most importantly, asking whether the US had the right, by ethics and international law, to invade Iraq.[12] Instead, not a single voice in the mainstream media highlighted the inconsistencies of the primary mainstream media spokespersons for the invasion of Iraq.

The second structural dynamic reveals that the mainstream media are capitalist institutions. Historically, this process, if not begun by President Reagan, was certainly accelerated by him, when he began a process of allowing mega corporations to form. The *coup de gras* came with President Clinton, who opened the gates to these mega corporations to concentrate US media sources into a few hands. The result is that "the media's interest is now united with that of the government and the oligarchs."[13] But one need only examine the balance sheets of the major media outlets to see that they are huge, highly profitable institutions. For example, in 2010, CBS net income rose 53 percent to $317 million, or forty-six cents per share in a single quarter, from $207.6 million, or thirty cents a share, a year ago, the company said on November 4, 2010.[14] Similarly, in July 2010, General Electric released its second-quarter earnings, and operating profit at its media unit was up 13 percent to $607 million compared with the period a year ago. Revenue at NBC Universal was up 5 percent to $3.75 billion, which marked the biggest increase of any GE unit.[15] It is a salient notation that almost all of these media mega corporations are owned completely by larger corporations. For example, GE owns NBC, Disney owns ABC and ESPN, Westinghouse owns CBS, etc.

5. THE STRUCTURAL ASPECTS OF AMERICAN
DEMOCRACY: CAPITALISTIC AND AUTHORITARIAN

It would be naïve to believe that such a corporate structure of the mainstream media had no effect on government structure. As we noted, Bernays saw a clear overlap between the methods used to create a profit and the methods used to keep elite politicians in office. Our conclusion that the US government is aligned with corporate, elite interests, and that the corporate media are a part of this complex will be supported in the following four steps.

First, state intervention plays a decisive role in the market system. Government heavily subsidizes corporations and works to advance corporate interests on numerous fronts, such as tax breaks and protectionist tariffs. In fact, the global market economy could not have occurred without powerful governments, such as the US, leveraging pressure on other nations to accept trade deals to make it easier for corporations to dominate the economies from around the world. Here are just three examples, on which we cannot elaborate at this time, but of which a simple reading will suffice to make the point: the North American Free Trade Agreement (NAFTA); the creation of the World Trade Organization (WTO) in the 1990s; and the Multilateral Agreement on Investment (MAI).[16]

Second, because corporations benefit from state intervention, they seek, in turn, to control the persons who are permitted to run for office, by either financially bankrolling their campaigns or by rejecting such financial support. The result is that government is being run *by* corporate interests, *for* corporate interests. As a consequence, the philosophy that has come to run the government is called neoliberalism, propagandized by neoliberals as "free market policies," which are said to encourage private enterprise and consumer choice, while handcuffing the hands of the incompetent, bureaucratic government. For example, Milton Friedman, in *Capitalism and Freedom*, stated that profit-making is the essence of democracy, so any government that pursues antimarket policies is being antidemocratic. Thus, it is best to restrict governments to the job of protecting private property and enforcing contracts.[17] Additionally, Robert Nozick, in his classic defense of libertarianism, *Anarchy, State, and Utopia*, argues that the notion of equality was not meant for the economic arena, in that it denies "the fact of our separate existences."[18] This conception of liberty is important: in the economic sphere, at least, we are atomistic players; there is no sense of community involved: "there is no moral outweighing of one of our lives by others so as to lead to a greater overall *social* good."[19]

However, there are many significant problems with the neoliberal-government complex. First of all, neoliberalism has disastrous effects for true democracy, because the latter requires an emphasis on *civitas*, or a felt connection of citizens, which is both manifested and enhanced by nonmarket organizations and institutions, such as community groups, neighborhood associations, libraries, public schools, cooperative, public parks, public meeting places, and trade unions. All of this is deliberately undermined by neoliberalism, whose only understanding of democracy refers to markets, not communities, and to consumers, not to citizens.[20] Furthermore, neoliberalism, "the free market," does and must ignore human rights, as in the case of Coca-Cola and many other corporate actions.[21] If it ignores human rights, *a fortiori* it can and must ignore civil rights, since the latter are predicated on the former. It "must" ignore rights because they interfere with profit-making ability, just as regulation does. In neoliberal philosophy, the rights that apply to persons and government relationship are only those involving property ownership and acquisition.

Third, what neoliberalism must do once it controls the government is to dismantle it as a monster institution that impedes corporate interests of profit-making. This is propagandized by such phrases as "getting the government off the backs of the people," where "the people" means "the elites," and by political speeches that keep the people in fear of losing their jobs, or more jobs. By reducing government influence in the private sector to protectionist lawmaking and the prosecution of self-chosen illegalities in profit-making (e.g. Martha Stewart; Bernie Madoff), it provides neoliberals with the only thing they desire: an unlimited ability to create wealth for themselves only, and to rig the game further in their favor.

Fourth, the consequence from these structural givens is that the US is formally democratic, in the sense that the people vote for their rulers but don't do much else; and that the choices of candidates for office are deliberately limited by elites—i.e. the media-government complex. A problematic aspect of this limited choice, and thus limited democracy, is that both major parties rely on the same corporate sources for money, so their ideologies become the same. In particular, the Democratic set of values that gave primacy to labor and to the people at large, has dissipated, as Democrats seek money from corporations, who in turn require Democrats to do their bidding. So there is no diversity in politics[22] and hence, no true democracy.

Most disturbingly, the Supreme Court decision of the *Citizens United* case locked this situation into place in the US for the foreseeable future.

6. RESULT (OF 1–5): A GOVERNMENT-MEDIA COMPLEX

If our argument so far is accurate, we would see a government-media complex revealing itself by the practices of either or both. So what can we see from the corporate media behavior that might indicate this government-media complex, informed by neoliberal philosophy?

a. There is no willingness on part of media to criticize government policies beyond general questions. For example, "Will the war be winnable?" instead of "Is the war right?"

b. More strikingly, in nearly every case, the mainstream media accepted forthrightly, and even touted as facts, the Bush administration's assertions regarding Iraq.

c. The "opponents" of the war permitted onto mainstream media only questioned the pragmatics of the war—e.g. the cost versus the good, the length of stay in Iraq, etc.

d. The corporate/mainstream media ignore critically important stories that do not play to the doctrines held by the elites. For example, this *Project Censored* book is necessarily based on the complex of elite power. Additionally, there is no media coverage of the illegal and wholly unethical and oppressive actions of the Coca-Cola Company in Mexico. For example: firing longtime employees so as to withdraw their pensions by forcing them, literally at gunpoint, to sign a pre-crafted resignation form; and closing plants in Mexico, then reopening the next day under a different name, and rehiring the same workers, but now at entry-level wages, etc.[23]

e. All debate is maintained within corporate-acceptable range: no direct attack on the policy and ideology behind the war is permitted.

f. The permitted statement of "lessons" from the Iraq debacle are quite narrow: the war was entered into "because of intelligence error," or "stupidly," or "without properly assessing costs or consequences," etc., and not because of its unethical nature or its illegality (in both cases, the "supreme crime" of aggression).

g. There is no question of the right of the US to interfere or invade other countries.

h. The antiwar movement is—and has been, beginning in 1991—excluded from news and/or consideration in the media.

i. The "9/11 Truth" movement is marginalized, and no open and public investigation of the events of September 11, 2001, is permitted.

7. THE ANTIDOTE TO PROPAGANDA AND AUTHORITARIANISM

Of the many things we citizens might do to battle against the government-corporate media complex, there are two that will functionally ground such battles.

First, media reporters and analysts need to return to the use of critical thinking tools. This has long since been abandoned by corporate media, but if one simply returns to the Founders and examines the esteem to which they held the ability to think rationally and logically (e.g. Thomas Jefferson, Thomas Paine), one cannot help but advocate this method of reviewing government policies and statements. For starters, let us propose three platforms for critical thinking:

a. General questions directed at institutional authorities concerning their use of power, especially "*qui bono?*" This question is the litmus test of whether a government is truly democratic or not;

b. Deep questions directed toward, and resulting from, analysis of institutional structures themselves, especially the values inherent to those structures in comparison with ethical values and values of justice, which they will indubitably proclaim as their own as well;

c. A willingness to critique and even criticize agents, not just institutions. A well-founded critique of agency follows from the presupposition that persons are moral beings, not just cogs in the machine of state or media. Once this agency perspective is introduced through moral lenses, one is in a stronger position to critique individuals who are acting as agents of state, media, and industry.

Second, media reporters and analysts should return to ethical foundations, recognizing universal principles that humans naturally embrace. Two such principles stand out. First, we must recognize freedom as a necessary part of being human. For example, John Locke, in his second *Treatise of Government*, maintains that liberty is a fundamental natural right, and that "one who would take that away declares war on me." Further, Jean Jacques Rousseau, in his *Discourse on Inequality*, maintains that our nature is "intelligent, free," and rational, with freedom being "the most noble of man's faculties."

The second necessary ethical principle that needs to be re-embraced is the principle of equality. In fact, we need to recognize that without equality, there is no liberty. Equality is fundamental to our human *and social* nature. The thinkers just named above would all agree with this. So would Wilhelm von Humboldt, who said that "the isolated [person] is no more able to develop than the one who is fettered."[24]

This notion of equality is diametrically opposed to the inequality demonstrated by both neoliberalism and the propaganda model of the government-media complex. Here, ideological control of the population done through propaganda only serves to demonstrate that the current structures of daily American life are neither equitable nor peaceful, but are designed to maintain the institutional structures of inequality.[25] The inequality embraced by neoliberalism has had the consequence of "massive increase in social and economic inequality, a marked increase in severe deprivation for the poorest peoples and nations, a disastrous global environment, an unstable global economy, and an unprecedented bonanza for the wealthy."[26]

In conclusion, the propaganda of the government-media complex is directly contradictory to human nature, and to be watchful of it, with the right critical tools, is the task of every truly democratically free citizen. In this regard, we may conclude with Humboldt: "Whatever does not spring from a man's choice, or *is only the result of instruction and guidance*, does not enter into his very being, but remains alien to his true nature."[27]

DR. ROBERT P. ABELE holds a PhD in philosophy from Marquette University and MA degrees in theology and divinity. He is the recipient of numerous scholarships and fellowships, including the National Endowment for the Humanities Fellowship to the U.S. Naval Academy for the study of war and morality (2004), and the Illinois Council of Humanities Scholarship, for his work on the issues of freedom and democracy (2003). He is the author of four books: *A User's Guide to the USA PATRIOT Act* (2005); *The Anatomy of a Deception: A Logical and Ethical Analysis of the Decision to Invade Iraq* (2009); *Democracy Gone: A Chronicle of the Last Chapters of the Great American Democratic Experiment* (2009), *Patterns of Dominance* (forthcoming this fall, 2011), and *War and Its Limits: East and West*, forthcoming this spring (2012). He has written numerous articles on politics and U.S. government foreign and domestic policies. He recently has contributed eleven chapters for the forthcoming *Encyclopedia of Global Justice*, from The Hague: Springer Press (October 1, 2011). The chapters are entitled: "Noam Chomsky," "Propaganda," "Oil; "Language and Justice," "The Hague Convention," "The Geneva Conventions," "State Terrorism," "Torture," "Global Justice and the Invasion of Iraq," "Conspiracy Theory," and "Capital Punishment." Dr. Abele is an instructor of philosophy at Diablo Valley College, located in Pleasant Hill, California, in the San Francisco Bay area.

Notes

1. The following article is an adapted transcript of a talk given at the Berkeley Fellowship of Unitarian Universalists, on November 16, 2010, for Project Censored. Mickey Huff, director of Project Censored, moderated the evening.
2. The term "the Fourth Estate" is historically a sociopolitical group that is not officially part of the government structure. The etymology of the term is uncertain, but as applied to the media, it was probably first used by Thomas Carlyle, in his 1840 book entitled *On Heroes, Hero-Worship, and the Heroic in History. Six Lectures: reported with emendations and additions* (Nabu Press, 2010; reprinted from Ann Arbor, Michigan: University of Michigan Library, 2005).
3. It is important to note that Chomsky himself denies that there is any connection between syntactic and socio-political analysis. I do not agree with this assumption, but this is not the proper forum for discussion of such views.
4. For a further discussion of this issue, see Abele, *A User's Guide to the USA PATR-TIOT Act and Beyond.*

5. Bernays, 11.
6. Ibid., 16.
7. Chomsky, "Force and Opinion," 8.
8. Bernays, 16, 37, 109.
9. Chomsky, "Force and Opinion," 8–10.
10. Chomsky, "What Makes Mainstream Media Mainstream?" 1–4.
11. Chomsky and Herman, *Manufacturing Consent*, 31; the issue is summarized in Chomsky, "Force and Opinion," 10. For further information, see Herman, "The Propaganda Model," 1–3, 7–9; Cromwell, "The Propaganda Model: An Overview."
12. For detailed examples of this, see Abele, *The Anatomy of a Deception*.
13. Roberts, "The Impotence of Election."
14. Lafayette, "CBS Profits Rise."
15. James, "NBC Universal Profits Bounce Back Signaling GE Agreed to Comcast Sale at Market Bottom."
16. McChesney, 2. See also Chomsky, *Profit Over People*.
17. Ibid.
18. Nozick, 33.
19. Ibid.
20. McChesney, ibid.
21. For a further discussion of Coca-Cola's illegal actions, see www.killerCoke.org.
22. Roberts, "The Impotence of Elections."
23. See www.KillerCoke.org.
24. Humboldt, 98.
25. For more information see Herman, *Manufacturing Consent*; and Laffey More in *Manufacturing Consent*; see also Laffey, "Discerning the Patterns of World Order: Noam Chomsky and International Theory after the Cold War," 596.
26. McChesney, 1.
27. Humboldt, 28.

Bibliography

Abele, Robert. *The Anatomy of a Deception*. Lanham, MD: University Press of America, 2008.

——. *A User's Guide to the USA PATRIOT Act and Beyond*. Lanham, MD: University Press of America, 2004.

Barnett, Michael N. and Raymond D. Duvall, eds. *Power in Global Governance*. Cambridge: Cambridge University Press, 2005.

Bernays, Edward. *Propaganda*. New York: Ig Publishing, 1928, 2004.

Chomsky, Noam. *Aspects of the Theory of Syntax*. Cambridge, MA: MIT Press, 1969.

——. *Chomsky on Anarchism*. Oakland, CA: AK Press, 2005.

——. "Force and Opinion." *Z Magazine*. July–August 1991.

——. "Language, Politics, and Propaganda." In *Conversations on the Edge of the Apocalypse*. Ed. David Jay Brown et al. New York: Palgrave Macmillan, 2005. 33–39.

——. "Market Democracy in a Neoliberal Order." *Z Magazine*. November 1997.

——. *Necessary Illusions*. New York: South End Press, 1999.

——. "On Propaganda." WBAI interview. January 1992.

——. *Profit Over People: Neoliberalism and Global Order*. New York: Seven Stories Press, 1999.

——. "Triumphs of Democracy." *Language and Responsibility*. New York: Pantheon, 1977.

———. "The Victors." *Z Magazine*. Printed November 1990, January 1991, and April 1991.
———. "What Makes Mainstream Media Mainstream?" *Z Magazine*. October 1977.
Chomsky, Noam, and Edward S. Herman. *Manufacturing Consent*. New York: Pantheon, 2002.
Cromwell, David. "The Propaganda Model: An Overview" in *Private Planet*. Jon Carpenter Publishing 2002.
Ellul, Jacques. *Propaganda*. New York: Vintage, 1973.
Greenwald, Glenn. "The Wretched Mind of the American Authoritarian." *Salon*. October 29, 2010.
Herman, Edward S. "The Propaganda Model: A Retrospective." *Against All Reason* 1 (2003): 1–14.
Huff, Mickey, and Peter Phillips, eds. *Censored 2011: The Top 25 Censored Stories of 2009–10*. New York: Seven Stories Press, 2010.
Humboldt, Wilhelm von. *The Limits of State Action*. Cambridge: Cambridge University Press, 1969.
James, Meg. "NBC Universal Profits Bounce Back Signaling GE Agreed to Comcast Sale at Market Bottom." *Los Angeles Times*. July 16, 2010.
Klaehn, Jeffrey. "A Critical Review and Assessment of Herman and Chomsky's 'Propaganda Model.'" *European Journal of Communication* 17, no. 2 (2002): 147–82.
Lafayette, Jon. "CBS Profits Rise." *Broadcasting & Cable*. November 4, 2010.
Laffey, Mark. "Discerning the Patterns of World Order: Noam Chomsky and International Theory after the Cold War." *Review of International Studies* 29 (2003): 587–604.
Leopold, Jason. "Cheney Admits to War Crimes, Media Yawns, Obama Turns the Other Cheek." *Truthout*. Last modified February 15, 2010, http://archive.truthout.org.
McChesney, Robert W. "Noam Chomsky and the Struggle Against Neoliberalism." *Monthly Review*. April 1, 1999.
Nozick, Robert. *Anarchy, State, and Utopia*. New York: Basic Books, 1974.
"Ownership Chart: The Big Six." Free Press. http://www.freepress.net.
Parenti, Christian. *Lockdown America*. New York: Verso, October 2000.
Roberts, Paul Craig. "The Impotence of Elections." Global Research. November 4, 2010.

CHAPTER 9

The Impending Demise of Net Neutrality

by Elliot D. Cohen, PhD

If a computer virus with the capacity to disrupt the free flow of information on the internet were about to be unleashed by a gang of hackers whose aim was to control and monopolize the internet, then we would be shocked to find out that the federal government was not only unwilling to stop the culprits from accomplishing their goal, but was actually making it easier for them to succeed. And, as if this were not enough, we would be mortified to learn that the mainstream media knew all along about the attack and the complicity of government yet nevertheless chose not to report it.

Indeed, because the internet is so vital to our culture, the impending demise of its free architecture would be the story of the century. Yet something not unlike such a government and media-enabled plan is currently happening and, unless the story gets the attention it deserves, there is, predictably, little chance that the free internet will survive.

What I am speaking of is the current movement afoot aiming at dissolving net neutrality. The real "hackers" in this case are the giant internet service providers (ISPs)—notably the telecommunications companies Comcast, Verizon, and AT&T—with cooperation from the federal government; and at least part of the reason why the media is mum is because it is either owned by these giant ISPs, as in the case of Comcast, which recently acquired NBC Universal, or it has business relations including joint ventures with these behemoth companies.[1]

WHAT NET NEUTRALITY IS AND WHY IT MATTERS SO MUCH

Net neutrality—the more common term for "network neutrality"—is the principle according to which all bits are treated equally and therefore everyone has an equal voice on the internet, whether you are a giant corporation, a small website operator, or anything in between. This means that no ISP can screen, block, or filter any lawful content, or discriminate against any competing content or service provider. Thus, just because a company such as Comcast may own the means by which information is transmitted (for example, the cables or wireless network), it does not have the right to interfere with the transmission of any lawful content over this conduit.

For the consumer, this means that everyone should be able to access the same lawful information and have the same quality internet experience, without being blocked or otherwise prevented from gaining access to this information.

The essence of net neutrality is therefore freedom of information: everyone is entitled to the same information and no telecommunication company should have the right to restrict access to it. It is because of net neutrality that the internet is a free and democratic forum of ideas. While other mass media involve communication from the few to the many (such as a cable or broadcast television network), the internet involves communication from the many to the many. It has therefore, by design, created a forum by which each of us can speak our minds and be heard by millions of other people, who in turn can speak their minds and be similarly received. At no other time in history has humankind laid access to such a democratic media for the sharing of information and diverse points of view. Unfortunately, an ongoing, well-organized attack against net neutrality has already made substantial headway toward ending this free, open, and democratic forum.

THE BEGINNING OF THE END:
THE BRAND X DECISION

A major blow to net neutrality came in 2005 with the Supreme Court decision *National Cable & Telecommunications Association v. Brand X Internet Services*.[2] Prior to this decision, the internet fell under the common law doctrine known as common carriage.[3] Common carriage meant that, like a telephone line, anyone could communicate freely on it without being told what content could or could not be transmitted. Moreover, whereas anyone could communicate over the phone lines and receive the same quality reception as anyone else, the giant

ISPs like Comcast could also not discriminate against other ISPs or content providers.

The Brand X decision changed all this by turning this public information highway into private property. According to Brand X, the internet was an information service more like a cable television network and less like a telecommunication service such as a telephone system. Moreover, because the 1996 Telecommunications Act applies common carriage to telecommunication services but not to information services, the Court effectively gave the giant ISPs permission to control the flow of information and traffic down the high-speed internet cables. Moreover, the Court also gave the green light for digital subscriber line (DSL) ISP providers such as AT&T to follow suit. Accordingly, three weeks after the Brand X decision, the George W. Bush administration's Federal Communication Commission (FCC) ruled that common carriage would no longer apply to DSL internet service over the telephone lines.

In reality, though, the internet was and still is a telecommunication service because internet exchanges always involve two-way interactions, whether the activity is communicating with and downloading content from a website or exchanging e-mail messages. This is and always was more like a telephone conversation than a one-way transmission such as that performed by a TV cable station operator. Like a telephone conversation, each end user determines the data that is to be transported over a line.[4] In fact, in the 1999 case *AT&T v. City of Portland*, the US Ninth Circuit Court of Appeals made it clear that broadband and DSL internet service are subject to common carriage pursuant to the 1996 Telecommunication Act. It stated:

> Under the Communications Act, this principle of telecommunications common carriage governs cable broadband as it does other means of Internet transmission such as telephone service and DSL, "regardless of the facilities used." . . . The Internet's protocols themselves manifest a related principle called "end-to-end": control lies at the ends of the network where the users are, leaving a simple network that is neutral with respect to the data it transmits, like any common carrier. On this rule of the Internet, the codes of the legislator and the programmer agree.[5]

There could therefore be no reasonable construction of the Act that could have eviscerated internet common carriage. Instead, the motivation for the change in status came from the desire of the giant ISPs to control the internet and thereby reap greater profits.

THE END: REPLACING THE FREE NET WITH A PAY-FOR-PRIORITY SYSTEM

As soon as these companies received the green light from the Supreme Court, they began the next step in their attempt to take control of the internet: to take concrete steps to dismantle net neutrality. The giant ISPs began to lobby Congress and the FCC to make further changes to the law permitting them to turn the broadband internet pipes into a two-lane highway consisting of a fast lane and a slow lane. The fast lane would provide better bandwidth (quicker connectivity) to website operators who could afford to pay for it. Accordingly, content providers who could not afford the rates would be relegated to the slow lane, which would mean poorer bandwidth and thus a diminished presence on the net.[6]

Within this proposal was the germ of a cybercast system wherein the voices of the wealthy would be dominant over those of the less well-to-do. Thus, mainstream media companies such as News Corp (Fox), Disney (ABC), Time Warner (CNN), Viacom (CBS), and Comcast itself (NBC) would dominate the internet as they now dominate broadcast and cable television. In contrast, independent media organizations, such as those from which most of the Project Censored stories are gleaned, would no longer be able to afford to maintain an audible voice on the internet.

Unfortunately, this cybercast system is steadily becoming a reality as a handful of giant ISPs continue to make further legal headway in eviscerating net neutrality. Because their mainstream media accomplices stand to increase their bottom lines exponentially through such a system of information control, it is not surprising that these profit-oriented behemoths have kept their media mouths closed about this burgeoning assault on internet freedom and equality.[7]

THE FCC'S TOOTHLESS ATTEMPT TO SAVE NET NEUTRALITY

On December 21, 2010, the Obama FCC, under Chairman Julius Genachowski, passed a set of "net neutrality" rules, which many activists had hoped would halt, at least temporarily, the steady dismantling of net neutrality by the giant ISPs. Unfortunately, these rules turned out to be paper tigers, and, in the end, Genachoski capitulated to these companies.

The rules that were approved by the FCC embraced transparency, no blocking, and no unreasonable discrimination consistent with reasonable network management. These rules stipulated:

Transparency: Fixed and mobile broadband providers must disclose the network management practices, performance characteristics, and terms and conditions of their broadband services.

No Blocking: Fixed broadband providers may not block lawful content, applications, services, or non-harmful devices; mobile broadband providers may not block lawful websites, or block applications that compete with their voice or video telephony services; and

No Unreasonable Discrimination: Fixed broadband providers may not unreasonably discriminate in transmitting lawful network traffic.[8]

While the FCC maintained that it would not be unreasonable discrimination to charge consumers based on amount of usage, it did include a general proscription against a two-tiered, "pay-for-priority" arrangement:

No central authority, public or private, should have the power to pick winners and losers on the Internet; that's the role of the commercial market and the marketplace of ideas. So we are adopting a ban on unreasonable discrimination. And we are making clear that we are not approving so-called "pay for

priority" arrangements involving fast lanes for some companies but not for others. The order states that as a general rule
such arrangements won't satisfy the no-unreasonable-
discrimination standard—because it simply isn't consistent
with an open Internet for broadband providers to skew the
marketplace by favoring one idea or application or service
over another by selectively prioritizing Internet traffic.[9]

Here was a clear enough FCC mandate against the two-tiered
system embraced by the major ISPs; the FCC was also clear about the
discriminatory nature of such a system. So, the FCC stood its ground
against corporate pressures, right? Wrong!

The devil is often in the details, and there was at least one important
detail left out of the FCC's equation: legal enforceability of the new
rules. The obvious way to have given teeth to the new rules would have
been to reinstate common carriage by suitably reinterpreting the
ruling made under the Bush FCC. The Obama FCC had the authority,
but there was intense pressure from the giant ISPs not to do so.

In fact, in April 2010, a DC federal appellate court ruled in favor of
Comcast, which had been slowing traffic to BitTorrent, a popular file
sharing website.[10] This decision established a dangerous precedent
against preservation of net neutrality and Genachowski admitted it at
the time. In response to the BitTorrent decision, Genachowski
announced that the FCC would be returning the broadband internet to
its former common carrier status under Title II of the 1996 Telecommunication Act. "The goal," said Genachowski, "is to restore the broadly
supported status quo consensus that existed prior to the court decision
on the FCC's role with respect to broadband internet service."[11]

However, Genachowski retreated from his announced goal with the
passage of the 2010 Net Neutrality rules. Instead of reinstating Title
II common carriage status to broadband internet service, the new rules
were based on Section 706 of the 1996 Telecommunications Act,
which limply instructs the FCC to "encourage the deployment on a
reasonable and timely basis of advanced telecommunications capability to all Americans." Obviously, there was a huge difference
between "encouraging" and "requiring" and only a return to common
carriage status could have secured the latter authority.[12]

Thus, it was not surprising that, on January 20, 2011, days after the passage of the new FCC net neutrality rules, Verizon took the FCC to court, arguing that its new rules overstep the Commission's authority,[13] which now appeared to be true thanks to its refusal to reinstate common carriage status to broadband cable and DSL service. The Verizon case was filed in the same federal district court that had heard the BitTorrent case, but because the ink had barely dried (the FCC had not yet published the new rules in the Federal Registry), the court declined to hear the case.[14] Inevitably, we have not heard the last of Verizon and the other big telecoms in their attempt to officially nullify the new net neutrality rules in court.

The same feat has also already been attempted legislatively when the US House of Representatives in April 2011 voted 240 to 179 to reject the new FCC rules. A similar bill was also introduced in the Senate with thirty-nine cosponsors,[15] so net neutrality now continues to hang by a virtual thread.

THE ORWELLIAN NIGHTMARE: MASS, WARRANTLESS SURVEILLANCE AND STATE CONTROL

The implications of the impending demise of net neutrality are daunting. In fact, it may well mark the end of freedom and democracy in the free world. This is not an overstatement. It is a realistic danger.

The legal climate of net neutrality in the US needs to be viewed in the larger legislative context of federal government and its interest in cyber-control. Pursuant to the 2008 Foreign Intelligence Surveillance (FISA) Amendments Act, telecom companies such as Comcast and AT&T are mandated to help government conduct warrantless, mass surveillance sweeps of all electronic traffic passing through their networks. In fact, presently, all e-mail messages, telephone conversations, and internet searches of all American citizens are being copied, stored, and analyzed by federal agencies with the assistance of these companies, allegedly for purposes of fighting the "war on terror." In return, these companies have been given full retroactive and prospective immunity from criminal investigations and civil lawsuits filed by customers for abridgments of their Fourth Amendment rights.[16]

Consequently, the companies that are now internet gatekeepers are also working for the federal government. This portends increased government cyber-control. While these companies work cooperatively with government in monitoring electronic communications, they do not regularly block content, at least not yet. However, without a clear legal mandate against blocking web content and against unreasonable discrimination, these same corporate gatekeepers will have patently "legal" authority to block, as well as monitor, internet content on behalf of the government. Accordingly, in the present legal context, there is a chilling potential for government censorship and abridgment of First Amendment rights.

THE MEDIA MELTDOWN

If the giant ISPs put their proposed two-tiered pay-for-priority plan into play, citizen journalism will be dead in the water. Smaller news organizations, including individual bloggers, which now cover stories that have been censored or downplayed by the mainstream media, will be relegated to the slow lane, hence unable to compete with giant corporations in the fast lane.

Effectively, these smaller news organs provide a system of checks and balances capable of encouraging some measure of public responsibility among mainstream news organizations. For example, during the Iraq war, the Downing Street memos, which clearly proved that the Bush administration had lied to the American people about its reasons for going to war in Iraq,[17] at first received scant attention by the mainstream media, including the *New York Times*. However, the internet began to buzz with the story, and eventually this noise got so loud that the mainstream media could no longer ignore it. It still took months before the mainstream media finally covered the story, and even then it was downplayed.[18]

But imagine if small website operators could no longer buzz at an audible decibel. Imagine if these websites were either inaudible or filtered out by the government. The lies and deception of the Bush administration would never have been exposed, even to the extent that they were exposed. Unless we preserve the integrity of the free and open internet, we can look forward to a future in which giant corporations and their government cronies reap great profits and amass incredible power through deception, lies, and fraud, while all along the citizens of the "free world" remain oblivious to what is going on. The crucial role that net neutrality plays in the survival of democracy can therefore not be understated!

KEEPING THE MASSES IGNORANT

About 86 million people in the US are presently without access to affordable internet, a large percentage of whom cannot afford it.[19] Only 60 percent of rural households have broadband connections.[20] The US ranked 22nd in 2008 in terms of cost of high-speed internet service, which is cheaper in Portugal and Turkey than in the US. Internet penetration dropped from #4 in 2001 to #15 in 2007.[21] The US presently ranks 25th in the world in average internet connection speed. In South Korea, the average download is 10 times faster than in the US. Such slow internet speed can prevent access to many online services and applications.[22]

Yet, despite these disconcerting facts, the giant ISPs want to keep the majority of content providers in the slow lane, thereby making it harder for most Americans to secure quick connectivity to all but the sites run by the wealthy corporate sector. Moreover, it is seeking to do so instead of trying to catch up with other industrialized nations to make broadband internet service faster, more affordable, and accessible to more Americans.

As discussed earlier, the new FCC rules permit ISPs to proportion service fees to amount of usage. This opens the door to even further exclusionary practices by the giant ISPs. Already, these companies have begun to impose usage caps on cable and DSL broadband. For example, AT&T has imposed a 150 GB cap on its DSL users and charges a $10 overage fee for every additional 50 GB.[23]

This trend toward imposing usage fees is likely to become more exclusionary with the introduction of a two-tiered system of fast and slow lanes. This is because major content providers (for example, YouTube) will pass the charges it pays for operating in the fast lane onto their customers. This means that the internet will become a pay-per-view internet much akin to pay-per-view cable television.

UNFAIR DISCRIMINATION IN EDUCATION

In addition to diminishing internet access among the general population, such a plan would seriously impact public institutions such as colleges and universities, which regularly use the internet to teach their curricula. Thus, professors who download information as part of their teaching would be forced to restrict the amount of bandwidth they use in teaching their classes. Students, in turn, who conduct research for writing assignments, would be limited to the amount of information they could afford—which would impact the poorest students. Access to information would become a function of how much money one has and not of how much one wishes to learn.

THE INDUSTRY'S BOGUS "SOLUTION"

So how can net neutrality be saved? In August 2010, Verizon and Google teamed up to propose a compromise between net neutrality advocates and the giant ISPs, a proposal that was supposed to allow the latter to control the flow of content while still permitting the former to maintain net neutrality. How so?

The proposal was to create two internets, one that resembled the current public internet and another, a form of private internet. The latter would contain innovative new broadband services such as health care monitoring, educational services, and new forms of entertainment and gaming. This private internet would be a pay-for-play variant of the current internet and thus would be restricted to those who were prepared to pay. Wireless broadband, however, would not be given net neutrality protections because this mode of broadband, according to Google/Verizon, is "too competitive and changing rapidly."[24]

One obvious problem with this proposal is that it would provide an incentive for the giant ISPs to invest in the private internet while leaving the fruits of the public internet to rot on the vine. If all the new technologies end up on the private internet, then in the long run the public version would become an infertile cyber slum, an empty vessel of the robust information highway that it once was. Thus, those who could afford to pay for the innovative new internet would have access to it while those who could not would be relegated to second class citizens.

Moreover, because the new private internet would not be subject to net neutrality rules, there would be no mechanism to guard against the control of content by government and its corporate cronies. The giant ISPs would have full reign in determining which content providers could operate on the private internet and which content providers could not, and thus the preservation of the democratic flow of information from the many to the many would become a pipe dream.

GETTING REALISTIC ABOUT A SOLUTION

The answer to the problem of net neutrality is therefore not to restrict its scope to one side of a bifurcated internet but rather to guarantee its application to a unified internet. One way to accomplish this would be for the FCC to pass rules that have legal teeth, which could be done by reinstating the internet's former common carriage status. As mobile internet continues to expand as a major way in which Americans log onto the internet, net neutrality rules, for mobile as well as fixed internet, against content blocking, filtering, and slowing, and against unreasonable discrimination by ISPs, will need to be clearly articulated and enforced pursuant to the Title II common carriage provisions of the Telecommunication Act.

Another way is for Congress to pass legislation ensuring net neutrality protections. However, the federal government (unfortunately encompassing agencies like the FCC) is presently in alliance with the same companies it is entrusted to regulate. This leaves the American people, along with the realized potential for a free and democratic America, in a serious quandary. If the American people simply sit by and permit their representatives to make decisions regarding the future of the internet, then the prospects are indeed grim for the survival of a free and democratic network.

ACTIVISM: USE IT OR LOSE IT!

Most Americans do not want to pay service charges to access the internet and then pay again each time they download information from it. They do not want to wait extended periods of time for their favorite websites to load or time out. Most of us do not want to see the end of the days when a local musician could achieve fame by putting her music online, or when a small online business could become a multimillion-dollar enterprise. Most of us want to see independent news sources flourish and continue to provide us with the stories that are being censored or downplayed by the mainstream news organizations. Indeed, most Americans want to be able to speak truth to power, to have an uncensored forum by which to make their views known to the masses, and to see free speech and democratic debate thrive on the internet.

So most Americans should be prepared to stand up and be counted for net neutrality. They should, but will they? Many of us think that our own voice alone will not count, so we quietly excuse ourselves from taking an active stand. While we may nod our heads in assent, we retreat when it takes more than a nod to make our views known. But this is an issue that those of us who care about democracy in America— which is the greater majority of us—cannot afford to soft peddle about.

So how can we stand up and be counted? The answer is, by using the free and unfettered architecture of the present internet to have our voices heard before this incredible conduit of democracy is no more. Thus, the adage "use it or lose it" could not be more fittingly applied than here.

The infrastructure for such collective activism on the internet is, to some extent, already in place. For example, Free Press's SavetheInternet .com is composed of "two million everyday people who have banded together with thousands of nonprofit organizations, businesses and bloggers to protect Internet freedom." This organization sponsors organized citizen campaigns to lobby Congress to save the free internet. However, two million people is a relatively small number of people who could band together to make a difference. What if most Americans who cared about the survival of a free internet were to sign up?

A new organization called Internet Neutrality Freedom Organization (INFO) on Facebook (facebook.com/info.org) consists of "friends of a free and democratic internet who are prepared to take a stand against ISPs who want to destroy the open, free, and democratic architecture of the Net." It seeks to use social media to amass large numbers of people to band together to actively support net neutrality—for example, by organizing boycotts against the ISPs and other showings of unified power against those who seek to undermine internet freedom and democracy. The giant ISPs need internet consumers in order to remain in business. This is where we the people come in. Together, we can make a difference by standing up to the giant ISPs and letting them know who keeps them in business!

Civil liberties organizations such as the Electronic Frontier Foundation (EFF.org), the Electronic Privacy Information Center (EPIC.org), the American Civil Liberties Union (ACLU.org), the Center for Digital Democracy (DemocraticMedia.org), and Public Knowledge (PublicKnowledge.org) provide opportunities for citizens to support and assist in helping to secure a free and democratic internet. These organizations also help to educate citizens about current events surrounding the attempts by giant corporations to usurp our online freedom. Some of them, such as Public Knowledge, also offer internships for students who want to give their time and energy to helping change the current legal climate surrounding net neutrality and related issues. Thus, each of us can become informed, active participants in the struggle to preserve the free internet.

America is on the precipices of a brave new world in which freedom and democracy may come to be an empty slogan for government and corporate officials who seek money and power through mass manipulation and deception. Without legally enforceable protection of net neutrality, the internet could very likely come under the control of these formidable, megalomaniac powers. The hour is late, and the time is near. We must individually and collectively take responsibility or forever bemoan the demise of the greatest bastion of freedom and democracy ever devised by humankind.

ELLIOT D. COHEN is a contributor to *Truthout* and *Truthdig*, editor in chief of *International Journal of Applied Philosophy*, ethics editor for *Free Inquiry* magazine, and blogger for *Psychology Today*. His most recent book is *Mass Surveillance and State Control: The Total Information Awareness Project* (Palgrave Macmillan, 2010).

Notes

1. Elliot D. Cohen, "Media Mum While Congress Considers Giving Telecoms Blank Check to Eavesdrop," *Buzzflash*, October 11, 2007, http://blog.buzzflash.com/contributors/1373.
2. 545 U.S. 967 (2005).
3. Mark Cooper, "Building a Progressive and Democratic Media Sector," in *News Incorporated: Corporate Media Ownership and Its Threat to Democracy*, ed. Elliot D. Cohen (Amhert, NY: Prometheus Books, 2005).
4. Elliot D. Cohen, "Web of Deceit: How Internet Freedom Got the Federal Ax, and

Why Corporate News Censored the Story," *Buzzflash*, July 18, 2005, http://www.buzzflash.com/contributors/05/07/cono5238.html.

5. AT&T, et. al. v. City of Portland, U.S. Court of Appeals, 9th Circuit, Appeal No. 99-35609, Section C, http://caselaw.findlaw.com/us-9th-circuit/1435844.html (accessed May 13, 2011).

6. Elliot D. Cohen, "The Great American Firewall: Why the Net is Poised to Become a Global Weapon of Mass Deception," *Buzzflash*, May 1, 2006, http://www.buzzflash.com/contributors/06/05/cono6169.html.

7. Elliot D. Cohen, "Web of Deceit."

8. Federal Communications Commission (FCC), *Report and Order: In the Matter of Preserving the Open Internet Broadband Internet Practices*, December 21, 2010, 2, http://transition.fcc.gov/Daily_Releases/Daily_Business/2010/db1223/FCC-10-201A1.pdf.

9. FCC, *Report and Order*, 137.

10. Edward Wyatt, "U.S. Court Curbs F.C.C. Authority on Web Traffic," *New York Times*, April 6, 2010, http://www.nytimes.com/2010/04/07/technology/07net.html.

11. Grant Gross, "FCC Chairman Defends Broadband Regulation Move," *PCWorld*, May 6, 2010, http://www.pcworld.com/article/195759/fcc_chairman_defends_broadband_regulation_move.html.

12. Elliot D. Cohen, "Help Stop Destruction of the Free Internet Now," *Truthdig*, December 26, 2010, http://www.truthdig.com/report/item/help_stop_destruction_of_the_free_internet_now_20101226/.

13. Joelle Tessler, "Verizon challenges FCC's net neutrality rules," *Salon*, January 21, 2011, www.salon.com/technology/feature/2011/01/21/verizon_net_neutrality_fcc.

14. Steve Augustino, "Court Dismisses Verizon Net Neutrality Appeal—for Now," *Telecom Law Monitor*, http://www.telecomlawmonitor.com/tags/court-of-appeals/ (accessed May 13, 2011).

15. Kevin Drawbaugh, "UPDATE 2-U.S. House rejects FCC's 'open' Internet rules," Reuters, April 8, 2011, http://www.reuters.com/article/2011/04/08/congress-internet-idUSN0825411720110408.

16. Elliot D. Cohen, *Mass Surveillance and State Control: The Total Information Awareness Project* (New York: Palgrave Macmillan, 2010).

17. The Downing Street Memo(s), http://downingstreetmemo.com/ (accessed May 14, 2011).

18. Elliot D. Cohen, *Mass Surveillance and State Control*.

19. Paul Davidson and David Lieberman, "FCC wants more access to affordable high-speed Internet," *USA Today*, March 16, 2010, http://www.ksdk.com/news/local/story.aspx?storyid=198055.

20. "Rural Activists: Treat Broadband as Basic Utility," Public News Service, April 29, 2011, http://www.publicnewsservice.org/index.php?/content/article/19808-1.

21. Elizabeth DiNovella, "US Slipping in Internet Access," *The Progressive*, June 25, 2008, http://www.progressive.org/mag_wxld062508.

22. 2010 Report on Internet Speeds in All States, SpeedMatters.org, November 2010, http://cwa.3cdn.net/299ed94e144d5adeb1_mlblqoxe9.pdf.

23. Ryan Singel, "Investigate AT&T Broadband Caps, Interest Groups Tell FCC," *Wired*, May 6, 2011, http://www.wired.com/epicenter/2011/05/investigate-broadband-caps/.

24. Ian Paul, "Google-Verizon Net Neutrality Pact: 5 Red Flags," *PC World*, August 10, 2010, http://www.pcworld.com/article/202970/googleverizon_net_neutrality_pact_5_red_flags.html.

CHAPTER 10

A Tea Party Among Us
Media Censorship, Manufactured Dissent, and the Right-Wing Rebellion

by Anthony DiMaggio

It was difficult to turn on the television in 2010 without seeing daily references to the Tea Party. As the darling "movement" of choice for the mass media, the Tea Party seemingly arose out of nowhere following the group's April 15, 2010, "Tax Day" rally, and continued to attract media attention throughout the year and in the run-up to the 2010 midterm elections. By early 2011, however, the group was forced to share the spotlight with those revolting in Wisconsin against Governor Scott Walker's draconian attacks on labor's very existence. Without any warning, the Tea Party found itself cast into a national spotlight due to its support for long-standing Republican attacks on basic rights such as collective bargaining, pension benefits, and other worker-related protections.

While most Americans have a general idea of the politics behind the Tea Party, much less is understood about the group's relationship with political and business power centers. Is the Tea Party a genuine manifestation of grassroots "movement" protest against a corrupt status quo? Are Tea Party officials a serious challenge to Wall Street and the "bailout" politics in Washington? Is the group independent of the Republican Party and elite business interests, as its members so often claim? Answers to these questions are badly needed at a time when mainstream journalists are consigning themselves primarily to a cheerleader role for the group, following its "grassroots uprising" leading up to the 2010 midterm and 2012 presidential elections.

MEDIA PROPAGANDA?

Any effective study of the Tea Party phenomenon must first begin with a general understanding of the workings of the American press. Claims that American media systematically engage in censorship and propaganda are met with suspicion by most journalists, academics, and political officials. Manipulation of the public by journalists and government is seen as something that only happens in authoritarian countries, not in the world's most powerful democracy. To suggest otherwise is to engage in a conspiracy theory.

The problem with the conventional narrative as described above is that it ignores the American media's thorough reliance on the state as *the* leading agenda setter for the news. Journalists' dependence on officialdom to determine the parameters of public discourse resides at the heart of any propaganda state. Noted media critic and scholar Noam Chomsky argues that "propaganda is to democracy what the bludgeon is to a totalitarian state."[1] This statement cuts to the core of the modern democratic propaganda state.

Business and government officials do not need to conspire behind closed doors to determine media content. Political leaders already accomplish this goal incidentally by way of the prestige they enjoy from American journalists, who rely on their regular statements to fill the daily news hole and to set the tone for discussions of Washington-related politics and business issues. Business elites, by virtue of their ownership of the mass media and their reliance on advertising dollars, also exert a structural influence over media content in favor of pro-corporate perspectives, and against potential criticisms.[2]

Media propaganda, simply understood, entails two major components. First, it includes a systematic bias in favor of official government sources. Journalists accept as standard operating procedure that the spectrum of views dominating the mass media should be determined by Democrats and Republicans holding power in Washington, DC. These officials provide the moral compass for journalists, who claim to objectively mirror in their reporting the policy debates and opinions raging among political officialdom. Objectivity, in their lexicon, is not defined by reflecting the full spectrum of views that exist throughout a society on major policy issues.[3] Quite the contrary, any consistent coverage of those opinions that reside outside of the bi-partisan spectrum of agreement and conflict is greeted by political elites, conservative media monitors, and business representatives with screams of "bias!" These elite actors have never shown much interest in sharing the national megaphone with those who offer substantive challenges to their communicative and ideological monopolies over the public sphere.

The second major component of media propaganda includes a reliance on the manipulation of public emotions. Any effective propaganda state must master the art of fear mongering if it is to force an often unwilling public to go along with unpopular public policies. In an insightful study of political and media propaganda, Erin Steuter and Deborah Wills argue that "propaganda is not concerned with disseminating information, but with rallying emotion . . . propaganda must be pure, distilled, and unpolluted by contaminants such as complexity and subtlety."[4] This definition of propaganda, as I found throughout my study, proved an effective description of the politics of the Tea Party. The Tea Party's embrace by the mass media, Republican operatives, and business elites is marked by precisely the kind of propaganda that make it difficult, if not impossible, for the public to engage in careful or reasoned discussion of the full implications of health care reform, or any other policy issues in question.

THE TEA PARTY: A FORENSIC ANALYSIS

Perhaps the most censored news story throughout 2009 and 2010 was the revelation that the Tea Party is not, in fact, a social movement. This conclusion will no doubt jar those who share the group's ideology, although no other conclusion is possible following a systematic analysis of the group and its politics. I had assumed that the Tea Party was a mass movement before starting my study of the group, which began immediately prior to the April 15, 2010, "Tax Day" protests and culminated one year later between the midterm elections in 2010 and the 2012 presidential election season. I had little reason to think the Tea Party was not a movement at a time when reporters and news outlets were reflexively assuming that the group was a product of decentralized, grassroots, and community forces. My assessment of the group would change radically, however, over the course of my examination in light of the discovery of numerous inconvenient realities.

In assessing the Tea Party, I engaged in a multipronged approach. My national analysis of the Party's participation levels and membership was buttressed by intensive case study analysis of the group, as it operated throughout the Chicago and Madison metropolitan areas. Aside from my observational study, I also looked at the group with regard to its media coverage, most specifically in terms of how they were framed by journalists as a social movement and the reports on the Tea Party's most important issue: health care reform. Finally, I undertook an extensive analysis of the effects of Tea Party-related messages emanating from the mass media, as reflected in public opinion surveys. In the end, my examination concluded that the Tea Party is largely a mass-mediated phenomenon, drawing most of its power not from grassroots, decentralized forces, but from sympathetic patrons operating in the mass media, Republican Party, and business community. I dedicate the rest of this essay to exploring these findings in greater detail.

ASTROTURF: A MOVEMENT IN NAME ONLY

In spite of its nearly endless media coverage, any serious analysis of the Tea Party phenomenon is bound to conclude that the "movement" is a mile wide and an inch deep. It contains few of the basic prerequisites of a social movement, as laid out by scholars. At the national level, the group is unrecognizable as a mass uprising. Most problematically, few local chapters in the run-up to and aftermath of the April 15, 2010, rallies displayed any evidence of engaging in regular organizational meetings. Of the 150 cities in which Tea Party rallies were held on April 15, I found that just 8 percent provided any information through their local website or the national *Tea Party Patriots* website of regular meetings (defined as at least one meeting per month, for at least two consecutive months). My findings were further reinforced by a national study by Patchwork Nation, which found that registration with Tea Party chapters across the country was incredibly small. Searching through online directories of local Tea Party organizations, Patchwork Nation analyzed records for "the overwhelming majority of registered members" throughout the country. The group's study concluded that the Tea Party consisted (as of April 2010) of "roughly

67,000 members in counties across America." When broken down, this total translated into less than three Tea Party members per 10,000 people in cities across the country, or just .03 percent of the adult population. These numbers are a far cry from the 4 to 5 percent of adults who claimed to be attending Tea Party rallies or meetings in 2010. My study of various national-umbrella groups produced similar data, as documented in a recently released book on the Tea Party.[5]

Additional problems quickly emerged for the mass media's dominant "social movement" narrative. In my Chicago metropolitan area case study, active Tea Party organizing was meager. Of all the metropolitan Tea Party groups, less than 15 percent posted any information about regular meetings on their websites or through the national website. In the spring of 2010, there were only twenty local Tea Party groups listed on the national *Tea Party Patriots* website for a metropolitan area claiming more than 250 jurisdictions. This presence was incredibly small, translating into just 7.5 percent of all municipalities containing a Tea Party chapter. The percent of cities and towns with regular meetings was even smaller, representing a miniscule one percent of all municipalities. When rallies and organizational meetings did take place in cities I observed, attendance was usually low, and willingness to organize beyond meetings was nearly nonexistent.[6]

Participation at rallies that occurred in the Chicago area throughout the spring through fall of 2010 were sparsely attended, with little evidence of grassroots local organizing. Consistent with the trend for national rallies, actual attendance at major events was usually a tiny fraction of the 4 percent of Americans nationally who claimed to be supporters of the "movement." Of those who did turn out, there was little evidence of the sort of activist behavior that is the hallmark of social movements. There was almost no leafleting and pamphleteering. Political speaker lists and tabling (the little of it that existed) were dominated by Republican Party activists and candidates who were running for office in the midterms. Rally turnout was hardly representative of the surrounding areas' demographics. In the city of Chicago, for example, only a small handful of African American or Hispanic demonstrators turned out for a city that retains a minority-majority status.

In the February demonstrations in Madison, Wisconsin, against Scott Walker, Tea Party turnouts were also extremely low, despite the "movement" highlighting the tremendous importance of the city's struggle for their conservative cause. Tea Party rallies were rarely visible over a few-week period in which tens of thousands of pro-union supporters were turning out daily. Tea Partiers were visibly the odd-man-out in a state in which a strong majority of citizens opposed Walker's attempt to destroy union organizing and remove collective bargaining rights.[7] Even among the few supporters of Walker's draconian measures, few could be bothered enough to publicly turn out. On the one day in February in which the Tea Party promised a "mass turnout," conservative protestors were dwarfed by a sea of union supporters, with less than 1,000 Tea Partiers demonstrating alongside more than 100,000 Walker opponents.[8] In my repeated visits to Madison to observe and participate in the labor protests, there were literally no Tea Partiers to be seen, despite the calls of national leaders for mass turnouts to show solidarity with Walker and state Republicans.

Tea Party national organizing in the spring of 2011 was also anemic at best. The April 15 "Tax Day" rallies came and went across the country *without* the mass coverage or seemingly larger turnouts showcased in many local chapters. Turnout in Madison of Tea Partiers "in solidarity" with Governor Walker was meager, despite the calls of regional and national Tea Party leaders for a mass showing. When the "I Stand with Scott Walker Rally" finally materialized on February 19, strong evidence of Astroturfing was evident. Fox News creations such as Andrew Breitbart and "Joe the Plumber" dominated the lineup, highlighting the top-down, mediated nature of the "movement."

Organizing in preparation for the February 19 event was dominated by national groups with extensive ties to the Republican Party and corporate interests. "American Majority," the group that played a lead role in organizing the event, is a creation of Ned Ryun, a former speechwriter for George W. Bush and the son of former Republican Congressional Representative Jim Ryun. The Ryun family shares a long history of Republican activism, with Ned Ryun's brother serving as the deputy director of the Republican National Committee in 2004 and also working for the Tea Party-affiliated American Majority. The organization receives most of its funding from the Sam Adam's Alliance, a group that is supported by the billionaire Koch brothers, who have become notorious for funding right-wing Astroturf groups that front as "grassroots," but in reality strongly serve corporate interests.[9]

On-the-ground observation of the few Tea Party organizational meetings taking place throughout Chicago consistently found a lack of interest in grassroots activism. Tea Party meetings for cities with regular meetings were scarcely attended by more than a handful of "activists," and when larger numbers did appear, few indicated a willingness to engage in activism beyond simply appearing for the meeting. Local chapter leaders and members regularly expressed frustration with the lack of turnout, while explaining that they had turned to an alternative strategy to gather larger numbers for rallies: "the e-mail blast."[10] Local chapter leaders would rely on visitors to their local websites, rather than on those attending meetings, to turnout at strategically planned rallies. This approach provided these leaders with effective PR opportunities, since rallies boasted far larger numbers of people than were actually involved in planning activities or organizing. This failure to organize, however, was inconsequential in the end. Journalists were intent on certifying these rallies as proof of "mass organizing," and the media megaphone was already succeeding in creating the false impression that the Tea Party was a genuine mass movement.

A MASS-MEDIATED AFFAIR

In my writings covering the Tea Party, I spent significant time tracing the role of wealthy business leaders and Republican operatives in organizing Tea Party rallies across the country. While individual stories have appeared (at times regularly) in reporting about the Tea Party as influenced by the Koch brothers and other wealthy industrialists and business elites, suggestions that the Tea Party is Astroturf are few and far between. In analyzing national network television, and print coverage throughout 2009 and 2010, my comprehensive analysis of the *Lexis Nexis* database found that references to the Tea Party as a "movement" radically outnumbered suggestions that it was "Astroturf" in origin. Furthermore, the Tea Party was far more regularly and undeservingly certified as a mass movement than other legitimate social movements that did boast mass turnouts, but were heavily critical of the political-economic status quo. Using *Lexis Nexis*, I collected data on the two-week periods immediately before and after national rallies of the Tea Party (for a total of one month), in comparison to similar periods covering major protests related to the antiwar movement, the anticorporate globalization movement, and the pro-choice movement. References to the Tea Party as a "movement" outnumbered similar references to these other movements by ratios of between two to 100:1. The most extreme example was the 2003 antiwar protests across the United States and the world. While those demonstrations attracted upwards of ten million people, the Tea Party rallies in April 2010 attracted up to one hundred thousand nationwide (perhaps less), according to available evidence.[11] Despite the massive imbalance in participation levels, the Tea Party was referenced twice as often as a "social movement," compared to the anti-Iraq war rallies, within the same periods of time.

NO REPUBLICAN TIES HERE

Central to the mass media's mythic Tea Party narrative is the notion that the group is fiercely antiestablishment and nonpartisan. Reports from the *New York Times* in early 2010 framed the Tea Party's upcoming national convention as a "coming together" of the Tea Party's "diffuse," or as "grassroots groups" that express fierce "antigovernment sentiments." This depiction of the group was endemic within reporting (as documented above) which regularly referred to the Tea Party as a mass movement, rather than a partisan affair. *The New York Times'* "Tea Party outsider" narrative was wildly popular throughout the rest of the mass media. *Time* magazine, for example, reacted to the Tea Party's rise by describing it as outside of electoral politics: it "is not a political party . . . and maybe never will be. Rejecting the idea— widely held by Democrats—that a government of brainy people can solve thorny problems through complex legislation, the Tea Party finds its strongest spirit among conservative Republicans."[12] *Fox* agreed, reporting that the group was deeply outside of Republican-politics-as-usual: "Anything could happen from now [November 2010] until the presidential election in 2012, and it remains to be seen whether a movement that prides itself on being outside the establishment will front its own Tea Party presidential candidate, revolutionize the Republican Party or merely fade back into the background. Leading Tea Partiers vowed to keep up the pressure on their favored new lawmakers to fight a Washington establishment they say is broken and doesn't work for the best interests of the American people."[13]

In addition to the anecdotal evidence above, journalists framed the Tea Party "movement" as an outsider force on a systematic level. In the four months prior to the 2010 midterm elections, the *New York Times* and the *Washington Post* ran 135 and 136 stories respectively, or an average of 45 per month, referring to the Tea Party as a "social movement." MSNBC and Fox, as respective leaders of the Left and Right wings of the media, ran 137 and 167 stories respectively, or 46 and 56 stories per month. During the same period, stories referencing the Tea Party in relation to the "Republican establishment" appeared in 98 and 159 stories in the *New York Times* and the *Washington Post* (an average of 33 and 53 stories per month), and 88 and 90 stories at MSNBC and Fox (29 and 30 stories per month). In short, depictions of the Tea Party "movement" as an insurgent force were standard operating procedure throughout the entire spectrum of the establishment press.

Some basic problems emerge with regard to the dominant media narrative. The Tea Party as an "outsider" depiction is only convincing if one actively ignores the mountain of evidence suggesting that the Tea Party has long been seen as an integral part of Republican politics, rather than an independent political force. The major symbolic leaders of the group, for example, include Michelle Bachmann, Sarah Palin, and Dick Armey, all long-time Republicans who have held (or currently hold) major positions within the party. One would also need to ignore the fact that major Tea Party organizations, including Americans for Prosperity, the Tea Party Express, American Majority, Freedom Works, and the Tea Party Caucus (in the House of Representatives), are all led by conservative activists with long histories of actively collaborating with Republican leaders. Finally, one would also need to discount national polling findings, which suggest that more than three-fourths of Tea Party supporters either consider themselves Republicans, lean toward the Republican Party, or regularly vote Republican.[14] While statistical analysis suggests that these individuals do represent the most conservative elements of the Republican Party, they are not far out of step ideologically with the rest of the party, which numerous studies demonstrate has been moving toward the radical Right for a number of decades.[15]

There is a serious discrepancy between the Tea Party "outsider" rhetoric and the reality that the Tea Party phenomenon is heavily integrated into Republican politics. This finding, however, was consistently ignored in reports following the November 2010 midterm elections. A *Lexis Nexis* search reveals that, in the two months prior to the November 2 elections and in the week following the elections (from September 1 through November 7, 2010), the Tea Party was described as at least one of the following: "revolt" or "rebellion" against the political establishment, an "insurgent" or comprising an "insurgency" against Washington politics, as "grassroots," and as a "movement" in 135 pieces from the *New York Times* (60 a month), 120 in the *Washington Post* (53 a month), in 127 MSNBC programs (56 a month), and 149 Fox stories (62 a month). Another study of media coverage found that reporting on the Tea Party as outside of the "Republican establishment" and as a "social movement" was a regular occurrence in the run-up to and immediately following the midterms. Such references appeared in dozens of articles and stories in the variety of news outlets examined above.[16] In short, few people in the mass media took seriously the reality that the Tea Party is largely a Republican phenomenon.

CREATING THE ECONOMIC CRISIS

Tea Party supporters will dispute the findings above, suggesting that while the Tea Party is now a part of the Republican Party, it is dedicated to promoting radical change from within. There is little merit to such claims, which are endlessly repeated throughout the mass media. What this argument conveniently neglects is that the Congressional Tea Party Caucuses' members are an integral part of the inner-Washington political circle. Members of the sizable "Tea Party caucus" in the House of Representatives have received massive funding from, and granted significant concessions to the very corporate banking and finance interests that succeeding in destroying the US economy. They benefit from serious campaign contributions from the health care interests that benefitted from the expansion of market-based care under Obama—this while working to ensure that any reforms passed by the Democrats would not go too far in challenging the for-profit health system. Furthermore, most of these caucus members voted for the very same deregulatory acts that helped create the economic crisis. Far from rebelling against Wall Street, these individuals voted in favor of deregulating the destructive derivatives that wreaked havoc on financial markets, and supported the reregulation of the national banking system in order to allow a select few corporations to become "too big to fail" by buying up smaller banks in the merger-mania that followed the repeal of the repeal of the Glass-Steagall Act in 1999.

Newcomer Tea Partiers do not fare much better with regard to their alleged independence from Wall Street. Statistically speaking, newly elected Tea Partiers in Congress were just as likely, and at times more likely, to rely on business interests as their top donors when compared to previous Tea Party Caucus members. More specifically, new Tea Partiers were just as likely as previous caucus members to rely on campaign contributions from the real estate, finance, banking, and securities and investment industries.[17] That these groups were instrumental in the 2008 economic meltdown, yet have served as major supporters for newly elected Tea Partiers, is a fact overwhelmingly ignored in popular media commentary. This finding goes against the entire narrative of the Tea Party as a fresh, rebellious force in Washington politics; hence it is ignored by the media and political powers that be.

THE TEA PARTY GOES MORBID: DEATH PANEL PROPAGANDA AND THE PLOT TO KILL GRANDMA

Nowhere was mass-mediated Tea Party propaganda more apparent than in national coverage of protests of "Obamacare" in mid-to-late 2009 and early 2010. Tea Partiers and Republican leaders symbiotically joined together during this period to promote some of the most extreme distortions of Democratic health care proposals. As I document in my book, *The Rise of the Tea Party*, by mid-2009 coverage of nonexistent "death panels" that were allegedly intent on denying senior citizens health care were rampant throughout media coverage across the board. Furthermore, my content analysis of news reporting from major national agenda-setting newspapers and television outlets found systematic evidence that reporting was tilted toward conservative perspectives, with mentions of concerns over the "costs" and "price" of health care, and of allegedly high levels of "debt" that would accompany Democratic reforms. These mentions greatly outnumbered any discussion of the proposed "public option," of Democratically supported health insurance "exchanges," or of more progressive policy proposals such as Medicare-for-all, universal health care coverage. As expected, conservative media outlets such as Fox News led the way in warning against fictitious "government takeovers" and "Obama socialism," despite the fact that "Obamacare" represented one of the largest expansions of the private insurance health care market in US history.[18]

Reactionary Tea Party-Republican propaganda on health care reform was flagrantly inaccurate with regard to the actual reforms being proposed by Democrats. This inconvenient detail was largely inconsequential, however, in a media climate in which the Democrats were publicly abandoning progressive reforms such as the public option and universal health care, and leaving a vacuum Tea Partiers and Republicans were more than happy to fill with their many scare tactics and messages. As Steuter and Wills remind us, propaganda is not interested in accurate, nuanced discussions of public policy. Emotion and fear are powerful tools, and they were extremely successful in blunting discussion of possible steps the government could take to help those in medical need.

THE PUBLIC REACTS

Media censorship of critical views of the Tea Party is accompanied by dramatic costs when looking at public opinion. By systematically denying the public access to the findings discussed, media outlets play an instrumental role in fostering public support for the Tea Party and opposition to health care reforms. My study of Tea Party reporting and rhetoric in the mass media finds effects of such coverage on public opinion, as reflected in analysis of national surveys, at two levels. First, one sees that increased attention to the national debate and reporting on the Tea Party is accompanied by growing support for the group. After controlling for respondent ideology, partisanship, income, sex, race, and a number of other demographic variables during analysis, a strong, positive statistical relationship is still found between consumption of Tea Party news and positive attitudes toward the group.[19]

On a second level, one sees that the increasingly negative media coverage of health care reform also influenced public attitudes. After controlling for the demographic variables mentioned above, one also finds a positive, statistically significant relationship between attention to the national debate on health care reform on the one hand, and opposition to government efforts at promoting reform on the other. Such increased opposition is not the result of citizens becoming more actively informed about the dangers of liberal and potentially progressive health care proposals. National statistics from the *Pew Research Center* find that those who paid the closest attention to the health care reform debate in the news were actually the most likely to be confused with regard to the basic contours of that debate. The problem only got worse over time, with the proportion of those finding the debate hard to understand increasing from July through September 2009.[20] This finding is precisely what one would expect to find in a media system that propagandizes citizens, stirring public opposition over fictitious "death panels," nonexistent "government takeovers," and Democratic Party "socialism."

PEELING BACK THE CURTAIN: BEHIND THE TEA PARTY ALLURE

The Tea Party's preferred treatment in the mass media, accompanied by the censorship of critical viewpoints with regard to the group, is the result of numerous structural factors. For one, the Tea Party is closely aligned with business elites in their efforts to fight off any potential health care and Wall Street reforms that could cost investors and insurance companies profits, or cost the wealthy in terms of increased taxation. The interests of business elites, then, serve as one important pressure upon the corporate media system to promote free market "movements" like the Tea Party.

On another level, the Tea Party's symbiotic relationship with the Republican Party ensures that it will be granted favorable treatment in the national press. Tea Party leaders and rank-and-file members speak a language similar to that of journalists in Washington who share an obsession with "unsustainable" debt, and who have also been calling for the leadership needed to enact deeply unpopular and dramatic cuts in social welfare spending in a time of economic crisis and stagnation. The Republican Party's embrace of neoliberal policies that directly assault the welfare state have also grown increasingly popular among Democrats who have indicated openness to cutting popular programs such as Medicare and Social Security, and entirely ended other programs such as Aid to Families with Dependent Children. Under such a political system, where Democrats abandon progressive positions in favor of center-right ones, journalists become subject to strong pressures from political elites to embrace their "movements" of choice, and ignore those that fail to fall within the bi-partisan spectrum of opinion.

Despite strong political, business, and media support, the Tea Party appears to have hit a plateau with regard to public sympathies. National polls suggest that support for the group has stagnated at between one-fourth to one-third of the public throughout 2010 and 2011.[21] Minority support, however, is hardly inconsequential. The dramatic successes of Republicans in the 2010 midterms in mobilizing their Tea Party-affiliated base should demonstrate the power of determined minorities. The national media has played a critical role with regard to motivating this minority to recommit to national electoral politics in order to return Republican officials to majority status in Congress. Republican officials' dressing up of the top-down Tea Party phenomenon as a "grassroots movement" represents a concession that the Republican Party is no longer able to effectively govern on its own. At a time of mass distrust of government, conservatives have concluded that populist facades reframing Republicans as opposed to bailouts and Washington or Wall Street corruption represent the best hope for garnering votes in the run-up to midterm and presidential elections. These officials can count on the mass media to play an instrumental role in fostering public rebellion at a time of economic instability and suspicion of government.

ANTHONY DIMAGGIO is the author of numerous books including *The Rise of the Tea Party* (Monthly Review Press, 2011), *Crashing the Tea Party* (with Paul Street, Paradigm Publishers,

2011), *When Media Goes to War* (2010), and *Mass Media, Mass Propaganda* (2008). He has taught US and Global Politics at Illinois State University, and has written for numerous publications, including *Z Magazine, Counterpunch, Truthout, Black Agenda Report, Monthly Review, Common Dreams,* and *AlterNet.* He can be reached at adimag2@uic.edu.

Notes

1. Noam Chomsky, *Media Control: The Spectacular Achievements of Propaganda* (New York: Seven Stories Press, 1997), 16.
2. The role of advertising, for example, in ensuring the censorship of views critical of corporate America has been thoroughly documented in previous studies. For examples, see: Robert W. McChesney, *Rich Media, Poor Democracy: Communication Politics in Dubious Times* (New York: New Press, 1999); Robert W. McChesney, *The Problem of the Media* (New York: Monthly Review Press, 2004), 83; Dean Alger, *Megamedia: How Giant Corporations Dominate Mass Media, Distort Competition, and Endanger Democracy* (Maryland: Rowman and Littlefield, 1998), 163–164; David Croteau and William Hoynes, *The Business of Media: Corporate Media and the Public Interest* (California: Pine Forge Press, 2001), 179–180; "Self-Censorship: How Often and Why," Pew Research Center, April 30, 2000, http://people-press.org/report/39/.
3. Academic studies typically find that objectivity, as understood by journalists, entails the restricting of political views (in reporting and editorializing) to those views already accepted by the two major political parties. For more on this wide literature, see: Jonathan Mermin, *Debating War and Peace: Media Coverage of U.S. Intervention in the Post-Vietnam Era* (Princeton: Princeton University Press, 1999); Daniel C. Hallin, *The "Uncensored War": The Media and Vietnam* (Oxford: Oxford University Press, 1986); W. Lance Bennett, Regina G. Lawrence, and Steven Livingston, *When the Press Fails: Political Power and the News Media From Iraq to Katrina* (Chicago: University of Chicago Press, 2007); and Anthony R. DiMaggio, *When Media Goes to War: Hegemonic Discourse, Public Opinion, and the Limits of Dissent* (New York: Monthly Review Press, 2010).
4. Erin Steuter and Deborah Wills, *At War With Metaphor: Media, Propaganda, and Racism in the War on Terror* (Maryland: Lexington Books, 2008), 18.
5. For a review of the Patchwork Nation study and my own survey of Tea Party chapters, see Anthony R. DiMaggio, *The Rise of the Tea Party: Political Discontent and Corporate Media in the Age of Obama* (New York: Monthly Review Press, 2011).
6. For more details, see chapter 2 of *The Rise of the Tea Party.*
7. For more details on the state of Wisconsin's opposition to Governor Scott Walker's attack on unions, see Anthony DiMaggio, "Masters of Spin: Rightwing Manipulation of the Wisconsin Revolt," *Counterpunch*, February 25–26, 2011, http://www.counterpunch.org/dimaggio02252011.html.
8. Paul Street, "It's Not About $, It's About Rights," *Z Magazine*, February 24, 2011, http://www.zcommunications.org/it-s-not-about-it-s-about-rights-by-paul-street.
9. Stephanie Mencimer, "Wisconsin: Tea Partiers, Breitbart Coming to Fight Unions," *Mother Jones*, February 18, 2011, http://motherjones.com/mojo/2011/02/wisconsin-tea-partiers-breitbart-fight-unions.
10. For more, see chapter 2 of *The Rise of the Tea Party.*
11. For more, see chapter 4 of *The Rise of the Tea Party.*
12. David von Drehle, "Why the Tea Party Movement Matters," *Time*, February 18, 2010, http://www.time.com/time/magazine/article/0,9171,1966475,00.html.

13. "After the Election Victories, Tea Party Activists Look Ahead to 2012," FoxNews.com, November 5, 2010, http://www.foxnews.com/politics/2010/11/05/election-victories-tea-party-activists-look-ahead/.

14. The Tea Party's many Republican ties are explored consistently throughout *Crashing the Tea Party* and *The Rise of the Tea Party*.

15. See chapter 1 of *The Rise of the Tea Party* for more on these studies.

16. See Paul L. Street and Anthony R. DiMaggio, *Crashing the Tea Party: Mass Media and the Campaign to Remake American Politics* (Boulder, Co.: Paradigm Publishers, 2011).

17. See chapter 1 of *The Rise of the Tea Party*.

18. For a more thorough description of my findings, see chapter 5 of *The Rise of the Tea Party*.

19. For more, see chapter 4 of *The Rise of the Tea Party*.

20. My findings with result to the impact of health care coverage on public opinion are explored in greater detail in chapter 6 of *The Rise of the Tea Party*.

21. For more on these findings, see the regular updates of Tea Party polling questions available at www.pollingreport.com.

Project Censored International
Human Rights and the Right to Know
INTRODUCTION BY MICKEY HUFF
WITH AN INTRODUCTION TO THE FAIR SHARING
OF THE COMMON HERITAGE BY MARY LIA

Unpopular ideas can be silenced, and inconvenient facts kept dark, without the need for any official ban. . . . At any given moment there is an orthodoxy, a body of ideas which it is assumed that all right-thinking people will accept without question. It is not exactly forbidden to say this, that or the other, but it is "not done" to say it. . . . Anyone who challenges the prevailing orthodoxy finds himself silenced with surprising effectiveness. A genuinely unfashionable opinion is almost never given a fair hearing, either in the popular press or in the highbrow periodicals.
—George Orwell, from his unpublished "Freedom of the Press" introduction to *Animal Farm*, eventually published in 1972, *New York Times Literary Supplement*

The final section of *Censored 2012* is designed to give unfashionable opinions a fair hearing, whether they are from the United States or around the globe. We hope we are giving these following contributions, all serious journalistic and scholarly investigations, a pedestal from which to spring forth into the world of public debate. Our authors here examine media censorship issues and their ramifications in the US and internationally through the topics of peace movements worldwide, Western policy and action in Africa, human rights abuses in Palestine, distorted natural disaster coverage, bias against universal health care, and natural child birth and midwifery, with a focus on human rights and the right to know, and especially highlighting the right of people everywhere to learn about and understand the conditions of their fellow planetary inhabitants.

There are ever many global issues that impact people locally. And so our media analysis in this section looks at these diverse subjects with the hope of broadening our awareness of international human rights and the importance of media freedom as a holistic, global issue in the struggle for peace and equality. After all, the United Nations Declaration of Human Rights, adopted in 1948 by the UN General Assembly, affirmed that "everyone has the right to freedom of opinion and expression; this right includes freedom to hold opinions without interference and to seek, receive and impart information and ideas through any media and regardless of frontiers." We need to live up to and enforce these rights, as together these are the cornerstones of democratic self-governance.

This year, we proudly welcome people whose views are oft not heard by readers of highbrow periodicals or the popular press despite their wisdom and importance: professor Cynthia Boaz looks at movements of nonviolence and their media depiction worldwide; independent journalist Ann Garrison outlines the massive blackout in US press coverage of what is happening across the African continent; Jon Elmer details the ongoing suppression of reporting about Palestine, and the neglect by the international community concerning human rights abuses there; professor Robin Andersen looks at HBO's television show *Treme* and what it says about the media's depiction of the post-Katrina flood disaster in New Orleans; Margaret Flowers points out the lack of corporate media coverage of the overwhelming support for single-payer health care in the US; and Ina May Gaskin rounds out our book this year looking at how the media ignore and distort the issues of maternity and natural childbirth in America. All of these are subjects for further study, and could be or already are full-length books. We include them here to put them on the radar, under the guise of un-censoring issues that matter to the public, generating real news for real people.

In that same spirit, this year we also introduce the Media Freedom Foundation and Project Censored collaboration on the Fair Sharing of the Common Heritage, which will be outlined below. In future editions of *Censored*, writings on this theme will be included as part of Project Censored International. Reclaiming the commons of a free press and public information, in support of the right of people "to seek, receive and impart information and ideas through any media" as outlined in the UN Declaration of Human Rights above, is of paramount concern to Project Censored. As journalist and scholar David Bollier wrote in his 2002 work, *Silent Theft: The Private Plunder of Our Common Wealth*, "The loss of a public commons in broadcasting must be counted as one of the great civic and cultural losses of the twentieth century."[1] We intend to continue combating censorship and propaganda as one means of protecting the human right to knowledge while working to realize an information commons—a true free press.

Together, working for media freedom across the globe, we can create more functional democracies, and, one community at a time, we can help birth a better world for the next generation to inherit. Project Censored engages over thirty colleges and universities in the US as well as activists and scholars in over a dozen countries in the effort to support media freedom. Quite clearly our survival as a species depends upon how successful we all are in this endeavor to foster the rights to information, education, and a free press for all. Here's to a prosperous, and well-informed tomorrow.

AN INTRODUCTION TO THE FAIR SHARING OF THE COMMON HERITAGE AWARDS
by Mary Lia

The Fair Sharing of the Common Heritage is a social action agenda supported by the Media Freedom Foundation and Project Censored. This global and local grassroots movement supports the mission of Alfred F. and Dorothy Andersen, which is based on one significant idea: every sentient being, human and nonhuman, has a right to the fair share of the material and economic wealth of the Common Heritage.[2]

Included in this Common Heritage are all Earth's natural resources: land surfaces, sub-surface minerals and fuels, water, and air—indeed the entire physical environment. This Heritage wealth should not be privately owned, especially not by an elite few. It should be held in democratically controlled local, regional, national, and global trusts. The renewable parts (land, water, and air) should be leased out and the income used to distribute financial and other benefits among the earth's inhabitants.[3] In addition, Common Heritage recognizes the knowledge and inventions created by previous generations. Cyberspace is such an example.

Alfred Andersen and his wife Dorothy have entrusted the Media Freedom Foundation to encourage discourse on the Common Heritage. In 2010, the Foundation began an essay contest for the Fair Sharing of the Common Heritage Award. Entries proposed ways in which the Fair Sharing of the Common Heritage could be accomplished. One proposal, from Alfred F. Andersen himself, was that natural resource extractors could be required to pay the full value of what they take into a Common Heritage fund for all living things.[4]

Media Freedom Foundation received twenty-six total nominations. Works varied in topic and scope, ranging from an entry by former US Senator Mike Gravel on citizen power to a creative play written by David Giesen named "Dino on the Line."[5] In order to judge these diverse works, the Media Freedom Foundation board members used a structured survey and voted two rounds before presenting the results to Dorothy Andersen. Copies of all nominations can be found at the website www.FairShareCommonHeritage.org. Two exemplary works by James K. Boyce and Clifford Cobb were chosen to bring the selection process to an exciting close, with the first and second place winners receiving $3500 and $1500, respectively. Five honorable mentions received $100 each, including one to author and longtime activist Mickey Z., who now writes for the Fair Share blog.

University of Massachusetts economics professor James K. Boyce won first place with his paper, "Is Inequality Bad for the Environment?" Boyce supported the idea that by respecting nature's limits and investing in nature's wealth, humans can protect and enhance the environment's ability to sustain our well-being. The way humans interact presently with nature is tied directly to how humans interact with each other. For example, those who are relatively powerful and wealthy typically gain disproportionate benefits from the economic activities that degrade the environment, while those who are relatively poor and powerless typically bear disproportionate costs. All else equal, wider political and economic inequalities tend to result In higher levels of environmental harm. For this reason, efforts to safeguard the natural environment must include polices that achieve a more equitable distribution of power and wealth in human societies.[6]

Second-place winner Clifford Cobb, who hails from San Francisco, offered historical context and some suggestions for how to expand the discourse on the Common Heritage in his article, "Broadening the Movement: A Blueprint for Achieving Social Justice through Sharing Common Heritage."[7]

Cobb explained that efforts to promote the idea of a shared Common Heritage and its assets have so far failed to gain a political constituency. In addition to introducing the philosophical precedents for a Common Heritage, Cobb discussed efforts by Alfred Andersen's Tom Paine Institute and other groups to propagate the relevant principles. He also illuminated the enormous political obstacles that any policy based on economic justice must contend with.

Cobb made the point that to connect with others in the social justice movement, advocates for sharing common assets should frame their arguments broadly so that they speak to a range of social issues. Indeed, to build a coalition we must develop a new language, just as political theorists in the seventeenth century created a language of "natural rights" in order to justify the growth of property rights. Yet Cobb rightly explained that the modern social justice movement needs to help activists and to understand that their work is related to the issues of the commons. "They will see it [is]to their advantage to make those connections only if a common, inclusive language treats their concerns as central, not peripheral," noted Cobb. He then quoted journalist Jay Walljasper: "It's not necessary that everyone adopt the word commons. What matters is that people understand that what we share together (and how we share it) is as important as what we possess individually."[8] Cobb underscored the idea that "creating a new language of shared connections will almost certainly mean dropping the heavy reliance on the unwieldy metaphor of 'the commons'" for "the problem of language is a more formidable obstacle to political cooperation than is generally recognized."[9]

And yet, coalition-building among groups with diverse interests is possible through the development of inclusive discourses, and by working to understand one another. Today as we ponder issues of the commons, we can almost certainly unite around a common cause: promoting the long-term existence of a beautiful Earth and a vibrant culture.

Notes

1. David Bollier, *Silent Theft: The Private Plunder of Our Common Wealth* (New York: Routledge, 2002), 148.
2. The Fair Share of the Common Heritage Mission Statement, May 2011, http://www.fairsharecommonheritage.org/the-fair-share-of-the-common-heritage-mission-statement/. See more on this in the "Nature and Technology" section of chapter 4 of this book.
3. Alfred F. Andersen, *Liberating the Early American Dream: A Way to Transcend the Capitalist/Communist Dilemma Nonviolently* (New Brunswick, NJ: Transaction, 1985), 145.
4. Alfred F. Andersen, "Fair Share Capitalism Merits Researching," *Eugene Oregon Register Guard*, September 9, 1996. Also see more on no-waste [full-cycle] accounting in the "Economy and Fair Exchange" section of chapter 4 of this book.
5. "Common Heritage Award Nominations," The Fair Share of the Common Heritage, May 1, 2011, http://www.fairsharecommonheritage.org/2011/05/01/common-heritage-award-nominations/.
6. James K. Boyce, "Is Inequality Bad for the Environment and Bad for Your Health?" Population & Development Program, Hampshire College, http://popdev.hampshire.edu/sites/popdev/files/uploads/dt/DifferenTakes_08.pdf.
7. Clifford Cobb, "Broadening the Movement: A Blueprint for Achieving Social Justice through Sharing Common Heritage," The Commons San Francisco, http://www.thecommonssf.org/commons_literature.
8. For more on this, see the "Community and Collaboration" section of chapter 4 of this book.
9. Ibid.

CHAPTER II

Media Distortion of Nonviolent Struggles
Putting Dark Lenses on Colored Revolutions

by Cynthia Boaz

> *If you're not careful, the newspapers will have you*
> *hating the people who are being oppressed, and loving*
> *the people who are doing the oppressing.*
> —Malcolm X

INTRODUCTION

In Iran, in early summer of 2009, students and citizens of the Green Movement continued taking to the streets despite open threats of violence from the regime and its security forces. At this point, much of the international media had already designated the uprising a failure. Mainstream news stories started acknowledging the regime's claims to be "restoring order" and their promise to dispense with the troublemakers and agent provocateurs. Of course, life for the people of Iran has not been "normal" for a very long time, but for the most part, this reality did not seem to concern journalists and editors who continued to rely on the regime for information on events transpiring on the streets of Tehran and elsewhere. On the ground, however, activists had a very different story to tell.

The frames on the story that emerged in international media reinforced several common and hardened beliefs about violence and power. These distortions—which can unconsciously serve the interests of oppressors and those committing the injustices—are sustained largely by the messages media audiences receive when reading or watching news coverage of civil resistance. Although the subject matter to be examined here cannot exactly be described as censored within the mainstream media, it is often so distorted and misinterpreted that the end result is arguably potentially worse than the outcome full-blown censorship would produce. Deprogramming hardened misperceptions is perhaps the greatest challenge for conscious media practitioners.

Media audiences who observe nonviolent struggles already face a number of challenges in obtaining a nuanced understanding of the dynamics underlying civil resistance. This is because most struggles are confronted by a tenacious conventional wisdom that can hinder an audience's perception of a movement's salience. For example, we often assume that certain structural conditions must be met in order for a movement to succeed. Factors such as favorable economic conditions, ethnic and/or religious homogeneity, a history of democratic institutions, and a thriving civic culture with a good degree of political space are all generally considered to be key to success. Additionally, observers tend to assume that extreme repression by the opponent is enough to stop a movement's momentum. This prevailing mythology—which elsewhere I have called "The Tiananmen Principle" because it is still being used to explain the failed uprising in China in 1989—says that as repression by the regime opponent increases, a movement's success decreases accordingly. Typically, media coverage of a struggle at this stage will reinforce the conventional wisdom by reporting on the use of violence as an effort by the repressor to "establish normalcy" or "generate stability or order," when they should be widening the lens and contextualizing both the underlying reasons for resistance and the fact that resistance perseveres despite the violence. These common media distortions run the risk of undermining the morale of members of a movement and diminishing the enthusiasm behind global shows of solidarity. *In other words, media-perpetuated distortions about the efficacy of repression can lead to a self-fulfilling prophecy in the context of a nonviolent struggle.*

Of course, this alone does not explain the Green Movement's inability to bring about a victory in 2009, nor does it explain the lack of success in Burma in 2007, or failures anywhere else for that matter. But while the international audience cannot win the Iranian or Burmese peoples' struggles for them, it is impossible to envision a scenario where any mass nonviolent struggle can succeed without the sympathy and solidarity of the global media audience—objectives that are attainable only with an accurate and contextualized understanding of the struggles by the public. And this is a result that is dependent largely on the narratives that emerge in mainstream media.

In this chapter, I will first give a brief overview of the core dynamics of nonviolent struggle (also known as "civil resistance") and how the phenomenon works to shift power from oppressors to the people. Then I examine several common misconceptions about nonviolent action, and how they are reinforced by media frames on the stories. Next, I look at several types of framing techniques (or media biases) and, using two recent case studies (Burma in 2007 and Iran in 2009), show several examples of how frames can be a power influence on the ways in which meaning is conveyed to the global audience. And finally, I consider the larger consequences of framing stories of civil resistance erroneously and the ways in which conscious media consumers and citizens can insert more truth and context into the stories of nonviolent struggles.

1. THE CORE DYNAMIC OF STRATEGIC NONVIOLENT CONFLICT

Strategic nonviolent conflict (sometimes called "civil resistance" or "nonviolent action," shorthanded here as SNVC) is a means by which ordinary people mobilize and fight for their rights using disruptive actions without using violence.[1] It is important to emphasize both the proactive (rather than passive or responsive) nature of SNVC and the notion that SNVC means fighting back with nonviolent tools—in other words, it is a means by which conflict is engaged (nonviolently) rather than avoided.

SNVC can take many forms, including protest (the most visible), persuasion, non-cooperation (the active withdrawal of one's consent— sometimes on a mass scale, such as a boycott), and nonviolent intervention (the most aggressive category of SNVC, which can include actions such as blockades and sit-down strikes.)[2]

SNVC is an active phenomenon that empowers people by uniting them in a vision and giving them a shared stake in the outcome of their struggle. It shifts power from oppressive rulers to civilian democratic rule in several phases: First, through SNVC, a broad-based civic movement drives up the cost of repression (both material and nonmaterial) and reduces the economic and political support that an oppressor needs to keep control. Next, when the system's own defenders begin to doubt whether it can survive (e.g. its pillars of support are undermined), the balance of power shifts to those using civilian-based resistance. Finally, the movement's (and methods') legitimacy increases, opening up the political space for genuine democracy.

This is a very basic overview of the sequence and dynamic of civil resistance, but even this highlights some key features of SNVC that are widely misunderstood or underemphasized in media reporting of the phenomenon: namely, that the practitioners of nonviolent action understand that the rulers cannot assert control without the active or tacit consent of the governed. Thus, disobedience is at the heart of nonviolent resistance. And simply rejecting the lie that those in power have a reasonable right to be there can be a very empowering phenomenon. By the time the global audience sees a mass civil resistance pouring out into the streets of a capital city, many other things (which have been largely ignored) have already been accomplished or overcome.

2. COMMON MISCONCEPTIONS ABOUT NONVIOLENT ACTION

There are numerous misconceptions in conventional media regarding civil resistance. Because of space constraints, I will limit this discussion to five of the most common.[3] These misconceptions tend to correspond with—and are reinforced by—the conventional media frames on nonviolent struggles. Because these beliefs tend to be so hardened and pervasive, it is rare that they are challenged in media coverage of stories about civil resistance. And where the stories clearly defy these deeply held beliefs, they are often treated as exceptions or accidents of history.

> ▶ Misconception One: Nonviolent action is inaction, the avoidance of conflict, or passive resistance.
>
> ▶ Misconception Two: Nonviolent action is only used as a last resort, when violent methods are unavailable.
>
> ▶ Misconception Three: The occurrence or success of nonviolent action is determined by culture, economic system, geography, or other structural conditions.

▶ Misconception Four: The effectiveness of nonviolent action is a function of the repressiveness of the oppressors.

▶ Misconception Five: Nonviolent campaigns need a charismatic leader.

As mentioned above, SNVC is actually a very proactive phenomenon, one which M. K. Gandhi called "the most activist force in the world," that uses nonviolent tools rather than violent ones to achieve its objectives. It is not the avoidance of conflict, or passivity; it is the waging of conflict nonviolently.

Additionally, as many movements have discovered, nonviolent action need (indeed, should) not be a last resort. This is for two reasons: First, activists and movements who are attempting to adhere to the Gandhian/Kingian understanding of nonviolent action realize that means and ends are inseparable; a state of justice cannot be manifested from an unjust process. Second, several recent empirical studies have demonstrated that democracies that were established through mass, nonviolent civic action (rather than armed insurrection or external intervention) are much less likely to be susceptible to democratic backsliding and are more likely to result in systems that are healthy and legitimate.[4]

Thirdly, there is an emerging subfield of research on the structure-versus-agency question in nonviolent action, but the brief answer to this misconception is that, given the universe of successful stories of nonviolent action, there are no structural conditions that are clearly prohibitive of nonviolent success, and conversely, there are no structural conditions that guarantee it. Rather, the success or failure of a nonviolent movement seems to be much more dependent on the strategic skills and discipline of the movement itself. The recent cases of Egypt, Tunisia, and others that make up the "Arab Spring" are excellent examples of this.[5]

The fourth misconception is related to the previous one. At the beginning of every successful struggle of the last century, there was someone ready to say "it cannot happen here—our oppressors are simply too brutal." In fact, pragmatic activists understand that desperate opponents will rely on brute force to try and quash a growing movement and that this is inherent in the risks a movement accepts when it launches a struggle against an oppressor. But repressive regimes have one important thing in common, which can be used by movements against their opponents: Violence, as an instrument of control, has a very simple and predictable dynamic. And clever movements will find strategies and tactics that maximize their potential to use this repression to the advantage of the movement— something Gene Sharp has named "political jujitsu."

Indeed, when asked about the effects of violence and repression on the Iranian movement, Nobel Laureate and human rights advocate Shirin Ebadi said, "I never agree with the idea that repression can lead to the death of a movement. If the foundations of a movement are laid correctly from the start, repression is not able to kill it. In fact, it makes it stronger. Just imagine the water flow through a pipe. When you open the faucet, the water flows out. What if you tried very hard with an external force to prevent the water flowing out? You might hold it back for ten minutes, but then the pipe explodes. That's precisely the effect of repression on movement. If the repression is extreme, the movement will break and shatter everything."[6]

Lastly, there is a common belief that in order to succeed, a movement needs a charismatic leader; its own Gandhi or Martin Luther King, Jr. This is not only wrong, but possibly backwards. Many (in fact, most) nonviolent movements of the past century have succeeded without one central personality at the helm. In fact, having one charismatic leader can work against the movement in a couple of ways: The vesting of so much authority in one person can be devastating to the organization and the morale of its constituents if that individual is jailed or, worse, killed by the regime. And correspondingly, there is a danger of the movement coming to identify with the persona rather than the larger unifying principles. While it is critical that a successful, strategic movement have good leadership, it does not need to take the form of one central persona.

3. FRAME ANALYSIS AND MEDIA BIAS

The reader may recall an image from the fall of 2007 from Burma that became symbolic of the conflict in that country. It shows about a dozen Burmese monks squatting together on the streets of Rangoon, facing half a dozen members of the Burmese army who are holding riot gear and weapons. Frames and metaframes shape the assumptions you make about who is confronting whom, whether you interpret the monks as victims or empowered action-takers, and if you see hope or demoralization, and violence or nonviolence, in the image.

In looking at the photo, most observers make their conclusions in the blink of an eye. Media audiences have, over time, been exposed to many subconscious messages—frames and metaframes—about how to understand nonviolent struggle. Frames tend to reinforce or harden our beliefs in such a way that it is actually easier to force reality to conform to predetermined conclusions than to shift our understanding. This explains why media audiences cannot make sense of the ongoing resistance in Iran and elsewhere, other than to assign credit to external forces (such as the United States) or to explain it away as accidental or insignificant.

4. BURMA'S SAFFRON REVOLUTION AND IRAN'S GREEN REVOLUTION

Because media are often obsessed with violence, the context and significance underlying the series of events like the ones that took place in Burma in 2007 and Iran in 2009 tend to be misinterpreted through that lens. An erroneous frame can lead us to believe things that are inaccurate, even when our hearts are "in the right place." And sometimes these conclusions have the consequence of creating a self-fulfilling prophecy. For example, when Iranian prodemocracy activists caught a glimpse of a CNN headline that read "Ahmadinejad Victorious!" they may have concluded that the regime's narrative had prevailed. This may in turn have demoralized the movement, and in the worst-case scenario, could even have caused some activists to turn to violence to fight back.

Although media frames are sometimes consciously manufactured, conventional wisdom suggests that the major culprit is the inability or unwillingness of reporters to engage in serious on-the-ground investigative reporting. For example, when in doubt, media tend to default to the perspective of the officials, no matter what their track records. This can be extraordinarily frustrating for members of a nonviolent struggle, who find themselves in the midst of an uprising having to try to unspin erroneous media coverage coming from all directions.

The following are several specific media techniques that help reporters and editors frame their stories in ways that reinforce existing assumptions mentioned above.

5. FRAGMENTATION BIAS

The work of W. Lance Bennett is instructive here. Bennett has named the fragmentation bias as the phenomenon that involves covering a story in isolated, seemingly unrelated pieces. At its worst, a story is completely removed from its larger historical or political context. The stories focus on the trees rather than the forest, and as a result, key information is missed. Consider some of the terminology used to describe events from Iran in June 2009: On June 14, 2009, a BBC headline announced, "Crowds join Ahmadinejad's victory rally." Another from CNN on June 21, 2009, tells us that "Chaos Prevails as Protestors, Police Clash in Iranian Capital" and similarly, on June 13, 2009, ABC proclaimed that "Election Battles Turn into Street Fights in Iran." Terms like "crowds," "chaos," and "street fights" paint a picture of a country in anarchy and awash in violence. There is a much larger story being missed when news is fragmented. In the case of Iran, it is that people continue (to this day, in fact) to resist with discipline and strategy, despite the personal risk and violence by the regime.

6. DRAMATIZATION BIAS

Stories about nonviolent struggle also tend to be framed by what Bennett has named the dramatization bias. According to Bennett, dramatization of a story occurs when the news is encapsulated in short, sensationalistic bits intended to provoke an emotional response on the part of the news consumer. There is little to no discussion of the deeper policy issues, institutional interplay, or larger social setting related to the story. Dramatized stories might appropriately be thought of as a type of marketing, in which media is selling a product to its audience. Not surprisingly, dramatization thrives on confusion and skepticism, and thus tends to produce cynical conclusions. It is also no surprise that fragmented stories tend to be dramatized stories and vice versa. In the context of the Iranian Green Revolution, a dramatization bias would refer to the events as a "spontaneous mass revolt" suggesting that it is disorganized, undisciplined, and ad hoc. This in turn could create the perception in the global media audience that there is no movement with whom to demonstrate solidarity.

Other examples of dramatization, from Burma's Saffron Revolution, include a BBC story from September 24, 2007 which proclaimed that "Burmese military threatens monks" and a London *Telegraph* story on September 27, 2007, which reported that "Burma troops issue 'extreme action' ultimatum." The emphasis on the sensational in these stories is not an absolute break with the truth, and thus it gives editors and reporters plausible deniability. But the heavy emphasis on drama that is perceived as more exciting leaves less room for other, possibly more important parts of the story, namely the ways in which monks and citizens responded with nonviolent, but still powerful, forms of resistance to the threats by the junta.

7. EUPHEMISM

With the euphemism bias, careful (or reckless) selection of language produces a shift in emphasis and a distortion in meaning. Occasionally, meaning is actually turned upside down. For example, in a nonviolent struggle an oppressor's use of violence is referred to as a "show of strength." The work of Sheldon Rampton and John Stauber (formerly of PR Watch) examines this phenomenon extensively.

The use of euphemism has historically played a deciding role in the way civil resistance is covered by media, especially when the events take place in a non-Western country. The terminology used to describe the images of thousands of people on the streets often wrongly connotes improvised and anarchic action, hidden agendas, and backroom deals. A common caption for photos from the massive demonstrations in Tehran during the height of the uprising in 2009 would often say simply, "Huge Crowds in Iran," a statement that, while technically not inaccurate, was woefully incomplete. A "crowd" can refer to any large group of people congregated together for no specific reason, so use of the term unconsciously implies that what brought the people together is not the result of strategy, organization, or discipline. Another example comes from Burma in mid-October of

2007, when the *Guardian* announced that "One month on, Burmese regime stages show of strength." The text that followed the headline went on to describe how the regime, fearing a resurgence of mass nonviolent prodemocracy protests, rolled tanks into the streets. A more accurate frame on that story would remind us that such shows of force are used only when a regime feels threatened—that is, when it perceives itself in a position of relative weakness. It would say something like "One month on, Burmese regime shows fear." Yet the actual frame turned this revelation of weakness into a "show of strength," ultimately defaulting to the perspective of the junta through the use of one strongly loaded word.

8. AUTHORITY BIAS

Lastly, where information is hard to obtain or has a sense of immediacy, media tend to default to the perspective of the official authority, no matter how ridiculous. An example from Iran is when the BBC announced on June 15, 2009, that "Iran's supreme leader [has] order[ed] investigations into claims of vote fraud." Or the example from Reuters on September 25, 2007, when they reported that "Myanmar junta sets curfew."[7] In both cases, there is an undeniable defaulting to the government authority as being responsible for contextualizing the crisis at hand. But how seriously should media audiences take the IRI's promise to investigate itself? Is it the Burmese people or the junta whose actions more appropriately call for a curfew? The use of the authority bias lends credibility to the oppressors' narratives, whether that result was intentional or not.

9. THE ROLE OF METAFRAMES

Beyond the story-specific frames and biases, we can observe a number of deeper metaframes that emerge from the patterns in media coverage of stories about nonviolent struggle. These metaframes can be thought of as widely shared assumptions that shape the lenses through which we draw conclusions and attribute meaning and significance. For our purposes, the most relevant metaframes are:

► Repression is more interesting/important than resistance[8]

► Power is top-down

► Power is monolithic

► Violent methods are more effective than nonviolent ones

Together, the disempowering metaframes above suggest to the media audience that the outcome in a mass civil resistance is not determined by the movement, but by the oppressor. Thus, the metaframes are significant for two reasons: On one hand, they make it difficult for media and audiences to predict nonviolent success or to make sense of it when it occurs, and on the other, they must be entirely rejected by participants in a movement if the struggle is to succeed. No people power struggle can win if its adherents hold these perceptions, because by definition they run counter to the dynamics that make nonviolent civil resistance effective. It is just as important that media audiences are conscious of metaframes as of surface frames, and that we look for and understand the interactions between the two phenomena, particularly when interpreting the meaning in the events that take place in the context of a mass nonviolent struggle.

10. CREATING CONSCIOUS MEDIA CONSUMPTION

Given the persistence of metaframes and the power of media biases to shape our perceptions, it is critical that we take a moment to consider how media audiences can begin to counter pervasive, erroneous, and disempowering frames on stories of civil resistance and mass nonviolent action. First and most importantly, it is the task of the media audience to be conscious of the frames on the stories they are being told. One must ask whether a frame's assumptions are valid, if they are being given enough information to draw a conclusion, and if so, whether the conclusion follows logically from the facts at hand. Correspondingly, it is critical that the media consumer be aware of his or her own biases and how they may be shaping his or her interpretation of the narrative.

More powerfully, conscious media citizens can take on the responsibility of "being" the media. Citizen journalism has replaced professional journalism in many parts of the world as the go-to genre for the most sophisticated and insightful analysis. As a contributor to the media universe, it is essential that the citizen journalist use accurate language consistently. For example, instead of talking about the Burmese or Iranian governments as "restoring order," a responsible journalist might talk about them as "attempting to suppress discontent."

There is also a role for new media: Video journalism, blogs, Facebook, and Twitter are all venues where political grievances and advocacy can be aired and discussed. One of the advantages of much of these media is that information communication goes two ways. The media audience becomes an active participant in the discussion—a phenomenon that encourages empowerment and civic engagement, both of which (in addition to being democratic virtues) undermine the efficacy of the metaframes discussed above.

The use of Twitter during the Iranian uprising is instructive. During June and July of 2009, when the streets of Iran were full of election protestors, Twitter became a key source of information on the resistance and subsequent crackdown. The regime banned all nongovernmental media activity, making it very difficult for information to get out of the country. But clever Iranian activists adopted Twitter as their primary mode of communication with the outside world. And as the regime told one story, the people of Iran told a completely different one. As Iranian state news was claiming that only a handful of people showed up at a well-publicized Tehran protest, for example, thousands of independent "tweeters" were all saying otherwise. The Green Revolution has been dubbed "The Twitter Revolution" for the degree to which even legitimate, mainstream international media (such as CNN and BBC) came to rely on tweets as their primary, up-to-date sources of information for what was happening inside the country. This is remarkable because not only was the movement able to undermine the official version of the news and make the regime look silly, but it was also able to play a key role in telling its own story.

Despite mainstream media frames to the contrary, neither of the struggles discussed above are news stories that should be characterized simply as examples of failed movements and successful repression. Nonviolent movements can sometimes take years to achieve victory, but as long as people continue to resist, even under great personal risk, the struggles should be considered ongoing. Without open displays of violence, it is much more difficult to keep the attention of an international audience, but without that attention (and ideally, subsequent solidarity), these movements' tasks are made much more challenging.

As activists continue to learn how to use media to take ownership of their own stories, the conventional surface frames will begin to shift. And as conscious media audiences challenge erroneous or simplistic assumptions and engage in active news integration, the metaframes can also be undermined. Ideally, the common misconceptions about nonviolent action will diminish as knowledge about the phenomenon evolves. But it is up to us—as global citizens—to understand our responsibility in this dynamic. Ultimately our unwillingness to be complicit in sustaining conventional wisdom about civil resistance and nonviolent struggles will be the key to more responsible media coverage about this global force for freedom, justice, and democracy around the world.

Bibliography

Ackerman, Peter. "Skills or Conditions? What Key Factors Shape the Success or Failure of Civil Resistance?" Paper presented to the Conference on Civil Resistance and Power Politics, University of Oxford, Oxford, 2007.

Bennett, W. Lance, Regina G. Lawrence, and Steven Livingston. *When the Press Fails: Political Power and the News Media from Iraq to Katrina.* Chicago: University of Chicago Press, 2007.

Bennett, W. Lance. *News: The Politics of Illusion.* New York: Longman, 2004.

Boaz, Cynthia. "Nonviolent Skills versus Repressive Conditions." In *Peace Movements Around the World,* edited by Michael Nagler and Marc Pilisuk. New York: Praeger, 2011.

Boaz, Cynthia. "Red Lenses on a Rainbow of Revolutions." *Open Democracy.* Accessed November 17, 2010. http://www.opendemocracy.net/cynthia-boaz/red-lenses-on-rainbow-of-revolutions.

Chomsky, Noam. *Manufacturing Consent: The Political Economy of the Mass Media.* New York: Pantheon, 2002 [originally published, 1988].

Karatnycky, Adrian and Peter Ackerman. *How Freedom Is Won: From Civic Resistance to Durable Democracy.* Freedom House Report, 2005.

Lakoff, George. "Obama, Tea Parties and the Battle for Our Brains." *truthout.* Accessed February 10, 2010. http://archive.truthout.org/obama-tea-parties-and-battle-our-brains57089.

Lakoff, George. *Don't Think of An Elephant!* Vermont: Chelsea Green Publishers, 2004.

Lakoff, George. *The Political Mind: A Cognitive Scientist's Guide to Your Brain and Its Politics.* London: Penguin, 2009.

Rampton, Sheldon and John Stauber. *Trust Us, We're Experts: How Industry Manipulates Science and Gambles with Your Future.* Los Angeles: Tarcher Press, 2001.

Rampton, Sheldon and John Stauber. *Weapons of Mass Deception: The Uses of Propaganda in Bush's War on Iraq.* Los Angeles: Tarcher Press, 2003.

Schock, Kurt. *Unarmed Insurrections: People Power Movements in Nondemocracies.* Minneapolis and London: University of Minnesota Press, 2005.

Sharp, Gene. *The Politics of Nonviolent Action.* Boston: Porter Sargent Publishers, 1973.
Stephan, Maria and Erica Chenoweth. "Why Civil Resistance Works: The Strategic Logic of Nonviolent Conflict." *International Security* 33, no. 2 (2008): 7-44.

DR. CYNTHIA BOAZ is an assistant professor of political science at Sonoma State University in California, where her areas of expertise include political development and quality of democracy, nonviolent conflict and nonviolent struggle, and political communication with an emphasis on media coverage of democracy struggles. Professor Boaz is an affiliated scholar at the UNESCO Chair of Philosophy MA program in Peace, Conflict, and Development Studies in Castellon de la Plana, Spain. She is also vice president of the Metta Center for Nonviolence Education and on the board of directors for Project Censored/Media Freedom Foundation. She is on the board of advisors for *truthout*, for whom she is also a contributing writer. Over the past several years, she has contributed dozens of articles on the themes above to various venues including *truthout*, *Open Democracy*, Common Dreams, *Waging Nonviolence*, and the *Huffington Post*.

Notes

1. A nod to the International Center on Nonviolent Conflict, from whom this terminology is borrowed, and by whom much of the scholarly understanding about the dynamics of strategic nonviolent action has been gleaned. They can be found online at http://www.nonviolent-conflict.org.
2. For a more comprehensive list of nonviolent tactics, see Gene Sharp's "198 Methods of Nonviolent Action," available through the Albert Einstein Institute: http://www.aeinstein.org/organizations103a.html.
3. The author gratefully acknowledges Kurt Schock, who offers a comprehensive overview of, and response to, the nineteen most common misconceptions about nonviolent action in his book *Unarmed Insurrections: People Power Movements in Nondemocracies* (2004).
4. Karatnycky, Adrian and Peter Ackerman. *How Freedom Is Won: From Civic Resistance to Durable Democracy.* Freedom House Report, 2005. http://www.freedomhouse.org/template.cfm?page=137.
5. Peter Ackerman, "Skills or Conditions? What Key Factors Shape the Success or Failure of Civil Resistance?" (paper presented to the Conference on Civil Resistance and Power Politics, University of Oxford, Oxford, 2007).
6. Shirin Ebadi, Naropa University, interview with author, October 9, 2009.
7. The legal name of the country is Myanmar (which was renamed by the regime after 1988), but the people and their supporters continue to call the country Burma, in a rejection of the junta's legitimacy. Most international organizations (including the UN) as well as most media, refer to the country as "Myanmar." The primary exception is British media.
8. A simple glance at the several hundred articles compiled from both struggles and linked from each one's Wikipedia page shows a clear bias toward headlines that mention repression or violence rather than resistance. Only a tiny sprinkling of headlines uses terminology such as "movement" or "struggle"— most talk about "protestors" and "uprising"—and not a single one on either page uses the terms "nonviolence" or "nonviolent."

CHAPTER 12

The US in Africa
Velvet Glove on a Military Fist

by Ann Garrison

United States foreign policy is global military and corporate dominance and the control of resources required to sustain it. The US divides the world into six regional military commands and four functional commands, with a four-star general or admiral at the head of each. There are over seven hundred military bases worldwide. All else is detail, however myriad and multifaceted, and this is nowhere more stark than in Africa, where, in October 2007, the US formalized and further organized its longstanding military operations with the creation of AFRICOM, the US Africa Command. Since December 2007, two months after the creation of AFRICOM, the US has imported more oil from Africa than from the Middle East, and African resources have long been essential to both military and nonmilitary manufacture, and thus, to empire.[1]

Empire is not a simple national concept in a world dominated by minimally regulated or taxed multinational corporations and an international executive and über rich class huddling annually at the World Economic Forum, the North Atlantic Council, or the exclusive and secretive Bilderberg Conference. However multinational empire may be, it is still defended, first and foremost, by unparallelled US military might.

Canada is now the mining superpower in Africa, and throughout the rest of the world.[2] The US is the military superpower and the largest weapons manufacturer and exporter. Canadian mining corporations depend on AFRICOM to secure access to resources; US weapons manufacturers depend on Canadian mining corporations for mineral manufacturing inputs.

In a March 2003 *Buffalo News OpEd*, Council fellow Scott B. Lasenksy wrote:

> Liberals who fault the United States for not spending as much of its gross domestic product on development aid as

387

Europe or Japan make the wrong case for foreign aid. They
fail to appreciate that the US carries a much greater share of
the global security burden.[3]

THE VELVET GLOVE: "HUMANITARIAN" AID IN GEOSTRATEGIC INTEREST

When humanitarian foreign aid is indeed extended, however piously
proferred, packaged, and promoted by celebrities like Ben Affleck,
George Clooney, Bono, Don Cheadle, and Angelina Jolie, or by
Christian evangelicals like Reverend Rick Warren, it must, as a matter
of policy, serve the US geostrategic agenda, and serve to keep recipient
nations aligned with Washington and its allies.

Hence, for example, the President's Emergency Plan for AIDS
Relief (PEPFAR), is most active in fifteen "focus countries" of
geostrategic importance to the US: thirteen African countries and
Haiti and Vietnam.[4]

As Lasensky wrote:

> The truth is that the vast majority of US aid goes to countries that
> are not poor, not free or both. This should not be cause for moral
> outrage. It simply reflects the cold fact that foreign aid—$18
> billion in 2004, under the president's budget—is still allocated
> primarily on the basis of American political and strategic needs
> and priorities, rather than pure humanitarianism. And this is
> how it should be.

Since most diplomats, elected officials, aid executives, and
celebrities are far less frank than Lasensky, PEPFAR and most other
US humanitarian aid mask "security" agendas, although, as *Foreign
Policy in Focus* editor Emira Wood says, in the video "Resist Africom,"
this is not new:

> What we see is a repeat of the Cold War experience, with the
> US arming and equipping militaries, essentially putting
> forward a military fist, but covering it up with a velvet glove of
> humanitarianism and development.[5]

In the US, the most censored or misreported news and the most massive disinformation campaigns about Africa serve to fit the velvet glove onto the military fist.

They include these "stories"—so called "stories" in that they have not been reported or so little that they are not widely understood—which are all intertwined in the African Great Lakes region, the Horn of Africa, and, most of all, in the long tortured Congolese border region with its eastern neighbors Uganda, Rwanda, and Burundi.

UNITED NATIONS "PEACEKEEPERS" IN COMBAT

United Nations "peacekeepers," formally dispatched by the UN Security Council, are often, in reality, combatants dispatched by the US.

On April 29, 2011, *Somalia Report* published the news that "the US government requested Rwanda to contribute peacekeeping forces to Somalia," but not that "the UN, or the Security Council, requested Rwandan forces." The Security Council gives the label "UN peacekeepers" to African forces recruited to fight Al Shabaab in Somalia, and will no doubt do the same for any Rwandans who will join them. Whatever the War on Terror rhetoric, their missions will be, above all, securing the Somali coastline, which much of the world's maritime traffic, including oil, passes by.[6]

During the first week of June 2011, an Associated Press story published on many outlets reported that a Somali American from Minnesota had repatriated and suicide bombed the UN peacekeeping mission in Somalia "because of abuses by Christians in Muslim countries." The study failed to report the peacekeeping mission's radical expansion of the war for control of Somalia's capitol Mogadishu.

They also failed to report that another Somali American, Mohammed Abdullahi Mohammed, a resident of New York State for twenty years, had also repatriated, after being appointed Prime Minister of Somalia in October 2010, much to the surprise of his neighbors in Buffalo, New York, where he had been working for the New York State Department of Transportation at the time.[7]

While at the State University of New York in Buffalo, Mohammed Abdullahi Mohammed had written a master's thesis titled "US Strategic Interest in Somalia: From Cold War Era to War on Terror,"[8] which called on the US to extend financial, political, and military support—i.e., UN peacekeepers—to defend the Transitional Government in Mogadishu. It also warned that US Marines would have to be deployed to combat Islamic extremism if they failed.

Mohammed's thesis is not altogether uncritical of the US and its past and present interests in Somalia. Nevertheless, it does raise questions of whose peace is to be kept, for what purpose, and by whose mandate.

The term "UN peacekeepers" implies global moral consensus, although UN peacekeepers are hired by the Security Council—which the US largely controls or ignores at will if it can't.

When given the chance, I call them combatants, as does veteran Africa journalist and investigator Keith Harmon Snow, whose response to this summary was, "This is not about peacekeeping, so no peace is to be kept. It's about empire."

For daily news reporting, "UN troops" will do far better than "UN peacekeepers," and, better yet, with a reminder that they're dispatched by the UN Security Council, not the General Assembly.

SOMALIA: UN COMBATANTS AND CATASTROPHE MANAGERS

As I was organizing this list of the most censored and/or misreported stories about Africa, I opened a dispatch from Thomas Mountain, sent to AfrobeatRadio.net, saying that a million Somali refugees were facing slow, UN-managed starvation in refugee camps.

Mountain, who identifies himself as "the only independent journalist working in the Horn of Africa," wrote that the UN High Commissioner for Refugees had cut food aid to a third of what it had been, while "the UN," meaning the Security Council, had, at the same time, increased funding for "thousands more Ugandan troops [peacekeepers], tanks, and helicopter gunships to fight the War on Terror."

A million people facing slow starvation?

Thomas Mountain's source on the ground was an aid worker who had just been to Dabaab, a Somali refugee camp in Kenya, and who was afraid to identify the aid agency he worked for:

I really hope and pray that someone is listening. I work for—and I have just returned from Dadaab, it is hell on earth, and this has been going on for 20 years. Today 320,000 are living in camps for 90,000. Geldof's images that so shocked the world in the 80s are the daily lives of people there today. Children severely malnourished. New arrivals having to walk miles to register instead of the UNHCR providing registration in all the camps. The rationale being that if they have made their way from Mogadishu they can surely walk a few more miles for registration . . . people who have already begun the process of a slow death; mothers with 8 kids in tow. It is disgusting (the people saying this are obviously in an air conditioned room and have probably not walked anywhere in a few decades). I don't know how this can be justified in a so-called modern society. Where is our humanity? Keep writing."[9]

I produced a few minutes of KPFA Radio's Weekend newscast, including the voice of Thomas Mountain reporting this from Eritrea and that of Ugandan American journalist Milton Allimadi saying that the Ugandan "peacekeepers" were again acting as a police force for the US, then sent the audio archive and transcript to Toronto-based Global Research, which published it the next day with the headline "Somalia: A UN Managed Catastrophe, A Million Refugees Facing Starvation." Hiiraan, a news and information website about Somalia, published it the day after that. We were briefly visible in Google News search for "Somalia" before being buried in news of Somalia's War on Terror, but, several weeks later, we'd sustained visibility in searches for "Somalia" and "refugees" because far fewer outlets were reporting the refugee story.[10]

I'm not an expert on Somalia, but the outlines of Thomas Mountain's story were familiar:

1) Military operations armed and organized by external forces, most of all by the US, in accordance with their own geostrategic agendas, cause human catastrophe in Africa, creating populations of internal and/or external refugees.

2) Underresourced, ineffective, and/or corrupt catastrophe managers follow, not only from UN agencies, but from USAID and large government contractors and nonprofit corporations like CARE, Catholic Relief Services, Save the Children, and Feed the Children.

Michael Maren, a former international aid worker and Africa journalist, makes a damning argument in his 1997 book *The Road to Hell, the Ravaging Effects of Foreign Aid and International Charity* that "these organizations are a complete waste of money that serves absolutely no purpose but to keep Westerners employed." However, so long as US and other foreign military operations continue to create huge, desperate, internal and external refugee populations, it seems heartless to argue that the catastrophe managers not at least follow along with aid, like that Thomas Mountain said the UN was failing to provide to Somalian refugees in June 2011.

A similar problem played out on the Gulf Coast, after Hurricane Katrina and flooding that resulted in 2005, as Blackwater Marines patrolled the streets in combat vehicles while refugees gathered to speak out about being abused by the Red Cross. It was still no time to refuse any food or other aid that might actually be delivered.[11]

Far too often, however, aid isn't delivered. Most of the six million or more people dead in the Democratic Republic of the Congo since 1996 have died of pneumonia, starvation, malnutrition, disease, or exposure to the hardships of refugee camps or in the bush, after being driven from their villages and homes.

US "RELIEF" TEAMS BUILD A MILITARY BASE IN RWANDA, AFTER THE RWANDA GENOCIDE AND BEFORE THE CONGO WARS

On July 28, 1994, within weeks of General Paul Kagame and his Rwandan Patriotic Front's seizure of power in Kigali, Rwanda, the *New York Times* helped the Pentagon slide a velvet glove onto its military fist, and told one of the tallest tales of all time, in this news report titled "US is Considering a Base in Rwanda for Relief Teams" by Eric Schmitt:

The United States is preparing to send troops to help establish a large base in Rwanda to bolster the relief effort in the devastated African nation, Administration officials said today.

Setting up a staging area in the capital, Kigali, would mark an important new phase, committing American troops in Rwanda for the first time. Military officials said 2,000 to 3,000 troops could be sent into Rwanda, in addition to the 4,000 that Washington has said would join relief efforts outside the country.

President Clinton's senior foreign policy advisers discussed the plan at the White House today but delayed approval. One Administration official said the White House may not decide until Defense Secretary William J. Perry visits the region this weekend.

But other officials said the White House was inclined to go ahead if several conditions were met. Engineers must first assess the battle-scarred airfield in Kigali. Assuming it can be used, American officials need permission of the Government of the victorious Rwandan Patriotic Front, and want assurances that the front will guarantee the safety of a small but growing stream of returning refugees.

Relief effort indeed, though I do have to thank the *New York Times* for at least creating this record, and acknowledging that "the victorious Rwandan Patriotic Front" was in power at the end of the massacres that the world came to know as the Rwanda Genocide, meaning that they had won the Rwandan Civil War of 1990–1994.

Seventeen years later upwards of six million Congolese people and tens of thousands of Rwandan Hutu refugees had died either in the massacres or, after being driven from their homes during the First and Second Congo Wars, during the ongoing conflict. US ally Rwanda, with its neighboring US ally Uganda, had invaded and occupied eastern Congo and established an infrastructure for plundering its mineral wealth, much of which is essential to both military and consumer manufacture.[12]

The US had also established itself as the dominant power in the region, along with its Anglophone allies, displacing France. Before the Rwandan Civil War, which ended in the Rwanda Genocide and the ensuing Congo Wars, Rwanda and Congo had been French-speaking, Francophone countries. France had been the dominant power in the region.[13]

Finally, Rwandan and Ugandan troops were defending US interests in Sudan, Somalia, Congo, and elsewhere on the African continent. Rwanda even sent expert police and prison wardens to Haiti in the aftermath of the 2009 earthquake there, and thousands of Ugandan troops have taken the place of US troops in Iraq.[14]

Relief effort indeed. It's very hard to believe that the Rwandan Patriotic Front colors are red, white, and blue, or that it celebrates Rwanda Liberation Day on July 4, by accident.

GATHERING DUST: SEVENTEEN YEARS OF UN REPORTS ON WHY SIX MILLION HAVE DIED IN CONGO

Despite the International Rescue Committee's January 2008 report that over 5.4 million people had died in the Congo conflict since 1998 alone—not including those who died in the First Congo War, 1996–1997—and that 45,000 continue to die each month, the US and its allies on the UN Security Council continue to ignore seventeen years of investigations documenting the responsibility of the Ugandan and Rwandan regimes, most recently including the UN Mapping Exercise Report on Human Rights Abuse in the Democratic Republic of Congo, 1993–2003, released on October 1, 2010.[15]

The Mapping Report wasn't literally censored; no one managed to keep it from being published or released, but not because no one tried. Someone leaked it to *Le Monde* on August 26, 2010, inspiring headlines in major media around the world, including the BBC, *Guardian*, *Democracy Now!*, the *New York Times*, and even CNN, but not the other major television networks.[16]

Who might have tried to prevent the report's release and why?

The governments of Angola, Burundi, Uganda, Rwanda, and the Democratic Republic of Congo all tried because the report included evidence that all of their armies, and thus their presidents and military commanders, were responsible for war crimes and crimes against humanity in Congo.

But the western powers on the Security Council, most of all the US, who have armed and trained the Ugandan and Rwandan armies, probably would have preferred not to see this report released either.

Why?

First, the report contains evidence that the Rwandan army, which was then made up of mostly ethnic Tutsi, committed ethnic massacres of Rwandan Hutu refugees and Congolese Hutus in Congo—crimes which an international criminal court might try as genocide, were a court convened, and the crime of genocide, if proven, weighs heaviest on the scales of international justice.[17]

Second, the evidence that the Rwandan army commanded by Rwandan President Paul Kagame is guilty of genocide undermines the false equation of the Rwanda Genocide and the Nazi Holocaust, said to create the same "Never Again" imperative, which is a pillar of the US and its allies' foreign policy in Africa.[18]

Third, the US and its allies, who backed Rwandan Patriotic Army General Kagame and his army's invasion of Rwanda and then Congo to establish dominance in the region, would be implicated as well. International Criminal Defense Attorney Christopher Black's response to the call for an international tribunal was: "They're never going to charge the RPF [Rwandan Patriotic Front], because it would be too dangerous. If you start charging the RPF, RPF officers, to save their necks, are going to start talking about others. And then you're going to get up to the Americans and the British and the Canadians and the Belgians. The whole thing would fall apart. They don't dare do that."[19]

And finally, Rwanda and Uganda's armies continue to be of such service to the US/UN Security Council agenda on the African continent. Both Kagame and Museveni threatened to withdraw their "peacekeepers" from Sudan in response to the leaked report, and the threat to the UN Security Council's sense of "global security" was so serious that UN Secretary General Ban-Ki-Moon was immediately dispatched to assuage and appease.[20]

When the Mapping Report was formally released, on October 1, 2010, the US State Department issued a perfunctory statement calling for accountability, but no international court has been convened, and the report is now gathering dust, as have seventeen years of reports exposing the crimes of Rwandan President Kagame and Ugandan President Yoweri Museveni.[21]

One of those ignored reports, the 2001 UN Report on Illegal Exploitation of Natural Resources and Other Forms of Wealth of the Democratic Republic of the Congo, noted that the World Bank ignored Rwanda and Uganda's increasing exports of resources that didn't exist in their countries, meaning resources plundered from Congo, and declared both countries success stories, rewarded them with debt relief, and even seemed to financed their war in Congo:

> In the case of Uganda and its exploitation of the natural resources of the Democratic Republic of the Congo, the World Bank never questioned the increasing exports of resources and in one instance a staff member even defended it. During the Panel's visit to Uganda, the representative of the Bank dismissed any involvement of Uganda in the exploitation of those resources. The Bank not only encouraged Uganda and Rwanda indirectly by defending their case, but equally gave the impression of rewarding them by proposing these countries for the Highly Indebted Poor Countries debt relief initiative. The Bank's shadow on the conflict in the Democratic Republic of the Congo is even more apparent on the budget. The balance of payments of both Uganda and Rwanda shows a significant increase in long-term borrowing in support of the budget. The defence budget however has increased in absolute terms, allowing Uganda and Rwanda to continue the conflict.[22]

One World Bank staffer warned that the Bank's silence would blow up in its face. But these UN reports are of even less interest to the corporate press than they are to the Pentagon, so there have been no noteworthy "explosions" in the Bank's face.

And, though the 2001, 2002, and 2003 UN reports on illegal resource exploitation in Congo all clearly demonstrate that Uganda and Rwanda plundered the Congo, and that foreign interests benefitted mightily, only a very few Ugandans and Rwandans did. Most continue to struggle as subsistence farmers, much of the public sector has been privatized, and inequality has increased.

PREDATOR DRONES TO STOP GENOCIDE?

People have asked me whether or not the Pentagon sees the irony in this, but no, this is real and its proponents are dead serious, not only at the Pentagon but also at Harvard. Drones are one of a number of proposals in a new publication, *Mass Atrocities Response Operations: A Military Planning Handbook*, produced by the Harvard Kennedy School's Carr Center for Human Rights Policy and the US Army Peacekeeping and Stability Operations Institute:

> In a MARO [Mass Atrocity Response Operation] situation, transparency or witness can be a particularly important alternative or adjunct to using force. It is also a capability that retains utility before and throughout an intervention. For these reasons, witness deserves special attention from political and military leaders.
>
> ISR [Intelligence, Surveillance, and Reconnaissance] provided by satellites, aircraft, or drones is the most flexible and lowest risk form of witness available to military planners.[23]

General Atomics happened to have a product ready to go when MARO was conceived at Harvard in 2007. Its Predator Drones were designed to be unmanned surveillance aircraft, but, beginning in 2000, President Bill Clinton and then George W. Bush had the Predators outfitted to drop Hellfire missiles, as they have in at least five countries—Afghanistan, Pakistan, Iraq, Yemen, and now Libya. In 2008 General Atomics began producing the much larger Reaper Drones, which carry up to two tons worth of bombs—ten times more than the Predators—cruise at higher altitudes and at three times the speed, and have more surveillance capability thanks to advances in computer technology.

In December 2010, the military tech section of San Francisco's trendy, techno lifestyle magazine, *WIRED*, reported that the US Air Force was phasing out the Predators in favor of the Reapers, and accepting the last of its order of 268 Predators in the early months of 2011.[24]

Though General Atomics had held onto the combat market with its Reaper Drones, this meant they needed a new market for the Predators, in which they had invested so much research and development. On February 10, 2011, *WIRED*, an ever willing marketing tool for US weapons manufacturers, published "Pentagon: Drones Can Stop the Next Darfur," an editorial advocating the use of Predator Drones to stop genocide, like that in Darfur and Rwanda.[25]

WIRED's advocacy was posted to the website of Operation Broken Silence, a stop-genocide organization that gives Martin Luther King's "break the silence" phrase a military configuration similar to Operation Iraqi Freedom or Operation Enduring Freedom (in Afghanistan).[26] It was also posted to STAND, the student division of Genocide Intervention Network, an organization identified with humanitarian hawk Samantha Power, Harvard professor and Senior Director of Multilateral Affairs on the staff of President Barack Obama's National Security Council. Samantha Power is the foreign policy advisor who persuaded Obama to drop Hellfire missiles from drone bombers on Libya by insisting that genocide would be on America's conscience if he did otherwise.[27]

Professor Ed Herman, coauthor (with Noam Chomsky) of *Manufacturing Consent* and (with David Peterson) of *The Politics of Genocide*,[28] responded in his essay "Samantha Power, Libya, and Selective Memory of Genocide":

> In her 2002 book *A Problem From Hell: America and the Age of Genocide*, Power called for greater U.S. intervention to prevent major human rights violations and genocide. She never suggests that this might require LESS intervention (e.g., Vietnam; the "sanctions of mass destruction" in Iraq) or reduced support for killers (e.g., Guatemala, El Salvador, Chile, Israel). She also finds that we inappropriately "just stood by" and failed to intervene in cases where we actually gave positive support to the mass murderers (e.g., Indonesia in East Timor; Kagame and Museveni in Rwanda and the Congo).[29]

Professor Herman and David Peterson are two of the dissident scholars of the Rwanda Genocide. Professors Christian Davenport and Allan Stamm are two more. They began their investigation believing essentially the Wikipedia version of Rwanda's 1994 massacres, which was that the dominant, ruling ethnic group—the Hutu—targeted the minority ethnic group known as the Tutsi for eradication; that the Western community—especially the United States—had dropped the ball by failing to intervene; that eight hundred thousand or more Tutsis and moderate Hutus who tried to defend them died; and that the Rwandan Patriotic Front, now the ruling party in Rwanda, had stopped the genocide by ending the civil war and taking control of the country. This is not only the Wikipedia version, but also that of Samantha Power, in her *Atlantic Monthly* account, "Bystander to Genocide."[30]

It's also codified in the Pentagon/Harvard Carr Center Mass Atrocity Response Handbook.[31]

After ten years of research, Stamm and Davenport wrote that "our views are completely at odds with what we believed at the outset, as well as what passes for conventional wisdom about what took place."[32]

This is the summary that Professor Allan Stamm now displays on a screen when he gives a lecture about how radically their conclusions changed:

Most likely 1,000,000,000 + people died
Vast majority who were killed were Hutu
US, French, Belgians, British all knew what was happening
 • the US's man [Paul Kagame] wins
 • no good guys
Current President of Rwanda
 • Likely Guilty of War Crimes[33]

Others who have come to different conclusions about how the Rwanda Genocide happened—who died, why, and what the aftermath was—include journalist and human rights investigator Keith Harmon Snow,[34] Rwandan American Law Professor Charles Kambanda,

International Criminal Tribunal on Rwanda defense lawyer Christopher Black, and Law Professor Peter Erlinder. Erlinder published his eighty-five-page analysis of the Rwanda Genocide, supported by original documents,[35] after being arrested and nearly disappearing in Kigali, Rwanda, in 2010 for traveling there to defend the leading dissident, Rwandan opposition leader Victoire Ingabire Umuhoza. Ingabire, in June 2011, remained in a maximum security prison in Kigali, charged with terrorism and disagreeing with the official history of the Rwanda Genocide.

The stakes in Ingabire's trial and in establishing the truth of the Rwanda Genocide story are very high, as Jean Nepo, a Rwandan microbiologist and immunologist, explained at KPFA Radio in May 2011.

JEAN MANIRARORA: First of all, Victoire Ingabire has never denied the Tutsi Genocide. But, when she returned to Rwanda in January last year to run for president, she visited the Kigali Genocide Memorial and asked why it commemorates only the Tutsi victims. She asked when the Hutu victims would be commemorated as well. Just saying this is a statutory crime called genocide ideology in Rwanda.

KPFA: What would be the consequence of acknowledging that Hutus were also killed, by extremist Tutsis, because they were Hutus during the 1994 Genocide?

JEAN MANIRARORA: If it were acknowledged that Hutu people were massacred because they were Hutus, then the collective guilt for the genocide would no longer be forced on Hutu people. There would no longer be any justification for packing Hutu people into prisons or forcing them to make restitution to Tutsis by surrendering their property or by indentured servitude to Tutsis. Hutus would finally be allowed to mourn the dead they lost in the genocide, and the bones in the memorial sites would finally be buried in dignity.

KPFA: People from all over the world go to these genocide memorial sites and photograph the bones in these memorial sites. Could you explain what you mean about finally burying them?

JEAN MANIRARORA: It is not normal in the Rwandan culture to display the bodies, bones, or body parts of loved ones, no matter how they died. Foreigners come with their fancy cameras and take photos of these bones, assuming that this is part of our culture, but it is not. Many of these bones are the bones of Hutu people; that is why they are allowed to be on display, although they are presented to the world as the bones of Tutsi victims. Hutu people need to be able to bury and publicly mourn their dead.

KPFA: Could you explain the importance of establishing the truth of the Rwanda Genocide to achieving peace in Rwanda's eastern neighbor, the Democratic Republic of Congo, which has, since 1996, been the site of the deadliest conflict since World War II?

JEAN MANIRARORA: If it is established that Kagame's troops committed atrocities in Rwanda during the Rwanda Genocide, then Kagame would no longer be justified in pursuing the former Rwandan army of Juvenal Habyarimana, the president of Rwanda whose assassination by Kagame's troops in April 1994 triggered the genocide. Kagame refers to the former Rwandan soldiers who took refuge in Congo as "genocidaires." He says he is going after them every time he invades the Congo and he has used them as his excuse to occupy and plunder Congo's resources, with the blessing of the international community.[36]

What if the story of the Rwanda Genocide, as told in the Harvard/Pentagon *Mass Atrocity Response Operations: A Military Planning Handbook*, is wrong? What if that's not at all what happened? Where might General Atomics find its next market for the Predator Drones that have been invested with so much research and development? An African friend of mine suggested that "we"—the US—bomb ourselves to stop mass atrocities.

SEXUAL VIOLENCE AS A WEAPON OF WAR

The common term for this is "gender-based violence," which usually seems to mean sexual violence against women, and this is of course an appealing humanitarian cause. In August 2009 Hillary Clinton traveled to eastern Congo to "address gender-based violence," met some victims, listened to some horrendous stories, and promised $17 million in aid.[37]

Which is to say, she promised another velvet glove on the military fist that so little of the world acknowledges because, again, the US isn't dropping bombs in Congo, and US soldiers aren't dying. Our Rwandan and Ugandan proxy armies control much of the region and serve in our interest instead. It has been documented that they are guilty of mass weaponized rape.

Clinton did not quote the 2001 UN Report of the Panel of Experts on the Illegal Exploitation of Natural Resources and Other Forms of Wealth of the Democratic Republic of the Congo on bilateral donors, the US and its allies:

> The main bilateral donors to Rwanda and Uganda have been the United Kingdom of Great Britain and Northern Ireland, Denmark, Germany and the United States of America in various sectors. The analysis of their cooperation shows that sectors benefiting from this assistance are related to poverty, education and governance. Priority sectors have been water and sanitation, health and governance, including institutional reforms, justice and human rights, especially for Rwanda. In some cases, direct aid to the budget is provided. The balance of payments of Rwanda shows that budget support has steadily increased, from $26.1 million in 1997 to $51.5 in 1999. While such support is legitimate, the problem is that expenditures and services which were supposed to be provided and covered by the Governments of Rwanda and Uganda and which are covered by the bilateral aid constitute savings in the national budget. *Were these savings used to finance this war?* (Author's emphasis.)

The New York Times also reported that Secretary of State Clinton addressed "root causes":

Mrs. Clinton also addressed some of the conflict's root causes, including Congo's illicit mineral trade. In the words of Congo's foreign minister, who also met with Mrs. Clinton on Tuesday, the country, with its rich trove of diamonds, gold, copper, tin, coltan and other minerals, is a "geological scandal."

But Congo's mines are often the unlawful prize of armed groups, and Mrs. Clinton said the world needed to take more steps to regulate the mineral trade to make sure the profits do not end up "in the hands of those who fuel the violence."[38]

She did not mention that US weapons manufactures depend on Congolese minerals—most of all those in the Katanga Copper Belt running from Southeastern Congo into Northern Zambia—or that it has been US policy to control the region, specifically the Katanga Copper Belt, since 1982.

Nor did Clinton remark on this passage from the UN Mapping Report, leaked on August 26, 2010, and released on October 1, 2010 (one year after the report from the *New York Times*), regarding our longstanding military "partners," Uganda and Rwanda, under the command of Rwandan officer James Kaberebe:

329. On 4 August 1998, hundreds of Rwandan troops and a small number of Ugandan troops placed under the orders of James Kabarebe arrived by plane at the military base in Kitona, in Moanda, having travelled from Goma. Some ex-FAZ soldiers stationed at the Kitona base for several months rallied to join them. During the days that followed, the Rwandan-Ugandan-Congolese military coalition was reinforced by several thousand men and embarked on its conquest of the Bas-Congo via the road between Moanda, Boma and Matadi. Some elements in the FAC, which included numerous children associated with armed groups and forces ("child soldiers") (known as "Kadogo" in Swahili) tried to resist, particularly in Boma and Mbanza Ngungu, but were swiftly overwhelmed; many died during the fighting.

330. Throughout their advance on Kinshasa, the Rwandan-Ugandan-Congolese coalition, referred to in the remainder of the report using the acronym ANC/APR/UPDF, killed numerous civilians and committed a large number of rapes and acts of pillaging.[39]

Clinton also failed to remark on AFRICOM Commander William "Kip" Ward's arrival in Kigali in January for his final meeting with Rwandan Defense Minister James Kaberebe, the commander of the Rwandan-Ugandan-Congolese military rape-and-pillage conquest of Bas-Congo, described above. This farewell was reported in the Rwanda News Agency:

Gen Ward will meet Defense Minister Gen James Kabarebe, with whom they have worked closely since the American came to office in October 2008. The AFRICOM chief will also meet the Army boss Gen. Charles Kayonga.

AFRICOM has been helping train Rwandan soldiers—as part of a wider US government military support program for Rwanda. This week, the State Department announced it had awarded a multimillion dollar contract for training of Rwandan soldiers in peacekeeping operations.

Finally Clinton failed to address the President's Emergency Plan for AIDS Relief's (PEPFAR) mobile assistance units that deliver HIV/AIDS services to the Rwandan and Ugandan armies deployed in remote regions. These units enable Rwandan and Ugandan soldiers to remain deployed, despite HIV infection—and despite documentation that Ugandan and Rwandan soldiers are guilty of using mass rape as a weapon.[40] Documentation not only includes the UN Mapping Report, but other sources including *Gender Against Men*, a documentary film produced by the Refugee Law Project at Makerera University in Kampala, Uganda, which won the best documentary film award at the Kenyan Film Festival in 2009.[41]

Samuel Olara, Ugandan exile, English citizen, attorney, and human rights activist, wrote about rape, including male on male rape, committed by the Ugandan Army, sometimes with the conscious intent of spreading HIV, in "Winning Acholi Region," in February 2011:

> During the two decades of conflict, rape against women (and young girls) was used as a weapon of war by warring parties. It was also used to humiliate and dehumanize men in Acholiland. "Gunga Tek" for instance, as it became known, was a phrase that had never been used against men, in the entire history of the Acholi people, until the NRA [National Resistance Army, renamed the Uganda Peoples' Defence Force in 1995] deployed a mobile battalion that became known as the notorious mobile "Gunga" (kneel for me) battalion. They operated in Gulu and Kitgum in the late 1980s. They raped men before their wives and other family members in broad-daylight and the only Acholi word they learned at the time was "gunga" which meant kneel down.

The Refugee Law Project at Kampala, Uganda's Makarera University, recounted the same atrocities in its 2009 film *Gender Against Men.*

In August 2009, while Hillary Clinton was in eastern Congo, Ugandan American journalist Milton Allimadi published "Targeted Rapes to Spread HIV Started in Uganda."

On October 7, 2010, six days after the release of the UN report on Congo atrocities, and a subsequent rash of newly urgent reporting on the issue of rape in eastern Congo, Allimadi republished with this introduction:

> *The New York Times*—and the US State Department—would like to wish away the inconvenient truth; that the proliferation of mass rapes as part of warfare in DR Congo originated with the invasion of Congo by US-allies Uganda and Rwanda. It's also no coincidence that the *Times'* sudden focus on the Congo rape crimes comes the same week that the UN issued a report exposing Paul Kagame's role in Congo genocide. We will watch carefully to see if the *Times* revisits that story. While current coverage of the Congo rapes atrocities is welcome, the

Times' should not use it as strategic diversion and abandon coverage of the October 1, 2010 UN report which implicates Rwanda and Uganda in genocide.[42]

In June 2011, the Congo rape story burst back into the news, with an *American Journal of Public Health* study, an extrapolation from five-year-old statistics, which concluded that forty-eight women are raped every hour in Congo. The study not only discounted the political context, but also reported only women victims, giving the Congo conflict a fundamentally feminist construction, which further deflected attention from the principle aggressors, Uganda and Rwanda, and their powerful "partner," the US and its allies, and from the loss of more than six million lives in Congo since 1996.

Veteran *New York Times* journalist Howard French, in a Youtube interview on the crisisincongo channel, asked:

What is the greatest violation of human rights that exists? That's my question to you. Is it a rape, which is an awful thing? A rape is a horrible thing, but is it the greatest violation of human rights? For me, the greatest violation of human rights is the loss of life. Millions of Congolese people have lost their life as a result of the crisis that we've been discussing and it has warranted almost no sustained and enterprising reporting from the media of the world.[43]

The New York Times, BBC, *Huffington Post*, and more international media reported the new *American Journal of Public Health* rape report, which was also applauded by the humanitarian hawks. Feminist antirape campaigner Eve Ensler was on *Democracy Now!* with eastern Congo antirape campaigner Christine Schuler Deschryver within the week talking about a women's spring beginning in eastern Congo, although Ensler said that the study was flawed and the time for further studies of this crisis had passed, that it was time for action.

Both Ensler and Deschryver, like Lisa Shannon, founder of Run for Congo Women, have commonly blamed the rape crisis on the defeated Rwandan army that crossed Rwanda's border into eastern Congo in 1994, not on the invading armies of Rwanda and Uganda. In this they both share the viewpoint of Samantha Power and another prominent humanitarian hawk, former National Security Advisor and National Intelligence Community employee John Prendergast. At the end of his book *The Enough Moment: Fighting to End the World's Worst Human Rights Crimes,* Prendergast offers a long list of humanitarian hawk nonprofits including Operation Broken Silence, Eastern Congo Initiative, and Jewish World Watch. He also includes Eve Ensler's V-Day.[44]

The October 2010 UN report implicating both Uganda and Rwanda in genocide—and sexual atrocities—had long since faded from the news when eastern Congo's rape crisis seized headlines again.

SO, WHAT IS TO BE DONE?

Someone inevitably asks me this every time I'm invited onto a radio show to talk about these issues. What's to be done about millions of innocent Africans dying and being dislocated in the scramble for African resources essential to weapons manufacture and other details of empire? My best answer: "Redefine national security as national health insurance."

Project Censored Director and KPFA radio host Mickey Huff asked me what's to be done about the disinfo, all the humanitarian abuse and excuse for militarization of Africa, on the *Project Censored Show* on August 10, 2011, and I didn't have a ready answer. Having thought about it since, I can suggest, for one, that we talk to our local school boards about adding to America's high school curriculum, a primer on strategic minerals and America's global dependency for nearly everything, and make it as core to the curriculum as the US Constitution. Whatever they may ultimately think of it, kids should at the very least understand the natural resource requirements for sustaining the greatest military force the world has ever seen.

This isn't top secret, classified information as it is readily available online; the primer doesn't have to be written. People at the National Defense Stockpile even return calls, as I'm sure they would to any high school or college student writing a term paper.

As for the corporate networks, my best answer is "turn it off," even if that means turning off the presidential debates. Isn't a boycott of these debate charades, if not the presidential election itself, long overdue?

Listen, read, support, and create independent media. Defend Net

Neutrality. News of a new internet backbone, up the West Coast of Africa to Europe, was some of the most promising out of Africa last year.

Reach out through the social networks and your web browsers; you can meet and talk to African people without mediation except that of the internet itself now. There's been a paradigm shift that we're just beginning to understand. Africa is no longer that far away from any place with a Net connection.

If you're a media maker, note that you can compete in Google search by writing unique news. You need an outlet that has earned a high Google page rank, which translates into web visibility, but that doesn't mean you have to be on ABC, CNN, or Fox News. Unique news appears ahead of duplicated wire service copy, or otherwise generic news on the Web, because the Google Search algorithm perceives unique news. I regularly come in ahead of Fox News, the networks, and often ahead of Reuters, AP, AFP, and even the BBC in Google Search with my researched, contextualized news on Africa—because no one else is writing the same copy. That much at least, I know, can be done.

As I was concluding this, I received an e-mail from Thomas Mountain in Eritrea, about another unreported genocide, this time in Ogaden, also known as the Ogaden Oil Basin, about 200,000 square kilometers of Ethiopia, bordering Djibouti, Kenya, and Somalia, where ethnic Somali and Muslim rebels who think the Ogaden is Western Somalia, seem to be fighting the Ethiopian government and challenging the infamous Swedish Lundin group's oil concession. It appears there is a media blockade and atrocities are alleged on both sides.

The outlines of this, again, sound familiar. I doubt the spectre of genocide would be raised if there weren't oil on this land, but I also doubt we're going to hear much about this one, at least for awhile—maybe never—because Ethiopia is a US ally, and that always puts a crimp on humanitarian concern. But I wrote down Thomas Mountain's most accessible phone number and resolved to call him for KPFA and/or WBAI *AfrobeatRadio*. Breaking down the barriers of censorship on Africa continues.

ANN GARRISON writes for the San Francisco Bay View, Global Research, Afrobeat-Radio.net and other publications, and produces radio for KPFA Weekend News and

WBAI AfrobeatRadio. She is working on a book titled "Sodomy and Hypocrisy," about American evangelicals, LGBT persecution, war crimes, and sexual atrocities in Africa.

Notes

1. "General Ward on AFRICOM," YouTube video, 1:30, posted by "DODvClips," October 3, 2008, http://www.youtube.com/watch?v=yzoeAfgkIjk; US Africa Comman homepage, accessed June 12, 2011, http://www.africaom.mil/#; "AFRICOM: BUSHES PLOT AGAINST AFRICA," YouTube video, 4:03, posted by "grannypeacebrigade," April 8, 2008, http://www.youtube.com/watch?v=XzdF4hA4XfY&feature=related; "Cynthia McKinney – Oppose Africom," YouTube video, 0:54, posted by "RunCynthiaRun," October 8, 2008, http://www.youtube.com/watch?v=sDGOMY4gNVQ&feature=related; Major R. A. Hagerman, "US Reliance on Africa for Strategic Minerals," Global Security, April 6, 1984, http://www.globalsecurity.org/military/library/report/1984/HRA.htm.

2. Denis Tougas, "Canada in Africa: The Mining Superpower," *Pambazuka News*, November 20, 2008, http://www.pambazuka.org/en/category/features/52095.

3. Scott B. Lanesky, "How Foreign Aid Serves the National Interest," *Buffalo News*, March 16, 2003, reproduced at http://www.cfr.org/democracy-and-human-rights/foreign-aid-serves-national-interest/p5711.

4. "US Presidents Emergency Plan For AIDS Relief," January 20, 2009, http://2006-2009.pepfar.gov/countries/c19418.htm.

5. "RESIST AFRICOM," YouTube video, 8:13, posted by "elliejoy11," October 28, 2008, http://www.youtube.com/watch?v=JRCZk8mM1EU.

6. "Daily Roundup," *Somalia Report*, April 30, 2011, http://www.somaliareport .com/index.php/post/636; Thomas C. Mountain, "UN Cuts Food, Expands War in Somalia," May 28, 2011, transcript, AfrobeatRadio.net, http://afrobeatradio.net/ 2011/06/07/un-food-cuts-and-expanded-war-in-somalia-continues/.

7. Jay Rey, "UB grad is named prime minister of Somalia," *Buffalo News*, October 15, 2010, http://www.buffalonews.com/city/article220990.ece.

8. Mohamed A. Mohamed, "US STRATEGIC INTEREST IN SOMALIA: From Cold War Era to War on Terror," Horseed Media, June 1, 2009, http://horseedmedia .net/wpcontent/uploads/2010/10/US_STRATEGIC_INTEREST_IN_SOMALIA.pdf.

9. Thomas Mountain, "UN Cuts Food Aid, Expands War in Somalia," *Counterpunch*, May 25, 2011, http://www.counterpunch.org/mountain05252011.html.

10. Mountain and Ann Garrison, "Somalia: a UN Managed Catastrophe," Global Research, June 5, 2011, http://www.globalresearch.ca/index.php?context=va&aid=25130.

11. Mountain, "UN Food Cuts And Expanded War In Somalia Continues," AfrobeatRadio.net, June 7th, 2011, http://afrobeatradio.net/2011/06/07/un-food-cuts-and-expanded-war-in-somalia-continues/; Michael Maren, "The Might Interview: The Lie of Foreign and International Charity," *Nomadnet*, http://mmaren .wordpress.com/reviews/michael-maren-the-might-interview/; Maren, *The Road to Hell: The Ravaging Effects of Foreign Aid and International Charity* (New York: The Free Press, 1997); Mountain, "UN Food Cuts Continues."

12. Report of the Panel of Experts on the Illegal Exploitation of Natural Resources and Other Forms of Wealth of the Democratic Republic of the Congo, April 12, 2001, http://www.friendsofthecongo.org/pdf/un_report_apr_01.pdf; Final Report of the panel of Experts on the Illegal Exploitation of Natural Resources and Other Forms of Wealth of the Democratic Republic of the Congo, October 15, 2002, http://www .friendsofthecongo.org/pdf/third_panel_report_october2002.pdf; Chairman of the Panel

of Experts on the Illegal Exploitation of Natural Resources of the Democratic Republic of the Congo to the Secretary-General, October 15, 2003, http://www.friendsofthecongo.org/pdf/un_report_oct_03.pdf; Special Rapporteur Roberto Garretón, United Nations Commission Resolution 1998/61 "Question of the Violation of Human Rights and Fundamental Freedoms in any Part of the World," February 8, 1999, http://www.unhchr.ch/Huridocda/Huridoca .nsf/0/8e3dbacbae51ce60802567460034073d?OpenDocument; Gerard Prunier, *Africa's World War: Congo, The Rwandan Genocide, and the Making of a Continental Catastrophe* (Oxford: Oxford University Press, 2009); Timothy Longman, *Christianity and Genocide in Rwanda* (Cambridge: Cambridge University Press, 2010); Anthony Court, "Book Review," *Oxford Journals, Humanities Holocaust and Genocide Studies* 24, no. 23 (2010): 493–498; "Cobalt: Policy Options for a Strategic Mineral," Congressional Budget Office, September 1982, http://www.cbo .gov/doc.cfm?index=5126&type=0; Garrison, "The Holocasut in D.R. Congo: War for the Sake of War Itself," *San Francisco Bay View*, March 11, 2009, http://sfbayview.com/2009/the-african-holocaust-in-dr-congo-war-for-the-sake-of-war-itself/.

13. Michel Chossudovsky, "The US was Behind the Rwanda Genocide: Rwanda: Installing a Protectorate in Central Africa," Global Research, May 8, 2003, http://www.globalresearch.ca/articles/CHO305A.html; Keith Harmon Snow, "The US Sponsored 'Rwanda Genocide' and Its Aftermath," Global Research, April 12, 2008, http://www.globalresearch.ca/index.php?context=va&aid=8657; Andrew Gavin Marshall, "Congo Research Wars," Global Research, March 1, 2008, http://www.globalresearch.ca/index.php?context=va&aid=8310.

14. Max Delany, "Why 10,000 Ugandans are eagerly serving in Iraq," *Christian Science Monitor*, March 6, 2009, http://www.csmonitor.com/World/Africa/2009/0306/p04s02-woaf.html; Garrison, "Just What Haiti Doesn't Need: Rwandan Police," *San Franciso Bay View*, March 12, 2010, http://sfbayview.com/2010/just-what-haiti-needs-rwandan-police/; Jean Ndayisaba, "'US Military Not Intending to Control Africa'—Says Army Chief," Rwanda News Agency, June 14, 2001, http://www.rnanews.com/archives/3580-us-military-not-intending-to-control-africa-says-army-chief-; Beth Tuckey, "AFRICOM's Uganda Blunder," *Foreign Policy in Focus*, April 20, 2009, http://www.fpif.org/articles/africoms_ugandan_blunder; "Ward Press Conference in Rwanda," US Africa Command, April 22, 2008, http://www.africom.mil/getArticle.asp?art=3011; "Kagame for Lunch with Obama," Rwanda News Agency, September 21, 2009, http://www.rnanews.com/politics/1981-kagame-for-lunch-with-obama-; Snow, "Proxy Wars in Central Africa? Profits, Propaganda, and Luxury Goods for the West Pacification, Rape and Slavery for the Rest," *World War 4 Report: Deconstructing the War on Terrorism*, July 18, 2010, http://ww4report.com/static/proxy.html; "Outsourcing US Wars: Ugandans in Iraq," YouTube video, 5:01, posted by "AnnieGetYourGang," June 2, 2011, http://www.youtube.com/watch?v=0532plca9mA; Mountain, "UN Food Cuts," 2011.

15. "DRC: Mapping Human Rights Violations 1993–2003," Office of the UN High Commissioner for Human Rights, Accessed June 12, 2011, http://www.ohchr .org/en/Countries/AfricaRegion/Pages/RDCProjetMapping.aspx; "IRC Study Shows Congo's Neglected Crisis Leaves 5.4 Million Dead; Peace Deal in N. Kivu, Increased Aid Critical to Reducing Death Toll," International Rescue Committee, January 22,

2008, http://www.rescue.org/news/irc-study-shows-congos-neglected-crisis-leaves-54 million-dead-peace-deal-n-kivu-increased-aid—4331; "Six Million Dead in Congo's War," Caritas Internationalis, Accessed June 12, 2011, http://www.caritas.org/activities/emergencies/SixMillionDeadInCongoWar.html.

16. "The Leaked UN Report The Contradiction of General Paul Kagame.flv," YouTube video, 9:07, posted by "AnnieGetYourGang," June 3, 2011, http://youtube/A2yYkdDHfyY.

17. "Democratic Republic of the Congo 1993–2003 UN Mapping Report," Office of the High Commissioner for Human Rights, Accessed March 18, 2011, http://www.ohchr.org/Documents/Countries/ZR/FS-2_Crimes_Final.pdf.

18. "Candles for Rwanda," YouTube video, 1:03, posted by "NancyPelosi," April 7, 2009, http://www.youtube.com/watch?v=RT_4CpAvEUI; Aimable Mugara, "Rwanda Circa 1994 is No Nazi Germany," *Opednews.com*, June 6, 2010, http://www.opednews.com/articles/Rwanda-circa-1994-is-no-Na-by-Aimable-100602-508.html; Mark Doyle, "Rwanda: 'The Israel of Africa,'" BBC News, January 20, 2009, http://news.bbc.co.uk/2/hi/7839922.stm.

19. Ann Garrison, "ICTR Laywers: No Justice for Congo From Independent Courts," *San Francisco Bay View*, October 11, 2009, http://sfbayview.com/2010/ictr-lawyers-no-justice-for-congo-from-courts; Mugara, "Bill Clinton, the Genocider Who Just Might Get Away," *San Francisco Bay View*, November 3, 2010, http://sfbayview.com/2010/bill-clinton-the-genocider-who-just-might-get-away/; Christopher Black, "The Rwandan Patriotic Front's Bloody Record and the History of UN Cover-ups," *Monthly Review Magazine*, December 9, 2010, http://mrzine.monthlyreview.org/2010/black120910.html.

20. "Uganda: Ban Ki-Moon Meets Kagame Over Leaked Genocide Report," *Monitor*, September 9, 2010, http://allafrica.com/stories/201009090953.html; "Rwanda to Keep its Peacemakers in Place," CNN, September 27, 2010, http://articles.cnn.com/2010-09-27/world/un.rwanda_1_hutus-tutsis-rwandan-army?_s=PM:WORLD; Xan Rice, "Uganda Rejects UN Report on War Crimes in Congo," *Guardian*, October 1, 2010, http://www.guardian.co.uk/law/2010/oct/01/ uganda-un-war-crimes-congo; Jeffrey Gettleman, "Uganda: A Threat to Pull Peacekeepers," *New York Times*, October 1, 2010, http://www.nytimes.com/ 2010/10/01/world/africa/01briefs-Uganda.html.

21. Philip J. Crowley, "UN Mapping Report on Violations of Human Rights in the Democratic Republic of the Congo," Bureau of Public Affairs, October 1, 2010, http://www.state.gov/r/pa/prs/ps/2010/10/148549.htm.

22. Kofi A. Annan, "Report of the Panel of Experts on the Illegal Exploitation of Natural Resources and Other Forms of Wealth of the Democratic Republic of the Congo," April 12, 2001, http://www.friendsofthecongo.org/pdf/un_report_apr_01.pdf.

23. "Mass Atrocity Response Operations: A Military Planning Handbook," Harvard Kennedy School of Government, 2010, http://www.hks.harvard.edu/cchrp/maro/pdf/MARO_Handbook_v9.pdf.

24. "Air Force is Through with Predator Drones," *Wired*, December 14, 2010, http://www.wired.com/dangerroom/2010/12/air-force-is-through-with-predator-drones/.

25. "Pentagon: Drones Can Stop the Next Darfur," *Wired*, February 10, 2011, http://www.wired.com/dangerroom/2011/02/drones-vs-darfur/.

26. Mark Hackett, "Can Predator Drones Stop the Next Darfur?" *Operation Broken Silence*, February 11, 2011, http://www.operationbrokensilence.org/?p=5658.

27. Sheryl Gay Stolberg, "Still Crusading, but Now on the Inside," *New York Times*, March 30, 2011, http://www.nytimes.com/2011/03/30/world/30power.htm; Clifford H. Bernath, "Mass Atrocity Prevention and Response and the US Government," presentation at Harvard Kennedy School of Government, March 31, 2011, http://www.hks.harvard.edu/cchrp/maro/events/2011/month03/Bernath_31.php.

28. Edward S. Herman and David Peterson, "The Politics of Genocide," *Monthly Review*, June 11, 2011, http://monthlyreview.org/press/books/pb2129/.

29. Herman, "Samantha Power, Libya, and Selective Memory of Genocide," *Institute for Public Accuracy*, May 25, 2011, http://www.accuracy.org/samantha-power-libya-and-selective-memory-of-genocide/.

30. Samantha Power, "Bystanders to Genocide," *Atlantic*, September 2001, http://www.theatlantic.com/magazine/archive/2001/09/bystanders-to-genocide/4571/.

31. Bernath, "Mass Atrocity Response Operations," 6.

32. Miller McCune, "What Really Happened in Rwanda," *Miller-McCune*, October 9, 2009, http://www.miller-mccune.com/politics/what-really-happened-in-rwanda-3432/

33. Professor Allan Stam, "Understanding the Rwanda Genocide," February 2009, video, Gerald R. Ford School of Public Policy Video Library, University of Michigan, http://www.fordschool.umich.edu/video/2009/44939157001/.

34. Keith Harmon Snow, *Conscious Being Alliance*, blog, http://www.consciousbeingalliance.com/cgi-bin/mt/mt-search.cgi?search=Rwanda&IncludeBlogs=1.

35. Peter Erlinder, "The UN Security Council Ad Hoc Rwanda Tribunal—International Justice or Judicially Constructed 'Victor's Impunity?'" *De Paul Journal for Social Justice* 4, no. 1 (2010).

36. Garrison, "Rwanda: Victoire Ingabire Umuhoza on Trial," *KPFA Radio* and *San Francisco Bay View*, May 15, 2011, http://sfbayview.com/2011/rwanda-victoire-ingabire-umuhoza-on-trial/.

37. Gettleman, "Clinton Presents Plan to Fight Sexual Violence in Congo," *New York Times*, August 1, 2009, http://www.nytimes.com/2009/08/12/world/africa/12diplo.html.

38. "Cobalt," US Congressional Budget Office, 1982.

39. *Democratic Republic of the Congo, 1993–2003*, mapping report, 2010.

40. "PEPFAR Strengthens UPDF with Critical HIV Services," United States Virtual Presence Post Northern Uganda, http://northernuganda.usvpp.gov/pepfar_updf.html.

41. Ibid., 318–324; "Gender Against Men, Refugee Law Project," Vimeo video, 43:47, posted by "SRLAN," March 25, 2010, http://vimeo.com/10430187; Samuel Olara, "Uganda, Winning Acholi Region," *The Monitor*, February 7, 2011, http://allafrica.com/stories/201102080261.html.

42. Milton Allimadi, "Congo: Targeted Rapes to Spread HIV/AIDS Started in Uganda," *Black Star News*, October 6, 2010, http://www.blackstarnews.com/news/135/ARTICLE/6840/2010-10-06.html.

43. "Howard French—Congo: Rape, Savagery, and Stereotypes, the Heart of Darkness," YouTube video, 2:17, posted by "crisisincongo," May 14, 2011.

44. John Prendergast and Don Cheadle, *The Enough Moment: Fighting to End Africa's Worst Human Rights Crimes* (New York: Three Rivers Press, 2011).

CHAPTER 13

Establishing Ghetto Palestine

by Jon Elmer

While arguably the most reported conflict in the North American press, the Israel-Palestine conflict is, at the same time, often the least understood. The pace of events, the overemphasis on diplomatic reportage, and the ritualistic coverage of an unending peace process obfuscate the overarching strategic imperatives that are being implemented by the state of Israel.

Israel's separation barrier surrounding Palestinian communities has been reported on extensively over the nine years since construction first began. Coverage has invariably been dominated by narratives of Israeli security, with occasional stories on the barrier's impact on Palestinians framed as a human interest-type narrative. Missing in this coverage is the larger Israeli project that has, since the end of the Second Intifada (the al-Aqsa Intifada), reshaped the core dimension of the conflict.

In an effort to maintain Israel as a Jewish state in the face of increasing demographic parity between Jewish and Palestinian populations residing between the Jordan River and the Mediterranean Sea, Israel has sought to establish Palestinian enclaves—or "cantons" as their architect, former prime minister Ariel Sharon, called them—that would euphemistically be called a state. In apartheid South Africa, indigenous enclaves were referred to as Bantustans; in North America they are called reserves or reservations; "ghettos" was the term during the Nazi occupations in Europe during the Second World War.

For their part, Israel's top political leadership has been reasonably straightforward about this project and its critical place in the country's strategic vision.

Speaking last year at the Herzliya Conference, Israel's most important annual security plenary, former prime minister and current defense minister Ehud Barak was clear: "If, and as long as between the Jordan [River] and the Sea there is only one political entity, named Israel, it will end up being either non-Jewish or nondemocratic. If the

413

Palestinians vote in elections it is a binational state, and if they don't vote it is an apartheid state."[1]

Former prime minister Ehud Olmert delivered an equally unambiguous message en route to the Annapolis peace conference in 2007: "If the two-state solution collapses, and we face a South African–style struggle for equal voting rights, then the State of Israel is finished."[2]

Indeed, for the first time in its history, Israel is now acknowledging that a Palestinian state—even one that looks like no other state in the world—is a necessity. Put another way, the creation of a Palestinian state is now an Israeli imperative.

GHETTO PALESTINE

The fall of 2003 was a turning point in the Israeli-Palestinian conflict. The three-year Palestinian uprising, or intifada, was beginning to wane, attacks on Israel had declined significantly (though not vice versa), and internal fissures within Israeli society were coming to the fore.

It is in this context that Sharon's leading portfolio holder, Olmert, floated a trial balloon to the Israeli public that came to be known as the "disengagement plan."

In an interview with the Israeli daily *Ha'aretz*, Olmert laid out the strategic vision and the reasons for the imperative. Its headline was instructive: "Maximum Jews, Minimum Palestinians." Olmert said:

> There is no doubt in my mind that very soon the government of Israel is going to have to address the demographic issue with the utmost seriousness and resolve. . . .
>
> We don't have unlimited time. More and more Palestinians are uninterested in a negotiated, two-state solution, because they want to change the essence of the conflict from an Algerian paradigm to a South African one. From a struggle against "occupation," in their parlance, to a struggle for one-man-one-vote. That is, of course, a much cleaner struggle, a much more popular struggle—and ultimately a much more powerful one. For us, it would mean the end of the Jewish state. . . .
>
> The formula for the parameters of a unilateral solution are: To maximize the number of Jews; to minimize the number of

Palestinians; not to withdraw to the 1967 border and not to divide Jerusalem.

Large settlements such as the cantons Sharon proposes would "obviously" be carved into Israel. The unilateral project, Olmert said, "would inevitably preclude a dialogue with the Palestinians for at least 25 years."[3]

Dov Weisglass, Sharon and Olmert's top aide, characterized the unilateral action in even blunter terms several months later:

> In the fall of 2003 we understood that everything is stuck. Time was not on our side. There was international erosion, internal erosion. Domestically, in the meantime, everything was collapsing. The economy was stagnant, and the Geneva Initiative garnered broad support. And then we were hit with letters of officers and letters of pilots and letters of commandos [of refusal to serve in the Palestinian territories]. These were not weird kids with green ponytails and a ring in their nose who give off a strong odor of grass. These were really our finest young people.
>
> When negotiations begin, it's very difficult to stop them. The result would be a Palestinian state.

This is the thrust of the Israeli predicament: Israel needs a Palestinian state to exist, but the question is what kind of state it will be—namely, how can they establish its borders in accord with Israel's maximum aspirations? Enter the disengagement plan. Said Weisglass:

> The disengagement is actually formaldehyde. It supplies the amount of formaldehyde that's necessary so that there will not be a political process with the Palestinians. . . .
>
> The disengagement plan makes it possible for Israel to park conveniently in an interim situation that distances us as far as possible from political pressure. . . .
>
> In regard to the large settlement blocs, thanks to the disengagement plan, we have in our hands a first-ever American statement that they will be part of Israel . . . There is an American commitment such as never existed before, with regard to 190,000 settlers [of 240,000].

Rather than critiquing Sharon for relinquishing Gaza—as many right-wing Israelis did at the time, the settlers, said Weisglass, "should have danced around and around the Prime Minister's Office."

Weisglass further elaborated the substance and intended outcome of the project: "The term 'political process' is a bundle of concepts and commitments. The political process is the establishment of a Palestinian state with all the security risks that entails. The political process is the evacuation of settlements, it's the return of refugees, it's the partition of Jerusalem. And all that has now been frozen. . . . When you freeze that process you prevent the establishment of a Palestinian state and you prevent a discussion about the refugees, the borders, and Jerusalem."

Because of this plan, Weisglass said, "there will be no timetable to implement the settlers' nightmare. I have postponed that nightmare indefinitely."[4] The disengagement was passed with the consent of the US Congress and was reaffirmed by US President Barack Obama in the late spring of 2011, when he said that mutually agreed swaps would form the basis of negotiations. It was passed in the House of Representatives by a vote of 405–7 and in the Senate by 95–5. Israel's most important ally was backing the canton plan.

CREATING LEGITIMACY

For the ghetto-state plan to be viable, it must be palatable to the international community. The attempt to construct a framework of legitimacy has been a three-pronged process centered on governance, economy, and, most importantly, security.

Governance

The first pillar, governance, is spearheaded by former International Monetary Fund (IMF) official Salam Fayyad. Appointed prime minister of Palestine in 2007 following Fatah's failed coup in Gaza, after having received only 2 percent of the popular vote in the 2006 elections, Salam Fayyad was installed by the US and Israel. Since then, he has been tasked with rebuilding the Palestinian Authority institutions in the West Bank that Israel destroyed during the al-Aqsa Intifada (2000–2005).

In a meeting with senior western diplomats, Israeli President Shimon Peres characterized Fayyad as the "Palestinian Ben Gurion."[5] The right-wing daily, the *Jerusalem Post*, carried a long feature by editor David Horovitz headlined, "Fayyad builds Palestine."[6]

Economy

The economic pillar is headed by Quartet envoy Tony Blair. In order to create legitimacy for the ghetto state, lofty economic benchmarks achieved in the West Bank are regularly touted. Blair has selected several "model cities" to highlight this economic growth, including Jenin and Bethlehem. The goal is to implement a kind of "economic peace," in Netanyahu's words.

In 2010 the Palestinian economy's growth rate was almost 10 percent, among "the world's hottest economies," the *Financial Times* said.[7] These statistics are brandished most commonly not by Palestinians, but by Israeli leaders.

The UN, however, disagrees with the simplistic accounting. "Contrary to media reports of a flourishing West Bank economy, evidence from the second half of 2010 shows deteriorating labour market conditions, with falling employment growth, accelerating unemployment and lower real wages. These trends disproportionately affected refugees."[8]

A systematic appraisal by the Carnegie Endowment found that "to the extent that Fayyadism is building institutions, it is unmistakably doing so in an authoritarian context. . . . A governmental system with no organized domestic constituency whose performance is completely dependent on continuing international largesse can hardly be seen as stable indefinitely."[9]

The damning report continues: "The entire program is based not simply on de-emphasizing or postponing democracy and human rights but on actively denying them for the present. But [Fayyad] has done so in an authoritarian context that robs the results of domestic legitimacy."

Security Forces

The most important aspect of the ghetto-state plan is the reconstituted security apparatus of the Palestinian Authority. Under the auspices of Lieutenant General Keith Dayton, also the US security coordinator, an entirely new security force has been established since 2005, ostensibly tasked with confronting the Palestinian resistance.

The project began in Gaza. Sean McCormack, a state department spokesman at the time, explained Dayton's role as "the real down in the weeds, blocking and tackling work of helping to build up the security forces."[10]

But within weeks of Dayton's arrival in Israel in the last days of 2005, things began to fall apart. Hamas's decisive January 2006 election victory ushered in a crippling international blockade on the Palestinians in Gaza. Soon after, the security forces of Hamas and Fatah began fighting in the streets, culminating in Hamas's June 2007 takeover of the enclave.

Dayton's initial aims lay in tatters, and while Fayyad became prime minister in a "caretaker" government in Ramallah, a new security strategy was formulated. As a grim status quo was established in Gaza, Dayton's new mission became clear: the job of the security coordinator was now "to prevent a Hamas takeover in the West Bank," according to Michael Eisenstadt, Dayton's former plans officer.[11]

The Palestinian forces have an open agenda to target Hamas and other Palestinian factions. In May 2010, six people were killed when Dayton's forces attacked Hamas activists in the West Bank town of Qalqilya, sparking a gun battle that lasted several hours and took place without Israel's interference. Hamas characterized the attack as "an awful crime" committed by "collaborators," while Abbas declared that his forces would continue to strike opposition groups "with an iron fist."[12]

Lieutenant General Dayton saw the Qalqilya event as a telling example of how the security forces would operate inside a future ghetto-state. They had, he said, engaged in a series of violent raids that were "surprisingly well coordinated" with Israel. Dayton characterized the results as "electric."[13]

"They have caught the attention of the Israeli defense establishment for their dedication, discipline, motivation, and results," Dayton added.

That Palestinian security forces are being trained in Jordan, not in the West Bank, cuts to the heart of their lacking credibility among their own people. It is presumed that they cannot be trained in their local milieu because they lack political legitimacy.

To this end, Dayton told the staunchly pro-Israel Washington Institute for Near East Policy (WINEP), an audience of American and Israeli diplomats and policymakers, American and Israeli alike, in 2009: "You might ask, why Jordan? The answer is pretty simple. The Palestinians wanted to train in the region, but they wanted to be away from clan, family, and political influences. The Israelis trust the Jordanians, and the Jordanians were anxious to help."[14]

A coordinated attack on Hamas's civilian apparatus was launched immediately after the takeover in Gaza in June 2007. Major General Gadi Shamni, the head of the Israeli army's central command, led an initiative to target the base of Hamas's support in the West Bank. The plan, dubbed the Dawah Strategy, involved pinpointing Hamas's extensive social welfare apparatus—the lynchpin of their popularity among many Palestinians.

Minutes from a security meeting between Israeli generals and Palestinian security forces leadership attended by Israel's leading security correspondent, Nahum Barnea, were uniquely blunt:

"Hamas is the enemy, and we have decided to wage an all-out war," Barnea quoted Majid Faraj, then the head of Palestinian military in-

telligence, as telling the Israeli commanders. "We are taking care of every Hamas institution in accordance with your instructions."[15]

Unlike the first iteration of security forces established by the CIA during the Oslo peace process of the 1990s and staffed by Fatah partisans, this latest manifestation is a strictly apolitical formation where each and every soldier is vetted by Israeli and American intelligence to ensure that there are no factional affiliations in their ranks.

While the 1990s edition was nevertheless indicted for widespread human rights abuses, torture, arbitrary detention, and even extrajudicial killings aimed predominately at Hamas and Islamic Jihad, when the al-Aqsa Intifada broke out in September 2000, many of those trained and armed security men either joined militias or at least redistributed their weapons for use in the armed struggle against Israel.

"What we have created are new men," Dayton told the audience of policymakers at the WINEP symposium. "For the first time, I think it's fair to say that the Palestinian security forces feel they are on a winning team." Namely, firmly on the side of the Israelis.[16]

"I'm an American, I'm here to advance America's interests," Dayton told Ha'aretz. "But I am also here because of the relationship between your country and mine."[17]

If there is a standard narrative presented in the media on this conflict, it is one of stagnation—a string of failed peace negotiations, endless shuttle diplomacy by senior diplomats, decade after decade of stalemate in achieving peace. By setting the focus on immediate events, usually without necessary context, the overarching strategic framework escapes attention. In reality, the Israeli occupation is slowly grinding ahead, more Palestinian land is stolen, more Israeli infrastructure—roads and settlement housing—is planted on the ground that Palestinians have rightful claim to in any iteration of internationally recognized peace. Palestinian territory is ever-shrinking, while Israel creates the facts on the ground—namely, the separation barrier—and turns the West Bank into a series of Gaza Strips, isolated from one another, land bisected by Israeli roads and settlements. The strategic vision to establish a Palestinian ghetto-state is happening daily outside the media spotlight.

JON ELMER is a Canadian journalist who has been based in the Middle East since 2003. He is a contributor to Al Jazeera English and Inter Press Service, among others. He lives in Bethlehem. Jon Elmer's website is www.jonelmer.ca. With additional editing assistance from NORA BARROWS-FRIEDMAN.

Notes

1. Tony Karon, "Israel Gets More Comfortable with Status Quo," *Time*, February 15, 2010, http://www.time.com/time/world/article/0,8599,1962232,00.html.
2. "Olmert Warns of 'End of Israel,'" BBC, November 29, 2007, http://news.bbc.co.uk/2/hi/7118937.stm.
3. David Landau, "Maximum Jews, Minimum Palestinians," *Ha'aretz*, November 13, 2003, http://www.haaretz.com/general/maximum-jews-minimum-palestinians-1.105562.
4. Ari Shavit, "Top PM Aide: Gaza Plan Aims to Freeze the Peace Process," *Ha'aretz*, October 8, 2004, http://www.haaretz.com/print-edition/news/top-pm-aide-gaza-plan-aims-to-freeze-the-peace-process-1.136686.
5. Akiva Eldar, "EU Sources: Terms Set for Renewal of Israel-PA Talks," *Ha'aretz*, September 13, 2009, http://www.haaretz.com/print-edition/news/eu-sources-terms-set-for-renewal-of-israel-pa-talks-1.8008.
6. David Horovitz, "Fayyad Builds Palestine," *Jerusalem Post*, November 19, 2009, http://fr.jpost.com/servlet/Satellite?cid=1258624595789&pagename=JPArticle%2FShowFull.
7. Sarah Mishkin, "A Safe Stock Market?" *Financial Times*, May 14, 2011, http://www.ft.com/cms/s/0/75886a56-7cbf-11e0-994d-00144feabdc0.html#axzz1PmPXofzY.
8. United Nations Agency for Palestinian Refugees, *Labour Market Briefing: West Bank—Second Half 2010*, East Jerusalem: United Nations Relief and Works Agency, June 8, 2011, http://www.unrwa.org/userfiles/201106082849.pdf.
9. Nathan J. Brown, "Are Palestinians Building a State?" *Carnegie Endowment*, July 1, 2010, http://www.carnegieendowment.org/publications/index.cfm?fa=view&id=41093.
10. Jon Elmer, "Fighting in the Gaza Ghetto," *Canadian Dimension* 42, no. 1 (February 2008): 18–20.
11. Michael Eisenstadt, "Why the Next President Will be a Wartime Leader," *Jerusalem Post*, November 4, 2008, www.jpost.com/Home/Article.aspx?id=119405.
12. Rory McCarthy, "Six Die as Palestinian Police Clash with Hamas in West Bank," *Guardian*, May 31, 2009, http://www.guardian.co.uk/world/2009/may/31/palestinians-killed-west-bank-hamas.
13. Lieutenant General Keith Dayton, Michael Stein Address on US Middle East Policy (keynote address, Soref Symposium, Washington Institute for Near East Policy, Washington, DC, May 7, 2009).
14. Ibid.
15. Nahum Barnea, "Report on Israeli-PA Security Coordination Meeting, 19 September 2008 (excerpts)," *Journal of Palestine Studies* 38, no. 2 (Winter 2009): 202.
16. Lieutenant General Keith Dayton, Michael Stein Address on US Middle East Policy (keynote address, Soref Symposium, Washington Institute for Near East Policy, Washington, DC, May 7, 2009).
17. Aluf Benn, "Top US General Lays Foundation for Palestinian State," *Ha'aretz*, August 8, 2008, http://www.haaretz.com/hasen/spages/1009578.html.

CHAPTER 14

HBO's *Treme*
Exposing the Fractured Press Coverage of the Storm and Post-Katrina New Orleans

by Robin Andersen

Five years after the storm that flooded 80 percent of New Orleans and devastated the Gulf Coast, killing 1,800 people, author Rebecca Solnit observed that evaluating the media coverage of Hurricane Katrina is important because "getting the story right matters for survival as well as for justice and history."[1] That same year, in April 2010, a few months before the storm's fifth anniversary, the first episode of the fictional series *Treme*, set in post-Katrina New Orleans, aired on HBO. Veteran television producers David Simon and Eric Overmyer of *The Wire* begin their drama three months after the storm, chronicling the lives of ten main characters who stubbornly reinhabit a city they refuse to let die. By doing so the producers of *Treme* breathed life into a story that was by then all but dead in the United States press. As early as 2006, Fairness & Accuracy In Reporting noted in a piece titled "Katrina's Vanishing Victims" that the recovery of New Orleans had lost its news value.[2] After a steady decline, the story was relegated to an "anniversary event," and by 2008 the Tyndall Report found that Katrina was no longer among the top twenty stories on TV news. There were only six hurricane-related stories on TV in the first seven months of 2009.[3]

Treme revives the story of the storm, a story many—especially those formerly in "official" positions—would rather forget. The filming of *Treme* looks eerily real, and people and places are shot in ways that foreground a city in distress. Nowhere is this more apparent than in the opening scenes of the series that are at once beautiful and disturbing. Mold spores on walls visually measure the high water marks of interior spaces; it is real footage, the same used in Spike Lee's *When the Levees Broke*. Along with the aerial images of floodwaters that surge into doorways and places where water should never be, the eye of the storm hits viewers week after week.

The program does not mince words about the flooding. From the beginning *Treme*'s spotlight has been harsh. Early on, the disaster that hit New Orleans is described in this way by the memorable character Creighton Bernette (played by actor John Goodman): "What hit the Mississippi Gulf Coast was a natural disaster; a hurricane pure and simple. The flooding of New Orleans is a manmade catastrophe, a federal f*** up of epic proportion, and decades in the making." The intensity of Bernette's ongoing blog posts, his hilarious profanity, and biting criticism of the forces unwilling to rebuild one of the country's "great cities," indicate from the start that the writers of *Treme* intended to rekindle a national dialogue about the disaster and its consequences. Indeed, it has also challenged the news coverage of the storm and its aftermath, and what better way to illustrate that than by having Bernette, a character who portrays a Tulane University professor, throw the microphone of a British television news anchor into the lake?

SETTING THE RECORD STRAIGHT

The series' writers are determined to closely follow events as they actually unfolded in post-Katrina New Orleans. Lolis Eric Elie, story editor for the series and a former *Times-Picayune* journalist, said, "We have a timeline of the events as they occurred hanging on the wall of our conference room. We use it as an outline and fill it in with personal stories of people's lives." For example, "We wanted to describe what it was like to come back and see your flooded house for the first time."[4] Other residents of New Orleans—authors, DJs, musicians, chefs, lawyers, and even Mardi Gras Indians—also populate this series both on- and off-screen. Many work behind the scenes as consultants and writers, while others appear in cameo roles and as extras in order to create a complex, compelling, vérité view of post-Katrina New Orleans, and to demonstrate to the rest of the country, in the words of New Orleans author and *Treme* scriptwriter Tom Piazza, "Why New Orleans Matters."[5]

In the same way it tracks events, the program also tracks the news discourse of the time, challenging past news reporting and journalism in just about every way: in detail, theme, point of view, and most importantly when it comes to telling the stories of the musicians, culture, and communities of New Orleans. After watching the first two episodes of season two (set fourteen months after the storm) at the premier in New York City, Eric Overmyer confirmed in an interview that they have an interest in "setting the record straight."[6] In doing so they offer an ideal lens through which to look at the multiple, evolving narratives of a disaster of epic proportions, one that can teach us much about how to cope with humanitarian crises, and how to represent the indignities of ongoing racial and economic inequalities. *Treme* creates alternative narratives that reveal a media system either unwilling or unable to fulfill the promise made by one significant broadcaster, NBC's Brian Williams: "If we come out of this crisis and in the next couple of years don't have a national conversation on the following issues—race, class, petroleum, the environment—then we, the news media, will have failed by not keeping people's feet to the fire."[7]

Identifying the holes and distortions of post-Katrina coverage, and explaining the lack of a meaningful public discourse of the storm's aftermath, requires that we look back at the initial coverage of the event. This first draft of history set the tone, directing media down a path difficult to alter, following a selection of themes seemingly impossible to change.

THE FIRST DRAFT OF THE DISASTER: DEMONIZING THE VICTIMS

Academic researchers and media critics alike have demonstrated that news reports from New Orleans in the immediate aftermath of the storm were dominated by themes of anarchy and chaos and by stories of looting in which the residents, particularly poor African Americans, were portrayed as criminals and worse. Consider this *Washington Post* report on August 31, 2005: "Even as the floodwaters rose, looters roamed the city, sacking department stores and grocery stories and floating their spoils away in plastic garbage cans. . . . In drier areas, looters raced into smashed stores and pharmacies and by nightfall the pillage was widespread."[8] By September 3, Maureen Dowd of the *New*

York Times concluded that New Orleans was "a snake pit of anarchy, death, looting, raping, marauding thugs."[9] Who can forget the news images, which are now available on the internet, of people waist deep in water trying to negotiate supplies that are floating in large garbage bags? Under the pictures of white people the caption explains they are "finding supplies," while under images of African Americans the caption identifies them as "looters."

Writing in *The Annals of the American Academy of Political and Social Science*, Kathleen Tierney, Christine Bevc, and Erica Kuligowski argued that reporting conformed to the conventions of a "disaster myth," a predictable media frame in which a crisis is habitually "accompanied by looting, social disorganization, and deviant behavior." The researchers attributed this mythic understanding to past news reporting of crisis, pointing out that in covering the storm "the media greatly exaggerated the incidence and severity of looting and lawlessness."[10] Author Rebecca Solnit, who writes about humanitarian crisis and media response to disaster, reported, "Many major media outlets repeated rumors of snipers firing on helicopters. These rumors were never substantiated, but they interfered with the rescue operations nonetheless."[11]

Portrayals of the city's residents going berserk—mostly African Americans who did not have the means to leave the city—coincided with punitive disaster responses from the authorities. Mayor Ray Nagin ordered 1,500 police officers to leave their search-and-rescue missions and return to the city streets to stop the looting. As Solnit put it:

> Only two days after the catastrophe struck, while thousands were still stuck on roofs, in attics, on overpasses, on second and third stories and in isolated buildings on high ground in flooded neighborhoods, the mayor chose protecting property over human life. There was no commerce, no electricity, no way to buy badly needed supplies. Though unnecessary things were taken, much of what got called looting was the stranded foraging for survival by the only means available.[12]

DIVERGENT FRAMES OF THE ALTERNATIVE AND MAINSTREAM PRESS

Though initial media narratives demonized the victims of the storm, these portrayals have since been challenged and revised in films by Spike Lee[13] and others, such as investigative reporter Jeremy Scahill and the producers of PBS's Frontline,[14] which feature other themes and points of view. In 2008, for example, journalist A. C. Thompson[15] recounted the story of thirty-two-year-old Donnell Herrington, who had stayed behind to help rescue his grandparents and was shot by vigilantes in the white enclave of Algiers Point.

Less than a year after Katrina, while other independent reporters were tracking stories of white vigilantes and police murders in the wake of the storm, the *New York Times* was missing the story, instead sticking to the familiar "law and order" framework of "disaster reporting" that emphasized the need for police response to the violence caused by the poor.[16] Reporter Christopher Drew followed law enforcement and found that New Orleans Police Department's SWAT team, known as "The Final Option," was "running dangerously low on firepower." Hitting old themes that Katrina helped wash away a violent underclass, Drew wrote, "As residents return, [the team] is once again kicking in the doors at the worst drug dens," for the new superintendent William J. Riley was not going to let the drug dealers and "gutter punks" take over. Drew explained that cops were bearing the brunt of "displaced anger" from citizens who "talk back."

Similar themes with rhetorical flourishes appeared six months later in Adam Nossiter's *New York Times* article "Storm Left New Orleans Ripe for Violence."[17] After Katrina, the city was a "stalking ground" where "teenagers with handguns" roamed with "impunity." Kids returned with guns in a "tidal wave of violence." Though they "begged" witnesses to come forward, "the police, feared and hated by the city's poor, [got] no cooperation from them in solving crimes." No explanation for the public's fear of the cops was offered. In another caricature, Nossiter wrote, it's "the classic Maoist strategy of guerilla insurgency: criminals swim like fish in the surrounding sea" of poor neighborhoods. Abstracted poor people, "fish," are criminalized, lumped with the perpetrators.

At the end of 2006 and into 2007, the time frame depicted in season two of *Treme*, there was, in fact, a heartbreaking resurgence of violence that shook the Big Easy, and the depictions in the fictional program are far more complex and balanced than those in the *New York Times*, for example. *Treme* shows the violence and its consequences from a very different point of view: from the victims experiencing the violence, the multiracial cast of characters. In post-Katrina New Orleans, bad things happen to good people who do not deserve it, such as the sexual assault of LaDonna Batiste-Williams (played by Khandi Alexander) in episode 3. In *Treme* we feel the pain of characters we have come to care about; African American men, usually stereotyped in news reports as simply criminal, are cast as musicians and also fall victim to the violence perpetrated by criminals as well as police.

Treme depicts the shooting deaths of two artists in NOLA at the time, Dinerral Shavers, a local high school teacher and Hot 8 Brass Band drummer, and filmmaker Helen Hill at her home in the Marigny-Bywater. The program dramatizes a botched police investigation of the Hill murder, illustrating the sloppy police work that failed to protect residents and prosecute criminals. These real people and real murders were so troubling to New Orleans residents and their impressions of the viability of the city's culture that on January 11, 2007, residents organized a March for Survival, five thousand marchers strong. Civil rights attorney Mary Howell—upon whom the character Toni Bernette (played by Melissa Leo) is based—said, "It was a unity march that included a broad, diverse cross section of New Orleanians."[18] They demanded that the police and city officials do their jobs and keep the public safe. *The New York Times* allotted 604 words to the march, claiming that most marchers were white, describing a "monochrome crowd" and an "unpromising augury for any possible resolution of the city's crime crisis."[19] Why? Because of poor black people: "Law enforcement officials have for years spoken of mute circles of witnesses around crime scenes in largely African American neighborhoods here."[20]

In *Treme*, the unity march begins with Antoine Batiste (played by New Orleans local Wendell Pierce) and his girlfriend Desiree (played by another New Orleans resident, Phyllis Montana-LeBlanc), with other musicians at the front of the line that begins in the poor, African

American neighborhood of Center City. They come together with marchers from other neighborhoods and walk on chanting as police stand mute on the sidelines. In the last scene, LaDonna, in emotional recovery with her face still bruised from the attack, watches on television.

The program criticizes the focus on crime in news coverage through the character of NOPD Lieutenant Terry Colson (played by David Morse). Early in the second season, Colson argues over the phone with a *New York Times* reporter, saying that the "crime could have happened in any city; it wasn't particular to NOLA, the guy was a disturbed Iraq war vet."

REPEATING THE "CULTURE OF VIOLENCE"

The March for Survival and community activism did nothing to shake the *New York Times* framework of "culture of violence." Less than a month after the march, Nossiter and Drew teamed up to produce their longest tome yet, a full 2,354 words: "In New Orleans, Dysfunction Fuels Cycle of Killing." It began with two boys watching a body carried out of their building, boys who do "not stop chewing their sticky blue candy or swigging from their pop bottles," while a teenage girl is "laughing up on a worn stoop." Police have said that evacuees from Katrina have been involved in many killings, and "successive killings became easier, once the first was accomplished." The implication is that even arrest and convictions won't stop the murder, that they can't break the cycle of violence. Nossiter and Drew quoted prosecutor Eric E. Malveau—"You can put a cop on every corner, and you will not stop the murder"—and concluded that "the killing is integrated deep into the community."[21]

DEMOLISHING LOW-INCOME HOUSING WITH 12,000 HOMELESS IN NOLA

The blanket condemnations of the poor as violent and deviant, evident in the rhetorical spin of such reporting, helped justify the demolition of four low-income housing projects in New Orleans, and fed into the racial coding that identified "revitalization" of the city as synonymous with preventing the "undeserving" poor from finding their way home.

These issues are documented in Spike Lee's film *If God Is Willing and Da Creek Don't Rise*. Sequences contain footage of the former secretary of the US Department of Housing and Urban Development (HUD), Republican Alphonso Jackson, arguing to "get rid of these drug-infested killing field environments," and claiming that anyone who wants to keep the low-income housing "really doesn't care about people having sanitary places to live."[22]

But as *In These Times* reported, it took over $700 million to demolish the public housing, and the cost of new "mixed-income" housing was over $400 million for each unit.[23] Insurance estimates have shown that it would have cost less than $10,000 per building to repair the low-income projects, most of which had never flooded. Later forced to resign from office because of corruption in managing post-Katrina contracts, Alphonso Jackson publicly stated in September 2005 that New Orleans was "not going to be as black as it was for a long time, if ever again." He later said, in front of Spike Lee's cameras, in an attempt to use his own skin color to deflect attention from his racist remarks, "When I woke up this morning, I was still black." The second season of *Treme* portrays the process of corruption of local politicians as well as the demolition and destruction of undamaged property.

Treme's portrait of the character Albert Lambreaux (played by Clarke Peters) follows his struggles to rebuild his destroyed house and the problems he faces finding a place to stay when he returns after the flood. At one point he illegally enters a vacant but habitable apartment in one of the housing projects. After several days, and under cover of night, cops enter the apartment, beat him, and forcibly remove him from the building. Similarly, *If God Is Willing and Da Creek Don't Rise* contains disturbing footage of police pepper spraying New Orleans residents who are trying to enter the city council to protest the destruction of the projects. Inside the council chambers, those trying to speak to politicians are seen being brutally tasered by New Orleans police.

THE FAUBOURG TREME AND GENTRIFICATION

The television series derives its name from the oldest inhabited African American neighborhood in the country, the Faubourg Treme, where free people of color owned property as early as the 1700s. At its center in Congo Square, African slaves drummed and danced, and American jazz was born.

In early episodes of the series, a belligerent DJ Davis (played by Steve Zahn) directs huge speakers that blast loud music onto the streets of Treme. They seem particularly targeted at his closest neighbors, a gay couple, a pair Davis perceives as outsiders to the culture and history of the Treme. Reasons for the hostility emerge slowly, as one of the threads subtly woven through the texture of the program. This thread is gentrification, a process that has taken its toll on the culture of the real-life neighborhood, especially damaging to the spontaneity that lies at the heart of jazz culture.

An October 2007 piece by *Times-Picayune* staff reporter Katy Reckdahl titled "Culture, Change Collide in Treme" offers some explanation, with a story about police breaking up a funeral parade in honor of tuba player Kerwin James, who died of complications from a stroke suffered after Katrina. As the second line made its way along a traditional route in Treme, about twenty police cars stormed the procession and grabbed local musicians, taking two away in handcuffs. Residents complained of the "over-reaction and disproportionate enforcement by police." Others called it "a sign of a greater attack on the cultural history of the old city neighborhood by well-heeled newcomers attracted to Treme by the very history they seem to threaten."[24]

After Katrina, as well-heeled newcomers moved into Treme, they often complained about the noise when musicians took to the streets spontaneously. When Davis blasts his speakers into the neighborhood, it is to protest this changing composition in the neighborhood. The conflict is resolved amicably in *Treme*, at a party at Davis's house when his neighbor admits and apologizes for calling the police about the loud music.

MUSIC AND MARDI GRAS INDIANS

"Music is a character in the show," said jazz musician Donald Harrison Jr.[25] Harrison, like his father before him, is a Mardi Gras Indian Chief, and the characters of Albert Lambreaux and his son Delmond (played by Rob Brown) are loosely based on them. During Super Sunday, when the Indians parade, New Orleans comes alive with drumming and chanting men in stunning feathered suits. The tradition, taking place close to St. Joseph's Night, is an African American homage to Native Americans who in the antebellum era sheltered runaway slaves in the surrounding bayous.

Treme's season one finale represents an important moment in the history of the Mardi Gras Indians and references the long tradition of police violence toward them. Two months before the levees breached in the wake of Katrina, "Big Chief Tootie" Montana, a man who "masked Indian" for longer than anyone else in New Orleans, appealed for an end to police violence and gave testimony about the police brutality that Indian tribes had endured over the years. He recounted events of St. Joseph's Night in 2005, when police blocked the annual Indian celebration because they didn't have a permit. He died of heart failure on the floor of the council chambers at the age of eighty-two, while testifying about the police violence that erupted in the aftermath.[26]

In the *Treme* episode, Lieutenant Colson pulls up in his patrol car and confronts Lambreaux. An impromptu negotiation takes place in the street in front of the well-known bar Pokes, as both characters appeal for calm and respect from each other's "tribes" in the hopes of avoiding violence between Indians and police. They both acknowledge it is what Chief Tootie would have wanted. The character Big Chief Lambreaux later emerges triumphantly in full regalia on Super Sunday 2006, and encounters Donald Harrison in his actual suit, as Big Chief of Congo Nation. They exchange "respect for respect." It is a moment of calm and reconciliation, as cops do not arrive to harass the Indians. The scene also references one of the most important events in New Orleans in 2006, when Donald Harrison strolled out of St Augustine's into Treme in his stunning new Congo Nation Big Chief suit, offering hope to all assembled that the culture of New Orleans would survive.

DEPARTMENT OF JUSTICE REPORT ON NOPD, MARCH 2011

Between 2006 and 2007, post-Katrina New Orleans reporting was marked by the consistent selection and emphasis on violence by the poor, with the near total exclusion of police violence, corruption, and culpability. In some cases, a mention was made of the past, the bad old days before the police force "modernized." But in a long overdue development, the Department of Justice (DOJ) investigated the NOPD and issued a report in March 2011.

Writing in *New Orleans Magazine*, Allen Johnson Jr. reported that police corruption drew the attention of the DOJ in the early 1990s, when they began moving toward a federal consent decree, which would have allowed the federal government to assume control of NOPD. After the events of September 11, 2001, as terrorism became the national priority, the DOJ ended its intense scrutiny of NOPD, accepting the department's own internal reports on reform. By 2011, the Feds found that NOPD's own oversight of the use of deadly force had been so perfunctory it could not even locate officer-involved shooting investigation files.[27]

The federal investigation uncovered disturbing evidence of "repeated instances" of excessive forces, including deadly force, during which officers "endangered the lives of civilian bystanders." Officers fired at moving vehicles, "yet no one in the chain of command held officers accountable." Police harassed and brutalized African Americans in great numbers.[28] The fictional portrayals in the series *Treme* offer a critical but balanced view of police officers through the sympathetic character of Lieutenant Colson, one more comprehensive than those of the news media. As civil rights attorney Mary Howell told *Extra!*, "For years we've had accusations, now we have findings, let's hope we can find solutions."

CONCLUSION

Testifying before Congress on the crisis of newspapers, *Treme* co-creator and former *Baltimore Sun* journalist David Simon explained that when he was in journalism school in the 1970s, he learned that the challenge of journalism was "to explain an increasingly complex world in ways that made us essential to an increasingly educated readership. The scope of coverage would have to go deeper, address more of the world, not less. Those were our ambitions. Those were my ambitions." He goes on to say that newspapers were not betrayed by the internet. "We had trashed them on our own, years before.

Incredibly, we did it for naked, short-term profits. . . . And now, having made ourselves less essential, less comprehensive, and less able to offer a product that people might purchase online, we pretend to an undeserved martyrdom at the hands of new technology."[29] The stilted, simplistic myths of journalism are not only being replaced by the internet, but now also seemingly by fictional forms more willing to present a complex world to viewers.

The narratives that emerge from events set in motion by the storm of August 2005 will continue to influence our ability to respond humanely to natural and human-influenced disasters alike, both nationally and globally. Reconstructing this story through the eyes of people on the ground, instead of the people behind the guns, affects our ability as a country to conceptualize and plan for future disasters in ways that protect people and their communities. Rejecting the stereotypes of poverty and race, and other forms of rhetorical demonization that lead to further suffering and human destruction, may be one of the most important messages of *Treme*.

ROBIN ANDERSEN, PHD, is a professor of Communication and Media Studies at Fordham University, where she also directs Graduate Studies in Public Communications and the Peace and Justice Studies Program. She is the author of four books and dozens of chapters and journal articles, and writes media criticism for a variety of publications. Her book *A Century of Media, A Century of War* won the Alpha Sigma Nu Book Award in 2007. Her research interests include the ways in which media influence public opinion and social policy, including the links among advertising persuasions, consumer culture, and environmental issues and policies. She has written about the implications of merging news and information with entertainment fictions depicting war and conflict. She co-edited the two-volume reference book *Battleground: The Media* in 2008. Her other books include *Consumer Culture and TV Programming* and the edited anthology *Critical Studies in Media Commercialism* by Oxford University Press. She often serves as a consultant for nonprofit groups, and helped develop curriculum for Fordham University's MA in Humanitarian Action, covering strategic communication design for humanitarian organizations. She is featured in numerous educational documentaries. Her website is http://faculty.fordham.edu/andersen/.

Notes

1. Rebecca Solnit, "Reconstructing the Story of the Storm: Hurricane Katrina at Five," *Nation*, August 26, 2010, http://www.thenation.com/article/154168/reconstructing-story-storm-hurricane-katrina-five.

2. Neil deMause, "Katrina's Vanishing Victims: Media Forget the 'Rediscovered' Poor," *Extra!* July/August 2006, http://www.fair.org/index.php?page=2933.

3. "Erasing Katrina: Four Years On, Media Mostly Neglect an Ongoing Disaster," Fairness & Accuracy In Reporting, September 2, 2009, http://www.fair.org/index.php?page=3891.

4. Lolis Eric Elie, interview by author, March 15, 2011.

5. For more information, see Tom Piazza, *Why New Orleans Matters* (New York: Harper, 2005).

6. Eric Overmyer, interview by author, April 21, 2011.

7. Julie Hollar, "Brian Williams Rehashes Katrina Violence Myth," Fairness & Accuracy In Reporting, August 25, 2010, http://www.fair.org/blog/2010/08/25/dateline-rehashs-katrina-violence-myth/.

8. Gugliotta and Whoriskey, quoted in Kathleen Tierney, Christine Bevc, and Erica Kuligowski, "Metaphors Matter: Disaster Myths, Media Frames, and Their Consequences in Hurricane Katrina," *Annals of the American Academy of Political and Social Science* 604, no. 1 (March 2006): 57–81, doi: 10.1177/0002716205285589.

9. Maureen Dowd, "United States of Shame," *New York Times*, September 3, 2005, http://www.nytimes.com/2005/09/03/opinion/03dowd.html.

10. Kathleen Tierney, Christine Bevc, and Erica Kuligowski, "Metaphors Matter."

11. Rebecca Solnit, "Reconstructing the Story of the Storm."

12. Ibid.

13. See Spike Lee, dir., *If God Is Willing and Da Creek Don't Rise*, 40 Acres and a Mule Filmworks, 2010.

14. Thomas Jennings, dir., *Law & Disorder*, documentary (Public Broadcasting Service, 2010), http://www.pbs.org/wgbh/pages/frontline/law-disorder/.

15. A. C. Thompson, "Katrina's Hidden Race War," *Nation*, December 17, 2008, http://www.thenation.com/article/katrinas-hidden-race-war.

16. Christopher Drew, "Police Struggles in New Orleans Raise Old Fears," *New York Times*, June 13, 2006, http://www.nytimes.com/2006/06/13/us/13orleans.html.

17. Adam Nossiter, "Storm Left New Orleans Ripe for Violence," *New York Times*, January 11, 2007, http://www.nytimes.com/2007/01/11/us/11orleans.html.

18. Mary Howell, interview by author, May 4, 2011.

19. Adam Nossiter, "In Downtown New Orleans, Thousand March Against Killings," *New York Times*, January 12, 2007, http://www.nytimes.com/2007/01/12/us/12orleans.html.

20. Ibid.

21. Christopher Drew and Nossiter, "In New Orleans, Dysfunction Fuels Cycle of Killing," *New York Times*, February 5, 2007, http://www.nytimes.com/2007/02/05/us/05crime.html.

22. Spike Lee, dir., *If God Is Willing*.

23. Lewis Wallace, "First Came Katrina, Then Came HUD," *In These Times*, January 16, 2008, http://www.inthesetimes.com/main/article/3504/.

24. Katy Reckdahl, "Culture, Change Collide in Treme," *A Katrina Reader*, October 2, 2007, http://katrinareader.org/culture-change-collide-treme.

25. Donald Harrison Jr., interview by author, April 21, 2011.

26. For more information, see Lisa Katzman, prod. and dir., *Tootie's Last Suit*, DVD, 92 min. (2007).

27. Allen Johnson Jr., "What the Studies Said," *New Orleans Magazine*, May 2011, http://www.myneworleans.com/New-Orleans-Magazine/May-2011/WHAT-THE STUDIES-SAID/.

28. Ibid.

29. David Simon, "David Simon's Testimony at the Future of Journalism Hearing," Real Clear Politics, May 9, 2009, http://www.realclearpolitics.com/articles/2009/05/09/david_simon_testimony_at_the_future_of_journalism_hearing_96415.html.

CHAPTER 15

Single Payer Singled Out
Corporate Control of the Message in US Health Reform

by Margaret Flowers

In late 2008, with the election of President Barack Obama, single-payer health system proponents expected that there would follow an honest discussion of the fundamental causes of the health care crisis and an opportunity to debate the merits of single payer during the national health reform process. Instead efforts were made—with the cooperation of the White House, Congress, and the United States corporate media—to exclude single-payer advocates, and to portray single payer mainly in a negative light. Through these institutions, industries that profited from the status quo were able to shape the public discourse in a way that distracted from the real health crisis and instead focused on perceived crises, or attempted to discredit single-payer systems such as Medicare and those in other industrialized nations. In comparison, the international media was more balanced in their coverage of health reform in the United States with inclusion of single-payer experts and single-payer activism.

Despite decades of intentional misinformation about single payer systems in the corporate media, the majority of people in the United States have demonstrated consistent support for national single-payer health insurance in both citizen juries and independent polls since the early 1990s. Support in polls conducted by groups such as ABC, NBC, AP-Yahoo and the Kaiser Family Foundation ranges from a low of 50 percent to a high of 69 percent for the general population.[1] Data shows that the more information is provided describing a single-payer health system, the higher the support.[2] And if polling results are assessed by political affiliation, we see that support among Democrats is even higher than the general public, with 81 percent of Democrats in 2008 believing that the government has a responsibility to make sure that everyone has adequate health care.[3] In fact, 70 percent of Democrats polled said that our country would be better off with "socialized medicine."[4] And physicians, once opponents of health care reform, are showing increasing support for single payer. National polls of physicians across most practice specialties found a 10 percent increase in support from 49 percent in 2002 to 59 percent support in 2007, with higher levels in the fields of primary care and psychiatry.[5]

Given the broad support for single payer, especially among the Democratic base, one would expect that under a Democratic White House and Congress, single payer would at least be considered in the health care debate. However, quite to the contrary, the debate was highly scripted to lead the public to a preconceived idea of health care reform outlined by Jacob Hacker, a fellow at the New America Foundation,[6] and single payer was actively excluded. Though the debate was directed by the White House and congressional leadership, the corporate media and other allies in Washington, such as the Center for American Progress and other "progressive" organizations, followed the script with rare deviation. It was recently discovered that Jim Messina, deputy chief of staff for operations for President Obama, held regular meetings with heads of progressive organizations during the health reform process to instruct them in conveying their messages consistent with policy supported by the White House.[7]

The call for public input into the reform process in early December 2008 demonstrated the degree of scripting that occurred. Americans were encouraged to hold health care house parties in which they invited friends to participate in discussions using materials created by the Obama campaign. Though former Senator Tom Daschle, then the point person on health, said, "These Health Care Community Discussions are a great way for the American people to have a direct say in our health reform efforts," the prepared materials led the participants down a specific path that concluded that Americans wanted health insurance exchanges—i.e. a centralized way to shop for plans from different insurance providers.[8] The final report on the community discussions contained a single small paragraph that stated, "Supporters of a single-payer system submitted numerous reports, in part due to the encouragement by advocacy groups to participate in Health Care Community Discussions."[9] Not only did the report fail to adequately portray the majority support for single payer, but it also discounted any support for single payer as being driven primarily by the urging of advocacy organizations.

As in the 1990s, during the recent health reform process the relationship among corporate media, industry lobbyists, and the White House was quite cozy. This was exposed in the summer of 2009 with the discovery that Katharine Weymouth, publisher of the *Washington Post*, was issuing invitations for the three entities to meet for a "salon" in her home at the price of $50,000 per event.[10] Similar meetings have been arranged by other corporate media outlets such as the *Wall Street Journal* and the *Los Angeles Times*. Industry influence on the media also takes the form of "interlocking directorates" in which board members of large corporations sit on the boards of media outlets as well.[11]

It is then no surprise that a study looking at the early months of 2009 showed little mention of single payer, with the views of single-payer advocates were rarely included. In the week leading up to the first White House Health Summit, there were hundreds of stories about health care reform in both major newspapers and on television outlets. Single payer was mentioned only eighteen times and single-payer advocates were quoted in only five interviews.[12] In that same time period, T. R. Reid quit Frontline over the public affairs series' limited coverage of alternative reforms for the US in their hour-long documentary called *Sick Around America*, a follow-up to Reid's previous *Sick Around the World*.[13] Frontline only offered the Massachusetts health reform as a model in the US. Not surprisingly, this was the same model being used for the Obama administration's preferred health reform.

Another obvious example of exclusion of single payer was ABC News' White House Health Forum in June 2009. President Obama's personal physician of twenty-two years, Dr. David Scheiner of Chicago, was invited to participate in the forum. One week prior to the forum, Dr. Scheiner was interviewed by *Forbes* magazine.[14] He criticized the president's plan and instead advocated for a Medicare for all approach. Dr. Scheiner was subsequently disinvited from the White House forum.

When single-payer health reform was discussed in the corporate media, most often the coverage was negative. Certain key phrases were used repeatedly to describe single payer such as "socialized medicine" or "government-run" medicine. The messaging was so successful that some senior citizens in the August 2009 town hall meetings held signs protesting government-run health care without realizing that their very own Medicare was government-run. An extreme example of this was a September 2009 article in the *New York Times* by Katharine Q. Seelye, "Medicare for All? 'Crazy,' 'Socialized' and Unlikely."[15] Corporate media focused on the flaws in Medicare such as the low reimbursement to physicians, which occurs in some areas of the country, and the fact that Medicare and single payer are financed through taxes. *The New York Times* article quoted an economist who directs a managed-care company and a fellow from the Heritage Foundation, who both falsely stated that the tax increase under a single-payer system would be a financial burden. *The Times* mentioned only parenthetically that single-payer advocates argue that the tax increase would be neutralized by decreased out-of-pocket expenses and lack of premiums.

Another technique employed to sway public opinion against single payer was the sensationalism of certain medical cases from Canada and the United Kingdom. Shona Holmes, a Canadian citizen, received extensive media coverage in the summer of 2009. She was portrayed as having a brain tumor and as having to wait for so long to receive treatment in Canada that she sought care at the Mayo Clinic instead.[16] In truth, she had a benign congenital cyst in her brain, which is very different from a cancerous tumor, but this distinction was not made in the media.[17] *Investor's Business Daily* published an article in August 2009 claiming that people with disabilities such as Stephen Hawking "wouldn't have a chance in the UK, where the National Health Service would say the life of this brilliant man, because of his physical handicaps, is essentially worthless."[18] They failed to realize that Hawking has received quality health care from the British NHS for his entire life.

Corporate media also employed specific messaging to distract from the real crisis. Wendell Potter discussed this health insurance industry practice in his recent book, *Deadly Spin: An Insurance Insider Speaks Out on How Corporate PR is Killing Health Care and Deceiving Americans*. He described how, rather than focus on the growing number of uninsured, citizens have been told that many of the uninsured are undocumented people or "young invincibles" who choose not to buy insurance. And rather than focus on the growing number of underinsured and the resulting personal bankruptcies, we have been told that health care consumers need to take more personal responsibility and have more "skin in the game" so that they can make wise decisions about how to spend their health care dollars. The soaring cost of health care has been blamed on the American love for technology, people overusing health care services, hospitals and physicians pushing procedures, and the aging baby boomer population. That much of the US population delays or avoids necessary care altogether because of out-of-pocket costs, which leads to a high number of preventable deaths, and that health care costs in the private sector rise much more rapidly than in the public sector, has been ignored. And finally, Wendell discussed how our crisis was frequently blamed on the need for tort reform despite the fact that malpractice costs are a small percentage of our overall health care costs and tort reform has not been proven to reduce health care costs or improve health outcomes.[19]

As a result of the exclusion of single payer, advocates sometimes went to great lengths for media coverage. In May 2009, thirteen people (including this author) were arrested at two Senate Committee on Finance health reform hearings. These events received some coverage because they took place while C-SPAN cameras were covering the hearings live. In fall 2009, national days of protest at health insurance offices were organized through a campaign called the Mobilization for Health Care For All. Over one thousand people signed up to risk arrest in order to spread the improved Medicare for All message. Days of action included up to two dozen protests across the country, including one action during which protesters were locked overnight in the lobby of Humana in Louisville, Kentucky, without access to bathrooms, food, or water.[20] Doctors were present at many of these actions and several were arrested. Despite this, there was only minimal coverage by local news stations. On two occasions, national networks agreed to cover the protests, but the story was bumped both times, first by the "Balloon Boy" hoax in October, then by the shooting at Fort Hood in November.

A common excuse for the lack of coverage during the health reform process was that the national media accepted the idea, perhaps prematurely, that single payer was no longer on the table as an option. Single-payer advocates who organized public educational events and rallies for single-payer systems heard this repeatedly when they sought media coverage. Due to public pressure over the lack of coverage of single payer by National Public Radio, the ombudsman was forced to address the issue.[21] "This issue is not getting a lot of attention from NPR because it's simply not on the table in Congress," said Julie Rovner, NPR's lead reporter covering the health care overhaul. In other words, NPR was only willing to cover what Congress would consider rather than what the majority of the public desired.

When single-payer events were covered by major television outlets, it was primarily Fox News and international media. Russia TV, Catalunya TV, Real News Network (Canada), Al Jazeera English, Atlantic Television News (Denmark), and Swedish Television interviewed single-payer advocates repeatedly and covered rallies in and around Washington, DC, throughout the health reform process of 2009–10. Al Jazeera English produced a full *Fault Lines* episode on the reform process that included a broad range of views, from single-payer advocates to health insurance industry lobbyists.[22] In contrast, the Frontline documentary *Obama's Deal*, released shortly after the health reform law passed in March 2010, edited out references to single payer in an interview with this author.[23]

Media coverage of American health care is very different in the European news, where industry influence does not reach. European media frequently highlight the high number of uninsured people in the United States and the suffering that occurs as a result.[24] When the health reform law was passed, French press hailed the US entry into the twentieth (not twenty-first) century. And while there was little mention in the US corporate media of industry influence over our politicians, this fact was not missed in European media.[25] The British medical journal the *Lancet* featured this quote on the cover of the December 2009 issue: "The health-care reform process exposes how corporate influence renders the US Government incapable of making policy on the basis of evidence and the public interest."[26]

The medical-industrial complex succeeded this time in shaping public discourse and the political process to its advantage. The new health law mandates the purchase of insurance, providing hundreds of billions of public dollars to the insurance industry to subsidize this purchase. The losers are the people of the United States, as we continue to live in the only industrialized nation that does not have a universal health system. Under the new law, the current trend away from employer-sponsored insurance and toward individual consumer-driven (underinsurance) health plans is expected to continue, and personal bankruptcy due to medical costs will continue to occur. Tens of millions of people, who are either exempt from the insurance mandate or undocumented, will remain uninsured.[27] None of this would occur in a single-payer national health system. Thus, the prevention of an honest debate about the health care crisis and the benefits of the single-payer option come at a very human cost: the unacceptable continuation of human suffering and countless preventable deaths.

MARGARET FLOWERS, MD, is a Maryland pediatrician who serves as Congressional Fellow for Physicians for a National Health Program and sits on the board of Healthcare-NOW!

Notes

1. Kip Sullivan, "Two-Thirds of Americans Support Medicare for All," report, Physicians for a National Health Program, 5, http://www.pnhp.org/sites/default/files/docs/2011/Kip-Sullivan-Two-thirds-support-medicare-for-all.pdf.
2. Ibid.
3. Douglas Schwartz, "Quinnipiac University Poll," May 8–12, 2008, http://www.pnhp.org/campaign/materials/AP%20polling%20is%20quite%20clear.pdf.
4. Robert Blendon et al., "Poll Finds Americans Split by Political Party over Whether Socialized Medicine Better or Worse than Current System," press release, Harvard University School of Public Health, http://www.hsph.harvard.edu/news/press-releases/2008-releases/poll-americans-split-by-political-party-over-socialized-medicine.html.
5. Aaron E. Carroll and Ronald T. Ackermann, "Support for National Health Insurance among American Physicians: Five Years Later," *Annals of Internal Medicine* 148, no. 7 (2008): 566–67.
6. Jacob Hacker, "Reform Beyond Access: A Plan to Extend Medicare that Would Also Limit Costs, Improve Quality," New America Foundation, February 13, 2007, http://newamerica.net/publications/articles/2007/reform_beyond_access_4877.
7. Ari Berman, "Jim Messina, Obama's enforcer," *Nation*, April 18, 2011, http://www.thenation.com/article/159577/jim-messina-obamas-enforcer.
8. Ceci Connelly, "Obama Asks Nation to Discuss Health-Care Reform and Provide Input," *Washington Post*, December 6, 2008, http://www.washingtonpost.com/wp-dyn/content/article/2008/12/05/AR2008120503322.html.
9. "Americans Speak on Health Reform: Report on Health Care Community Discussions," US Department of Health and Human Services, March 2009, 69, http://www.healthreform.gov/reports/hccd/report_on_communitydiscussions.pdf.
10. John Geyman, *Hijacked: The Road to Single Payer in the Aftermath of Stolen Health Care Reform* (Monroe, ME: Common Courage Press, 2010), 92–93.

11. Kate Murphy, "Single Payer and Interlocking Directorates: The Corporate Ties Between Insurers and Media Companies," *Extra!*, August 2009, http://www.fair.org/index.php?page=3845.

12. "Media Blackout on Single-Payer Healthcare: Proponents of Popular Policy Shut Out of Debate," study, Fairness & Accuracy In Reporting, March 6, 2009, http://www.fair.org/index.php?page=3733.

13. "Frontline Responds on Sick Around America," Fairness & Accuracy In Reporting, April 9, 2009, http://www.fair.org/index.php?page=3757.

14. Jim Acosta, "Obama's Former Doctor Critical of White House Health Care Plan," CNN, Politics, July 30, 2009, http://articles.cnn.com/2009-07-30/politics/obama.doctor_1_single-payer-health-care-public-option?_s=PM:POLITICS.

15. "NYT Slams Single-Payer: Fails to include advocates among 'diverse' experts," Fairness & Accuracy In Reporting, September 22, 2009, http://www.fair.org/index.php?page=3907.

16. Dana Bash and Lesa Jansen, "Reality Check: Canada's government health care system," CNN, Politics, July 6, 2009, http://articles.cnn.com/2009-07-06/politics/canadian.health.care.system_1_government-run-health-health-care-system-mayo-clinic?_s=PM:POLITICS.

17. Heather, "Reality Check on Shona Holmes: Holmes' 'brain tumour' was actually a Rathke's cleft cyst on her pituitary gland," Crooks and Liars, July 27, 2009, http://videocafe.crooksandliars.com/heather/reality-check-shona-holmes-holmes-brain-tu.

18. Rachel Weiner, "Stephen Hawking Enters US Health Care Debate," *Huffington Post*, August 12, 2009, http://www.huffingtonpost.com/2009/08/12/stephen-hawking-enters-us_n_257343.html.

19. Wendell Potter, *Deadly Spin: An Insurance Company Insider Speaks Out on How Corporate PR Is Killing Health Care and Deceiving Americans* (New York: Bloomsbury Press, 2010), 110.

20. Gabe Bullard, "Demonstrators Sit In at Humana," WFPL News, October 29, 2009, http://www.wfpl.org/2009/10/29/demonstrators-sit-in-at-humana/.

21. Alicia C. Shepard, "Is NPR Ignoring the Single-Payer Health Care Proposal?" National Public Radio, Ombudsman, July 17, 2009, http://www.npr.org/blogs/ombudsman/2009/07/is_npr_ignoring_the_singlepaye_1.html.

22. Avi Lewis, "Healthcare Reform," *Fault Lines*, Al Jazeera English, August 6, 2009, http://english.aljazeera.net/programmes/faultlines/2009/08/20098663722846685.html.

23. Michael Getler, "Single Minded About Single Payer," Public Broadcasting Service, Ombudsman, April 23, 2010, http://www.pbs.org/ombudsman/2010/04/singleminded_about_singlepayer.html.

24. Vivienne Walt, "E.U. Gloats Over Belated U.S. Health Care Reform," *Time*, March 23, 2010, http://www.time.com/time/world/article/0,8599,1974424,00.html.

25. Daniel Ward, "The Money Taboo in Health Reform Coverage: Industry donations to powerful players often go unmentioned," *Extra!*, November 2009, http://www.fair.org/index.php?page=3935.

26. *The Lancet* 374, no. 9705 (December 5, 2009).

27. "Pro-single-payer doctors: Health bill leaves 23 million uninsured," statement, Physicians for a National Health Program, March 22, 2010, http://www.pnhp.org/news/2010/march/pro-single-payer-doctors-health-bill-leaves-23-million-uninsured.

CHAPTER 16

Censorship of the True State of Maternity Care in the US

by Ina May Gaskin, MA, CPM, PhD (Hon.)

The myth that we have the greatest maternity care in the world pervades most media coverage of birth issues. If you get your news from the mainstream media, it will probably surprise you that, according to the Centers for Disease Control (CDC), women in the United States today face more than twice the chance of dying from causes directly related to pregnancy and birth than their mothers did.

US BIRTH STATISTICS AND THE NEED FOR FEEDBACK

In some states, the maternal death rate has more than doubled what it was years earlier. For instance, in 2010, California reported a tripling of the death rate between 1996 and 2006, attributing a significant part of the sudden rise to an excess of cesarean sections (C-sections).[1] New York State's report in 2011 was no better: the maternal death rate between 2005 and 2007 was an unacceptably high 16.6 deaths per 100,000 births, when according to the US Department of Health and Human Services, that rate should not exceed 4. For African American women in New York City in 2008, the rate was an incredible 79 per 100,000 births. The leading cause of death in the state was pulmonary embolism, a complication whose incidence rises significantly after C-section or prolonged bed rest.[2] Neither of these startling state reports received national news coverage.

In the US today, one in three babies is born surgically, despite the World Health Organization's recommendation that rates not exceed 10 percent in hospitals serving the general population, or 15 percent in hospitals serving high-risk cases. C-section rates in some US cities are rapidly moving in the direction taken by Brazil, South Korea, Thailand, and Chile, where rates in private hospitals exceed 90 percent of all births. When this happens, the profession of obstetrics is essentially eliminated, along with that of midwifery, and replaced with surgery, with drastically negative results for women and their babies. When C-section rates are too low, women and babies will pay with their lives, but the same result occurs when C-section rates climb too high. This is a lesson we have yet to learn in the US.

Further, far more babies than ever are born after a host of technological interventions such as induction and the use of pitocin to speed up labor, which bring along their own risks. Amnesty International published a damning report in 2010 titled *Deadly Delivery: The Maternal Health Care Crisis in the USA*, which outlined various failures in the way our health care system treats pregnancy and birth. The facts surrounding the sharply increasing dangers to women giving birth are brutal and shocking, but they cannot be denied. According to a recent report published in the *Lancet*, about forty-one other countries, including Bosnia and Macedonia, do a better job of preventing maternal death and serious maternal disease or injury associated with giving birth than we do in the US, even though every one of these countries spends considerably less on maternity care than we do.[3] We need to ask ourselves why our maternal death rates are increasing while the death rates in most countries of the world are decreasing.

Unfortunately, our health care industry (we gave up calling it a "system" years ago) is woefully ill-equipped to answer this question. California and New York are two states that in recent years have made enhanced efforts to identify maternal deaths that might have been misclassified in the first pass. Additionally, these two states are two of only a handful that have taken steps in recent years to set up statewide systems to review the causes of maternal deaths, in order to determine which deaths could have been prevented with more appropriate care. The reason for conducting such reviews is to find out whether any errors were made in a woman's care, so that lessons can be learned from them and evidence-based recommendations for safer future care can be disseminated.

Unfortunately, most of our states have no such systems of review and analysis, which means that even in cases where a review is done, hospitals are left to investigate themselves. Only six of the fifty states even make it mandatory to report maternal deaths at all. In other words, in almost every state, it is still optional for a hospital to report a pregnancy-related death as such and to enter the accurate cause of death on a death certificate. The result is that our maternal death rates are grossly underreported, and there is good reason to believe that the excessively poor outcomes we've seen in California and New York are happening in other states as well. Due to the lack of media curiosity concerning the question of safety in maternity care, most Americans are ignorant about how drastically inferior our data-gathering of maternal deaths is compared with that of other industrialized countries. The CDC produced its own report card about the shortcomings of our system in 1998, admitting that it's possible that two-thirds of the maternal deaths that actually occur weren't even classified as such.[4]

This much is clear: literally every industrialized country in the world has a better system of counting maternal deaths than ours, because other countries don't allow their various provinces, states, or cantons to each decide what questions (if any) will be asked on their death certificates regarding the prior pregnancy status of a deceased woman. Other industrialized countries have formulated standard methods for identifying maternal deaths—standards that are consistent throughout each country.

Countries that actually try to count every maternal death know that it is often far from obvious when a woman dies from causes related to a pregnancy. This can be the case, for instance, when a woman dies from a ruptured ectopic pregnancy and no autopsy is performed. Another possible scenario is that a woman may die from an infection or a hemorrhage after hospital release, and the cause of her death may not be recognized as related to her pregnancy because most medical records are still not computerized in the US. A suicide due to postpartum psychosis may not be classified as a maternal death for similar reasons. It's necessary, therefore, for epidemiologists to widen the field of inquiry beyond the standard information gathered on a death certificate for other demographic groups (such as men, infants, and children), in order to find out whether a woman was pregnant during the year preceding her death. Unfortunately, though, the CDC has never required that the various states use the same death certificate form. This failure to require a single standard has led to a hodge-podge of mismatched data, which has inevitably lowered the quality of US data.

When we attempt to understand what excuse we might have for

allowing such chaos in the most elementary step in data-gathering, it's difficult to pinpoint anything beyond an uncritical allegiance to states' rights. While prioritizing states' rights over public health considerations may not affect the counting of deaths among other demographic groups, when it comes to distinguishing maternal deaths from deaths of women of childbearing age who died from other causes, such sloppiness can make a huge difference in the annual counts that are reported to the CDC. Lower maternal death counts than are real inevitably lead to a false sense of security and increased risk for childbearing women.

Incredibly, when the CDC finally created a US Standard Death Certificate in 2003—its first step toward remedying our system of ascertainment of maternal deaths—with five questions specifically designed to gather the necessary information, it stopped short of *requiring* its use. At this writing, at least one-third of the states have still opted not to adopt the use of the US Standard Death Certificate.[5] Some states stubbornly continue to use their old death certificate forms that do not ask all of the questions recommended by the CDC, while others use death certificates with no questions whatsoever regarding the previous pregnancy status of a deceased woman. Such gradualism in reform does women little good.

The question arises as to why we have so many shortcomings when it comes to dealing with maternal deaths. Is it because we don't put very much value into ensuring maternal safety? Or is it perhaps that we have never found the political will to design a good system? There is quite a lot of literature in English about how such systems of feedback are designed and executed. Our epidemiologists at the CDC attend international conferences and thus have some familiarity with other countries' ways of counting and reviewing maternal deaths. If the reason for our laidback approach to studying maternal deaths is lack of political will, one way to explain this is that there has been literally no media curiosity about the many flaws in maternal death reporting and analysis here. This creates a situation in which virtually no one understands why a highly developed, standardized system is necessary and why it should be federally funded. *New York Times* best-selling author T. R. Reid put his finger on this kind of problem when he wrote, "The US health care system developed without much planning, and without the serious assessment of national values that prompted other nations to create systems for universal care."[6] Reid wasn't focusing on maternal death reporting when he wrote that, but his analysis does a good job of explaining why we have so far neglected to create a feedback system to help make sure that childbearing is as safe as it should be.

We find a useful comparison in the United Kingdom where, for decades, the Confidential Enquiry into Maternal and Child Health (CEMACH) has been publishing a large report titled *Saving Mothers' Lives: Reviewing Maternal Deaths to Make Motherhood Safer* (formerly titled *Why Mothers Die*) every three years. The book details all of the causes of maternal deaths—devoting a chapter to each of the leading causes of maternal deaths in the four countries that make up the UK—and includes narratives of some of the deaths that are related in such a way as to provide lessons of prevention. Confidentiality of hospitals, mothers, and caregivers is preserved. This example of a well-designed feedback system demonstrates at least one reason why the maternal death rate in the UK decreased during the same period that ours increased.[7] How can we know how we are doing if we don't develop a good system of feedback to inform us?

Former supermodel Christy Turlington Burns became an advocate for better global maternity care after a complication following her first child's birth prompted her to study why so many women worldwide die around the time of birth from preventable causes, and to make a new documentary *No Woman, No Cry*. When she began her project, she hadn't expected to learn that the US itself has an unacceptably high rate of maternal deaths. Speaking to Canadian reporters, she told them about how her film covers pregnant women in several parts of the world and added that US statistics on maternal mortality are "quite shocking." Whereas her remarks were well reported in Canada when her film debuted, there was no mainstream coverage of her film's release on our side of the border.[8] Undaunted, Turlington Burns, who is also spearheading the Every Mother Counts campaign, told Canadians that she was hopeful that the Maternal Health Accountability Act, introduced in the House of Representatives in March 2011 by Representative John Conyers of Michigan, will improve the situation.[9] For her hope to be realized, though, it is certain that her efforts will need to receive coverage in the US media.

THE US BIRTH MYTHOLOGY

The primary problem with the mainstream media's treatment of birth issues here is not that the subject of birth and maternity care is entirely avoided but that apparently every potential story in this area must conform to the standard ideological narrative if it is to be published.

Many elements of the preferred narrative emphasize technology. One prevalent belief is that the greater the application of high technology during the birth process and the more drugs used, the better the birth. Another pair of common beliefs is that newborns hardly ever die when they are born in hospitals, and that home birth is dangerous and shouldn't be allowed. (The corollary is that newborn deaths following home births are generally the only ones that will receive mainstream media attention, because people here have learned to assume that hospital-born babies never die, although this is hardly the case.) Other myths include: Breech births are only safe when cesarean sections are done; assisted reproductive technologies do not increase risks for mothers; cesarean sections are safer than vaginal births; and once a cesarean, always a cesarean.

Another narrative thread in the coverage of birth in the mainstream media is that the mother is at fault, or is not to be trusted. When newborns do die in hospitals, there's the widespread belief that their mothers were likely abusing drugs during pregnancy. Other myths include: If mothers or their babies come to harm during the course of pregnancy or labor, it is most likely because the mothers are too old, too fat, or too selfish in seeking their own comfort or "birth experience," at the expense of their babies; the way labor progresses has little to do with how a woman is treated during her labor, and whether or not she feels secure and respected; it is smart, modern, and safe to schedule births, whether by elective cesarean sections or elective inductions.

The above beliefs serve as an integral part of US birth mythology. They are untrue and lack the support of any credible evidence, and yet each is accepted without question by a huge portion of our population. It is remarkable how closely this framework for filtering stories can be applied to a sampling of stories that received national attention during the last decade or so:

A wire service press release noted how much the US

maternal death rate had improved *over the last century*—a story that was released just after the CDC published its 1998 findings about the lack of improvement in maternal death rates over the previous two decades.

A 1998 press release from the American College of Obstetricians and Gynecologists (ACOG) reversed ACOG's previous policy that it was safe for women to have a vaginal birth after a previous cesarean in most cases. Although ACOG implied that the reasons for this 180-degree turn were based on scientific evidence, their position statement provided no evidence to support that claim.[10]

Prevalent reporting of a statement from ACOG reiterated its long-held opposition to home birth while neglecting to supply evidence to support this opinion.[11] National radio, television, and news interviews by a former ACOG president, W. Benson Harer, Jr., advanced the idea that abdominal surgery is safer than natural vaginal delivery, without citing any credible evidence for his view. "For the mother, it reduces the damage to the pelvic structures which would lead to urinary or fecal incontinence," he told the *Boston Globe*. "And, for the [full-term] baby, an elective C-section is probably as safe or maybe even safer than attempting a vaginal delivery."[12] Dr. Robert K. DeMott, chief of staff at Bellin Memorial Hospital, Green Bay, Wisconsin, sharply disagreed with Dr. Harer but did not receive national coverage when he commented: "Patients are being hoodwinked into choosing cesareans by overblown fears of incontinence and other risks associated with trial by labor. Putting it bluntly," DeMott said, "it's unethical to recommend a practice that leads to more patient deaths."[13] Dr. DeMott was referring to an increase in maternal deaths.

A deeply flawed but widely reported Canadian study published in 2000 stated that there was a slight increase in newborn deaths following vaginal breech birth, as compared with cesarean section breech birth. This study caused hundreds, perhaps thousands, of hospitals worldwide to discontinue their policies of allowing vaginal breech delivery,[14] and also suddenly stopped the teaching of breech skills to doctors and midwives in many countries. Unfortunately, too many leading obstetricians failed to remember that there will always be some undiagnosed or rapidly progressing breech births, and that every birth attendant, whether midwife or doctor, should receive breech birth training.

This abandonment of essential breech skills has already put an uncounted number of mothers and babies at risk. Angela Wilburn, a mother of twins who lived in Coon Rapids, Minnesota, was just one of them. She gave birth to the first of her twins in 2005 without a problem, but when her second twin's feet appeared, along with the umbilical cord, her doctor resorted to an emergency cesarean section, apparently unaware that neither the footling breech presentation nor the cord were dangerous to mother or baby in this situation. Ms. Wilburn died from blood loss during the cesarean section.

By 2007, the Dutch Maternal Mortality Committee had already recorded four maternal deaths after elective cesarean section for breech presentation between 2000 and 2002 inclusive. No death after emergency cesarean section for breech presentation was registered during that same period by the committee.[15]

An internationally reported yet highly misleading and much discredited 2010 study—published in the *American Journal of Obstetrics & Gynecology* (AJOG) and now known as the "Wax paper" because of its principal author's name—purported to show that home birth isn't safe for babies. The bundled "meta-analysis" infamously included an already discredited home birth study known as the "Pang study," as well as other studies that included the following scenarios under the banner of "planned homebirth": unplanned sudden births at home and in transit to the hospital, premature sudden births, births following pregnancies for which there was no prenatal care, involuntary home births by mothers in poor health, and other unplanned births without medical assistance. The Wax study also included, as was noted in a letter to the journal, "mistakes in definitions, numerical errors, selective and mistaken inclusion and exclusion of studies, conflation of association and causation, and additional statistical problems," causing many critics to demand the journal publish a full retraction. Critics noted especially the press release advertised data from about 500,000 births, while the text of the study actually stated that the neonatal death rates they used to support their claim were drawn from only 50,000. Incredibly, the Wax study attempted to fluff its credibility by adding a large Dutch study, but then ignored that study in the tabulation of results related to neonatal mortality.[16]

A home breech birth attended by a midwife, which resulted in a newborn death and criminal charges against the midwife, received national coverage.[17] In more than thirty years of close media scrutiny, I cannot remember a mainstream news account of a newborn death from a hospital birth that received national coverage. It's nearly impossible for people to find out that breech babies born in hospitals by C-section sometimes die.

UNDERREPORTED US BIRTH STORIES

Except for the Angela Wilburn death, each of the above stories received wide coverage by well-known media outlets. But during the same period, several rather shocking stories that should have been reported nationally were not; they didn't conform to the acceptable stereotypes that I described earlier in this chapter. Here are some that would have made interesting reading for the general public:

Seven North Carolina obstetricians and an ultrasound technician managed to misdiagnose a false pregnancy in late 2007, something that was only discovered when the woman's abdomen was cut open for a cesarean section. Not one of them seems to have manually checked the accuracy of the diagnosis of pregnancy. This was a case of *pseudocyesis*, or false pregnancy, a condition that is best diagnosed by manual examination. There is reason for concern that neither of the major obstetrics textbooks studied by doctors-in-training today even mention this once well-known phenomenon, which used to be standard information in all obstetrics textbooks. Because an increasing reliance on ultrasound has convinced many medical schools to give up teaching traditional manual skills, women today who have a false pregnancy may have this kind of unnecessary cesarean section.[18]

Two teachers who worked at the same small-town New Jersey school died within two weeks of each other in 2007 after cesarean sections at the same local hospital. Later that year, that hospital was given an award by the Johnson & Johnson corporation for "excellence in maternity care."[19]

Dr. Charles Mahan, a distinguished Florida obstetrician who has long worked to prevent maternal deaths, wrote in a letter to the editor to a Tampa Bay online news site: "Florida's maternal deaths are almost twice the rate of the US rates and going up. From 2001 to 2004 the overall maternal death rate in Florida went from 16 deaths per 100,000 live births to 23 deaths per 100,000. The Healthy People 2010 goal was 3.3 maternal deaths per 100,000 births. Florida's maternal death rate rose from about five times the rate set by the goal in 2001 to seven times that rate in 2003." Despite its importance, no national media reported this information.[20]

An article on a landmark home birth study, published in the *British Medical Journal*, demonstrated the safety of home birth attended by Certified Professional Midwives but was followed with only minimal coverage in the mainstream press.[21]

The deaths of Virginia Njoroge and Tameka McFarquhar, both single mothers who died at home after early release from the hospital, were reported in local media, but did not receive wider media coverage. Each woman had a baby who died of starvation because of the length of time elapsed between their mothers' deaths and the discovery of their bodies. There is no way of knowing how many deaths of this kind take place every year, but these two stories let us know how possible it is, given that postpartum home visits are rarely included in the standard maternity care package offered by hospitals.[22]

Tatia Oden French, her baby Zorah, and Pamela Jean Young Lippert all died because Tatia and Pamela's obstetricians pressured them into taking Cytotec (generic name: misoprostol) to induce labor when their pregnancies continued a week past their estimated due date. Cytotec was approved by the Food and Drug Administration to prevent gastric ulcers in people who are taking lots of aspirin, but the manufacturer warned from the beginning that it should not be used on pregnant women. Unfortunately, this warning did not prevent a large number of obstetricians from using it regularly to induce labor, ultimately killing more than one hundred mothers in the US, according to the Food and Drug Administration, and even more babies. The major media have so far given little mention to the problems that have surfaced with this use of Cytotec.[23]

Amnesty International's damning 2010 report, *Deadly Delivery: The Maternal Health Care Crisis in the USA*, outlined various failures in the way the US health care system treats pregnancy and birth. Despite the worldwide reputation of Amnesty International, this report received surprisingly little national media coverage.

In January 2010, twenty-seven-year-old Amy Lynn Gillespie died of untreated pneumonia. According to the *Pittsburgh Post-Gazette*, she was in jail for "violating the terms of her work release by becoming pregnant." When she complained that she was having trouble breathing and that she was coughing up phlegm, she was denied diagnostic tests. When it was finally recognized that she was suffering from bacterial pneumonia rather than a simple cold, it was too late to save her life (and that of her eighteen-week fetus). This story remained local.

The cruel practice of keeping women prisoners in shackles

during labor seems never to receive national coverage. It should be obvious that a women in labor is not going to escape custody, so the shackling in these cases is apparently being done with the motivation of further punishing the woman (and her baby) for whatever act resulted in her imprisonment.

PROFITING FROM BIRTH

Sadly, US maternity care has come to prioritize ways of profiting from birth over concerns such as doing the best job possible of creating and maintaining a maternity care system that is woman-centered and produces good outcomes. Many Americans tend to forget that for-profit insurance companies are not in business to see that good health care is given. It is worth remembering that it was only when health insurance companies began to deny malpractice coverage to hospitals that allowed doctors to assist vaginal breech deliveries that obstetricians started applying C-sections to virtually all breech births, and medical schools stopped teaching breech delivery.

And the widespread practice of defensive medicine has become so serious that some physicians are beginning to write about their concerns of misplaced priorities in professional journals, a rather startling—and welcome—development. Dr. Annette E. Fineberg, for example, broke from the usual herd mentality in her poignantly titled article "An Obstetrician's Lament," published by *Obstetrics & Gynecology* (a highly influential trendsetter in US obstetrics, as well as in many other countries), in which she stated that choosing hospital birth usually means an obligatory cesarean section for women with breech babies, twins, or previous cesarean section, even in hospitals with good safety records for all of the above situations. She wrote, "Many obstetricians do not have the willingness, time, or skills to provide maternal choices. . . . Our contracting skill set as obstetric providers, as well as the prevailing risk-averse culture among physicians and hospitals, have given support to home birth."[24]

Another editorial in the same issue of *Obstetrics & Gynecology* was just as newsworthy for the departure it represented from standard obstetric opinion over the last century. Its author, Dr. David Hayes, cited the unsatisfactory outcomes of US obstetrics in its present condition and added this ringing declaration:

> Yes, women are increasingly avoiding the medical model of childbirth and the hospital setting for deliveries. They are fully capable of reading and of obtaining good, accurate information. They are well aware that the decisions their obstetricians are making on their behalf often are not supported by the literature and do result in worse outcomes. They do understand the problems endemic in the US obstetrical system. The fact is, 90 percent of births in the US could be accomplished at home, at lower cost, with better outcomes, and with more satisfied moms and babies. . . . We debate the causes, bemoan the rise in cesarean delivery rates, but through it all we are missing a hugely important fact—a fact that is not lost on a generation of intelligent, educated women. Outcomes are better in a home birth attended by a skilled birth attendant than a hospital birth attended by ANY attendant, midwife or obstetrician. Until we admit that basic premise, we will make no progress.[25]

CENSORSHIP OF BIRTH

Self-respecting journalists and editors who are employed in the mainstream media should take a cue from Drs. Fineberg and Hayes, because these two obstetricians are pointing out how so many of their colleagues are limiting real choices for US women. It's time for journalists to break out of the code of censorship that has so greatly added to the fear and confusion that characterize the way that most Americans view birth and maternity care. If the media stop their robot-like incantations of the scariness of birth and do enough homework to examine credible evidence, it's possible that US women will someday have a chance to learn that their bodies are as well designed for birth as those of aardvarks, mice, moose, and elephants.

It is worth noting that at the present time, the only kind of birth footage allowed to air without digital "draping" at the moment of birth is the heavily edited cesarean section. When birth first began to be shown on US television during the nineties, decisions were made in broadcasters' boardrooms that it would be acceptable for people to see an incision made into a woman's abdomen and uterus, and a baby's head pushed through that incision, but not to clearly see a baby emerge from a woman's capable body, from her vagina. This kind of censorship in the service of "modesty" has the effect of teaching the public that the cesarean section is safer and more socially acceptable for mother and baby than a vaginal birth. It also reinforces the notion that the woman's body is something she should be ashamed of. While watching these cesarean "reality" shows, women are never shown how they would feel just after the epidural wears off, or what it would be like for them to be urged to get out of bed as soon as they are able to move (as is necessary to prevent a blood clot).

It has become clear that instead of creating safer births and healthier moms and babies, our overuse of technology has caused a host of problems. My friend Dr. Tadashi Yoshimura, a Japanese obstetrician, talks about how he suddenly became aware of how terrifying standard hospital routines can be to women in labor when he looked at a television monitor showing the face of a laboring woman who was hooked up to various devices and left alone. As he began to substitute routine use of technology with a caring and observant midwife for each woman, he got to see what he termed "the mystic beauty" of a laboring woman who is not frightened and is thus powerful in bringing forth life. I know exactly what he is talking about because I saw that on the face of the first woman I ever observed giving birth. He learned what I learned: that for the most part, nature gets it right in birth when women are healthy. Women's bodies are not lemons. The creator is not a careless mechanic. The same process that has brought hundreds of thousands of years of human beings to earth can continue to do so today. The human species is no more unsuited to give birth than any other of the five thousand or so species of mammals on the planet. We are merely the most confused.

It's high time that we gave common sense and compassion a try in maternity care for a change. If other female mammals were treated the way most US women are during labor, they wouldn't have a very easy time of it either. No matter how much pressure our society may bring upon us to pretend otherwise, pregnancy, labor, and birth produce very powerful changes in women's bodies, psyches, and lives, no matter by which exit route—natural or surgical—babies are born. It follows then that the way birth care is organized and carried out will have a powerful effect on any human society. A society that places a low value on its mothers and the process of birth will suffer an array of negative repercussions for doing so. Even men and women with no interest in parenthood should understand that the right to a positive and safe birth is just as important as the right to choose whether or not to have a child.

It is critical that we examine how the mainstream media has shaped and often distorted our knowledge of our bodies and ourselves, especially in the realm of pregnancy and birth. Women and families should demand that the media report factual information, and that their representations of birth reflect the full scope of women's experiences. This would include the mystic beauty I have witnessed again and again for nearly forty years as the director of the Farm Midwifery Center.

We need to train more midwives with respect for the natural process to provide care for pregnant and laboring women in every part of the US. It would take 150,000 new midwives to reach the midwives-to-physicians ratio that characterizes the industrialized countries that outdo us both in newborn and maternal mortality.

Most of all, we need to disabuse ourselves of the idea that high technology is always better than natural processes, while, at the same time, being fully thankful for those times that technology saves lives. I am eager to work with forward-looking obstetricians such as Drs. Fineberg and Hayes to build, for the first time in the US, the kind of maternity care system that US women and their babies need and deserve. I hope that our voices make it into the nightly news, along with the voices of women who have experienced the beauty and strength of their capable bodies.

Called the "midwife of modern midwifery" by *Salon*, INA MAY GASKIN has practiced for nearly forty years at the internationally lauded Farm Midwifery Center. She is the only midwife for whom an obstetric maneuver has been named (Gaskin maneuver). She is the author of *Spiritual Midwifery* (4th ed., 2000), *Ina May's Guide to Childbirth* (2003), *Ina May's Guide to Breastfeeding* (2009), and *Birth Matters: A Midwife's Manifesta* (2011).

Thanks to VERONICA LIU, CRYSTAL YAKACKI, and MEG HUFF for additional editing and input on this chapter.

Notes

1. Nathanael Johnson, "More Women Dying from Pregnancy Complications; State Holds on to Report," California Watch, February 2, 2010, http://californiawatch.org/health-and-welfare/more-women-dying-pregnancy-complications-state-holds-report.
2. *Trends in Maternal Mortality: 1990 to 2008*, report, World Health Organization, 2010, http:/whqlibdoc.who.int/publications/2010/9789241500265_eng.pdf.
3. Tiffany O'Callaghan, "Making Sense of the New Maternal Mortality Data," *Time*, Healthland, April 16, 2010, http://healthland.time.com/2010/04/16/making-sense-of-the-new-maternal-mortality-data/.
4. "Maternal Mortality—United States, 1982–1996," *Morbidity and Mortality Weekly Report* 47, no. 34 (1998), 705–07, http://www.cdc.gov/mmwr/preview/mmwrhtml/00054602.htm.
5. Donna L. Hoyert, "Maternal Mortality and Related Concepts," US Department of Health and Human Services, *Vital and Health Statistics* 3, no. 33 (2007): 1–13.
6. T. R. Reid, *The Healing of America: A Global Quest for Better, Cheaper, and Fairer Health Care* (New York: Penguin, 2010).
7. *Saving Mothers' Lives: Reviewing Maternal Deaths to Make Motherhood Safer, 2003–2005* (London: CEMACH Publications, 2007).
8. "Christy Turlington Burns Hopeful for Change in US Maternal Health," Canadian Press, May 13, 2011.
9. The Maternal Health Accountability Act of 2011 is HR 894, http://www.house.gov. Its progress may be tracked here: http://www.govtrack.us/congress/bill.xpd?bill=h112-894.
10. "Vaginal Birth after Previous Cesarean Delivery," *ACOG Practice Bulletin* no. 2 (October 1998).
11. "Planned Home Birth," Committee Opinion #476, American College of Obstetricians and Gynecologists, *Obstetrics & Gynecology* (February 2011).
12. Michael Lasalandra, "C-Sections on Demand Are Rising Fast," *Boston Globe*, April 20, 2004.
13. Greg Borzo, "Elective C-Sections Stir Up Controversy," *Ob/Gyn News*, October 1, 2000, http://findarticles.com/p/articles/mi_m0CYD/is_19_35/ai_66931827/.
14. M. E. Hannah et al., "The Term Breech Trial Collaborative Group: Planned Cesarean Section Versus Planned Vaginal Birth for Breech Presentation at Term: A Randomised Multicentre Trial," *The Lancet* 356 (2003): 1375–83.
15. J. M. Schutte et al., "Maternal Deaths After Elective Cesarean Section for Breech Presentation in the Netherlands," *Acta Obstetricia et Gynecologica* 86 (2007): 240–43.
16. Joseph R. Wax et al., "Maternal and Newborn Outcomes in Planned Home Birth Vs. Planned Hospital Births: A Metaanalysis," *American Journal of Obstetrics and Gynecology* (2010), 203–07.
17. Josh White and Susan Kinzie, "Midwife Pleads Guilty to Felonies in Death of Alexandria Newborn," May 5, 2011, *Washington Post*, http://www.washingtonpost.com/local/midwife-pleads-guilty-to-felonies-in-death-of-alexandria-newborn/2011/05/05/AFetRQ2F_story.html.
18. "Doctors Perform C-Section on Non-Pregnant Woman," WTVD, Fayetteville, North Carolina, April 1, 2010. See also Steven G. Gabbe, Jennifer R. Niebyl, and Joe Leigh Simpson, *Obstetrics: Normal & Problem Pregnancies*, 4th ed. (New York: Churchill Livingstone, 2007).
19. Marie McCullough, "Joined in Birth, Death," *Philadelphia Inquirer*, May 10, 2007.

20. Charles Mahan, "Maternal Deaths in Florida a Grave Concern," letter to the editor, June 15, 2007, http://www.itsyourtimes.com.
21. Kenneth C. Johnson and Betty-Anne Daviss, "Outcomes of Planned Home Births with Certified Professional Midwives: Large Prospective Study in North America," *British Medical Journal* 330, no. 7505 (June 2005): 1416–19.
22. John Golden, "Postnatal Problem Ruled to Be Cause of Soldier's Death," *Watertown Daily Times* (March 8, 2005). See also http://www.kpho.com/news/23995023/detail.html.
23. See the Safe Motherhood Quilt Project, http://www.rememberthemothers.org and the Tatia Oden French Memorial Foundation, http://www.tatia.org.
24. Annette E. Fineberg, "An Obstetrician's Lament," *Obstetrics & Gynecology* 117, no. 5 (May 2011): 1188–89.
25. See the following articles: Patricia A. Janssen et al., "Outcomes of Planned Home Birth with Registered Midwife Versus Planned Hospital Birth with Midwife or Physician," *Canadian Medical Association Journal* 181, no. 6–7 (September 2009), DOI:10.1503/cmaj.081869; A. de Jonge et al., "Perinatal Mortality and Morbidity in a Nationwide Cohort of 529 688 Low-Risk Planned Home and Hospital Births." *British Journal of Obstetrics & Gynaecology* (2009), DOI: 10.1111/j.1471-0528.2009.02175.x; M. Hatem et al., "Midwife-Led Versus Other Models of Care for Childbearing Women," *Cochrane Database of Systematic Reviews* (2008), art. no. CD004667, DOI: 10.1002/14651858.CD004667.pub2; and David Hayes, "An Obstetrician's Hope," *Obstetrics & Gynecology* 117, no. 5 (May 2011): 1188–90.

ACKNOWLEDGMENTS

by Mickey Huff

I would like to broadly and sincerely thank everyone that has ever been part of Project Censored as we celebrate our thirty-fifth anniversary this year. From the founding days at Sonoma State University by Dr. Carl Jensen in 1976, who directed the Project for twenty years, through an additional fourteen annual yearbooks with Dr. Peter Phillips, to the present, where we now have over thirty colleges and universities worldwide helping to validate independent news and combat censorship in support of a free press, I emphatically thank everyone for their contributions to the success and longevity of this amazing and important Project. It is an honor to serve as the director as we forge into the twenty-first century where there is much work to do in establishing true media democracy. Without Carl and Peter, Project Censored would not exist, let alone be expanding in its didactic mission in 2011. For his vision and dedication, I thank Carl for creating such a significant vehicle to understand the value of a constitutionally protected free press while also laying the foundation for actually achieving one.

I want to personally thank Dr. Peter Phillips for not only continuing that mission and building upon it, but for mentoring me into the position of director the past several years, as his advice, counsel, and friendship have been invaluable. I continue to work closely with Peter through the Media Freedom Foundation, where he is president of the board. This work could not continue without his direct involvement and support. Most importantly, I thank my wife, Meg, and my family, for without their constant support, advice, and many sacrifices, I would not be where I am in my life, and would not be able to continue my work with such an important organization. For that, especially to Meg, I have the utmost love, respect, and gratitude. This book is dedicated to her, my daughter, and my late father.

Project Censored continues to be managed by the board of directors at the Media Freedom Foundation (MFF), a nonprofit corporation based in Sonoma County, California, which has close operational ties to Diablo Valley College, Sonoma State University, and San Francisco State University. The Project now operates with the help of thirty other colleges and universities around the world. We are an investigative research and media analysis project dedicated to journalistic integrity and the freedom of information throughout the world. Thanks go to all of those involved on the MFF board, the National Judges, all respective college and university affiliates, and a special thanks goes to all the independent journalists in this year's volume.

At Diablo Valley College, where I teach, I would like to thank the Dean of Social Sciences Ellen Kruse, Hedy Wong, outgoing history chair Greg Tilles,

Dr. Matthew Powell, Dr. Lyn Krause, Dr. Steve Johnson, Dr. Manual Gonzalez, Dr. Robert Ahele, Jacob Van Vleet, David Vela, Adam Bessie, Obed Vazquez, Dr. Jeremy Cloward, Dr. Amer Araim, Bruce Lerro, Jeffrey Michels, and especially my teaching assistants Kelli Baumgartner, James Sy Cowie, Kira McDonough, Ryan "Green Lantern" Shehee, and Laura Whitsett, as well as past students that continue to provide great assistance and support to the Project including Nolan Higdon, Kajal Shahali, and "Metal" Mike Smith.

Also, thanks goes to the Social Justice Committee at the Berkeley Fellowship of Unitarian Universalists for their support in hosting Project Censored for the monthly "Empire, Power, and Propaganda" lecture series; Bill Gibbons for his longtime contributions to Project Censored, and Trish Boreta for her continued assistance in editing; and many thanks to friends of the Project including Ralph Nader, Dahr Jamail, Dr. John Ely, Dr. Paul Rea, Dr. Marc Sapir, Dr. Michael Parenti, Kristina Borjesson, Nora Barrows-Friedman, David Mathison, Rob Williams, Brian Murphy, Chris Finan, the American Library Association and Banned Books Week, Netfa Freeman, Dave Heller, Carol Brouillet, Ken Jenkins, Stephen Lendman, Shawn Hamilton, Michel Chossudovsky, Bonnie Faulkner, Bruce Brugmann, Peter B. Collins, Allan Rees, Terri Perticone, Vic Sadot, Atilla Nagy, Rebel Fagin, Chris Cox and the Junkyard Empire, Josh Switky, Richard Becker, the Artist General Michael Masley, Mihai Manoliu, Barry Cleveland, Alan Warner, Jahni Misja, Nate Mudd, Blake Bresnahan, Dr. Fred Viehe, Dr. Martin Berger, Dr. Louis Zona, Joan Berezin, Mary Alice and the Mount Diablo Peace and Justice Center, the Cheeseboard Collective, all at Cesar in Berkeley, City Lights Books, Moe's Books, Busboys and Poets, independent bookstores everywhere, ECPC for providing community, a personal thanks to Kate, Sheffield, Ali, Brandon, Matt, Bruce, Jan, Tei, Fran, Toe, and anyone else that has touched the Project in some supportive way this past year. Cheers to you all!

A big thank you goes to the people at Seven Stories Press. They publish some of the most important works concerning political, cultural, and societal issues today, and they edit our annual book in record time. The people at Seven Stories continue to be great advisors in the annual release process of the *Censored* volume. Publisher Dan Simon is dedicated to building democracy in America through knowledge and literature. He deserves accolades for assembling an excellent support team including Jon Gilbert (layout and design), Veronica Liu (our lead editor), Ruth Weiner, Anne Rumberger, Stewart Cauley, Gabe Espinal, Liz DeLong, Astrid Cook, Linda Trepanier, Crystal Yakacki, Silvia Stramenga, and Jeanne Thornton, as well as interns Sophia Ioannou, Erica Olschansky, Eva Fortes, and Rhoda Feng. Additional thanks goes to Random House Publisher Services.

Special thanks to Jodi and Bill at the Jodi Solomon Speakers Bureau in Boston for their longtime support with arranging speaking engagements at various colleges and universities nationwide. Proceeds from these appearances are a continuing financial supplement to Project Censored. We look forward to continuing that relationship into the future.

Peter Phillips and I would like to personally thank all of the people that have supported us in our co-hosting endeavors at KPFA 94.1 FM and Pacifica Radio for *The Project Censored Show* (on The Morning Mix and Flashpoints programs), especially Arlene Engelhardt, Andrew Phillips, Carrie Core, Anthony Fest, Adrienne Lauby, Tara Dorabji, Carmen Reed, Leslie Stovall, Dennis Bernstein, Miguel Molina, Davey D, Erica Bridgeman, J. R. Valrey, Braxter Timerlake, Anita Johnson, Richard Phelps, Tracy Rosenberg, Steve Zeltzer, Tiny and the Poor News Network, Stan Woods, Bonnie Faulkner of Guns and Butter, and all other supportive staff and community members.

Also, thanks goes to all those that made the Project Censored book tour in New York City a success last fall, especially Lenny Charles and INN World Report, Dr. Mark Crispin Miller of New York University, Robin Andersen at Fordham University, McNally Jackson books in SoHo, Revolution Books, Mickey Z., and Seven Stories Press as well as the MFF board.

Thanks to our International and National Judges; some have been involved with the Project for thirty-five years and are among the top experts in the world concerned with First Amendment freedoms and media principles. We are honored to have them as the final voice in ranking the top twenty-five *Censored* stories along with our college and university affiliate participants each year.

We also would like to show gratitude to our webmaster, the extraordinary Adam Armstrong. We acknowledge Shah Baig for technical support and intern David Quintana for office support.

We also welcome our new relationship with Dorothy Andersen on the Fair Sharing of the Common Heritage project and awards. We are honored to work with her to further her late husband Alfred F. Andersen's work and we thank Mary Lia for taking leadership in fostering this very promising relationship.

This year's book, *Censored 2012*, again features the cartoons of Khalil Bendib. We appreciate his continued support and talents as his brilliant editorial work so enhances our content.

Thanks to this year's contributing authors who made the *Censored 2012* volume what it is, including (with some repetition for thanks from elsewhere here) Peter Phillips, Elliot D. Cohen, Andrew Roth, Kenn Burrows, Tom Atlee, Elaine Wellin, Kristen Seraphin, Joel Evans-Fudem, Amy Ortiz, Dean Walker, Adam Bessie, Abby Martin, Nolan Higdon, Clifton Roy Damiens, Tracy Rosenberg, Jeff Cohen, Lisa Graves, Josh Wolf, Khalil Bendib, Emma Cape, Logan Price, Ryan Shehee, yari ojeda-sandel, Alexandre Silva, Salma Habib, Casey Goonan, Randal Marlin, Jacob Van Vleet, Robert Abele, Anthony DiMaggio, Mary Lia, Cynthia Boaz, Ann Garrison, Jon Elmer, Robin Andersen, Margaret Flowers, Ina May Gaskin, and all the Project Censored interns, faculty, and students.

Last but not least, we thank you, the readers and supporters from all over the US and the world. Hundreds of you nominated stories for consideration as censored news stories, and we thank you and urge you to continue your vigilance in our collective struggle against censorship.

Media Freedom Foundation/Project Censored Board of Directors

Carl Jensen (founder), Peter Phillips (president), Mickey Huff (director), Dennis Bernstein, Cynthia Boaz, Kenn Burrows, Noel Byrne, Mary Lia, Abby Martin, David Mathison, Miguel Molina, Andrew Roth, Kristen Seraphin, Bill Simon, Elaine Wellin, and Derrick West, with thanks to recent past board members Gary Evans, Judith Volkart, and student representative Frances Capell.

Project Censored Webmaster: Adam Armstrong

Project Censored's Websites:
http://projectcensored.org- Censored Stories/Validated Independent News updated year-round
http://censorednews.org- Independent, non-corporate news and views, daily RSS feeds
http://mediafreedominternational.org- University affiliates, current stories, investigative research
http://dailycensored.com- Censored blog, created and overseen by Adam Armstrong
http://proyectocensurado.org- Project Censored in Spanish
http://fairsharecommonheritage.org- Site dedicated to the Fair Sharing of the Common Heritage

Participating Colleges and University Faculty and Students

College of Marin
Students: Elizabeth Fernwood, Stephanie Keena
Faculty Evaluator: Susan Rahman
Community Evaluators: Lourdes Alvarez, WIC Dietician; Kevin Coyle, Registered Nurse; Gary Evans, MD; Kaiser Permanente; Richard Gross; Eitan Har-Oz; Dr. Thaddeus Norman Jr., PhD Biochemist–SRI International

California State University, Fresno
Students: Amy Block, Aimee Caneva, Alyssa Jarrett
Faculty Evaluators: Michael Becker, Sharon Benes, Sari Dworkin, PhD, Matthew Jendian, Timothy Kubal, Ross LaBaugh, Dennis L. Nef, Malik Simba, Steven D. Walker

California State University, Fullerton
Student: Douglas Swanson

DePaul University
Students: Rashanah Baldwin, Zach Clapp, Lucy Chen, Tracey Dewland, John

Dickow, Maureen Foley, Michael Harris, Robert Larson, Tianyuan Ma, Monica Macellari, Brennan Martin, Mara Mote, Ìbíjoké Òké, Marisa Rouse
Faculty Evaluators: Marla Donato, Kevin Howley, Richard Martoglio, James Mills, Fred Soster

Diablo Valley College
Students: Kelli Baumgartner, James Sy Cowie, Clifton Roy Damiens, Brian Donovan, Casey Goonan, Salma Habib, Caitlyn Kelly, Kira McDonough, Ryan Shehee, Alexandre Silva, Daniel Stenrud, Michael Thurman
Faculty Evaluators: Robert Abele, Adam Bessie, Mickey Huff, Jacob Van Vleet

Experts in Field
Jim Bertoli, 4-H State Climatology Medalist; Glenn Cekala, IPT Leader, Boeing; Matt Greely, member of Novato Horsemen; Dan Greely, Marin County Sheriff's Posse; Brian Mulvey, senior aquatic biologist; Ryan Piche, Lemoyne University, Kenyan Missionary; Elena Verba, RN at Santa Rosa Memorial Hospital; Jacquelyn Walker, Attorney at Law, Syracuse University

Florida Atlantic University
Students: Alyssa Andrews, Michelle Brown, Nathasha Terry-Ulett, Kathleen Walter
Faculty Evaluator: James Tracy

Indian River State College
Students: Sandra Baer, Bertunie Berluce, Jeffrey Bouchard, William Briggs, Jessica Capers, Victoria Castaneda, Tinya Clements, Theo DeBarros, Jessica Drew, James Dobbs, Ciara Egerton, Ryan Ferraro, Nick Gedo, Brandon Grey, Gabriela Hery, Jessica Hooper, Angelina Hulbert, Amanda Junco, Ameline Limorin, Rachel Lounsbury, Morgan Chase Miller, David Murray, Ashley Noble, Kayelan Micha Nyako, Luis Chacon Perez, Christopher Petrovich, Jamaal Rawlings, Jessica Santos, Kinner Spaulding, Bonnie Tellez, Carly Thomas
Faculty Evaluator: Elliot D. Cohen, PhD

Media Freedom Foundation
Nora Barrows-Friedman, Andrew Roth, PhD, Kristen Seraphin, MA

Niagara University
Students: George Antzoulis, Vincent Caruso, Joshua Carey, John M. Curtin, Julie Fonzi, Amanda Galster, Sabree Gemel, Amanda Gorlewski, Sara Gromek, Tiffany Hyman, Monique Larkins-Funches, Gabrielle Lustrinelli, Lela Mayfield, Cieara Moore, John Powers, Raymond Potter, Maria Rose, Catherine Ruszczyk, Vincent Schiano, Kat Smith, Jillian Teeter, Molliann Zahm, Derek Zeller
Faculty Evaluator: Brian Martin Murphy

San Francisco State University
Students: Rcnc Arellano, Brittney Barsotti, Natasha Berg, Frances Capell, Lauren Dizon, Bay Ewald, Joey Fino, Allison Gill, Allison Holt, Jared L. Kowalski, Jourdan McPhetridge, Ashley Myers, Noe Otero, Hobie Owen, Aaron Peacock, Celeste Richmond, Michael Smith, Robert Usher, Brittney White
Faculty Evaluator: Kenn Burrows

Siena College
Students: Brittany Bardin, Danielle Booher, Jenn Brandi, Jacquelyn Casey, Lauren Connell, Tricia Davidson, Sara Fitzpatrick, Melanie Macri, Katie Pierre, Jenna Placke, Mike Reda, Jessica Starr, Gabrielle Vono, Emily Waterman, Christan Zbytniewski
Faculty Evaluator: Dr. Mo Hannah

Sonoma State University
Students: Stefanie Adams, Camille Avis, Shah Baig, Jamie Bee, Sam Bergman, Robert Block, Hallie Boldt, Ashley Bjorge, Angelina Bravo, Craig Cekala, Erica Chavez, Cameron Cleveland, Kendra Coleman, Jason Corbett, Josh Crockett, Nzinga Dotson-Newman, Accacia Downer, Ana Elliott, Joel Evans-Fudem, Taylor Falbisaner, Michelle Fielder, Cheryl Fonseca, Danielle Frisk, Keith Garrett, Nick George, Thomas Gojkovich, Jordan Hall, Katie Havens, Tyler Head, Karen Kniel, Kevin Knopf, Sean Lawrence, Stephanie Marion, Lauren McNamara, Elizabeth Michael, Alex Miller, Brittany Morgan, Caitlin Morgan, Andrew Nassab, Ashley Nelson, Amanda Newhall, Nzinga Dotson-Newman, Erin Newton, Chante Noel, Amy Ortiz, Kayla Peirano, Pedro Perez, Cassie Petersen, Courtney Rider, Chris Riske, Danielle Ritenour, Katherine Ross, Jenna Russett, Bradley Shadoan, Chelsea Silva, Cynthia Solano, Aluna Soupholphakdy, Dane Steffy, Lindsey Tanner, Alex Todd, Gina Uliana, Kaitlyn Vargas, Dean Walker, Jacquelyn Waring, Rebecca Wilson, Ashley Wood, Taylor Wright, Yuliana Zamudio
Faculty Evaluators: Gloria Allen, Jeffery Baldwin, Cynthia Boaz, Suzel Bozada-Deas, Denny Bozman-Moss, Julie Bright, Kelly Bucy, Noel Byrne, Caroline Christian, Dr. Daniel Crocker, Marjorie Crowder, James Dean, Andrew Deseran, Robert Eyler, Michael Ezra-AMCS Professor, Michelle Fielder, Heather Flynn, Marty Frankel, Keith Gouveia, Karen Grady, Diana Grant, Sue Hayes, Janet Hess, Patrick Jackson, Tom Jacobson, Shelia Katz, Deborah Kindy, John Kornfeld, Jeanette H. Koshar, Dr. John Kramer, Tyler Lewis, Joseph Lin, Ronald Lopez, Dan Lopez, Mutombo M'Panya, Daniel Malpica, Robert McNamara, Dr. Lena McQuade, Alex Miller, Mike Nackord, Matthew Paolucci, Ervand Peterson, Peter Phillips, Patricia Pollock, James Preston, Kimberly Ramos, Danielle Ritenour, Don Romesburg, Elenita Strobel, Parissa Tadrissi, Chong-Uk Kim, Frances Vazquez, Laura Watt, Elaine Wellin, Eric Williams, Terry Wright

St. Cloud University
Students: Nancy Shedrack Anwary, Wend-Kouni Deo-Gratias Nintiema, Bretta

Diekmann, Helen Kitilla, Amanda Peterson, Jessica Wiehr
Faculty Evaluator: Julie Andrzejewski

State University of New York, Potsdam
Students: Alexander Allen, Jonathan Alt, Brooke Armstrong, Amanda Avery, Ashley Benoit, Allison Breivogel, Matthew Cauwels, Francesca Centofanti, Paul Craig, Stacey Finley, Kathleen Frear, Matthew Glaeser, James Godek, Whitney Hargett, Shawn Hatch, Amanda Helms, Hilary Hitchman, Benjamin Houck, Kathleen Hoyt, Kenneth Jenkins, Nichole Kelder, Tyler Kellogg, Ashlie Klepper, Donald LaBarge, Courtney Laughlin, Annmarie Lewis, Tyrisha McFev-Mosley, Courtney McLamb, Jose Minguez, Kenneth Palmieri, Kyle Phelix, Matthew Raymond, Alexander Rounds, Dylan Soper, Nicholas Steblenko, Philip Stever, Amanda Stockwell, Sarah Vine, Louis Walker III, Brooklyn Wheeler, Kristopher Wilson
Faculty Evaluators: Dr. Christina Knopf, Richard Moose, Brett Smith, Dr. Susanne Zwingel

Complutense University of Madrid
Students: Joan Pedro, Luis Luján
Faculty Evaluator: Dra. Ana I. Segovia

University of California, Berkeley
Students: Stephanie Hanawalt, Yari Sandel, Kajal Shahali, Josh Wolf, Laralyn Yee

University of California, Davis
Faculty Evaluator: Andrea Allen, OBGYN

University of La Laguna
Students: Alberto Ardèvol Abreu, Ciro Enrique Hernández Rodríguez, Samuel Toledano
Faculty Evaluators: José Manuel de Pablos Coello, José Manuel Pestano Rodríguez

University of London
Students: Cruz Alberto Martínez Arcos

York University/Humber College Student
Students: Scott Fielder

We offer our sincere apologies to anyone that was overlooked. If you believe your name should be on this list, or if you'd like to be on it next year, please contact us!

Project Censored 2009–10 International Judges

JULIE ANDRZEJEWSKI, Professor in Social Responsibility, Saint Cloud State University. Publications: five editions of an anthology entitled, *Oppression and Social Justice: Critical Frameworks*

ROBIN ANDERSEN, Associate Professor and Chair, Department of Communication and Media Studies, Fordham University, Director of Peace and Justice Studies, Publications: *Critical Studies in Media Commercialism*

OLIVER BOYD-BARRETT, Director of School, Professor in Journalism and Telecommunications, Bowling Green State University, Publications: *The International New Agencies: the Globalization of News, Media in Global Context*

KENN BURROWS, Faculty member for The Institute for Holistic Health Studies, San Francisco State University, Producer and Director of the annual conference Future of Health Care

ERNESTO CARMONA, Chilean journalist and writer, director of the Chilean Council of Journalists, Executive Secretary of the Investigation Commission on attacks against journalists, Latin American Federation of Journalists (CIAP-FELAP)

LIANE CLORFENE-CASTEN, Cofounder and President of Chicago Media Watch, award-winning journalist with credits in national periodicals including *E Magazine*, *The Nation*, *Mother Jones*, *Ms.*, *Environmental Health Perspectives*, *In These Times*, and *Business Ethics*. She is the author of *Breast Cancer: Poisons, Profits, and Prevention*.

ELLIOT D. COHEN, Professor, Indian River State College, contributor to *Truthout* and *Truthdig*, Editor in Chief of *International Journal of Applied Philosophy*, Ethics Editor for *Free Inquiry Magazine*, and blogger for *Psychology Today*. Among his recent books is *Mass Surveillance and State Control: The Total Information Awareness Project* (Palgrave-Macmillan)

JOSÉ MANUEL DE PABLOS, Professor, University of La Laguna (Tenerife, Canary Islands, Spain) Founder of *Revista Latina de Comunicación Social*, RLCS, a scientific journal Laboratory of Information Technologies and New Analysis of Communication

GEOFF DIVIDIAN, Milwaukee investigative journalist, Editor of the *Putman Pit*, an online newspaper

LENORE FOERSTEL, Women for Mutual Security, facilitator of the Progressive International Media Exchange (PRIME)

ROBERT HACKETT, Professor, School of Communication, Simon Fraser University; Co-director of News Watch Canada since 1993. His most recent publications include *Democratizing Global Media: One World, Many Struggles* (Co-Edited with Yuezhi Zhao, 2005), and *Remaking Media: The Struggle To Democratize Public Communication* (with William K. Carroll, 2006)

KEVIN HOWLEY, Associate Professor of Communication, DePauw University; editor of *Understand Community Media*, and author of *Community Media: People, Places, and Communication Technologies*

CARL JENSEN, Professor Emeritus, Communication Studies, Sonoma State University; founder and former director of Project Censored; author of *Censored: The News That Didn't Make the News and Why* (1993–1996) and *20 Years of Censored News* (1997)

NICHOLAS JOHNSON,* professor, College of Law, University of Iowa; former FCC Commissioner (1966–1973); author of *How to Talk Back to Your Television Set*

CHARLES L. KLOTZER, editor and publisher emeritus, *St. Louis Journalism Review*

NANCY KRANICH, past president of the American Library Association (ALA); Senior Research Fellow, Free Expression Policy Project

MARTIN LEE, investigative journalist, media critic and author. He was an original founder of Fairness and Accuracy in Reporting in New York and former editor of *Extra Magazine*. Author of *Acid Dreams: The Complete Social History of LSD: The CIA, the Sixties and Beyond*

DENNIS LOO, Associate Professor of Sociology at California State University Polytechnic University, Pomona, Co-editor of *Impeach the President: The Case Against Bush and Cheney*, Seven Stories Press, 2006

PETER LUDES, Professor of Mass Communication, Jacobs University Bremen, Founder in 1997 of German initiative on news enlightenment publishing the most neglected German news (Project Censored Germany)

WILLIAM LUTZ, Professor of English, Rutgers University; former editor of *The Quarterly Review of Doublespeak;* author of *The New Doublespeak: Why No One Knows What Anyone's Saying Anymore* (1966)

SILVIA LAGO MARTINEZ, Professor of Sociology, Universidad de Buenos Aires, Co-Director of the Gino Germani Research Institute Program for Research on Information Society

CONCHA MATEO, faculty in the Universidad Rey Juan Carlos (Madrid); journalist for radio, television, and political organizations in Spain and Latin America. Coordinator for Project Censored Research in Europe and Latin America

MARK CRISPIN MILLER, Professor of Media Ecology, New York University, author, and activist

BRIAN MURPHY, Associate Professor of Communications Studies, Niagara University specializing in Media Programming and Management, Investigation and Reporting, Media History and Theory, and International Communication

JACK L. NELSON,* Professor Emeritus, Graduate School of Education, Rutgers University; author of 16 books, including *Critical Issues in Education* (1996), and more than 150 articles

PETER PHILLIPS, Professor Sociology, Sonoma State University; Director of Project Censored 1996 to 2009; President of Media Freedom Foundation; Editor/Co-Editor of 14 editions of *Censored*, and Co-editor of *Impeach the President: The Case Against Bush and Cheney*, Seven Stories Press, 2006

ANA I. SEGOVIA, Associate Professor, Department of Journalism, Complutense University of Madrid (Spain)

NANCY SNOW, Professor of Communications at California State University, Fullerton and Adjunct Professor of Communications and Public Diplomacy at the University of Southern California's Annenberg School for Communication and Journalism. She is the author or editor of seven books, including *Information War* and *Propaganda, Inc.*

SHEILA RABB WEIDENFELD,* president of DC Productions, Ltd.; former press secretary to Betty Ford

ROB WILLIAMS, Faculty at Champlain College in Burlington, VT; former Board Co-President with the Action Coalition for Media Education (ACME)

*Indicates having been a Project Censored judge since our founding in 1976

HOW TO SUPPORT PROJECT CENSORED

To nominate a *Censored* story, send us a copy of the article and include the name of the source publication, the date that the article appeared, and the page number. For news stories published on the internet of which we should be aware, please forward the URL to mickey@projectcensored.org and/or peter@projectcensored.org. The final deadline period for nominating a potential *Censored* story of the year is April 1 of each year, which means we look at stories from April to April for our calendar year and the *Censored* volume that comes out the following fall is titled like an almanac, in advance of the coming year. (Stories from April 2010–April 2011 are published in *Censored 2012.*)

Criteria for Project Censored news stories nominations:

1. A censored news story contains information that the public has a right and a need to know, but to which the public has had limited access.

2. The news story is timely, ongoing, and has implications for a significant number of residents in the world.

3. The story has clearly defined concepts and is backed up with solid, verifiable documentation.

4. The news story has been publicly published, either electronically or in print, in a circulated newspaper, journal, magazine, newsletter, or similar publication from either a foreign or domestic source.

Project Censored is supported by the Media Freedom Foundation, a 501(c)3 nonprofit organization. We depend on tax-deductible donations and foundation grants to continue our work. To support our efforts for freedom of information, send checks to the address below or call (707) 874-2695. Donations can also be made online at http://projectcensored.org. Please consider helping us fight news censorship.

Media Freedom Foundation
P. O. Box 571
Cotati, CA 94931
E-mail: mickey@projectcensored.org and peter@projectcensored.org.
Phone: 707-874-2965

ABOUT THE AUTHOR

MICKEY HUFF is the director of Project Censored and is a member of the board of directors for the Media Freedom Foundation. He is currently an associate professor of history at Diablo Valley College (DVC), located in the San Francisco Bay Area. Huff is radio co-host of the *Project Censored Show* with former Project Censored director Dr. Peter Phillips. The program airs as part of The Morning Mix on Pacifica Radio's KPFA in Berkeley, California, and rebroadcasts on approximately sixty stations weekly as part of the award-winning investigative reporting program *Flashpoints*. Huff is also on the board of directors of No Lies Radio and is a former advisor to the Students for a Democratic Society at DVC. He regularly holds forums on campus with authors and activists from across the country to discuss issues surrounding history, critical thinking, and current events.

Huff has been interviewed by affiliates of NPR, PBS, Pacifica, the New York Times Co., the *Christian Science Monitor*, ABC, the *San Francisco Bay Guardian*, Progressive Radio Network, Voice of Russia, Republic Broadcasting, and many other commercial and independent news media outlets. Previously the co-director of the alternative public opinion polling group Retropoll, he has been a visiting scholar in library science at the University of Nebraska, Lincoln, and a lecturer at numerous colleges, including in sociology at Sonoma State University. Huff speaks regularly at venues in the San Francisco Bay Area and across the United States on issues of censorship, propaganda studies, media literacy, and history. This past year, Huff keynoted and gave presentations at numerous events—including at the Northern California 9/11 Film Festival in Oakland, CA, the Kent State Truth Tribunal in New York City—and hosted the monthly lecture series "Empire, Power, and Propaganda" in Berkeley, CA. He is available for public speaking engagements through the Jodi F. Solomon Speakers Bureau (http://JodiSolomonSpeakers.com).

This past year, Huff and Phillips coauthored several chapters in academic publications, which focused on media censorship, propaganda, and the ongoing Truth Emergency relating to the US empire. Huff's writings and research were included in *Peace Movements Worldwide, Volume 3: Peace Efforts that Work and Why*, edited by Marc Pilisuk and Michael N. Nagler (Praeger); *Media and Social Justice*, edited by Sue Curry Jansen, Jefferson Pooley, and Lora Taub-Pervizpour (Palgrave Macmillan); and *Research in Social Problems and Public Policy, Volume 19: Government Secrecy*, edited by Susan Maret (Emerald); and *Algorithms of Power: Key Invisibles*, edited by Peter Ludes (Jacobs University Bremen in Germany). Huff has also been published by many online news and commentary sites including Global Research, *Truthout*, Buzzflash,

Dissident Voice, Lew Rockwell, Information Clearinghouse, and the *Daily Censored*, and has appeared on *CounterPunch*, Common Dreams, and AlterNet, among others.

Huff has a long history with Project Censored: he began reading the annual publication in 1993, became a faculty evaluator of censored stories in 2004, and later coauthored a chapter with Dr. Paul Rea in *Censored 2009*. Huff went on to coauthor and co-edit *Censored 2010* and *Censored 2011* with Dr. Peter Phillips. Before becoming the director in 2010, Huff was the associate director of Project Censored for two years, during which time the Project was honored with a PEN Oakland Literary Censorship Award.

Huff currently teaches courses on US history, critical reasoning, sociology of media, and propaganda studies, with special topics courses on "Money, Power, and Politics" and on contemporary historiography, specifically "America, 9/11, and the War on Terror: Case Studies in Media Myth-Making and the Propaganda of Historical Construction." He is also a musician and composer of over twenty years and lives with his family just outside Berkeley, CA.

INDEX

abortion
  fetus pain at, 122
  insurance coverage elimination for,
    124–25
  justifiable homicide for, 123–24
  South Dakota anti-, 42, 123
accountability, Jones on, 18–19
ACLU. *See* American Civil Liberties Union
ACOG. *See* American College of Obstetricians and Gynecologists
activism
  media use of, 385
  net neutrality and, 347–49
  of Tea Party, 355
activist
  animal rights, unjust incarceration of, 95
  anti-, legislation, 95
  anti-abortion, 121–22
advertiser influence, media reform movement and, 17
AEI. *See* American Enterprise Institute
Affordable Energy and Economic Justice, 104
Affordacare bill, 75
Afghanistan, 188–89
  DU weapons in, 52–53
  international aid to, 93
  secret US prisons in, 177–78
  Taliban in, 165–67
Afghanistan War, 29
  civilian deaths in, 51–52
  cost of, 193
  Obama administration financing of, 167
  US soldier suicide after, 46
Africa
  Canada mining in, 387
  central, 93–94
  Congo, 392–97, 402–6
  external capitalist forces in, 159–63
  humanitarian foreign aid to, 388–89
  Kenya, 132, 180

  land grabs in, 159
  North, 275–77
  oil exportation from, 387
  Predator Drones to stop genocide in,
    397–401
  Rwanda, 389, 392–94
  Somalia, 93, 179–80, 389–92
  Uganda, 391, 393
  United Nations peacekeepers in, 389–90
  United States in, 387–408
African Command (AFRICOM), US, 94,
  387, 404
Agence France-Presse, on global poverty, 78
Aid to Families with Dependent Children, 364
AJOG. *See American Journal of Obstetrics &*
  Gynecology
ALEC. *See* American Legislative Exchange
  Council
Allimadi, Milton, 391, 405
All Quiet on the Western Front, 303
Alter, Jonathan, 214, 216
AlterNet, 72, 74, 75, 80
altruism, 249
American Civil Liberties Union (ACLU),
  49, 123, 349
  National Security Project of, 50
American College of Obstetricians and
  Gynecologists (ACOG), 451
American Enterprise Institute (AEI), 200,
  208, 211, 214, 216
American Federation of Teachers, 208
*American Journal of Obstetrics & Gynecology
  (AJOG)*, 452
American Journal of Public Health, 406
American Legislative Exchange Council
  (ALEC), 205
American Psychology Association (APA), 48
American Recovery and Reinvestment Act,
  112–13
American Wasteland (Bloom), 76

475

misrepresentation of, 109–12
Olmert, Ehud, 414–15
online government wiretapping, 191
online personal management service, of
    Ntrepid, 58
Open Records Request, 205
Open Society Foundation, US, 178
Operation Broken Silence, 398, 407
Operation Earnest Voice (OEV), as psycho-
    logical warfare weapon, 58
Operation Enduring Freedom, 398
Operation Iraqi Freedom, 398
"Operation Northwoods," 310
"Operation Restore Hope," 162
oratory, 295–96
Orwell, George, 289, 297, 367
Ott, Riki, 111
Overmyer, Eric, 423, 425
Oxfam International
    on aid for political purposes, 42
    on international aid, 92
    on permanent food crisis, 79

P2P. *See* peer-to-peer
Pacific garbage dump, 41
Pakistan, US secret war in, 157–58
Palestine, Ghetto, 413–21
    creating legitimacy in, 416–20
    disengagement plan, 415–16
    IMF and, 416
Palestine, human rights abuses in, 163–65
Palestinian Authority, 417
Papaya Farmers, 80
parenting, mindfulness and, 248
Park Center for Independent Media
    (PCIM), 23, 265–67
participatory budgeting (PB), 42, 146–47,
    258
Patchwork Nation, 354
pay-for-priority system, 340, 341, 344
PB. *See* participatory budgeting
PBS. *See* Public Broadcasting Service
PCIM. *See* Park Center for Independent
    Media
peace movement, 24
peer-to-peer (P2P) protocols, 156
"Pentagon: Drones Can Stop the Next Dar-
    fur," 398
Pentagon Papers, 199–200
The Pentagon Propaganda Machine (Ful-
    bright), 309
people power, politics and, 254–58
People's Media Revolution, for US change,
    14

PEPFAR. *See* President's Emergency Plan
    for AIDS Relief
Perfect Citizen, cyber security system of, 65
Pericles, 295–96
permaculture design movement, 253
Pershing Square Capital Management,
    CCA investment by, 88
persuasion, 296
    credibility, 297–98
    from fear, 297
Peruvian sterilization program, 131
Peterson, David, 398, 399
Pew Research Center for People and the
    Press, 184, 291n1, 363
    Project of Excellence of, 193
Phillips, Peter, 22, 194, 261
Piazza, Tom, 424
Pickard, Victor, 20
piracy, Kenya on, 180
Pisistratus, 295
Planned Parenthood, 123
plastic
    bags, banning of, 42, 144–45
    BPA chemicals in, 144
plastic recycling, 107
    marine life damage from lack of, 108
    public awareness for, 108
political propaganda, 317–18
politicization, of international aid, 92–93
politics
    CIRs, 257
    civility in, 258
    corporate spending, 257
    dictators, 254
    Israeli occupation and, 255–56
    PB, 258
    people power, 254–58
The Politics of Genocide (Herman/Peterson),
    398
pollution. *See* environmental pollution
Population Fund, UN, on eugenic steriliza-
    tion, 131
Posse Comitatus statutes, 91
post-traumatic stress disorder (PTSD), 46
    MDMA-Assisted psychotherapy for, 244
Potter, Wendell, 268, 440–41
poverty
    Census Bureau on rate of, 72–73
    food waste and, 76–77
    global rates of, 78
    of LDCs, 79
    NAS calculations for, 73
    Obama on, 73
    power, abuse, and accountability, 39, 84–96